TH

D1765470

ADAM'S GRACE

FALL AND REDEMPTION IN MEDIEVAL LITERATURE

Brian Murdoch

D. S. BREWER

First published 2000
D. S. Brewer, Cambridge

ISBN 0 85991 559 X

D. S. Brewer is an imprint of Boydell & Brewer Ltd
PO Box 9, Woodbridge, Suffolk IP12 3DF, UK
and of Boydell & Brewer Inc.
PO Box 41026, Rochester, NY 14604–4126, USA
website: http//www.boydell.co.uk

A catalogue record for this book is available
from the British Library

Library of Congress Cataloging-in-Publication Data
Murdoch, Brian, 1944–
    Adam's grace : fall and redemption in medieval literature /
Brian Murdoch.
      p. cm.
    Papers originally presented as the Hulsean lectures for 1997–
1998, Faculty of Divinity, University of Cambridge.
    Includes bibliographical references and index.
    ISBN 0–85991–559–X (alk. paper)
    1. Literature, Medieval – History and criticism.   2. Fall
of man in literature.   3. Redemption in literature.   I. Title.
PN682.F3 .M78 2000
809'.933823314–dc21
                                                        00–020944

This publication is printed on acid-free paper

Printed in Great Britain by
St Edmundsbury Press Ltd, Bury St Edmunds, Suffolk

CONTENTS

Ursula

PREFACE

These chapters were originally given as the Hulsean lectures for 1997–8 in the Faculty of Divinity in the University of Cambridge under the slightly differently angled, but also appropriate, title *Adam sub gratia*; although they have now been expanded somewhat and provided with notes, an attempt has been made to preserve at least some of the informality of the lecture format. The theme is Adam: Adam is presented – in the terms of the Hulse bequest – in the light of Christianity, although not necessarily in what is usually seen as theological writing in the narrower sense. The interplay of theology and literature, and its use to put across to a largely lay audience centrally important theological ideas, is of special significance in the Middle Ages, and also (though there are changes in attitude) in the period of the Reformation and Counter-Reformation. This applies in particular to the divine economy of Fall and Redemption, the universality of original sin, and the identity of mankind with their first parents. The aim of the lectures was to look precisely at the interaction of literature and theology, and at the presentation, use and lay reception of these central ideas in medieval and later European literature, using as wide a range of genres and vernaculars as possible.

The process begins with the expansion of Genesis within the Christian tradition of apocryphal Adam-lives and the Holy Rood stories, at the interface between canonicity and literature, with the partial secularisation of a religious story. Vernacular versions of works like the *Vita Adae* have been neglected, in spite of burgeoning interest in the apocrypha as such, yet they demonstrate how the apocryphal material lives on and develops. Adam and the divine economy may be used as a literary model in various ways, and the lectures considered various important and well known Christian figures of the Middle Ages: knights, popes, emperors, kings and saints, all of them unusual, even extreme, yet all representative in some ways of mankind, all Adam-figures, however unlikely this might seem. They include Gregorius, the 'medieval Oedipus' who is so much more than that, whose case demonstrates the redeemability of all sin, original and actual, in the resolution of the paradox of the *felix culpa*; Perceval or Parzival, the Grail King, another unlikely Everyman, searching for the lost Paradise and for God in the hostile world into which he has been ejected; and the many medieval figures (literary and even historical) associated with the legends of leprosy, blood and healing that reflect the sacrifice in the Redemption.

The series of lectures concluded with two sessions devoted to drama at the end of the Middle Ages, the first examining the divine economy in medieval cyclic dramas of the Fall and the Passion, visual representations of central theological ideas to a very broad lay audience which is drawn into the action in a realisation of the identity expressed in Romans 5:12. Finally, Adam's Fall and the Redemption were looked at in the drama of the Reformation and the Counter-Reformation period, with attention paid to that influenced by Luther or Zwingli, contrasted – but more importantly *compared* – with, for example, the contemporary Jesuit-school drama.

The last session of the Hulse series took the form of a seminar in which I tried to draw some of the threads together, but also to offer some new material, looking on to modern literature to a certain extent. I have recast this in the light of comments, and turned it into an introduction. Of course the seminar (and now the introduction) leapt over Milton, but my concern in looking ahead was to demonstrate the tenacity of some of the motifs by looking at some modern adaptations presented in the same spirit, not perhaps Henry de Vere Stacpoole's *Blue Lagoon*, which was invoked in the first lecture, but certainly a diversity of texts, including even cartoons and advertising matter. I profited from the discussion (and from the questions and comments after the lectures) enormously, and I wish to thank all those who participated.

More formal thanks are due, too, to the Hulsean Electors for awarding me the 1997–8 lectureship. In the department I have to thank especially Dr Eamon Duffy and his colleagues, particularly Dr Janet Soskice and Ms Rosalind Paul for their hospitality as well as their scholarship. Thanks for hospitality, too, are due to my own college, Jesus, and to Trinity Hall, at which I had a Visiting Fellowship in 1989; I was delighted to renew acquaintance with both.

I began work on Adam and Eve in Cambridge in 1965 as a postgraduate student working under Professor Roy Wisbey (later of King's College, London, then at Downing College), and it was at his suggestion that I started work on some early medieval German adaptations of Genesis. This proved to be the foundation of a study that has preoccupied me for many years. My continued interest will be clear from a glance at the Bibliography, and it has also, happily, brought me into contact with many eminent scholars in the field: Professors Michael Benskin, Esther Quinn and Ute Schwab, and above all in the area of pseudepigrapha Professor Michael Stone must be named. Also I wish to recall with gratitude three other mentors in different areas: the late Professors Friedrich Ohly, David Greene and Leonard Forster. In or from Stirling, I am grateful to my colleague Professor Keith Whitelam, to my erstwhile pupil Dr Mary-Bess Halford(-Staffell), and to those undergraduates over the years with whom I have worked on aspects of the material, especially Judith Byrne and Carol Latimer (both now postgraduates). I owe a special and great debt of gratitude to my friend and colleague Dr Jacqueline Tasioulas, who listened to, read and discussed much of the material with me, and was as generous with her encouragement as she was with her scholarly comments and information, especially, but not only, in her field of medieval English. To all these and many others thanks are due whilst errors remain, as ever, my own.

Stirling 2000   BOM

Διὰ τοῦτο ὥσπερ δι᾽ ενὸς ἀνθρώύπου ἡ ἁμαρτία εἰς τὸν κοσμον εἰσῆλθεν, καὶ διὰ τῆς ἁμαρτίας ὁ θάνατος, καὶ οὕτως εἰς πάντας ἀνθρώπους ὁ θανατος διῆλθεν εφ ᾧ πάντες ἥμαρτον.

Propterea, sicut per unum hominem peccatum in hunc mundum intravit, et per peccatum mors; et ita in omnes homines mors pertransiit, in quo omnes peccaverunt.

Romans 5:12

INTRODUCTION: INTERPRETING ADAM

IT IS APPROPRIATE to begin any work which centres upon Adam and Eve with a comment by Milton, although this is not from *Paradise Lost*, but from his essay on education:

> The end then of learning is to repair the ruins of our first parents by regaining to know God aright . . . But because our understanding cannot in this body found itself but on sensible things, as by orderly conning over the visible and inferior creature, the same method is necessarily to be followed in all discreet teaching. . . . I deem it to be an old error of universities, not yet well recovered from the scholastic grossness of barbarous ages, that instead of beginning with arts most easy (and those be such as are most obvious to the sense), they present their young unmatriculated novices, at first coming, with the most intellective abstractions of logic and metaphysics . . .[1]

Milton probably did not foresee the age of popular learning, but his point remains. The easy arts, most obvious to the sense, are the best way of getting across the education designed to repair the Fall of Man. The theme of these chapters is the interpretation of theology through literature in the representation of the story of Adam and Eve and especially of its soteriological implications. Although the distinction is not an easy one, a literary work, rather than a specifically theological one, may use interpretations of the Bible or even theological arguments, but it will in doing so treat them pragmatically, and simplify them for the use of the individual reader or observer. The aim here is to show how in literature the story of the Fall as such has been presented as the necessary counter of the Redemption in Christian writing from the apocryphal Adambooks down to late medieval and post-Reformation drama; it also examines how the story of Adam and Eve has been used as a basis for literary narratives in which the same interaction of Fall and Redemption, and also some of the attendant problems with the theology of simultaneity, is clarified by the freedom allowed to the creative writer whose characters are not, or at least less strictly, bound by biblical roles.

There has always been debate (and particularly in the Middle Ages) about the precise nature of the Redemption in terms of mediation, sacrifice, ransom, reparation and restoration. The debates have moved from the Augustinian concept of expiation by the sacrifice of Christ to the theory (voiced by Anselm of Canterbury and refining the concept of substitution) of satisfaction (with added discussions on the devil's rights and the notion too of the redemption of a pledge), and ultimately to the doctrine of salvation by grace alone. Here again, secular writing, and espe-

---

1 John Milton, 'On Education' (1644) in *The Prose Works of John Milton*, ed. J. A. St John and Charles R. Sumner (London: Bohn, 18[48]–64), III, 462f. There is a reference to this passage in E. M. W. Tillyard, *The Elizabethan World Picture* ([1943] Harmondsworth: Penguin, 1963), p. 29.

cially secular writing with a literary intent (even if this is not necessarily the sole intent of any given work), takes a fundamental approach to man's loss of grace and the restoration of that grace (or the reconciliation of man with God) within the basic juxtaposition of Adam and Christ, using the word 'Redemption' as it is understood by those who are not primarily theologians. The role of Christ as priest (as well as sacrifice) is an additional point of interest, and the role of Adam himself as priest will emerge in some of the works we shall consider.

Any contextualisation of the Fall itself has to face basic problems, such as that of how to show naked innocence in a fallen world? How does literature cope with the figure of Adam – who existed outside time – in the framework of the world, given that his descendants co-exist in Adam, *in quo omnes peccaverunt*. In the second stage, then, the naked *infans* in the hostile *mundus* both is and is not Adam. Added to all this, and whether we are looking at medieval or indeed modern literature, there is the further problem that with the story of Adam and Eve we are increasingly not only not imparting anything new in the narrative sense, but we are telling a story that has already in some ways become *too* familiar. There are things that we all know about Adam and Eve and the Fall, and yet we do not of course *know* them at all. Lutheran *Bibelfestigkeit* and nineteenth-century biblical criticism both made it quite clear that there was no apple in Eden, at least not a dangerous one, and no devil either, in spite even of Milton, who assures us, in this case not very convincingly, that 'sin originated, first, in the instigation of the devil, as is clear from the narrative in Gen. iii.'[2] There is a world of interpretation in that word 'clear,' and if it is not one hundred per cent certain that Milton even wrote the words just cited (they are from the *De doctrina Christiana*), then even *Paradise Lost* has been described as 'not so much a teaching as an intangling'.[3] Even without the devil, the literary construct of the evil (*malum*) in the apple (*malum*), and the serpent (worm) as an instrument of evil in Eden has long been complete in itself. To give a thirteenth-century illustration, Geoffrey of Vinsauf used the story of the Fall in his *Poetria nova* as the vehicle for teaching the *ornatio facilis*, the use of elementary rhetorical devices: 'O apple! Wretched apple!' and so on.[4] Nor indeed has the passing of time weakened the usage of the Adamic narrative in literature, however much the Renaissance and later antiquarians (who would soon turn into archaeologists and anthropologists) might have begun to reach the conclusion

> that all the books of Moses
> were nothing but supposes . . .
> That as for Father Adam
> And Mistress Eve, his Madam
> And what the Devil spoke, Sir

[2] *Prose Works*, IV, 253, from the posthumous treatise *The Christian Doctrine*, chapter XI. On the problems associated with this work, see F. E. Hutchinson, *Milton and the English Mind* (London: English Universities Press, 1949), pp. 151–72. Recent work suggests that the text is not by Milton.
[3] Cited in the title of a 1967 paper by Stanley Eugene Fish, ' "Not so much a Teaching as an Intangling": Milton's Method in *Paradise Lost*', in *Milton*, ed. Alan Rudrum (London: Aurora, 1970), pp. 104–35.
[4] See the elegant translation by Margaret F. Nims, *Poetria Nova of Geoffrey of Vinsauf* (Toronto: Pontifical Institute, 1967), pp. 56f.

Twas nothing but a joke, Sir
And well invented flam.

I cite that piece of what Stuart Piggott refers to as 'jolly Chestertonian verse' by William King from Piggot's *Ancient Britons and the Antiquarian Imagination*, a work highly relevant to the study of the fortunes of Adam in spite of the title in general terms, even though Piggot misdates King by about seventy years,[5] and we might even (thinking of the books of Moses) be constrained to ask 'what devil?' King is mocking new ideas, of course, not evincing scepticism, which would take a long time to come. Even so, titles of modern anthropological works like *Adam's Ancestors, African Genesis, River out of Eden*, significantly retain the biblical link.

There is a case to be made for seeing the survival of literal interpretations of the Fall narrative precisely in the literary rather than the theological sphere in an age after such antiquarian studies, and more recently after Darwin, the Higher Criticism, Freud and modern investigative sciences. We have moved into philology, or history in the sense of *Religionsgeschichte*,[6] and the more resolutely theological presentations of the Adamic narrative can run into trouble. Thus a popular work from 1932 called *The Genesis of Genesis*:

> the Fall is not then to be regarded as mere allegory . . . Rather it is to be regarded as actual history symbolically portrayed; so that all mankind may get to the heart of the matter concerning the entrance of sin with its dire results, and the need of the Divine Redemption.[7]

The opening statement is pretty well completely opaque; but the conclusion is presumably as appropriate to 1932 as to, say, 1332.

In fact we may demonstrate the ongoing literary survival of the material very well with an actual illustration, created relatively recently in a famous concrete poem by a modern German poet, Reinhard Döhl, who used typography to set up and publish an apple-shaped piece made up of repetitions of the word *Apfel* (apple),[8] which is therefore entirely self-referential in the manner of the oldest concrete poems (there are Greek poems shaped like butterflies); but a serpent is tucked away, in a single occurrence, towards the bottom of the picture-poem, of the word *Wurm*, which serves in German as in early English for both creatures. The

---

5 Stuart Piggott, *Ancient Britons and the Antiquarian Imagination* (London: Thames and Hudson, 1989), cited pp. 53f. Piggot claims 1776 as the date the work was written (citing a secondary source) and places him after Rousseau. But William King died in 1712, in 'Melancholy Circumstances near Ludgate', or so we are told by G. J., the author of *The Poetical Register* (London, 1723; repr. Farnborough: Gregg, 1969), II, 87f. The same volume also tells us that King 'was generally too fond of low Humour in his Writings, which he affected out of a Natural Propensity to Mirth'. King was born in 1663 and was known for writing light verse and burlesques. Given King's involvement in the 'Battle of the Books' – Swift's satire was published in 1704 – this seems to be the context and hence 1706 a more likely date.
6 Gerhard Hasel, *Old Testament Theology: Basic Issues in the Current Debate* (Grand Rapids: Eerdmans, 4th rev. ed. 1991), see pp. 23–7.
7 D. E. Hart-Davies, *The Genesis of Genesis* (London: Clarke [1932]), p. 95
8 It is printed in various anthologies, including *Konkrete Poesie*, ed. Eugen Gömringer (Stuttgart: Reclam, 1972), p. 38. Döhl was born in 1934.

3

worm in the fruit is inevitable, says the poem, even if not spotted at once; it is part of the whole.

The shorthand of the Fall brings with it interpretative problems dependent upon shared knowledge, but also upon not necessarily shared interpretation. Döhl's poem does not show the Redemption; it is not even clear that there will *be* one. Medieval iconography was far clearer on that point, as in the example of a famous miniature by Berthold Furtmeyer in 1480, where virtually all the relevant images of the Fall and the Redemption have been piled into a single picture, at the centre of which is a tree with host wafers on it as well as fruit. Eve picks the fruit and delivers death, the Virgin takes the host to the faithful (who thus co-exist with her and with Eve), whilst Adam sleeps beneath the tree, which has a serpent around it. Death himself stands to one side. More reductive illustrations show the Cross as a living tree, and it grows from the seeds buried with Adam in the apocryphal Adam and Holy Rood traditions which will form part of this study.

Three further modern references to illustrative uses of the theology of the Fall are instructive, because they are all expressly and in the proper sense popular, something which is harder to establish with medieval works; they all seem to illustrate the conciseness of the Fall admirably. In one of Hugh Burnett's admirable ecclesiastical cartoons, a pre-Fall Adam and Eve in Paradise gaze at a tree which Adam has decorated, whilst Eve wonders what a Christmas tree is *for*? Beside this we may set – the example is fortuitous but could be multiplied – an advertisement, offering a product for sale simply by showing an apple with a bite out of it, and the caption 'tempting'. Both depend on knowledge of the Adamic narrative and its possible interpretations, yet they each have a different agenda: one to make the recipient laugh because of that knowledge, the other – a more ambiguous one, perhaps – to encourage the recipient to buy something. In the case of the cartoon, that *we* know what a Christmas tree (albeit the custom is non-Christian in origin) is supposed to celebrate, but Adam does not, evokes the required response. The joke depends not really on anachronism, but on the understanding, possible for us but not for Adam, of the interrelatedness of Fall and Redemption. The advertisement is more difficult in that the viewer is being tempted – something to be avoided in theological terms – actually to buy something (the bitten-into or indeed still intact apple is a very common advertising motif), but the best one can say is that the implicit indulgence is presented as a fortunate fall in the long run. That the advertisement on which these comments are based was in fact one encouraging a subscription to the magazine *Time* gives the whole thing an accidental but additional edge; in early dramas of the Fall, Time can be one of the personified results.[9]

---

[9]   There is a large coloured reproduction of Furtmeyer's miniature in Roger Cook, *The Tree of Life: Symbol of the Centre* (London: Thames and Hudson, 1974), illus. 44 and cover; there is an interesting modern parallel by the illustrator Monika Beisner in her collection *Von fliegenden und sprechenden Bäumen* (Munich: Hanser, 1994) in which an enchanted apple-tree contains Death as a skeleton with his scythe. The cartoon (one of a whole collection on the theme) is from Hugh Burnett's *Adam and Eve* (London: Merlin, 1963). There is a whole sub-genre of humorous adaptations and parodies of the story, often with incidental theological content: see for example Mark Twain's *Extracts from Adam's Diary* (London and New York: Harper, 1904). On the intrinsically odd semiology of the Fall made positive as an advertising ploy, the cynic might also point out that naked female figures still sell products; but the apple alone often suffices, even if the pun on *malum* is now irretrievably lost.

4

The semiotics of apple/temptation/purchase is a very common motif in advertising. The use of an Eve-figure might make its own point about concupiscence, but often the apple alone suffices as a (non-biblical) trigger. However, the world of marketing tends not to use the story of Adam and Eve as cautionary.

This is not the case in a third and in some ways more sinister use of a picture of Adam, Eve and the serpent. This rather less ambiguous use is found, for example, on a poster that was at one time widely displayed in public lavatories, and showed Adam and Eve, or at least a man and a woman, standing with a snake between them: the caption was a warning against venereal disease. The concept bases itself upon the sexuality that came after the Fall, with a new element of danger beyond the moral one of carnal concupiscence. This poster was in use some time ago, but the same image has been used to warn against AIDS. Freud's interpretation of the snake has doubtless given an extra (and for some recipients perhaps the only) dimension to this exploitation of the narrative. Whether the fact that Adam and Eve (who were sketched figures only) appeared in the original poster to be clothed may be due either to general propriety or to the desire to preclude gratuitous additional embellishment by outside hands is unclear; but it can also indicate, accidentally or not, that a potentially dangerous concupiscence was part of the *poena peccati* after the Fall.

Given the importance of the Fall and the Redemption in written literature alone (without, that is, attempting to embrace the iconographical aspects as well), we might set up a whole range of categories. The distinction of national language would probably (except perhaps to an extent after the Reformation) not be a significant distinguishing factor: we are dealing with a universal of the medieval Christian world. More significant would be the distinction between straightforward theological interpretation of the biblical matter (which might emphasise one pole of the history or the other – a Gospel poem starting with Adam, a Genesis-play with the Redemption), reworkings of that matter with express literary intent (to delight and to instruct), and the literature of analogy. Subdivisions of the literary modes might depend upon genre – prose, epic verse, lyric verse, drama – or register, by which we would separate *Paradise Lost* or *Parzival* from a folk-play, or from *Adam lay Ibounden*. And where Reinhard Döhl's little apple-poem and Geoffrey of Vinsauf's literary exercise would go is unclear, let alone that widespread work of ecclesiastical zoology, the *Physiologus*, known in most of the languages of Europe in prose and verse, where the supposedly non-sexual reproduction of the elephant is contrasted with Adam and Eve, or at least is used to show how things should have been.

The questions associated with the narrative of the Fall and the Redemption are large ones: *unde malum* is the first, whence evil, and then: *cur deus homo*? The supposition is of an original state of wisdom, unity and innocence, which was lost, bringing instead sin, death, time and sexuality into the world. The question that arises is whether there is a possibility of man's regaining what was lost, or indeed even recalling what it was like; hence the problem of innocent nakedness in a postlapsarian world.

Just as the original narrative of the Fall has all kinds of associative elements (the display of wisdom by naming the beasts; the serpent; the fruit; the trial of the protoplasts; the question of why evil came about), all these raise additional questions,

5

most notably those of recognisability, and of absolute responsibility. Interpretation already clouds this picture somewhat by the introduction of the devil and by a previous fall on the part of Lucifer. The answer to the second question, of how Paradise is to be regained, also involves a range of theological concepts: the notion of satisfaction, of recapitulation, of love and restitution, and of sacrifice. All these fit into the divine economy, the resolution of Fall and Redemption expressed in the tag *felix culpa*, the answer to the question posed by Anselm of why God became man being that it was essentially to rescue the situation, and indeed to rescue Adam quite literally in the Harrowing of Hell. A literary embellishment to this in all kinds of works is the introduction of the paradisaical debate between the daughters of God which leads to the incarnation, and that of itself requires a personification of concepts such as Justice and Mercy.

The question of simultaneity is equally significant; the divine plan exists outside time, thus the notion of the Redemption is implicit in the Fall. The early German poem known as *Ezzos Gesang*, the eleventh-century 'Song by Ezzo', concludes a strophe on the Creation of man with the barest juxtaposition:

> ze allen eron gescuofe du den man:
> du wissos wol sinen fal[10]

> (you created man in all honour: you knew well that he would fall.)

There are of course two aspects of simultaneity involved here: the inclusion of the Redemption in the Fall is one, and the other is the inclusion of all mankind in the sin of Adam, the Pauline inclusivity of Romans 5:12, at least in the Vulgate reading. Both points are hard to communicate in literature.

It is not really possible or helpful to attempt to set up a complete taxonomy either of approaches to the Fall – hexaemeral, paradisiacal, lapsarian, postlapsarian, human – or indeed of methodological approaches to the biblical narrative and its literary reflection, though this might well begin with medieval exegesis as a critical method in its own right, looking at the text word for word according to a set hermeneutic. Hraban's *Commentary on Genesis* is one example here; linguistic, doctrinal or historical approaches are now more likely. A fairly recent study of the Fall in literature may stand as an example of the problems: J. M. Evans wrote in 1968 on *Paradise Lost and the Genesis Tradition*,[11] placing a well known, but individual, literary adaptation first, and when he considers the tradition he makes divisions in terms of style (the neoclassical treatments of the Fall, such as that by Avitus), motive (as with the defiance and ambiguity in heroic treatments such as the Anglo-Saxon *Genesis B*) and genre, as with the dramatic versions.

The basic approach to the texts considered in this study is historical insofar as it accepts the premises, themselves theological or historical, of the age in which the works were written. This approach – as Charles Donahue pointed out in a summary

---

[10] *Ezzos Cantilena de miraculis Christi* (the older, Strasbourg version), in Friedrich Maurer, *Die religiösen Dichtungen des 11. und 12. Jahrhunderts* (Tübingen: Niemeyer, 1964–70), I, 269–303 (= S IV, 6, p. 287).
[11] Oxford: Clarendon, 1968.

of a debate about the use of patristic exegesis in interpreting medieval literature – follows Hugh of St Victor's own interpretative triad of *littera, sensus* and *sententia*, the letter, the meaning and the significance, we might say. The historical dimension is represented by the question put by J. Hillis Miller in 1967: 'of what use is this work to someone who believes this way?' The approach is one of informed pragmatism. What are the writings trying to do with the narrative, and in what context, and to what extent are they successful?[12] Different literary approaches might lead in specific directions, of course: philosophical or indeed psychological approaches to the reflection of the Fall in literature are not uncommon, nor, more recently, are gender-based analyses.[13]

In broad terms, indeed, there is in literature a recurrent neoplatonic view of the world after the Fall as an increasingly imperfect reflection of lost glory the further we move away from the experiences of Adam and Eve themselves, whose immediate and actual *memories* of Paradise lead them to undertake a penance in apocryphal texts. From Augustine's neoplatonism we might move to Spenser, whose *Hymne of Heavenly Beavtie* (the last of the *Fowre Hymnes* of 1596) stresses that our eyes are too frail to sustain 'the Sun's bright beames', to Milton, whose earth is the shadow of Heaven in *Paradise Lost* V, 575, and on to Wordsworth's *Intimations*.[14] Indeed, one of the most recent writers of an epic of Creation, the late Tom Scott in his long poem *The Tree* of 1977, places Adam and Eve into an already fallen world, but sees evil as the result not of sin but of an obscuring of the light; Scott's complex and rewarding work does seem to take the line that the loss of a restrictive Paradise was the origin of freedom, rather than of all our woe, and sees Adam as the first self-assertive hero rather than as the first sinner.[15] The romantic, assertively humanist and individualistic approach – we could apply other tags to it – on the other hand, stresses the independence of Adam, or indeed of Eve, the freedom of man after the Fall. And even in Milton, of course, Adam is a hero in the specific sense, the 'goodliest man'. On the other hand, as C. M. Bowra pointed out

---

[12] The collection edited by Dorothy Bethurum, *Critical Approaches to Medieval Literature* (New York: Columbia University Press, 1960) contains three papers on 'Patristic Exegesis in the Criticism of Medieval Literature', pp. 1–82, attacked by E. Talbot Donaldson, defended by R. E. Kaske, and summarised by Charles Donahue. The reference is to p. 77. The comment by Miller is from his essay on 'Literature and Religion', in *Relations of Literary Study*, ed. James Thorpe (New York: MLA, 1967), pp. 111–26, see p. 114.

[13] As examples we may cite such interesting papers or studies as William H. Poteat, 'Birth, Suicide and the Doctrine of Creation', in *New Essays on Religious Language*, ed. Dallas M. High (New York: Oxford University Press, 1969), pp. 162–77 and Maud Bodkin's *Archetypal Patterns in Poetry* (London: Oxford University Press, 1934) as representatives of quite different approaches. Bodkin discusses Eve as an archetype, pp. 153–216, and more recent studies are numerous.

[14] Spenser, *Poetical Works*, ed. J. C. Smith and E. de Selincourt (London: Oxford University Press, 1912 and reprints), p. 597; the reference to Milton is developed in Basil Willey, *The Seventeenth-Century Background* ([1934] Harmondsworth: Penguin, 1962), p. 69. On Wordsworth's neoplatonism, see Helen Gardner, *Religion and Literature* (London: Faber, 1971), pp. 134–5.

[15] Tom Scott, *The Tree* (Dunfermline: Borderline Press, 1977). I have discussed the work in detail in 'Naming the Beasts: Tom Scott and the Poet's Paradise', *Chapman* 26 (= 6/ii, Spring, 1980), 37–45. Scott died in 1995. An earlier assertion of the point was that by Archibald MacLeish in his 1926 plays of *Nobodaddy*, on which see Colin C. Campbell, 'The Transformation of Biblical Myth: Macleish's Use of the Adam and Job Stories', in *Myth and Symbol*, ed. Bernice Slote (Lincoln, Neb: University of Nebraska Press, 1953), pp. 79–88.

in his study of the hero in Vergil, Milton and elsewhere, Adam has lost his 'first naked glorie' and become like the American savage with 'featherd cincture' in *Paradise Lost* IX, 1114–18. The savage is not yet noble, and America is not yet the new Eden.[16] America is even seen as pre-dating Eden in works like the Calvinist Isaac (de) Lapeyrère's *Prae-Adamitae* of 1655, which has a separate pre-Adamic race (supported apparently by the fact that the Elohist Creation account in the first chapter of Genesis does not mention Adam and Eve, ancestors therefore only of the Jews) in remote regions like the Americas, not even affected by the Flood.[17] Yet another literary possibility is the presentation of Adam and Eve as proto-lovers, elements from which come into other interpretations of the narrative, as in the explanation of why Adam permitted Eve to persuade him to eat; or what their respective feelings were about the loss of Paradise and the gaining of earthly love.[18]

Other differences of focus might cause us to look more closely at the nature of the expulsion, at its simplest level the depiction of the history of alienation, the tale of what we have lost, the once-held Paradise, described in the Middle Ages often as part of a *locus amoenus* tradition by writers as far apart geographically as Otfried of Weissenburg in his Gospel-Book, the anonymous Irish poet of the *Saltair na Rann*, or Peter Damian in his *De gloria paradisi*.[19] Changing interests, even changing fashions in thought, will also cause shifts in focus; variations in the attitude to the Virgin (and hence to Genesis 3:15) have caused differences (both positive and negative) in the presentation of Eve throughout the centuries, and the feminist approach has refocussed on her, usually positively, and combined with the independent presentation of the protoplasts. So, too, considerations of genre alone will cause necessary differences of emphasis: *Paradise Lost* is not *Adam lay Ibounden*, and questions can be asked and answered in an epic work that a lyric piece has to accept or ignore.

How, then, do we read the Fall in mediated theology aimed at what we have to call a non-specialist audience? The specific question of how pre-lapsarian naked innocence is expressed can often be resolved, for example, by using the figure of the child. Wordsworth's *Intimations of Immortality* is probably the most conscious attempt to build a bridge to the real world (and we might also recall not only Blake's rather disturbing 'Infant Sorrow', but also T. S. Eliot's 'Animula'; the soul

---

[16] C. M. Bowra, *From Virgil to Milton* (London: Macmillan, 1945). See. p. 200 in his chapter on 'Milton and the Destiny of Man'; the simile of nakedness is on p. 207.

[17] See Piggott, *Ancient Britons*, pp. 45f.

[18] There is, for example, a long excursus on Eve as the mother of all women in Gottfried von Strassburg's epic of the love story of Tristan and Isolde: see Walter Haug, 'Gottfried von Strassburgs *Tristan*: Sexueller Sündenfall oder erotische Utopie?' in *Kontroversen, alte und neue: Akten des VII Internationalen Germanisten-Kongresses (Göttingen 1985)* (Tübingen: Niemeyer, 1986), I, 41–52. The title of the paper is significant, and we may add the following: F. Assensio, '¿Tradición sobre un peccado sexual en el Paraíso?', *Gregorianum* 30 (1949), 490–520 and 31 (1950), 35–62, 163–91, 362–90; Kenneth J. Northcott, 'Paradisaical Love in Early Middle High German Literature', in *Taylor Starck Festschrift*, ed. Werner Betz (Mouton: The Hague, 1964), pp. 164–75 and Reinhold Grimm, 'Die Paradiesesehe: eine erotische Utopie des Mittelalters', in *[Festschrift] für Wolfgang Mohr*, ed. F. Hundschnurcher and U. Müller (Göppingen: Kümmerle, 1972), pp. 1–25.

[19] See my *The Old Irish Adam and Eve from Saltair na Rann II: Commentary* (Dublin: DIAS, 1976), pp. 52–5; Peter Damian is in *PL* 145, 980.

that issues from the hand of God is a simple one, but it is still potentially 'a fiend hid in a cloud'). After early childhood, even the intimations of paradisiacal inno- cence are lost, and fuller texts are of course more complex. Even with modern English works – to take again a relatively accessible set of examples – a variety of textual approaches manifests itself, especially in longer texts. There is, for example, a quasi-science-fiction work which really presents a reworking of the Fall as it might have been, but with an outcome that both precludes the necessity for Redemption in the world in which it is set, and which depends upon its having happened already in our own; C. S. Lewis's *Perelandra (Voyage to Venus)* of 1943 is based effectively on the same religious premises as our medieval works, and adds really only one new human protagonist to the original set of characters in the medieval Genesis interpreted according to the *sensus litteralis*, with the difference that the devil occupies a different animal on this occasion.[20] More recently, and with different premises, Penelope Farmer's book *Eve: Her Story* (the title exploits the not entirely successful word-play of *his*tory/*her*story) offers a defiant presenta- tion of the romantic rebel, the individualised protoplast, with Eve eating the fruit because she wanted to, not on the prompting of the serpent. In this case, Eve is not just the biblical Eve, but an accretion of elements from other legends, rabbinic and otherwise, which Farmer lists in her afterword. Her work also transfers the biblical narrative into the world at large by using the parallel of growing up, albeit we have here not the male child we shall meet with Gregorius or Parzival, but the three stages of child, girl and woman. Farmer's Eve has medieval counterparts: her Eve claims that Adam wanted to regain Paradise, but that she did not, something the medieval Austrian writer Lutwin had already exploited in the fourteenth century when he permitted the pair to quarrel precisely over that point.[21]

Another modern English novelist, Emma Tennant, presents a version of the Fall in *Sisters and Strangers*, but here Eve is at the same time the first woman and also one living in a modern world as Mrs Eve First, for example, and the game aspect of the novella (Tennant refers to it as 'A Moral Tale') is underlined by the framework of the story. It is told to two young girls by their grandmother. There is no Redemp- tion, and the point at the end is the constant recreation of the new Eve, a self- assertion of the *Ewig-weibliche*.[22] In an interesting contrast, two very popular contemporary writers, Terry Pratchett and Neil Gaiman, published in the same year as Tennant's novella a work which is ostensibly a double parody, first of *The Omen*, and secondly of Salman Rushie's *Satanic Verses*. *Good Omens*, however, has a central character who is supposedly the Antichrist incarnate, but who is named Adam, and who follows his free will, and at the age of dawning reason – he is eleven, and in the literary sense he is also close to Richmal Crompton's William

---

[20] C. S. Lewis, *Perelandra* (London: Bodley Head, 1943), also as *Voyage to Venus* (London: Pan, 1953). A New York edition in the 1950s retitled the novel *Perelandra: World of the New Temptation*.
[21] Penelope Farmer, *Eve: Her Story* (London: Gollancz, 1985). The issue of gender (angels and pre- sumably God are perceived to be above gender) plays a considerable part in the work, of course. Eve's comments about Adam come in the final part of the third section of the work, which is divided into the development child–girl–woman. Farmer notes in her afterword J. A. Phillips, *Eve: The History of an Idea* (San Francisco: Harper and Row, 1984). On the point of Eve's views about the world, see my paper 'Eve's Anger: Literary Secularisation in Lutwin's *Adam und Eva*', *Archiv* 215 (1978), 256–71.
[22] Emma Tennant, *Sisters and Strangers* (London: Grafton, 1990).

– he forestalls the Apocalypse, the forces of which include a personified Death. The two authors are concerned to stress the continuity of humanity, which comes trailing clouds of damnation rather than of glory, through free choice, but the supernatural and all too human child does comment at one point that one day it might even be possible to conquer Death. And at the end, the brutish but eternal Adam slouches off, leaving the reader to supply the rest of Yeats' quotation: to Bethlehem.[23]

Finding works which use the Genesis narrative without direct reference even through a name, but which still show the Fall and the Redemption, can be more difficult, and studies of works like Golding's *Lord of the Flies*, or the selection of American Adamic heroes (including perhaps most fully Melville's *Billy Budd*) presented by R. W. B. Lewis in a book called, significantly enough, *The American Adam* are not always convincing.[24] The romantic Adam and Eve and the assertion of human individuality expressed through positive rebellion *are* made plain in works like Karel Čapek's *R.U.R. (The Robot Play)* of 1923, at the close of which the robots Helena and Primus are dismissed into the world by the human clerk of the robot factory, Alquist, since they represent a new start and a new humanity. The play ends with his voicing the words of the *Nunc dimittis*, and the Redemption lies in this fresh start. But they are still Adam and Eve sent into the world, and the word 'robot', of course, adopted into English from this play, derives from the verb 'to work hard'. The motif was in fact parodied a century before in Georg Büchner's play *Leonce und Lena*, in which the titular couple as Adam and Eve propose at the conclusion a reversal of the biblical judgement and a return to a state of childlike play, whilst an old governess speaks an ironic *Nunc dimittis* once again.[25] In the post-Hiroshima world, the idea of restarting the human race here on earth or (in another literary genre), somewhere in space has also become a commonplace, albeit with the notion expressed sometimes that the world has fallen too far for a second Redemption. There was a pithy example of the latter negative view in a song by Bob Dylan set after World War III in which a survivor invites a girl to 'play Adam and Eve', only to have her reject this because of what happened last time.

There are various (incomplete) collections listing Adam and Eve material of all kinds, and demonstrating incidentally the tenacity of the motif-complex. One of the fullest is that by Watson Kirkconnell, who produced in 1952 a brave and (in spite of its imperfections) entirely creditable and still useful volume called *The Celestial Cycle*, containing analogues of *Paradise Lost*. By this the compiler meant almost anything with a literary and (although his selection principles are not completely clear) a specifically poetic intent to do with the Creation or the Fall. He

---

[23] Terry Pratchett and Neil Gaiman, *Good Omens* (London: Gollancz, 1990).

[24] Erich Smith, *Some Versions of the Fall: the Myth of the Fall of Man in English Literature* (London: Croom Helm, 1973); R. W. B. Lewis, *The American Adam: Innocence, Tragedy and Tradition in the Nineteenth Century* (Chicago and London: University of Chicago Press, 1955). See now also Ingrid G. Daemmrich, *Enigmatic Bliss: the Paradise Motif in Literature* (Frankfurt/M: Lang, 1997).

[25] The Brothers Čapek, *R.U.R. and The Insect Play* (London: Oxford University Press, 1961). The first of these, *R.U.R. (Rossum's Universal Robots)* by Karel Čapek was translated by P. Selver and was performed in London in 1923. Georg Büchner's play was completed in the last year of his life, 1837, and published posthumously. It is in the edition of Büchner's *Werke und Briefe*, ed. Fritz Bergemann (Wiesbaden: Insel, 1958).

listed 329 analogues, starting with the Sumerian Creation (Genesis itself is only number four), and the literary material proper really begins with his twelfth entry, Victorinus of Petavio's poem on the Creation. We enter the twentieth century with Shaw's *Man and Superman* (number 307), specifically Act III as a parody of Milton, and the last piece is a posthumously published fragment by Paul Valéry. Kirkconnell's dating is not always helpful (an interesting but obscure poem by Lorca, which was published in 1922, is dated 1939, three years after the poet's death and presumably the date of the publication of a translation); and as Kirkconnell would have been the first to admit, the list is not complete. As fortuitous examples of omissions let me list – or possibly the more appropriate term is 'resurrect briefly' – Alonso López's *Glosa peregrina*, consisting of sixty-nine stanzas on the Fall and the Redemption, and dating from about 1550, a work for which there is no modern edition and on which my own information is second hand. Nor, I need hardly add, is there much likelihood that Milton had heard of this Spanish work, of course, but it is of interest not only as a chronological forerunner of *Paradise Lost*, but because it uses lines from ballads incorporated into the work, even though it is not, like other *a lo divino* texts, strictly speaking a contrafactura work.[26] It was also expanded and attributed to someone else a decade after its first appearance. My second example, and this time as a bibliographical curiosity, is *Adam and Lilith: A Poem in Four Parts* by A. F. Scot, of whom little is known, published in 1899; the piece, nearly a hundred pages long, draws on apocryphal and rabbinic stories. Finally, the Dutch poet Bertus Aafjes wrote, whilst in Cairo in 1948, an extended piece called *In den beginne*, which was published by Querido in Amsterdam.[27] As already indicated, there seems to be no sign of any diminution in the numbers of literary representations of the narrative, or indeed of studies of it in all kinds of genres.[28]

It is appropriate to begin a more practical approach to the question of how the Fall and the Redemption are treated in literature by the examination of a selection of smaller medieval and indeed modern pieces, the first of which – and reference has been made to it already – is very well known, nowadays probably primarily because of its inclusion and musical setting in Benjamin Britten's *Ceremony of Carols*:

> Adam lay i-bowndyn, bowndyn in a bond,
> fowre þowsand wynter þowt he not to long;
> And all was for an appil, an appil þat he tok,
> As clerkis fyndyn wretyn in here book.
> Ne hadde þe appil take ben, þe appil taken ben,
> ne hadde never our lady a ben heuene qwen;

[26] See John Crosbie, *A lo divino Lyric Poetry: An Alternative View* (Durham: DMLS, 1989), pp. 50f. Crosbie gives details of the text on p. 88 and discusses other comparable works.
[27] A. F. Scot, *Adam and Lilith* (London: Burleigh, 1899); Bertus Aafjes, *In den beginne* (Amsterdam: Querido, 1949).
[28] Thus there is an examination of folktales of the Fall by Paul Schwarz, *Die neue Eva: der Sündenfall in Volksglaube und Volkserzählung* (Göppingen: Kümmerle, 1963).

Blyssid be þe tyme þat appil take was,
Þer-fore we mown syngyn, 'deo gracias!'[29]

Carleton Brown classifies the piece as a nativity poem in his standard anthology, and one of its many other editors, Theodore Silverstein, introduces it in the *York Medieval Texts* with a summary that, for an eight-line piece, gives us a wealth of possibilities as to what it is actually about: 'Reversal of expectation brings charm to this statement of the consequence of a crime, in a brief poem of praise for Mary. The theme is the *felix culpa* joyously acclaimed on Easter eve.' And of course it is all those things: a poem about the results first and then the nature of the Fall, expressed very concisely; it praises Mary indeed, though without the Eve–Mary juxtaposition we get in topoi like the Eva–*Ave* reversal; and it expresses the *felix culpa* not only in the Marian part but in the implication that Adam is no longer *ibowndyn*. He had, however, been bound for four thousand years, an echo of the time found in apocryphal writings, usually 5,500 years, but with considerable variation. The apple is a standard point of reference, too, however unbiblical it might be, but the reference to written authority in the mention of the *clerkes* might well cover all the internal acts of interpretation. The second verse is Marian in that it uses the notion of the *felix culpa* to refer to the glorification of the Virgin in particular, but the *deo gracias* with which the work concludes is general.

A second preliminary example is provided by a Latin sequence from the school of Notker the Stammerer of St Gallen, perhaps of the ninth century, though it seems not to be by him; it is a strict sequence, with syllabic parallels between the half-strophes, like those of Notker.[30] It may be cited in full:

Pange deo debitum,
lingua, modulando plectrum.

1   Tolle sonos in aera   2   Sancta manus igitur nos
     Imple sinus a lacrimis   meditata effigiem

3   Pressit nobis suam: 4   Sursum caput tulis

[29] Cited from *Religious Lyrics of the XVth Century*, ed. Carleton Brown (Oxford: Clarendon, 1939), p. 120 (no. 83), where it is classed as a nativity song. See also Theodore Silverstein, *Medieval English Lyrics* (London: Arnold, 1971), pp. 99f. The work is very frequently anthologised, as in E. K. Chambers and F. Sidgwick, *Early English Lyrics* ([1907] London: Sidgwick and Jackson, 1947), p. 102. Brown and Silverstein are closer to the unique manuscript (BL Sloane 2593); there are stops to show the breaks. See on the work Rosemary Woolf, *The English Religious Lyric in the Middle Ages* (Oxford: Clarendon, 1968), pp. 290–1 and Peter Diehl, *The Medieval European Religious Lyric* (Berkeley etc.: University of California Press, 1985), pp. 155f, noting the time of four thousand years mentioned in the piece. He points out that it appears in lyrics in many European languages, but does not refer to the apocryphal material. The poem might also be compared with the German poem *Ezzos Gesang*, on which see Peter Dronke's analysis, *The Medieval Lyric* (London: Hutchinson, 1968), p. 49. There are various other English lyrics which are also comparable with the brief text (see no. 82 in Carleton Brown's collection, for example, 'Qwhereas Adam cawsed . . .').
[30] Dronke, *Lyric*, p. 41 discusses the form and analyses one of Notker's. This is in the *Analecta Hymnica Medii Aevi*, ed. Clemens Blume and Guido Dreves (Leipzig: Reisland, 1886–), XLII, 47, and it appears with a German translation in Horst Kusch, *Einführung in das lateinische Mittelalter* (Berlin: Verlag der Wissenschaften, 1957), pp. 118–21.

	flavit et indidit. ruri animam.			vultum ut cogitet semper Domini.

5   Tradit amoena locus
    corruit aspidis ingenio.

6   Mox actus in foveam
    asperis, heu miser, illiditur.

7   O facinus, vitae,
    pro dolor, memoriam
    quod aspirare non sinis
    neque fletibus, heu,
    expiare nefas miserum.

8   Artis ligata
    serpentis spiris, mens misera,
    Umbra volveris ibi nunc
    horrida, cupido
    quo profudit saeva animi.

9   Dira sorbes venena,
    sentis vulnera
    quae male nutricas, misera,

10 Facis caeco lumine
    fusa nebulis,
    expers dulcibus, mens misera.

11 Repit virus pectore
    sensu captus emoreris,
    cinis redis ad funera:
    heu, post stringeris in tartara.

12 Tantis potens doluit
    factor tui calumniis;
    venit, solvit a vinculis
    bonos; respires ad gratiam.

13 Siccat iam oculus,
    facescat et pudor taeter;
    vera sustineas gaudia.

14 Flecte hinc faciem;
    imaginem auri primam,
    dulcem repetito patriam.

15 Plasmator durare perennem
    quam concedas
    lux sis nobis, meritum.

16 Tu solus extas trinus unus,
    te voce, te
    corde, rex, laudamus.

In saecula.

(Sing out, my tongue, and create the song that is justly due to god./ 1 Raise voices into the air and fill every bosom with tears/ 2 For the holy hand has made us in its image and with its form/ 3 impressed upon us all: He breathed, and thus he gave a soul to the clay./ 4 Upwards man raised his head, that he might think upon the Lord for ever./ 5 God gave him Paradise, lost by the trickery of the serpent./ 6 Too soon he was thrown into the grave, hurled down, alas, against the rock./ 7 O crime, so wicked that the memory of that life, alas, will not come back to man, nor yet by human tears can such a wretched act be made good./ 8 And now, pitiful soul, caught tightly in the serpent's close coils, you struggle in the darkness now, where horrid lustfulness keeps you in chains as a prisoner./ 9 You drink an evil poison, the wounds are smarting, nor can you tend them, and must suffer/ 10 half-blind in flickering light, hemmed in by dark, far from all sweetness, o wretched soul./ 11 If the poison takes your heart you will die, robbed of all sense, and ashes shall become again, alas, and then shall be bound in hell./ 12 The great creator was sad that you were suffering so; he came and released the chains of the good; may you come to His grace./ 13 All the tears are wiped away, all the shame shall be put aside, and you shall experience joy./ 14 Turn your face from the world; seek out the golden origin and the sweet lost home in Paradise./ 15 Creator, who lives and reigns, grant to us your light and your reward./ 16 For you alone are the three in one, we call on you, O king, praising with heart and voice, for ever and ever.)

This time we begin with the Creation, so that the work forms a complete *summa*. It is Adam whom we see created and placed into Paradise, however, with the breath of God in him, and the suddenness of the shift from *tradit* to *corruit*, from 'hand over' to 'shatter' in the fifth strophe is striking. The results are the grave, and the ongoing effects of the serpent, whose coils are still around mankind. Even the memory has gone, and man is far further away from Paradise than were Adam and Eve, who could remember the glory. This is even more extreme, perhaps, than Wordsworth's *Intimations*. Adam and indeed man, since we have now merged these, are both bound in hell – *stringere* is the verb used. It is grace, however – *deo gracias* – that can return man to Paradise. We are not shown the Harrowing by Christ but by grace for the good, and the notion of the return as such echoes once again one of the salient questions, that of whether there can be a return, given a literal meaning in the *Vita Adae*, for example, where Seth, representing both Adam and mankind, tries to do so. The conclusion is homiletic, urging us towards the lost golden origins, back to Paradise – *sis lux nobis*: the conclusion is extended to all men.

A third work, in German this time, is hardly well known, although we do have quite a lot of information about the author. The work is a poem by Hugo von Montfort (1357–1423) who came from Austria. He is not usually thought of as a major poet, and in fact the standard literary histories, when they mention him at all, tend towards the word 'mediocre'; but his works do provide us with an example of a vernacular presentation of the Fall in a short mode. His poem on the subject of the Fall (XXXII) is very long, comprising forty-three quatrains, and we start at strophe 18. The work is most comparable, perhaps, with William of Shoreham's even longer English poem, an extended but orthodox and largely biblical work of 149 strophes on the Creation and Fall, written in about 1320. Even in the shorter German piece, however, there is space to expand ideas about the Fall and Redemption, though the constraints of the lyric are still there to an extent:[31]

> Wan unglük kunt von sünden
> Und von verschulten sachen:
> das tuot sich sicher gründen,
> Ich kans nicht anders machen.
>
> Hett Eva gots gebot nit gebrochen,
> Die welt die het kein liden.
> Das wart gar ser gerochen,
> Das mag ich nicht verswigen.
>
> Das widerbracht die magt,
> Die junkfrow muoter rein,

---

[31] *Hugo von Montfort*, ed. Karl Bartsch (Tübingen: Stuttgarter lit. Verein, 1871), pp. 185–91. For William, see the edition by M. Konrath, *The Poems of William of Shoreham* (London: Kegan Paul, 1902 = EETS/ES 86), poem VII.

Als sant Matheus sagt,
Mit irem kindlin ein.

Wol uns das sie ie ward geborn,
Ein bluom der selikeit.
Si verricht uns grossen zorn
Und behuot uns vor ewig leit.

Si truog zwar iren herren
Und aller welte got.
Unser glük das tet si meren,
Das ist ân allen spot.

Das kind is geborn
Von einr junkfrowen:
Das tet den tiefeln zorn,
Ir gewalt der ward zerhowen.

Des sind die juden blind
In gesehenden ogen.
Geboren ist das kind,
Das wellents nicht geloben.

Sie betrügt der talamuot
Mit gar gelogenn sachen:
Zwar das tuot in nimer guot,
Si slaffen oder si wachen.

All prophecien sind beschehen,
Die sach ist volbrâcht;
Das wil ich wol mit warheit jehen,
Ich hâns gar recht bedâcht.

Ir heiden, ir sült das verstân:
Als Crist ward geborn,
Umb üwer götter was es getân,
Ir gwalt der was verlorn.

Appollo der tet vallen,
Als im sant Gregori gebôt,
Vil geist in jamer wallen:
Crist half uns uss ewig nôt.

Mit sinem tod erworben,
Hab ich gar wolbedâcht:
Wir weren ewig gestorben,
Davon hât er uns brâcht,

Und fuor gen hell, daruss er nam
Die sinen willen hetten getân,
Als sinr gerechtikeit wol gezam:
Die wurden aller sorgen ân.

Ir heiden, es sind tiefel gwesen,
Die ir da angebettet han,
Das hab ich in der warheit glesen:
Ir gewalt mocht nicht lenger stân.

. . .

Almechtig got,
Hilf mir mit dinen gnaden,
Das ich nicht werd der tiefel spot:
Kum mir ze trost mit dines geistes gaben.

Wan an din macht
So wer min sach vernichte,
Das ich mit dinen gnaden tracht.
Min irren weg die mach mir in ein slichte.

Ich ruef dich an als Adam tet:
Er stuond gen dir in buosse.
Almechtig got, gwer mich der pet
Hilf miner sel uss böser sünde ruosse.

Ich halt dich ein
Got und minen herren,
Got vatter sun gemain
O heilger geist, tuo mir genade meren!

(Misfortune comes from sin and from guilty deeds; this is well attested; I cannot change that./ Had Eve not broken God's commandment the world would have had no pain. Vengeance was taken strongly – I cannot conceal that./ The maiden redeemed it, the virgin, pure, mother (as St Matthew says) with her baby./ O joy, that she was born! A flower of blessedness. She wiped out great anger, preserved us from eternal pain./ Truly she bore our lord and the God of the world. She increased our happiness; that is without any lie./ The child was born of a virgin: that angered the devils and their power was smashed./ The Jews are blind to this, though their eyes can see. The child was born, though they won't believe it./ The Talmud deceives them with lies; truly, this is bad for them, sleeping or waking./ All the prophecies are fulfilled – it is completed. I assert this in truth, I have thought about it well./ Unbelievers, understand this: when Christ was born that was the end of your gods, their power was finished./ Apollo was cast down, as St Gregory commanded. Many spirits were in misery: Christ led us from eternal pain,/ bought with his death. I have thought it out: we would have died eternally, but he saved us from that./ And went into hell, and took out those who had done his will, in accordance with his justice: They were freed of care./ O heathens, they were devils you prayed to, I have read that in truth. Their power had to fade./

16

.../ Almighty God, help me with your grace not to be the devil's prey: help me with your gifts of mercy./ For without your power all my deeds would be as nought, all that I think, with your grace./ Smooth my crooked path. I call to you as Adam did when he did penance before you; Almighty God, grant my plea, help my soul from sin's abyss./ I hold by you, my God and lord, God the Father, God the Son, O Holy Spirit, grant mercy!)

The extended opening of the work is simply a panegyric to God, but from quatrain 18 Hugo sets up a hypothetical situation: what if Eve had not fallen? She *did* fall, however, and this was redeemed by the Virgin, although the notion of the *felix culpa* is not underscored. Instead the concentration is first of all on the nature of the Redemption, and then on the fact that it is not universally believed. The work is not specifically anti-Semitic, but there is a strong assumption of learned dispute in the reference first to the Talmud and then to the fulfilment of the prophecies, although these are not spelt out. Rather the poet insists on it – *jehen* simply means 'to state'. Christ has destroyed the demons, and also harrowed hell, and that of course is the turning point in history, and the poet can now refer to his own sinfulness in a prayer for mercy. However, the Adamic references are not yet finished, and here towards the end of the work is an allusion – it is no more than that – to Adam's attempt at penance. It is unlikely that this passage could refer to anything else than an episode in the apocryphal life of Adam, although the outcome is not described, and one wonders how extensive or secure this piece of knowledge was. We might note, too, that Eve fell, and Adam did penance.

It is a large leap to make, but it is worth noting that the tradition of the short literary work – often a poem – concerned with Adam and Eve continues to flourish with considerable tenacity. Modern lyric poems concerned with Adam range in their approach to the story from the Christian-redemptory to the completely defiant, and in a brief article on the subject some years ago I discussed poems by (rearranged in alphabetical order) Vicente Aleixandre, Giacomo Belli, Noel Coward, D. J. Enright, Ted Hughes, Elizabeth Jennings, C. S. Lewis, Czeslaw Miłosz, Edwin Muir, Jacques Prévert, Tom Scott, and others. Some of these poems conform in outlook entirely to medieval views, where others might, for example, present God as pensioned off to live in a hut in Eden on his own, or even show us how Adam and Eve, bored with Eden, decide to create God. The continued acceptance of the divine economy stands side-by-side with the humanist-romantic ideal, the difference between the Fall as an expulsion from glory, and the emergence from Eden as the start of human freedom. Sometimes, admittedly, the poems are very hard to interpret, as with the piece by Lorca referred to already, a poem of which Watson Kirkconnell said that it was 'enigmatic as to sense'. Federico García Lorca's well known sonnet, called simply 'Adán', is relatively simple in purely linguistic terms, at least in most parts; in terms of understanding there are more difficulties,[32] and yet it is interesting precisely because of its conciseness, so that

[32] The poem is from the *Primeras Canciones* of 1922: Federico García Lorca, *Obras Completas*, ed. Arturo del Hoyo (Madrid: Aguilar, 1971), p. 353. There is a translation by Stephen Spender in the Penguin anthology *Lorca*, ed. J. L. Gill (Harmondsworth: Penguin, 1960), p. 126.

trying to unravel it brings in a whole range of interpretative possibilities based on connotation and pre-knowledge of the Adamic narrative. The basic features are easily picked out: there is a tree, a woman, Adam asleep, a child. But the tree is one of blood, and by it, in the morning (of the world?) the woman has just borne a child who might be Adam himself, or Cain, or Christ. That very narrative itself, the *fábula*, is forgetful, and that there is a human urge towards the apple underscores the inevitability of the Fall. The first part of the sestet focusses upon Adam, made of clay, asleep, dreaming of the child who will present a threat. But in the final lines another side of him – a different Adam – dreams of a different child, a *niño de luz*, who will flame and illuminate all, and who is perhaps the typological centrast, the child of the Virgin rather than the child of Eve.

One of the best – and far clearer – modern poems of Adam and Eve, and a useful one on which to end this introductory survey, is that by the late Alexander Scott, a piece in Scots, which, with the title 'Blues for the Blue Lagoon', is a poem which takes us, via an Edwardian popular novel, to the impossible desirability of recovering Paradise on earth, to medieval exegesis, to the sources, and to some of our original questions.[33] It also underlines yet again the unity of mankind with Adam. The text falls into three parts, the two outside and metrically distinct ones set very firmly in the reality of the fallen world – in this case Sauchiehall Street in Glasgow, a very long and enclosed street on a wet day in winter – and these two sections surround a distinctive middle part, at the centre of which is the flickering cinematic representation of the *Blue Lagoon*, the new Paradise, but re-interpreted in a mildly pornographic film with a happy ending. The street is dark and mournful – *dowie* – and as the rain falls the cats creep along, just about keeping their balance, while the people have their coats buttoned against the rain, and their minds buttoned against the misery of the human condition. The evocation of a wet winter's day offers us a stark picture of postlapsarian reality.

Are there any intimations of an earlier golden age? Where now, in the twentieth century, is the lost Paradise? In this case it is not something even dimly remembered, nor are we even shown it in a drama, but it is offered through the distanced medium of the cinema. The image now projected – the word is deliberate – is clearly a modern version of the *locus amoenus*, perpetual summer with flowers in the garden, and the setting is quite specifically *Eden's bonnie yaird*, even if the whole thing is, we are soon told, nothing but 'a technicolor lie'. Adam and Eve are figures in the film, but we, the audience, are watching their representations in a fallen world, so that naked innocence is impossible even there. Worse still, we have gone beyond the simple difficulty, encountered by the medieval dramatist, of how to portray nakedness on stage. Not only are these not at all innocent, but they are clothed just enough to titillate. There is a very medieval ring to the notion expressed here by Scott that their provocative semi-nudity is designed precisely to open the eyes of desire, echoing Genesis 3:7 and its exegesis.

Scott's entry of the devil has an interesting reference to authority, in this case the

---

33 Brian Murdoch, 'Eden to Sauchiehall Street: Variations on a Myth in Modern Poetry', *Lines Review* 86 (September 1983), 12–23. The poem is in Alexander Scott, *Cantrips* (Preston: Akros, 1968), pp. 50–3, where it is described as a pop poem. Scott died in 1989. See below, chapter 1 p. 21, on Stacpoole's *Blue Lagoon*.

Bible and Milton, since we know from these sources that there has to be such a creature, whether the devil is in the Bible or not. The inevitability of the action plays on the existing knowledge of the whole narrative: 'there maun be a Deil', 'an nou, the Faa' (with a capital letter). However, all the older views are now dismissed as *auldfarrant blethers*, and this is a different Eden, not a memory, but an improved version, where Eve *can* escape from the devil. However, we are soon reminded that all this is no more than a dream, at best only a neoplatonic flickering of lost reality, causing the viewer to wish the devil dead and Eve in his arms, and then we are back in the coarser climate of the real street;

> Here's simmer's short, and syne there's aye the Faa,
>> The hairst comes in –
> We canna cheit the Deil and jink awa
>> As Eve could rin.

Scott plays on the brevity of summer and then the Fall (still with a capital, but interpreted then as *hairst*, the Scots word for autumn, the fall), and the awareness that we – the homiletic inclusive puts the reader into the audience of the film – cannot cheat the devil; instead we have to struggle with him, or rather, with the devil inside ourselves, which is a struggle as long as life:

> A strauchle lang as life i the street o stane,
>> Sae lang at least,
> Sen aa maun fecht to the deid a Deil o their ain,
>> The hert i the breist.

Scott's moving interpretation of the Fall is of the rueful and isolated Adam, with the pictures of Paradise not as a memory, nor quite as shadows on the wall reflecting a higher reality, but as properly unreal flickerings on a screen which now are only wish-fulfillment, although they are for all of mankind: Romans 5:12 has moved into a Glasgow cinema. Adam has already been interpreted, and although we are *sub gratia*, we must all fight to the death our own devil, our own heart.

We have moved away from the Middle Ages, and hence further from theological assuredness. There are any number of Adam poems, and if in one sense St Paul was both reductive and backward-looking in Romans 5:12 in the idea that all had already sinned in Adam – provided we accept that reading – he could not have foreseen the interpretative diversity thereafter. To conclude with two quotations: in 1984 G. R. Evans commented, in his study of *The Language and Logic of the Bible*, that

> The most important effect [of the Fall] in the eyes of a number of early Christian writers, was the breakdown of communication between man and God ...
> It is upon this supposition, that man, through his own fault, is no longer able to understand what God says to him except dimly and imperfectly, that the whole of medieval exegesis is founded.[34]

---

[34] G. R. Evans, *The Language and Logic of the Bible: the Earlier Middle Ages* (Cambridge: Cambridge University Press, 1984), p. 1.

As far as recent poetry is concerned, a modern literary critic, Helen Gardner, commented in one of the 1966 Ewing Lectures at the University of California at Los Angeles precisely on the difficulty, on the gulf between the medieval views and the modern: she had earlier in the lecture, incidentally, established 'religious poet' as meaning 'Christian religious poet' in the context in which she wrote:

> The religious poet today has to meet a problem of communication that did not exist for earlier centuries. Words and symbols that lay to hand for earlier writers as sure to evoke an earlier response have lost their power.[35]

With the story of Adam and Eve, however, her comment is perhaps not quite so straightforward, in that we have in this case a narrative the outline and some details of which have for so long been so important as to permit the narrative to withstand – at least up to a point – what Gardner calls 'the disappearance of a general acceptance of Christianity' in a way that other biblical narratives have not. It is unsurprising that the Middle Ages treated the story in so many literary ways, from the *Vita Adae* down to the Reformation drama and beyond. But the extent of the literary tradition also clearly fixed the narrative into the imagination, and the insistent question of *unde malum* at least has remained, even if the subsidiary question *cur deus homo* is no longer always presented as the sole answer, and a scientific age can retreat into a statement of ignorance.[36] And given the pun on the Latin apple, a new scholasticism might even interpret that *unde malum* as meaning: who provided the apple?

Many of the chapters which follow open (since they were originally designed as lectures) with an image, sometimes iconographical, which is intended to set the stage for the main theme. At this point it is perhaps suitable to refer to the situation of a particularly celebrated instance of Adam and Eve iconography, a situation which underscores the position of the narrative at the start of salvation history. Amongst the best known medieval illustrations of the story of the Fall are the bronze reliefs by Lorenzo Ghiberti from the first half of the fifteenth century: that they are on the east doors of the baptistry in Florence makes its own point, as the Fall gives way, literally, to the first response, baptism, and then afterwards to the world.

---

[35] Gardner, *Religion and Literature*, p. 137, from the lecture 'Religious Poetry: a Definition', one of the four Ewing Lectures delivered in March 1966 in Los Angeles.

[36] See the admirable foreword by the biologist Steven Rose to the Pocket Canon *Genesis* (Edinburgh: Canongate, 1998), pp. viii–xiv.

ONE

AFTER EDEN: THE APOCRYPHAL ADAM

W E MAY BEGIN with three quite separate problems associated with the reflection in medieval European literature of the Fall and the Redemption, both of which are based on literary constructs, the brief narrative of Adam and Eve at the beginning of Genesis, and the rather longer Gospel narrative. The first problem is a simple one: the story of Adam and Eve is too short, a remarkably slender basis on which to place Paul's anthropology, Irenaeus's theory of recapitulation, and the entire doctrine of original sin. The second problem is both a logical and a literary one: Adam was created pure but lost his original innocence, and this innocence is inconceivable for us, as Adam's supposed descendants, precisely because we do not *have* that innocence.[1] Put succinctly, fallen mankind cannot imagine what it is like to be naked and unashamed, and this leads to logical impasses for theological and secular literary writers alike. And in any case – and this is the third problem – it is not always easy to distinguish between theological and secular literature, as T. S. Eliot, David Cecil, C. S. Lewis, Helen Gardner and others have found, the last-named devoting the 1966 Ewing Lectures to that question and reaching a very open-ended conclusion.[2] There is a difference of putative audience and authorial intent, admittedly, between Hrabanus Maurus's *Commentaria in Genesim* and – let us say – Henry de Vere Stacpoole's *The Blue Lagoon*, insofar as the latter is indirect, intended as entertainment, and incidentally mildly erotic, whilst Hrabanus's work is direct, intended as instruction, and can be, incidentally, mildly soporific. Neither, however, is very original, since both, even though they are eleven hundred years apart, rest upon the story of Adam and Eve. As a matter of fact, de Vere Stacpoole made a far better stab at expressing primal innocence in a fallen world than did Hraban; but then, he was less convinced of the doctrine of original sin.[3] Admittedly, extremes are easy: had we taken C. S. Lewis's *Perelandra* instead of *The Blue Lagoon* as a modern example the point would have been far less clear. The whole question of intentionality becomes more of a problem with early and medieval narratives which expand on the theme of the Fall.

The third chapter of Genesis can, in spite of its brevity, be reduced in essence

---

[1] On the attempt to exonerate or excuse Adam through the idea that the fallen or neutral angels cohabited with the daughters of men and only then brought evil into the world, see D. S. Russell, *The Old Testament Pseudepigrapha* (London: SCM, 1987), pp. 21f.

[2] Gardner, *Religion and Literature*. See especially the first Ewing Lecture (1966), pp. 121–42 entitled 'Religious Poetry: a Definition', although it is by no means clear whether she ever provides one. Lewis's views in his lecture to the Oxford Socratic Club in 1944 on the question 'Is Theology Poetry?' is equally confusing, especially in medieval terms: *They Asked for a Paper* (London: Bles, 1962), pp. 150–65.

[3] H[enry] de Vere Stacpoole's novel of two children marooned on a desert island first appeared in 1908 and enjoyed considerable popularity.

even further, to simple references to Adam *in quo omnes peccaverunt* (in a medieval context we may adhere to the Vulgate, even when the biblical reading – as here – is a questionable one), or, embracing the Redemption as well, to the paradox of a *felix culpa, qui talem redemptorem meruit*. But equally it is enlarged upon in all kinds of different ways outside and more especially within the Christian tradition, with the addition of clarifying details, some of which are entirely factual and hence primarily of narrative interest, although the implications may be significant in theological terms too. When did all this happen? Where was Paradise, and what was it like to live there? Some questions, indeed, are less obvious, such as Adam's height at creation, nine feet and eight inches according to the Old English dialogue *Solomon and Saturn*.[4] Even in the post-medieval period there are often absolutely firm answers to some of the questions. Bishop Ussher's 1658 dating of the creation to 4004 BC – at noon on October 23 – was still current enough in the time of the original benefactor of these lectures, and the *Universal Bible*, which appeared in two editions within John Hulse's lifetime, in 1758 and then again in 1761, included as its second engraving a map of the site of Eden, with confident coordinates of 33 degrees longitude and 37 degrees latitude, just outside modern Beirut. The Assyriologist Friedrich Delitzsch was still trying to pin it down in the nineteenth century, although Herbert Edward Ryle, lecturing in Cambridge as the Hulsean Professor in 1891 confessed that he thought (and indeed hoped) that it never *would* be identified. His still eminently readable lectures on the first chapters of Genesis also saw the biblical narrative of the Fall as a manifestation of divine mercy.[5] And as to what Eden was like, the anonymous translation of Giovanni Loredano's *L'Adamo* in 1640 described the climate of Paradise rather enigmatically as 'enriched with a perpetuall Autumnall spring'.[6] More familiar answers to the question of what exactly happened there are found in the tradition of medieval interpretation according to the *sensus litteralis*, by which the serpent becomes a mouthpiece for the devil and so on, although even here additional knowledge comes in by obscure routes. Thus the non-biblical apple from the tree of knowledge, a pun on the Latin word for 'evil', has established itself very thoroughly indeed.

The theological question of why the Fall happened at all has even been answered *without* reference to the Redemption. Of the various collections in and after the twelfth century of so-called *Salernitan Questions*, addressing largely

---

4   James E. Cross and Thomas D. Hill, *The Prose Solomon and Saturn* (Toronto: University of Toronto Press, 1982), pp. 67–76 has a great number of similar details.

5   Herbert Edward Ryle, *The Early Narratives of Genesis* (London: Macmillan, 1892), see pp. 43 and 51. The *Geneva Bible*, produced by and for English Protestants in 1560, also has a map of 'the sitvacion of the Garden of Eden' but it is far less specific and seems to imply the entire Tigris-Euphrates basin. A caption implies that Eden means the fertile crescent as such. Occasional attempts are still made to locate Eden, and the 'results' appear with some regularity in the colour supplements of Sunday newspapers or on popularising television programmes. Interest even in these matters has never completely waned.

6   Giovanni Francesco Loredano, *The Life of Adam*, trans. by T. S. in 1659, ed. Roy C. Flannagan and John Arthos (Gainesville, Florida: Scholar's Facsimiles, 1967), p. 7. The text was written in 1640, and was much translated and widely read. In spite of the title given it in English, it is unconnected with the apocryphal *Vita Adae* tradition.

medical issues, one manuscript now in the Bodleian library in Oxford opens with a theological affirmation of the necessity of Adam's Fall so that Christ could conquer death, but the related version in Peterhouse library in Cambridge is a little different. It claims that Adam, who had been created with a balance of humours (*temperatum in omnibus qualitatibus*), suffered, on being offered the fruit, an excess of *sollicitudo* – we might translate it as 'stress' – which threw his humours off-balance, so that he fell.[7] Presumably a mild sedative would have coped with this, but there is, of course, no 'would have' about the Fall; its essence is in its having happened, as is the case with all aetiological answers to philosophical questions, in this case, not just *unde malum* (a question which, as Elaine Pagels has pointed out, Tertullian claimed was the kind of thing that *made* people heretics),[8] but what was to be done about it. The key theme of the apocryphal lives of Adam and Eve is – to borrow the subtitle from a highly stimulating study by the late Friedrich Ohly on medieval literary texts, *vom Leben mit der Schuld* (living with guilt) – how did the protoplasts, the 'first created', live with guilt, and by extension how do we cope with the awareness of sin?[9]

The most speculative of the questions left open by the third chapter of Genesis – how final was the judgement of God? – is that ultimately answered by the Redemption itself, but there has long been speculation on whether the protoplasts *themselves* repented, and what efforts they made to get back to Paradise. This is important both if we take them as historical characters and if they are just seen as examples. Their fall is, indeed, seen customarily both as causative and illustrative, a literary separation easier to cope with than the identity suggested in Romans 5:12, even if trying to reconcile precisely this point has loomed large in theological arguments from Augustine's conflict with Pelagius onwards.[10] Northrop Frye comments in his study of the Bible and literature that 'it is not easy to hear . . . in the Genesis story what Paul and the author of II Esdras heard in it, the terrible clang of an iron gate shut forever on human hopes' and, as he points out, even the curse on the land in Genesis 3:17 is lifted in Genesis 8:21.[11] An exegetical answer to the

---

7 Noted in my paper '*Drohtin, uuerthe so*! Zur Funktionsweise der althochdeutschen Zaubersprüche', *Jahrbuch der Görres-Gesellschaft* NS 32 (1991), 11–37, esp. pp. 36f. The relevant passage of text reads: 'Nouisti Deum creasse Adam temperatum in omnibus qualitatibus . . . Sed postquam Eua verba a serpente audita ei retulit, cepit super huius uerba cogitare et sollicitus esse, et ita nimia cogitatione et sollicitudines plus naturali temperantia incaluit. Anima uero existens in distemperato instrumenta, distemperata petiit, petendo distemperata peccauit.' Cited from Brian Lawn, *The Prose Salernitan Questions* (London: British Academy, 1979), pp. 1 and 220.
8 In the provocative introduction to her book *Adam, Eve and the Serpent* (Harmondsworth: Penguin, 1988), p. xxiv. Pagels' study is still concerned with theologians; the present investigation begins more or less where she leaves off, and is concerned largely with the dissemination of theological ideas by writers *other* than theologians.
9 Friedrich Ohly, *The Damned and the Elect*, trans. Linda Archibald (Cambridge: Cambridge University Press, 1992) = *Der Verfluchte und der Erwählte: vom Leben mit der Schuld* (Opladen: Westdeutscher Verlag, 1976). It was subtitled 'guilt in western culture' in the English version.
10 See W. H. C. Frend, *Saints and Sinners in the Early Church* (London: Darton, Longman and Todd, 1985), pp. 129–40 for a clear and concise summary of the Pelagian problem with special reference to Adam and Eve.
11 Northrop Frye, *The Great Code: the Bible and Literature* (London: Routledge Kegan Paul, 1982), p. 109.

general point about the finality of the Fall was in any case soon found by the Fathers in what they saw as the protevangelical verse Genesis 3:15 and the eventual bruising of the serpent's head. However, many of the immediate questions are answered in the Christian apocryphal stories of Adam and Eve, stories which point far more clearly onwards to the Redemption.[12] They remove the last vestiges of potential terror from the biblical Fall, and not only do they lift the curse on the land rather earlier than Genesis 8 by having the Archangel Michael show Adam how to till the soil, but they actually show Adam the hope of the Redemption, placing him *sub gratia* in his own lifetime.

It is the apocryphal writings, then, that offer the first bridge between the theological and the literary, and specifically the apocryphal or (if we retain Fabricius's term),[13] the pseudepigraphic lives of Adam and Eve, which are extant in many languages of the near and middle east, in Greek and Latin, and also – importantly – in most European vernaculars. This is a large and complex area of study, and some narrowing-down is necessary. Whilst there has been some interest in this area in recent years – the appearance of several journals and now websites concerned with the pseudepigrapha is significant – much remains to be done.

For example, in their Latin, Greek, Syriac or Armenian prose forms we should find the pseudepigraphic lives of the protoplasts classified under theology in the library. We should find early Irish or English versions, which may be in prose or verse, under the respective national literatures, although the content and sometimes the implicit audience are the same. There are French and German chronicles which contain the same material, but for these we might have to look in the history section; and there are Italian, German and Breton dramatisations which we should probably not find at all because of their obscurity, even though they disseminated the material to a far wider audience than many of the other versions. Apocryphal, of course, does not betoken 'arcane'; in this case it becomes very much part of popular culture.

There is of course no such thing as '*the* apocryphal life of Adam and Eve'. What we have is a ramified tradition of Adamic apocryphal writings which has only recently been analysed in detail. Michael Stone's seminal study distinguishes between primary and secondary Adamic texts, between those, that is, that are more or less independent versions of a recurrent group of motifs, and those writings that are clearly derived later from one of these independent versions. It is possible to

---

[12] The point has been made that elements of the Adam-legends are early enough to have influenced Pauline anthropology from a Hebrew base: see U. Bianchi, 'La Rédemption dans les livres d'Adam', *Numen* 18 (1971), 1–8 and J. L. Sharpe, 'The Second Adam in the *Apocalypse of Moses*', *Catholic Biblical Quarterly* 35 (1973), 35–46. Much of the value of the argument must rest in the latter case upon the dating of the texts involved, and a separate issue lies in what Sharpe refers to as their reading public.

[13] See on the history of the terms James Hamilton Charlesworth, *The Old Testament Pseudepigrapha and the New Testament* (Cambridge: Cambridge University Press, 1985), pp. 6–10. There is a *Journal of Pseudepigraphic Studies* and a *Revue internationale des littératures apocryphes* with the title *Apocrypha*. On forthcoming studies (including the Adambooks) see the *Newsletter of the Leiden Institute for the Study of Religion* 1997/ii, p. 19, with reference to the series *Studia in Veteris Testamenti Pseudepigrapha*, published by Brill in Leiden. There are Internet websites devoted to Adam and Eve and to pseudepigraphic writings: see on these for example James R. Davila, 'Enoch in Cyberspace: the Internet meets the Old Testament Pseudepigrapha', *Computers and Texts* 15 (August 1977), 8–10.

question not the distinction as such, however, but how much importance really attaches to it, especially in considering what for want of a better term may be called the western vernacular tradition of one branch of Adamic writings as it continues and develops.[14]

The pseudepigrapha known under the general title of 'The Life of Adam and Eve' all contain some at least of the narrative elements in the following epitome.[15] After the expulsion of Adam and Eve from the garden and the initial hardship of their life on earth, they attempt to return to Paradise by undertaking a formal act of penance and cleansing by fasting whilst immersed in a river, a river which sometimes stands still, with all the fish in it, and sometimes the birds and beasts as well, as a gesture of support. Adam completes the penance, but Eve is tempted a second time by the devil (disguised this time as an angel) to abandon hers, after which Adam confronts the devil. The devil then gives his own reasons for his hatred of mankind, telling us how he was expelled from heaven for refusing to adore God's younger creation. The story of Cain and Abel is included, as is the subsequent birth of Seth, who at the death of Adam returns to Paradise, with or without his mother, to try to obtain the oil of mercy. He is told that he cannot receive it for another 5,500 years, when Christ will redeem mankind and rescue Adam from hell, and is given seeds or twigs from the tree of life. Some versions contain Eve's story of the Fall, and at the end, Seth (having opportunely just invented writing) records the whole thing for posterity, taking care to protect what he has written.

Distinctive pseudepigrapha containing some or all of this material are found in Greek, Latin, Armenian, Georgian, Slavonic, Coptic and Hebrew, and we might even add as a primary version (although Stone does not), a western vernacular language, namely Old Irish.[16] There is a separate but linked tradition which

---

[14] The standard and indispensable introduction is now Michael Stone, *A History of the Literature of Adam and Eve* (Atlanta: Scholars Press, 1992) and there is an extremely useful *Synopsis of the Books of Adam and Eve*, ed. Gary A. Anderson and Michael E. Stone (Atlanta: Scholar's Press, 1994); see also Michael Stone's papers, 'The Fall of Satan and Adam's Penance', *Journal of Theological Studies* 44 (1993), 143–56 and 'Jewish Tradition, the Pseudepigrapha and the Christian West', in *The Aramaic Bible: Targums in their Historical Context*, ed. D. R. G. Beattie and M. J. McNamara (Sheffield, 1993) (= *Journal for the Study of the Old Testament/* Supplementary Series 166), pp. 431–49. I remain indebted to Professor Stone for his kindness in keeping me in touch with his invaluable studies. There is a useful but brief survey (with further up-to-date bibliography) in Marinus de Jonge and Johannes Tromp, *The Life of Adam and Eve and Related Literature* (Sheffield: Academic Press, 1997).

[15] The standard text remains that edited by Wilhelm Meyer, *Vita Adae et Evae*, in the *Abhandlungen der bayerischen Akademie* (Munich), philos.-philol. Kl. 14/iii (1879), 185–250, and Latin references are to this text. There are translations in the major collections edited by R. H. Charles, *Apocrypha and Pseudepigrapha of the Old Testament, II: Pseudepigrapha* (Oxford: Clarendon, 1913, repr. 1963); by H. F. D. Sparks, *The Apocryphal Old Testament* (Oxford: Clarendon, 1984), pp. 141–68 (incomplete); and by James H. Charlesworth, *The Old Testament Pseudepigrapha* (London: Longman and Todd, 1983–5), II, 249–95. There are important variant texts edited by Carl Horstman, 'Nachträge zu den Legenden 10. *Vita prothoplausti Ade*', *Archiv* 79 (1887), 459–70; J. Mozley, 'The Vita Adae', *Journal of Theological Studies* 30 (1929), 121–47; Gerhard Eis, *Beiträge zur mittelhochdeutschen Legende und Mystik* (Berlin: Akademie, 1935), pp. 241–55; S. Harrison Thomson, 'A Fifth Recension of the Latin *Vita Adae et Evae*', *Studi Medievali* NS 6 (1933), 271–8.

[16] Another potentially early relative of the whole tradition is a Coptic text ascribed to Timothy of Alexandria (if the ascription is correct this would place it into the fourth century, though the manuscript is of the tenth), which contains the devil's story of his envy towards mankind. It does not contain

contains within the general framework of the post-Fall lives of Adam and Eve a few elements related to those already mentioned, most notably the penance (in the independent Ethiopic *Conflict of Adam and Eve*) and the promise of Redemption after a set period (in the Syriac *Book of the Cave of Treasures*, of which versions exist in Arabic, Coptic and Ethiopic). To both of these works is attached a so-called *Testament of Adam*.[17]

Inconclusive arguments have been made for perceiving a Hebrew original behind this tradition, but the one closely related extant text in Hebrew – the so-called *Pirkê Rabbi Eliezer* – is medieval. Although it does contain the story of the penance, it is strikingly unmotivated within a rabbinic work, and fairly clearly adapted from a Christian version.[18] One fourteenth-century English version does tell us that

> fferst þis was mad in Ebrew
> and sethen turned to latyn new,
> and now to englisch speche . . .

but this is a standard medieval legitimisation.[19] The arguments for a Hebrew or Aramaic original are, since we have no early texts, more or less exclusively philological, seeking Hebraisms behind Greek and indeed Latin words and phrases in the works we actually *do* possess. There are isolated small elements in the whole tradition which might depend upon Hebrew origin – plays on names most particularly – but apart from these rare verbal hints there is no real evidence for a pre-Christian Adambook as such, and the supposed Hebrew (sometimes Aramaic) original has in the past years receded further into the distance.[20] Michael Stone, who has examined the question in detail, is even constrained to use that telling word 'ingenious' when describing some of the arguments put forward. In the absence of clear evidence one can only say that the penance in the river, the central theme, is more likely to have a Christian, and initially at least a typological basis. At all events, virtually all the texts we have are Christian, and they provide evidence for a kind of creative typology, a link to the Redemption that goes beyond the interpretation of Genesis 3:15.

---

other elements associated with the life of the protoplasts, however. See Stone, *History*, pp. 39–41 and de Jonge and Tromp, *Life*, pp. 80–3. There are other Coptic fragments.

[17] See Stone, *History*, pp. 122–5 for details. There are further unconnected texts to do with Adam and Eve in various languages, and there are also small elements of additional information about the protoplasts in the Nag Hammadi material, in the Qur'an and in the Mandaean *Ginza*.

[18] *Pirkê de Rabbi Eliezer*, trans. Gerald Friedlander (London: Kegan Paul, Trench, 1916). The ascription to the first-century rabbi Eliezer is odd, but the work was especially popular after the ninth century. Chapter XX, pp. 143–9 describes the penance. Israel Lévi, 'Éléments Chrétiens dans le *Pirke Rabbi Eliezer*', *Revue des études Juives* 18 (1889), 83–9, esp. pp. 86–9, takes the passage as Christian. Reference to the Gihon is only found in this work.

[19] Lines 1189–91 of the Middle English *Canticum de Creatione* (see below, note 43). It is discussed by Friedrich Bachmann, *Die beiden Versionen des mittelenglischen Canticum de creatione* (Hamburg: Lütcke and Wulff, 1891 = Diss. Rostock), p. 43, although Bachmann sensibly only concludes from it that the source of the English work was a Latin one.

[20] The whole background of scholarship on this is analysed by Stone, *History*, pp. 42–53, including a detailed excursus (with G. Bohak). Paul Riessler, *Altjüdisches Schrifttum außerhalb der Bibel* (Heidelberg: Winter, 1928), pp. 668–81 takes a different view.

26

The pseudepigraphic lives of Adam and Eve have a variety of functions. They provide a great deal in the way of incidental historical detail, and in doing so can humanise the protoplasts. They also place Adam very firmly not just at the start of real history outside the timelessness of Eden, but at the start of what Eusebius and Origen called the history of salvation, doing so in literal and in typological terms. Further, they offer some more or less directly didactic precepts. And furthermore, they may easily be integrated both into historical and biblical contexts, both lending considerable authority to what they contain.[21]

The primary Latin versions[22] of the Adamic pseudepigrapha – we are still not in a position to talk about a single text, unfortunately – are the most interesting to the student of western literature and theology. Of the others, the Greek text, the oddly named *Apocalypse of Moses*, is possibly the oldest, although not in manuscript terms. The Georgian and Armenian analogues are extremely ramified, as are the Slavonic versions, which include the story of the cheirograph, the written pact between Adam and the devil, a pledge literally redeemed by Christ. The early Middle Irish poem, finally, known as *Saltair na Rann*, the *Psalter of Quatrains*, from the late tenth century, had a Latin source of some kind (since there are Latin words in it) but that source matches none of the known Latin versions, nor indeed the Greek *Apocalypse of Moses*, although there are some similarities. It may, therefore, provide evidence for a lost additional primary version which is, admittedly, closer to the Latin, Greek and Slavonic versions than, say, the Georgian or Armenian texts. It also has a variety of later prose redactions found in various contexts, including a legal codex, so that the pseudepigraphic tradition continued to develop in medieval Ireland.[23]

Even if we narrow our field of investigation down to what Wilhelm Meyer bravely edited in the 1880s as the *Vita Adae et Evae*, we are still faced with the problem that there is really no such thing. Rather we are faced with a large number of texts containing a selection of narrative episodes, loosely combined and placed into different contexts. Additional narrative elements found in this Latin tradition but not in the other pseudepigraphic versions include Adam's vision of the future – a very clearly Christological section – plus the details of Seth's placing his written account into or onto two pillars, one of marble and one of brick or clay, to withstand flood and fire respectively. That element, incidentally, is found also in Josephus's *Antiquities of the Jews*, and it provides an important legitimisation for the authority of the narrative with a built-in answer to the question of how we know all

---

[21] On the salvation history, see Glenn T. Chesnut, *The First Christian Histories* (Macon, Ca.: Mercer University Press, 2nd rev. edn 1986), pp. 65–95.

[22] See Meyer, *Vita* and others listed in note 15, above, for the Latin texts. That edited by Meyer is still the nearest we have to a standard edition. For lists of manuscripts, the most recent is that by M. E. B. Halford, 'The Apocryphal *Vita Adae et Evae*: Some Comments on the Manuscript Tradition', *Neuphilologische Mitteilungen* 82 (1981), 412–27 and 83 (1982), 222. These lists give an idea of the extent of the tradition. See also Stone, *History*, pp. 14–22.

[23] The Irish text is in *The Irish Adam and Eve Story from Saltair na Rann*, ed. and trans. David Greene and Fergus Kelly (Dublin: IAS, 1976), of which my *Commentary* is volume II. Details of the prose analogues are given in the commentary volume. See also my paper 'An Early Irish Adam and Eve', *Medieval Studies* 35 (1973), 146–77, as well as Martin McNamara, *The Apocrypha in the Irish Church* (Dublin: IAS, 1975), pp. 14–20 and Myles Dillon, 'Scéal Saltrach na Rann', *Celtica* 4 (1958), 1–4.

this. Josephus claimed that the pillar made of clay was still extant in his time 'in the land of Siriad', although his best-known translator, the eighteenth-century mathematician William Whiston, reminds us soberly that this particular pillar would not, of course, have survived the flood, informing us that Josephus had simply confused the biblical Seth with an Egyptian king of that name.[24]

Wilhelm Meyer distinguished between four versions of the *Vita* and more have been added since. Furthermore, familiarity with the very numerous manuscripts shows how still more legends regularly become attached to the core. These include the tale of Adam's creation from eight elements and of his name from the four cardinal points (found elsewhere in apocryphal writing, in the *Book of the Secrets of Enoch*). Individual motifs associated with the *Vita* appear, too, in other apocrypha of the Old and New Testament; the motif of the static river, for example, has an interesting history, and the promise made to Seth in some versions of the *Vita* that the Redemption will come about after a fixed time appears also in the *Decensus* portion of the *Gospel of Nicodemus*.[25] Most important of all, the Latin Adamic narratives, even in their earliest forms, contain the seeds (so to speak) of an overlap with another sequence of ideas, a sequence developed more fully (and also in a very varied manner) only after the twelfth century. This is the history of the Cross before Christ, the wood of which grows from seeds given to Seth in Paradise and placed in the mouth of the dead Adam.

Adamic pseudepigrapha are all notoriously difficult to date, and even of the Latin *Vita* almost the best we can say is that manuscript transmission takes us back to the eighth century. The interrelatedness of Fall and Redemption, however, becomes increasingly clear in progressively augmented versions of the *Vita Adae* and especially in the vernacular offshoots of that tradition. If we can talk of a single Latin *Vita*, then that pseudepigraph ends with the death of Adam and a quest to Paradise to find the oil of mercy. The Holy Rood legends in their fullest and independent form, again widely disseminated in the vernacular,[26] *begin* with a modi-

---

[24] There are innumerable editions of Whiston's translation of Josephus: I cite here the full *Works of Flavius Josephus*, with Whiston's *Dissertations* (Halifax: Milner and Sowerby, 1859), p. 27.

[25] Montague Rhodes James, *The Apocryphal New Testament* (Oxford: Clarendon, 1924, repr. 1975) has a convenient edition of this much-used text, which was widely known in most of the western European vernaculars. See now *The Medieval Gospel of Nicodemus: Texts, Intertexts and Contexts in Western Europe*, ed. Zbigniew Izydorczyk (Tempe, Arizona: Medieval and Renaissance Texts and Studies, 1997).

[26] See as an early example of a full study of the material Adolfo Mussafia, 'Sulla leggenda del legno della croce', *Sitzungsberichte der kaiserl. Wiener Akademie der Wissenschaften*, phil.-hist. Cl. 63 (1869), 165–216, but a good modern survey is that by Esther C. Quinn, *The Quest of Seth for the Oil of Life* (Chicago: University Press, 1962), which includes a full bibliography, including early material. See also the extremely valuable but unpublished D.Phil. dissertation by Andrew Robert Miller, 'German and Dutch Legends of the Wood of the Cross before Christ' (D.Phil. Diss., Oxford, 1992). Further: Joseph Szövérffy, *Hymns of the Holy Cross* (Brookline and Leiden: Brill, 1976) and Angelique M. L. Pragsma-Hajenius, *La Légende du bois de la croix dans la littérature française médiévale* (Paris: Van Gorcum, 1995). Texts are available in: Wilhelm Meyer, 'Die Geschichte des Kreuzholzes vor Christi', *Abhandlungen der bayerischen Akademie* (Munich), philos.-philol. Kl. 16/ii (1882), 101–66, and J. R. Mozley, 'A New Text of the Story of the Cross', *Journal of Theological Studies* 31 (1930), 113–27. Relevant vernacular versions of this text include in English Richard Morris, *Legends of the Holy Rood* (London: Oxford University Press, 1871) (= EETS/OS 46); Arthur S. Napier, *History of the Holy Rood-Tree* (London: Kegan Paul, 1894) (= EETS/OS 103); Betty Hill, 'The Fifteenth-

fied form of that same quest at the death of Adam. In the *Vita*, the eschatological point is made in the form of a promise which Seth has to transmit to Adam; that promise is made concrete in the continued narrative of the Rood itself. Most versions of the Adamic pseudepigrapha contain at least a specific promise to Seth after his quest to Paradise that Adam will be healed after a fixed time, usually (though not always) 5,500 years.[27]

Wilhelm Meyer noted within the tradition of the *Vita* as he knew it a group of manuscripts which he separated off as Class III. These interpolated a story of Seth seeing in Paradise a child in the branches of a dry tree,[28] and then receiving the seeds that, planted with the dead Adam, will grow into the wood used for the Holy Rood. A further manuscript category, not described by Meyer, probably English and known after one of the relevant manuscripts as the 'Arundel group', has Seth see in Paradise not a child in the tree, but the Virgin holding her son, that is a quite specific *pietà*: 'in summitate arboris uirginem sedentem et puerum crucifixum in manibus tenentem . . .'.[29] In manuscripts where this version of the Latin *Life* appears it is sometimes followed immediately by the full story of the Holy Rood after the death of Adam. The tree is nurtured by Moses and David, and Solomon tries in vain to incorporate it into his temple before it is abandoned into the Pool of Kidron to await the Crucifixion. Yet another narrative sequence, incidentally, goes on to discuss the Invention of the Rood *after* the Crucifixion. All this can, it is true, lead sometimes to what we would nowadays call continuity problems, as the tale of Seth's quest appears twice in a slightly different form, once (together with Eve) at

Century Prose Legend of the Cross before Christ', *Medium Aevum* 34 (1965), 203–22. In Low German see Arnold Immessen, *Der Sündenfall*, ed. Friedrich Krage (Heidelberg: Winter, 1913), and on his text, see Ludwig Wolff, *Arnold Immessen* (Einbeck: Geschichtsverein, 1964) and my entry 'Immessen', in *Die deutsche Literatur des Mittelalters, Verfasserlexikon*, 2nd edn by Kurt Ruh (Berlin: de Gruyter, 1977–), IV, 366–8. Immessen's work can be related to a Low German metrical version of the Holy Rood legend: *Dat boec van den houte*, ed. Lars Hermodsson (Uppsala: Lundequist, 1959). See below, notes 45 and 69, for references to the English *Cursor Mundi* and to Jans Enikel.

27 In the oriental texts this is usually five and a half days, which is interpreted, by way of II Peter 3:8, as 5,500 years – and the notion becomes a regular motif both within and outside the Adambooks, although the precise number of years varies. In the less closely related Adambooks, too, this is sometimes clarified even further and the precise nature of the Redemption is spelt out by Adam to his children after a revelation from God.

28 This is itself a complex allegorical (and soteriological) motif, developed in various ways in medieval thought. See as additional material Christoph Gerhardt, 'Der Phönix auf dem dürren Baum' and 'Arznei und Symbol', in *Natura loquax: Naturkunde und allegorische Naturdeutung vom Mittelalter bis zur frühen Neuzeit*, ed. Wolfgang Harms and Heimo Reinitzer (Frankfurt/M: Lang, 1981), pp. 73–108 and 109–82.

29 The variation, named after MS Arundel 326 in the British Library, from which I cite this vision of the Redemption before Adam himself has died, is a fourteenth-century codex from the Benedictine abbey at Abingdon (on its provenance see N. R. Ker, *Medieval Libraries of Great Britain* (London: Royal Historical Society, 2nd edn, 1964), p. 2) and it has a number of relatives: BL Sloane 285, a fifteenth-century copy of the Arundel codex; the fifteenth-century MS Petyt 538 vol. 36 in the Inner Temple library in London, and the rather earlier Bodleian MS 3462 (Selden Supra 72). The precise dates of these manuscripts are not always clear, nor can one be sure how extensive or homogeneous the so-called Arundel group of *Vita*-texts is: it seems to have been influential in England at least, however, as I have made clear in my paper 'Legends of the Holy Rood in Cornish Drama', *Studia Celtica Japonica* 9 (1997), 19–34.

the end of the *Vita* and again (on his own this time) at the start of the most common form of the Holy Rood story.

Most important of all, however: the Adamic narrative represented by the Latin *Vita* continues to change and develop when it moves into the vernacular. The Latin tradition provides the basis for an equally complex series of vernacular adaptations, with differences of genre and context causing further variations. These texts bring to a wide audience of listeners, readers and in the case of the drama, observers, a concrete promise to Adam of the Redemption, and are of cultural importance as a means of popularising, clarifying, strengthening, and also humanising the theology of the simultaneity of Fall and Redemption, often for a lay public. Texts are known in medieval English, French, German, Italian and the Celtic languages, with variants that are far more than simple manuscript variations. There are, for example, quite different English metrical versions.

Sometimes these works introduce apparently quite new motifs of greater or lesser theological significance, the source of which is initially hard to establish; and although the precise version of the *Vita* known to one of the later adapters can sometimes be identified, this is usually not possible.[30] Why does the tenth-century Irish text explain that Cain used to cut the grass for Adam? How in a medieval German text does Adam come by a seamstress daughter called Noema, and why, in a somewhat later German translation of the *Vita Adae*, is there an apparently unmotivated reference to 'the sons of the earth'? Such new elements in the vernacular texts are relatively rare, but the main features of the original may be developed in different ways. The importance of the vernacular versions is that they disseminate, clarify and do indeed modify motifs in the original as a living and developing apocryphal tradition. There is no cut-off point to the development.

In his edition of the *Vita* Meyer drew attention to a number of vernacular analogues, and Michael Stone has augmented that list. There is a great deal of material, too, in Hans Martin von Erffa's monumental study of the iconology of Genesis, and attention has also been paid to the relatively limited iconographical reflections of the story.[31] Equally, however, most recent discussions of the *Vita* have either ignored the vernacular dissemination or misinterpreted the information which that tradition might provide. That the recent handbook by Marinus de Jonge and Johannes Tromp refers rather abruptly to the ongoing tradition only in a final sentence was presumably dictated by space,[32] but one of the recent translations of the *Vita* is provided with an introduction which thoroughly confuses the picture. M. D. Johnson, introducing the *Vita* in the second volume of James Charlesworth's *Old Testament Pseudepigrapha*, is aware in general terms of the continuity, but confidently lists a number of works in various genres which purportedly derive

---

[30] See for example studies as early as Bachmann's 1891 Rostock dissertation, *Die beiden Versionen*, and A. C. Dunstan, 'Lutwin's Latin Source', in *German Studies presented to H. G. Fiedler* (London, 1938, repr. New York: Books for Libraries, 1969), pp. 160–73, and also his 'The Middle English *Canticum de Creatione* and the Latin *Vita Adae et Evae*', *Anglia* 55 (1931), 431–42.

[31] See Mary-Bess Halford, *Illustration and Text in Lutwin's Eva und Adam. Codex Vindob. 2980* (Göppingen: Kümmerle, 1980), and the major work by Hans Martin von Erffa, *Ikonologie der Genesis* (Stuttgart: Deutscher Kunstverlag, 1989–95), I, 248–342, with a very full bibliography on the apocrypha and their vernacular parallels.

[32] *Life of Adam and Eve*, p. 94. They do refer to the addition of new features in vernacular writings.

from the Latin, plus others in which a 'less direct influence' of the *Vita* is visible. This latter group, oddly enough, places works which betray no influence of the pseudepigraphic tradition whatsoever beside the Middle English *Canticum de Creatione*, which is a close verse adaptation of the whole thing, and even a prose *Life of Adam and Eve*, which (as one might be able to hazard from the title) is a complete and very close translation.[33]

The vernacular tradition may itself be broken down in all kinds of ways, in terms of genre, extent and context. We have prose and verse adaptations of all or part of the *Vita*, with or without additions from the Holy Rood material, and dramatic adaptations come a little later. Vernacular texts range from isolated references to single motifs, to free-standing independent adaptations of the penance, to translations or adaptations of the whole collection of episodes. Isolated references to *Vita*-motifs may be found, by the way, in any kind of work, including lyric poems; there is a reference in the German poem by Hugo von Montfort from around 1400 to Adam's penance, and the Middle English poem of the *Devils' Parliament*, which is roughly contemporary with it, has a two-line reference to Adam's weeping and his request for the oil of mercy.[34] Other references crop up even in early medieval vernacular literature to Adam's obtaining the oil of mercy (which might always, of course, echo the *Gospel of Nicodemus*).[35] But the fuller adaptations are often placed into biblical contexts in prose, verse or drama, and here they might be preceded with the Genesis story of the Fall, and continue thereafter either with more of the Old Testament, or proceed indeed to the Redemption, often with the Holy Rood elements as a bridge. Adam and Eve are at the beginning of human history, too, however, so that the narrative is found in chronicles, also frequently combined (and therefore given implicitly equal status) with the biblical story of the Fall.

The contexts in which these texts are found vary a great deal.[36] A thirteenth-century French prose text apparently translated from Latin by a monk called Andrius combines the *Vita Adae* material with the story of the Holy Rood, and is found in a manuscript which otherwise contains predominantly Arthurian romances.[37] The Middle English rhymed *Life of Adam* in the Auchinleck manu-

---

33 William of Shoreham's poem *On the Trinity*, for example, is claimed as a kind of commentary on the themes of the work, but has virtually nothing to do with it. Johnson bases his clearly unverified comments on a source which is somewhat unreliable. Other modern collections of the pseudepigrapha similarly fail to mention the vernacular tradition at all; for example, E. Hammershaimb, Johannes Munck et al. *De gammeltestamentlige Pseudepigrafer* (Copenhagen: Gads, 1953–73), II, 509–47 (= Hammershaimb, 'Adamsbøgerne'). There are a few references in the most recent edition of the Greek Adambook: *La Vie grecque d'Adam et Ève*, ed. Daniel A. Bertrand (Paris: Maisonneuve, 1987).

34 *Hugo von Montfort*, ed. Bartsch, pp. 185–91; *The Devils' Parliament*, ed. C. W. Marx (Heidelberg: Winter, 1993), pp. 76f. Interestingly, the B version tells how Adam 'wepte and siede soore/ askid mercy & oile of grace' (B, 347f), whilst the A version has 'wept & repentid' (A, 315f).

35 As in the septenary poem by the early medieval German writer known as Priester Arnold (*Siebenzahl*, strophe 30): see Maurer, *Die religiösen Dichtungen*, III, 71.

36 See Bertrand, *La Vie grecque* on the (largely hagiographic and apocryphal) contexts of early versions.

37 Esther C. Quinn and M. Dufau, *The Penitence of Adam: a Study of the Andrius MS* (University, Mississippi: Romance Monographs Inc., 1980). That work was discussed in some detail as early as 1855 by Victor Luzarche, 'Le Drame et la légende d'Adam au moyen-âge', *Revue contemporaine* 20

script is grouped with some saints' lives, though the codex again contains romances.[38] The long fourteenth-century *Eva und Adam* – thus his order of names – in German verse by the Austrian Lutwin integrates the *Vita*, without the full story of the Rood, into the biblical Genesis, and its self-contained (though late) manuscript is also illustrated.[39] A thirteenth-century German poetic version of the penance portion of the story, given the modern name of *Adams Klage* (The Complaint of Adam), not only appears in collective manuscripts of various kinds as an independent tale, but is also included in its logical place after the biblical Fall in the rhymed world-chronicle by Rudolf of Ems, and also in an expanded version of that same chronicle known as the *Christherrechronik* (the Chronicle of Christ); it is found, finally, resolved into prose and associated with the German *Historienbibel*, the story-book Bible.[40] There are straightforward prose translations into English, too, mostly of a full Latin version, and usually combined with the biblical story and/or the Holy Rood narrative and with the addition of other legends about the formation and naming of Adam,[41] and there is a prose version in French incorporated into the chronicle of Jean d'Outremeuse.[42]

The chronological spread may be demonstrated by the metrical adaptations. The tenth-century Old Irish *Saltair* is probably the earliest work in a western vernacular that is related to the *Vita*. In spite of some small hints to the contrary it does not seem to have anything of the Holy Rood material, and presumably predates altogether the merging in of that narrative sequence, although the soteriological message is still perfectly clear. The anonymous English poet of the lengthy

---

(1855), 5–38, and again in 1912 by Albert Pauphilet, 'La Vie terrestre d'Adam et Ève', *Revue de Paris* 5 (1912), 213–24.

[38] The Auchinleck *Life of Adam* is in *A Penni worth of Witte*, ed. David Laing (Edinburgh: Abbotsford Club, 1857), pp. 49–75, and in C. Horstmann, *Sammlung altenglischer Legenden* (Heilbronn: Henninger, 1878), pp. 139–47 (cited). There is a facsimile of the manuscript: *The Auchinleck Manuscript: National Library of Scotland Advocates' MS 19.2.1*, ed. Derek Pearsall and I. C. Cunningham (London: Scolar Press, 1977), with details of recent collations of the text noted on p. xix. The first piece is currently (since five of the numbered pieces have been lost) the English legend of Gregory, with the Adam-text now third.

[39] Mary-Bess Halford, *Lutwin's Eva und Adam: Study, Text, Translation* (Göppingen: Kümmerle, 1984), and see also the same author's *Illustration and Text*.

[40] See on the German material in general my paper 'Das deutsche Adambuch und die Adamlegenden des Mittelalters', in *Deutsche Literatur des späten Mittelalters*, ed. W. Harms and L. P. Johnson (Berlin: Schmidt, 1975), pp. 209–24, and the articles 'Adam', 'Adambuch', 'Adams Klage' and 'Adam-Predigtparodie', in *Die deutsche Literatur des Mittelalters: Verfasserlexikon*, 2nd edn by K. Ruh (Berlin: de Gruyter, 1977–), I, 44–7, 61–2. The important texts are in Friedrich von der Hagen, *Gesammtabenteuer* (Stuttgart and Tübingen, 1850, repr. Darmstadt: WBG, 1961), I, 1–16 (independent verse); Hans Vollmer, *Ein deutsches Adambuch* (Hamburg: Lütke und Wolff, 1908) (prose reduction); J. F. L. Theodor Merzdorf, *Die deutschen Historienbibeln des Mittelalters* (Stuttgart, 1870; repr. Hildesheim: Olms, 1963) (elements only).

[41] See below, note 47, for details of the fourteenth-century *Life* in the Vernon MS in the Bodleian library, and that in the Wheatley Manuscript (BL Additional MS 39574). There are two later English texts edited by Carl Horstmann from a fifteenth-century manuscript in the Bodleian library (MS Bodl. 596) and from BL Harleian MS 4775 in his 'Nachträge zu den Legenden. 3. *The lyfe of Adam*', *Archiv* 74 (1885), 345–65. Both versions include the other legends of creation and name-giving. The links in the notes with the *Golden Legend* are misleading, however.

[42] The *Chronique de Jean des Preis dit d'Outremeuse* was edited by A. Borgnet (Brussels: Academie, 1864), I, 318ff.

strophic *Canticum de Creatione* tells us that he composed it in 1375;[43] and just before the Reformation, five centuries after the *Saltair*, we have a German writer, Hans Folz, first translating a version of the Latin *Vita* (not always very accurately, though his errors seem primarily to reflect his source text) into German prose in a private manuscript-book for his own benefit, but then adapting it into verse which he then printed and published – both verbs are significantly modern – himself.[44]

The Italian, German and Breton dramatisations of the story represent a final stage, but not only do they add a new dimension, they reach a larger audience. These are the longest-living of the vernacular versions, performances being recorded as late as in the nineteenth century. In English drama there are only isolated motifs, but there are continental versions of the penance on stage. Cornish drama, whilst not having the penance scene, does have the Sethite quest leading to the Holy Rood story; the same is true of other works, such as the English metrical *Cursor Mundi*, and there are reflections of the Holy Rood legends at the beginning of other chronicles, such as the German world-chronicle of Jans Enikel. The additions, re-interpretations and shifts of emphasis in all these texts make clear that the developmental process of the Adamic pseudepigrapha as a soteriological supplement to Genesis continued well into the Middle Ages and beyond.[45]

Whatever the answer to the question of the original language of the Adamic stories may be, some of the apparent Hebraisms in the text certainly cause problems in the vernacular at the post-Latin stage, and the solutions are sometimes – to relocate Stone's term – ingenious. One much-quoted example occurs after the penance, at the birth of Cain, who runs off and brings a blade of grass to his mother just after he has been born. This may derive from a play on his name and the Hebrew word for corn, a derivation rather different from the etymology recorded in Genesis 4:1.[46] The Latin text of the *Vita* reads at this point:

> et peperit filium et erat lucidus et continuo infans ex surgens cucurrit et manibus suis tulit herbam [*in some versions*: dulcissimam] et dedit matri suae; et vocatum est nomen Cain.

> [and she bore a son, and straightway the child ran and brought in his hands (sweet) grass, and gave it to his mother; and the name he was given was Cain.]

---

[43] The *Canticum* was edited by C. Horstmann, 'Canticum de Creatione', *Anglia* 1 (1878), 287–331 from MS 57 in Trinity College, Oxford. It is also in his *Sammlung altenglischer Legenden*, pp. 124–39.

[44] See Brian Murdoch, *Hans Folz and the Adam Legends: Texts and Studies* (Amsterdam: Rodopi, 1977).

[45] Dramatic versions and the Cornish plays are noted later when cited. See note 69 for Enikel. The *Cursor Mundi* is edited by Richard Morris for the Early English Text Society, the relevant volume being the first: *Cursor Mundi*, ed. Richard Morris (London: Oxford University Press, 1874–93, repr. 1961–6 = EETS/OS 57–68). Citation is from the Cotton version (Cotton Vesp. A III). See on the text and the sources the codicological study by John J. Thompson, *The Cursor Mundi: Poem, Texts and Contexts* (Oxford: Blackwell, 1998), and earlier David C. Fowler, *The Bible in Early English Literature* (London: Sheldon, 1977), pp. 165–71. The link between I Corinthians 15:22 and the Holy Rood story is perhaps less close than Fowler seems to imply on p. 171. He refers also, p. 218, to the smaller reflection of the material in Ranulph Higden's *Polychronicon*.

[46] See Robert Graves and Raphael Patai, *Hebrew Myths: the Book of Genesis* (New York: McGraw-Hill, 1966), pp. 85 and 88 discussing the two etymologies of 'I have gotten' and 'a reed, or stalk'.

The Latin, then, links the astonishing deed implicitly, though not very clearly, with the name-giving; the same incident, told with slightly more vigour, but without any immediate reference to the name, appears in Georgian and Armenian. In the latter, in fact, the grass promptly withers, a variation of a motif found elsewhere associated with Adam and Eve themselves, as the grass withers beneath their feet as they leave Paradise; in Georgian the angelic midwife, able to foresee his future, is delighted not to have to hold Cain.

Vernacular versions deriving from the Latin treat this point in a variety of ways, and in doing so provide an illustration of how no longer clear apocryphal motifs may be adapted. The Irish poem refers with some inspiration to the usefulness of Cain to his parents, because he cuts the grass for them, although the primary miraculous element is still there as he begins to walk immediately after birth. There is no reference to the name. An anonymous German text simply mentions that the child brings a herb of some sort, whilst one in Old French underlines the miraculous aspect of Cain's precocious walking, but omits the grass completely. Neither refers to the name. The Middle English *Canticum de Creatione* has the newly born Cain bring his mother a bunch of flowers, but it is the Austrian Lutwin, composing in around 1300, who makes the most of the incident. He opens with a formulaic marker indicating that something odd is coming:

> Nu hörent zu, was geschach.
> Eua zu hant ein kint gebar
> Do su des rehte wart gewar
> Und sin bilde ersach,
> Jn grossem wunder su do sprach:
> Eya, woffen, here, waffen!
> Wer hat dis geschaffen,
> Das ich also wunderlich
> Einen menschen mir glich
> Getragen han by mynem hertzen
> Mit manigem ungefugem smertzen?
> Das ist ein grosses wunder . . . (1789–1800)

> (Now listen to what happened. Eve immediately gave birth to a child. When she became aware of it and beheld it, she exclaimed in great wonder: 'Ah, help me, lord, help! How did this come about that in some mysterious way I have been carrying under my heart and with such pain a human being like myself. It is a great marvel . . .')

But the mere stress on the miracle of birth, here seen of course for the first time, is not enough. Cain shows an interestingly specific post-partum concern, as well as miraculous abilities:

> Das kint sumete sich lenger niht,
> Do es von der müter lam,
> Einen louff es yme name
> Snelliclich zu walde

Und bröht siner müter balde
Wurtzeln an dem armelin.
Es sprach: "lieber müter myn
Nym das laub und nusz ouch der,
Die bracht ich von dem walde her.
Ich weis das wol, du bist krang.
Des dich manig stos betwang,
Des ich dir gein hertzen plag,
Do ich in dinem libe lag,
E ich kam her an den tag." (1805–18)

(The child did not waste time, for when he had been born he ran
quickly to the wood and soon brought back in his little arms
some herbs [or roots] for his mother. The child said: 'Dear
mother, take this plant which I have brought you from the woods
and eat it. I know well that you are ill. I used to inflict many
blows at your heart as I lay in your womb before I emerged into
[the light of] day.')

However, once again there is no etymology. Even though Lutwin has been
adapting the *Vita Adae*, and clearly enjoying the human aspects of it, he remains
aware of the biblical etymology of Cain, and even refers at this point specifically to
the Bible:

das kint wort Cayn genant
Als uns die schrifft düt bekant. (1832–3)

(The child was called Cain, as the Bible tells us.)

When Hans Folz translated a Latin text of the *Vita Adae* into German prose in
1483, he either used a hitherto unknown version, or he was adapting a great deal.
All that is said of the new-born Cain is that he was 'nearly grown-up' at birth; it is
Adam who fetches the sweet herbs for Eve, and the naming is completely wanting.
Whether Folz or his Latin original made these adjustments is not clear. At all
events, Folz left the whole incident, even the miraculous deed, out of the metrical
version he made later. In Middle English the Wheatley prose (BL Harley 4775)
follows the Latin exactly, but that from the fourteenth-century Vernon manuscript
(Bodley 3938) leaves out the whole thing, and it is possible that already Latin
versions were beginning to omit this by now opaque point.[47]

In trying to assess the importance and significance of the *Vita Adae* in Latin and
in the vernacular it is appropriate to follow a medieval hermeneutic paradigm and
look at the narrative from the point of view of the four senses of Scripture so admirably summarised for us in that much disseminated medieval verse attributed to
Nicholas of Lyra:

---

[47] Murdoch, *Hans Folz*, p. 64; there is a recent edition of the Vernon *Life* in N. F. Blake, *Middle
English Religious Prose* (London: Arnold, 1972), pp. 103–18; the Wheatley life is in Mabel Day, *The
Wheatley Manuscript* (London: Oxford University Press, 1921) (= EETS/OS 21), pp. 76–99.

35

Littera gesta docet, quid credas allegoria,
Moralis quid agas, quo tendas anagogia.[48]

Expanding slightly: the literal or historical sense tells us what actually happened, allegory or typology tells us how the New Testament was foreshadowed in the Old, the tropological or moral sense explains how we are supposed to behave, and the anagogical what will happen to us at the last.

First, the *sensus historicus, sensus litteralis*, the staple of the Antiochene school and revived in full value by the Victorines in the twelfth century, influenced by rabbinic *hagadah*, but still interpretative, of course, still explaining by adding to what is known, and thus helping to solve the problem of the brevity of Genesis. The *Vita* material is full of essentially human information. Adam and Eve had only roots to live on and were very hungry; but this physical state prompts a moral decision, namely to undergo a penance to try and return to their former position. Adam's relationship with Eve, too, is tested in the scene after the penance when she separates herself from him. This undergoes considerable and secularised development in vernacular works, and in one of these Eve leaves Adam not in shame and despair but rather because he doesn't love her enough; and yet her return to Adam is brought about by a cosmic miracle and associated with the power of intercession by Adam acting as a quasi-priest, thus supporting the notion of mediation with the divine through a human agency, a theme which recurs in the *Vita*. How Eve managed the first birth in human history is also explained in the *Vita*, and taken up in detail in vernacular versions, in one of which the Archangel Michael advises on breastfeeding. We are told as well what happens to Adam's soul after he dies. Even the direct statement that man will be redeemed, and the gifts to Seth of the seeds or twigs, are, of course, literal.

The events at the death of Adam literalise what elsewhere has to be offered as a typological interpretation. The biblical protevangelium in Genesis 3:15 requires exegesis. In the *Vita* with the extensions from the Holy Rood narratives, Seth returns for the oil of mercy and is given the promise of Redemption *expressis verbis*, while in the expanded Holy Rood versions the seeds he receives are to be placed in the mouth of the dead Adam (in the Vernon *Life* he is told of the seeds 'do that on [one] in his mouth and the othure in his nosethurles'), and they grow into the tree of the cross to form a factual, rather than an allegorical, link between the Testaments. In the fullest versions, Seth actually sees the child who will be the Saviour at the top of a barren tree, and in some versions even as a *pietà*. The concretised prefigurations of the Redemption in the Adamic writings offer a new historical reality which actually does away with the need for any potentially divergent allegorical interpretations.[49]

---

[48] *PL* 176, 801. See Cassian's definition in *CSEL* 12, 404f. There is a brief and useful summary in Robert M. Grant, *A Short History of the Interpretation of the Bible* (London: Black, rev. edn 1965): see pp. 92–101 with the verse cited on p. 95. See also Robert E. McNally, *The Bible in the Early Middle Ages* (Westminster, Maryland: Newman, 1959) on medieval exegesis (the verse is again cited, p. 53). For a more detailed study see Henri de Lubac, *Exégèse médiévale: les quatre sens de l'Écriture* (Paris: Aubier, 1959–64). For the later periods in particular see Beryl Smalley, *The Study of the Bible in the Middle Ages* (Oxford: Blackwell, 3rd edn, 1983).
[49] See Grant, *Interpretation*, 69–79. Grant reminds us that the earliest example of Antiochene exege-

Between the penance and the quest for the oil of mercy we find a number of smaller expansions in exegetical terms according to the *sensus litteralis*, answering questions of how Eve coped with childbirth, for example, or how Adam learned to plant and harvest, and these are often more clearly literary additions, even though they are necessary for the proper understanding of the situation in which the protoplasts, and hence mankind, found themselves after the Fall. The solutions to some of these points serve primarily to humanise the protoplasts but also to underline the goodness of God in individual respects. As an example, when Eve has failed to complete her penance, in the *Vita*, she simply leaves Adam and goes towards the west, but is already three months pregnant. This is most usually simply imitated in vernacular versions, but Lutwin's German poem again develops the incident. After a love-scene in which Lutwin plays a nice game with the audience by permitting Adam to use clichés of courtship – Eve is the only woman for him – which are in his case not only original but also literally true, Eve is unwise enough to voice a cliché herself, to say that her new love is better than Paradise. Adam demurs, leading to the first marital argument in history, and she goes more than a thousand miles westward. The scene remains in the mind, but it is worth pausing to consider its implications. Lutwin's whole poem is a poetic adaptation of the biblical story with the *Vita* narrative interpolated, and thus he has not only expanded the pseudepigraph but placed its events on an equal footing with the biblical material,[50] thus begging the distinction of terms like canonical and apocryphal. The general process of humanisation – and indeed of a kind of secularisation – of the biblically rather sketchily presented first couple is perhaps most clearly visible in Lutwin, and this is reflected in the fifteenth-century Vienna manuscript of his work, which has one of the few sets of illustrations of the *Vita*.

To digress briefly on those illustrations, there are certain dangers, in that the illustrations show the protoplasts wearing nothing at all before the expulsion and during and long after the penance scene; Adam has a garment of skins (in accordance with Genesis 3:21) when the pair are deliberating about the penance; but both wear fourteenth-century middle class German apparel not only at the end of their lives but also in a scene showing their labours just after the expulsion, a scene belonging iconographically to a traditional Genesis-cycle.[51] As a matter of fact, the pair are naked when deliberating the penance in a more or less contemporary German woodcut accompanying Hans Folz's text, whilst even in written texts such as the *Saltair na Rann* Adam and Eve seem to be without clothes after the Fall, although they claim (also against the Bible) to have been clothed in Paradise:

> Ron bae biäd, ron bai tlacht
> cein bamar can tarimthecht
>   iar tarmthecht dun is iar ndíal
>   nichar fail tlacht no dagbíad   (1557–60)

sis is that of Theophilus of Antioch on Genesis. On the later period, see the comments of Evans, *Language and Logic of the Bible*, pp. 67–71, referring again not only to Alcuin's *Quaestiones in Genesim*, but also to Hugh of St Victor on the Pentateuch.

50 See my paper 'Eve's Anger' on the point.
51 Halford, *Illustration and Text*, see plates 6–10.

> (We had food, we had clothing as long as we were without trans-
> gression; since we transgressed and fell away, we have not
> clothing or good food.)

It is true that there is a tradition in medieval thought that Adam and Eve were clothed in angelic garments which are sometimes described allegorically and sometimes thought of as real before the Fall, and were therefore unashamed because they were not actually naked. This is one way round the problem of showing prelapsarian innocence in a postlapsarian world. But the medieval audience might well have wondered precisely when and how Adam and Eve managed to dress. The problem is again one of continuity, but having the pair clothed before the Fall underscores their innocence for a fallen world unable to cope with nakedness otherwise; showing them naked afterwards underscores their predicament; and portraying them in contemporary costume emphasises the identity of mankind with the progenitors. Nothing of this is biblical.

The clothing of the protoplasts causes a series of problems, and leads to the somewhat puzzling introduction of Noema as a daughter of Adam in Jans Enikel's *Chronicle* (a work which uses the Holy Rood material rather than the *Vita*). Noema is a very useful child in that she is the first to weave cloth; the German chronicle, forgetting Genesis 3:21 once again, but tackling the human problem of the origin of clothes, devotes a lengthy passage to describing how Noema weaves and cuts the very first garment, which is apparently a trifle primitive, not yet having arms; and moreover, we are told that Adam also has no shoes. He is grateful, however, that the new garment covers his modesty, and he tells Noema so. One wonders about the gift by God of the skins of the animals. But Noema is still possibly an error. Enikel attributes to Adam all of the children of the Cainite Lamech, of which Noema is one, and although Noema's skills are non-biblical, she is traditionally the creator of the arts of sewing and weaving. One of Lamech's wives – though not in fact the mother of Noema – is called Ada, and the Latin genitive of Adam and Ada is the same, *Adae*. It has also been suggested that Jans Enikel or his source were actively trying to exclude from history the Cainite Lamech, who was, after all, the proto-bigamist.[52] Those clothes are always a problem, however, even if they are not tackled in the *Vita* tradition. Elsewhere in medieval writing Eve herself makes the breakthrough. Boccaccio is hesitant about this in the *De claris mulieribus*, but a fifteenth-century French play has Eve construct 'ung engin soubtil/ et matiere a faire du fil/ pour couvrir nos deux povres corps' (a subtle engine and the making of thread, to cover our two poor bodies), and this sounds rather like a prototype sewing machine.[53]

---

[52] See Raymond Graeme Dunphy, *Daz was ein michel wunder: the Presentation of Old Testament Material in Jans Enikel's 'Weltchronik'* (Göppingen: Kümmerle, 1998), pp. 90f on the *Weltchronik* 1429–1516. Enikel has several of the later generation listed as Adam's children, and the whole passage is somewhat complex: the first editor of Enikel assumed, too, that Noema was being thought of as a son.

[53] Giovanni Boccaccio, *Concerning Famous Women*, trans. Guido A. Guarino (New Brunswick, NJ: Rutgers University Press, 1963), p. 2, and Arnoul Greban, *Mystère de la Passion*, ed. Gaston Paris and Gaston Raynaud (Paris: Vieweg, 1878), p. 14, lines 907–9. The phrase may reflect *ingenium subtile*, the noun meaning originally an innate skill.

The first essentially theological element in the *Vita Adae et Evae* is that found also in most of the other early Adamic pseudepigrapha, namely the formalised act of penance by Adam and Eve as an attempt, in the face of the hardship of their new life, to regain the lost Paradise. It arises first from the literal question of whether the couple, less than comfortable in their new environment and having experienced Paradise, made any attempt to get back, and it is presented as a literal narrative. But the scene also provides an aetiology of penance, since it is the first instance of it in human history, an act of devotion pre-dating even Abel's offering. Adam, assisted by the miraculously static river, regains the grace of God, even if Eve is placed into a negative light (a process perhaps beginning with I Timothy 2:14) when the devil, disguised as an angel, successfully tempts her for the second time. In spite of the appearance of this narrative in the *Pirkê Rabbi Eliezer* and the speculation, again on linguistic grounds, of a Hebrew origin, all the implications are Christological. The interpretation of this narrative unit depends in its turn on two further elements from medieval biblical hermeneutics, typology and tropology, the two senses of Scripture interacting with one another.

The *sensus typologicus* in medieval biblical exegesis has as its starting point a completed New Testament incident and seeks for each antitype an Old Testament type which is then presented as a foreshadowing. From the tree in Eden came death, from the Rood Tree came life. Adam is a type of Christ. The method is applied in the Middle Ages outside strictly biblical material, and the penance in the river has clear typological implications. Adam fasts in the Jordan, the river in which Christ is baptized, rather than one of the rivers of Paradise, so that the narrative element may very well have been constructed (or reconstructed) to underscore the established anthropology of the δεύτερος ανθρωπος.[54] Adam and Eve frequently undergo the penance standing on a stone, and this too is linked with Christ's baptism. By offering a kind of supplement to the Old Testament, the *Vita* expands and legitimises interpetations of the theology of the Fall. To take just one example, the Old French *Pénitence d'Adam* has Adam fasting for forty days, whilst Eve is told to do penance for thirty-four. No further comment is made, but the medieval audience would have no trouble in making the connexion with the penance in the wilderness, which is followed by the defeat of the devil, nor would it fail to see thirty-four as the traditional years of the life of Christ.

In the subsidiary narrative motif that the river Jordan stood still to assist Adam in his penance we have a case in which an Old Testament pseudepigraph, the *Vita Adae*, has taken in an element based probably on an antitype in an earlier New Testament apocryphon. The situation is relatively complex, but there are two relevant New Testament apocrypha. The river Jordan stands still at the time of Christ's nativity in the so-called *Protevangelium Jacobi*, in which Joseph recounts with graphic clarity how it and indeed all creation stands still for a time. A Greek apocryphon attached to the third-century *Didascalia apostolorum* applies the legend of the static river to the Jordan at the time of Christ's baptism.[55] This apparently

---

54 See Claus Westermann, *Genesis 1–11* (Darmstadt: WBG, 1972), pp. 38f. The work is interesting in general terms on the literary limitations of the biblical Genesis.

55 See Adolf Jacoby, *Ein bisher ungeachteter apokrypher Bericht über die Taufe Jesu* (Strassburg:

somewhat obscure motif was extremely widely known in the Middle Ages, though in an odd context, namely that of the hemostatic charm, formulas pronounced to stop bleeding. In spite of the word 'charm' and the association of such devices with what people love to think of as medieval superstition, medieval medical charms are essentially just prayers or collects, which invoke a situation and then back up the healing request with recognised prayers, usually with a series of Our Fathers or a repeated Amen. The charms are familiar in most western vernaculars (and eastern ones as well), and prominent amongst those to stop bleeding are the so-called Jordan charms, which relate how the Jordan stood still either when Christ wished to cross it (echoing also the biblical stilling of the waters or perhaps the reference in Psalm 113:5), or at the baptism. The charms, which are attested from the tenth century, do not invoke Adam, so it is likely that the static river had an independent existence first. That the river Jordan stands still for the first Adam in the *Vita* texts may very well be a constructed type to match the later incident, a prefiguration of baptism (since Adam's penance is also a cleansing act) added after the event. That the Jordan stands still for Adam and for Christ provides us, then, with a type and antitype without canonical justification and probably created in the wrong order, but popular nevertheless. As an indication of the familiarity of the Christ legend, here is a charm in a mixture of Latin and one word of German from the tenth century:

adiuro sanguis per + + + ut non fluvas plus quam Iordanis *aha* quando Christus in ea baptizatus est

(I conjure you, blood, that you should flow no more, as happened with the *water* of Jordan when Christ was baptized in it.)

Five hundred years later an English Jordan-charm from a Welsh manuscript links the birth of Christ and the baptism with the static river:

as uerily as God was borne in bethleem and baptised was in flum Jordan// as verile as the floode stoode/ Reste thou blood.

All these charms have additional invocatory prayers.[56] As far as the vernacular versions of the *Vita* material are concerned, the fish, birds and beasts often stand still as well and there are even illustrations of this. The theological point is that the rest of creation, although itself guiltless, can pray for the sins of others. Oddly enough, the motif of the static river crops up even in drama. It is called for by Adam in the text of the Obergrund Christmas play known to have been performed in the 1820s and 1830s. The play – one of the most recent examples of the material, and

Trübner, 1902), pp. 70f; F. Ohrt, *Die ältesten Segen über Christi Taufe und Christi Tod in religions-geschichtlichem Lichte* (Copenhagen: Levin and Munksgaard, 1938), esp. p. 36, and my paper 'The River that Stopped Flowing: Folklore and Biblical Typology in the Apocryphal Lives of Adam and Eve', *Southern Folklore Quarterly* 37 (1973), 37–51.

[56] *Peniarth 53* in the National Library of Wales, a fifteenth-century paper manuscript largely of Welsh material but with a few fragments in English, ed. E. Stanton Roberts and Henry Lewis (Cardiff: UWP, 1927), pp. 31f. The earlier charm is cited in Jacoby, *Bericht*. Ohrt, *Segen*, refers to many other Latin charms.

probably the most remote, coming as it does from a Silesian village near what is now Zlaté Hory on the border betwcen Poland and the Czech Republic – is in fact at this point little more than a translation of the *Vita*,[57] and how the effect was indicated in practice is unclear.

The Holy Rood material itself, from the granting of the seeds to Seth down to the flourishing of the tree that will become the Cross, is itself an example of realised typology. Modern theologians have warned against the over-use of typology in anything but the strictest form in establishing the relationship between the two Testaments,[58] but the medieval approach is rather different, and can embrace what Friedrich Ohly referred to as semi-biblical or even extra-biblical (we can perhaps add pseudepigraphic) typology.[59]

Two elements in the *Vita Adae*–Holy Rood complex have significant but slightly different *tropological* implications. The first is once again the injunction to do penance at all, and the second is Adam's comment that the devil has to be recognised, however difficult this might be. On the first point, the imposition of formal penance, the *Vita* itself makes the context clear as Eve asks directly: 'domine mi, dic mihi quid est penitentia' (tell me, sir what penance is). Adam explains, and also differentiates the length of penance, a point made in medieval penitential handbooks and prescriptions.[60] The synodical constitutions of Odo, bishop of Paris, for example, laid down in around 1197, are very simple and he warns priests (who impose the penance) to remember that 'the nature of the penance ought to be according to the nature of the guilt and the capacity of the confessant'. The point is made in other penitential handbooks. The formal necessity is presented in an interesting manner in another of the dramatisations of the *Vita*, a Breton play, the

---

[57] The *Obergrunder Weihnachtsspiel* is a Fall and Redemption piece from German-speaking Upper Silesia, printed by Peter Anton, *Volksthümliches aus Österreich-Schlesien I* (Troppau: publisher not known, 1865), p. 377. See Carl Klimke, *Das volkstümliche Paradiesspiel* (Breslau: Marus, 1902; repr. Hildesheim: Olms, 1977), pp. 82f.

[58] Hasel, *Old Testament Theology*, pp. 179f.

[59] See Friedrich Ohly, *Schriften zur mittelalterlichen Bedeutungsforschung* (Darmstadt: WBG, 1977) – the paper 'Halbbiblische und ausserbiblische Typologie' of 1976 is on pp. 361–400 – and Ohly's *Ausgewählte und neue Schriften zur Literaturgeschichte und zur Bedeutungsforschung*, ed. Uwe Ruberg and Dietmar Peil (Stuttgart and Leipzig: Hirzel, 1995). Attention is drawn to the 1976 paper by D. H. Green in his review of the latter volume in *Modern Language Review* 92 (1997), 783–5 with reference to shaking off the 'clerical straitjacket' of strict typology. The complexity of what we might call the back-creation of typology is well illustrated in the development of the Holy Rood legends beyond the *Vita* in the legend of Maximilla (her name varies a little) as a prefigurative (proto-)martyr: see below, Chapter 5.

[60] Odo is cited from John T. McNeill and Helena M. Gamer's immensely useful translation of selected *Libri poenitentiales: Medieval Handbooks of Penance* first published in 1938 (New York: Columbia University Press, 1990), p. 412. For other examples see my paper on the aetiology of penance in the *Vita*-tradition, 'The Origins of Penance: Reflections of Adamic Apocrypha and of the *Vita Adae* in Western Europe', *Annals of the Archive of Ferran Valls I Taberner's Library* 9/10 (1991), 205–28. Adam's role as a priest in this matter is underlined further in the Irish *Saltair na Rann*, though at a later narrative stage, namely when he dies. Eve asks again what to do, and Adam tells her to perform a cross-vigil (not mentioned in the corresponding passage of the *Vita*) as a kind of vicarious penance on behalf of his soul. Cross-vigils (prayers with outstretched arms) seem to have been known, also as penances, in the early church in Britain and Ireland, and they are referred to in the penitential of Pseudo-Bede, for example: see *Saltair na Rann*, 2061–4; Greene and Kelly, p. 97; and Murdoch, p. 140; also McNeill and Gamer, *Penance*, p. 221.

earliest manuscript of which carries a date of 1663, but which was copied again in 1825 and possibly performed as late as 1833. The audience is told in a prologue to the action that God Himself makes clear to an already penitent Adam just before the expulsion what Adam has to do:

'Nep a deuio d'amanti dre ur guir binijen,
A renquo, eme Doue, er barados antren.'
    Doue lar da Adam quent fin d'eus he vue
Digas unan-bennac dimeus he vugale
Da guerhat an eoul d'eus a visericord
Digant ar Cherubin . . .[61]

('Anyone who wishes to make amends by true penitence will be able to re-enter Paradise that way', said God, who advised Adam at the end of his life to send one of his children to obtain from the Cherub the oil of mercy.)

Adam and Eve again discuss the nature of the penance, and once Adam has imposed a suitable period upon Eve, the Breton dramatist introduces a nice human touch (which perhaps also tells us about the performance) by having Eve very fearful of the terrifying noise made by the river in which she must immerse herself. It is not meant to be an *easy* penance.

On the recognition of the devil, it is sometimes claimed that the point of the first part of the *Vita*, in which Adam completes his penance but Eve does not, is to exonerate Adam and place the blame for the Fall more squarely upon her shoulders, but although Adam does prove firmer here, he is not exonerated, and the real Fall has already taken place; nor does the successful penance of Adam re-admit him to Paradise. Rather, the idea is to convey the notion of proper (and incidentally feasible) penance as existing from the time of the Fall onwards, and to stress the need to recognise the devil, even when disguised.[62] Adam is older and wiser and he takes the role of the priest, imposing an appropriate penance upon them both, giving himself a longer period in the water than Eve, whose penance varies, but which is less than forty days. Penance, an act imposed, is part of the process of salvation within the Christian context, and it is entirely unmotivated, for example, in the *Pirkê Rabbi Eliezer*. The enigmatic statement that Eve's flesh is like grass when she emerges prematurely from the Tigris (in western vernaculars simply taken as a sign of cold), in which she has been standing to complete her penance, has been seen as a play on the name 'Gihon', another river of Paradise, and that in

---

[61] The Breton play has been printed (incomplete) in the edition and translation by Eugène Bernard, 'La Création du monde: mystère Breton', *Revue Celtique* 9 (1888), 149–207 and 322–53; 10 (1889), 102–211 and 411–55; 11 (1890), 254–317; plus Noel Hamilton, 'A Fragment of La Création', *Celtica* 12 (1977), 50–74. These are vv. 1185–90. See also my 'The Breton *Creation Ar Bet* and the Medieval Drama of Adam', *Zeitschrift für celtische Philologie* 36 (1977), 157–79.
[62] The problem has been discussed (with examples from Milton where recognition is not possible) in the important paper published originally in 1963 by Rosemary Woolf, 'The Fall of Man in *Genesis B* and the *Mystère d'Adam*', in *Art and Doctrine: Essays on Medieval Literature*, ed. Heather O'Donoghue (London: Hambledon Press, 1986), pp. 15–28.

which she stands in the *Pirkê Rabbi Eliezer*. Since she stands (or occasionally sits) in the Tigris or the sea in most other versions, it is possible that the writer of the rabbinic tract changed the river precisely to provide for this explanation. The supposed word-play, coming as it does in the middle of the penance section, need not imply that the Gihon was the original river, nor is it a significant motif.

The real importance of the incident, and its tropological purpose, is the failure of Eve to complete the penance because she fails to recognise the devil's ploy. Indeed, in the Greek *Apocalypse of Moses* the devil disguises himself as an angel of light – the reference is of course to II Corinthians 11:14 – even for the first temptation. In the *Vita*, Eve fails to recognise the devil, although Adam does so immediately, and the point is the recognisability of temptation when it lies in the offer of what one most desires. Eve wants respite from her penance, but she should have been on her guard. The Breton play has Adam warning Eve quite specifically that Satan will try to trick her again, so that she should be careful:

> Rac-se ho suplian, a beurs Roue an Envo
> Teulet evoes ous Satan, rac mar guel, ho tromplo!   (1607–8)

> (And I beg of you, for the sake of the King of Heaven, be on
> guard against Satan, for he will deceive you if he can!)

In a late medieval Italian play from Bologna – which, like the Obergrund play, incorporates only the penance scene into the biblical narrative – it is not even made clear that the devil is in disguise.[63] Sometimes, too, the disguise is not specific; the English prose *Life* in the Bodley manuscript of around 1430 has the devil come only in 'a feire louely liknesse'.[64]

Lutwin's metrical version, however, is again very interesting, and he uses it as a starting point for a tropological homily based largely on the way women are taken in by the lies and flattery of faithless men during courtship; he warns women against too ready a belief, and men against false women. The same technique – that of the homiletic excursus – is used regularly in medieval adaptations of biblical texts,[65] but this, of course, is precisely not biblical. Lutwin also makes it perfectly clear that Adam is sufficiently wise as to recognise the devil at once, and the later illustrator of the fifteenth-century manuscript actually draws the devil in angelic disguise, but gives him cloven feet just about visible beneath his robe. In a miniature in a fifteenth-century German prose version of the story now in Hamburg there is an odd variation of the scene with Adam and Eve in the river together (this does not match the text), with a very obvious devil who is, however, still wearing angelic clothes. These illustrations have a parallel in a fifteenth-century blockbook *Biblia Pauperum* where a very urbane devil is dressed as a friar when he tries to tempt

---

63 *Laude drammatiche e rappresentazioni sacre III*, ed. Vincenzo de Bartholomaeis (Florence: le Monnier, 1943), p. 205. The speech tempting Eve a second time (it is not clear where she is undergoing her penance) is attributed simply to *el demonio*. Even the Obergrund play specifies that he is disguised as an angel.
64 Horstmann, 'Nachträge', p. 346. The Harleian manuscript has the devil as an angel.
65 See Peter Jentzmik, *Zu Möglichkeit und Grenzen typologischer Exegese in mittelalterlicher Predigt und Dichtung* (Göppingen: Kümmerle, 1973).

Christ in the wilderness, and Marlowe's Dr Faustus actually *demands* a similar disguise after he has been shown Mephistopheles in his real shape.[66]

The value of prayer as such is stressed in the *Vita* in various places. The pregnant Eve is baffled by her own condition (and the fact that in the English version in the Vernon manuscript she gives birth after twelve months is a rare and equally baffling variation),[67] and this is another reminder of the Christian presuppositions behind the *Vita*. Eve asks for the assistance of the sun and stars to tell Adam – in some versions it is just the stars, making Adam into a kind of astronomer – but either way a star is made to herald the first birth of all. Adam's intercession leads to the sending of the Archangel Michael to assist at the birth, just before which Eve herself makes a comment in some versions of the *Vita* of which Freud would have approved: 'kill the serpent before he does this to you', she says in one of the German texts. Eve is also convinced that she is going to die, a *desperatio* that she has exhibited previously and which has to be overcome. But here Adam prays and his prayers are effective, a point made by Michael in the Latin and in some of the western vernaculars, and expanded very considerably in the Armenian and Georgian analogues. That this is another illustration of God's goodness is made clear in some of the vernacular versions.

Anagogical motifs are fewer, although the promise of a Redemption at a specific time falls perhaps into this category, at least in its development. In the *Vita*, Michael promises the oil of mercy to Adam after 5,500 years. It is clear too what form the giving of the oil will take, as Michael promises that Christ, the Son of God, will revive Adam, anoint him and baptize him in the Jordan. Michael's speech is virtually the same as one in the New Testament apocryphal *Acts of Pilate* or *Gospel of Nicodemus*, another work very well known in the vernacular, and it appears too not only in the independent stories of the Holy Rood, but in the *Golden Legend*, again a familiar (hagiographic) handbook, and this overlap is presumably the reason that the motif as such regularly appears in isolation in medieval works – it is given as 5,500 years in many of the texts most closely derived from the *Vita*, but also in works like the English Chester Play, for example, which is otherwise uninfluenced by the *Vita*. The period is 5,000 years in the late thirteenth-century *Chronicle* of the German writer Jans Enikel, which includes as history the Sethite quest for the Holy Rood, and a 1464 Passion-play in Low German from Redentin, near Wismar in northern Germany, which has none of the *Vita* material, does have Seth mentioning this promise, albeit with a figure of 5,600 years. The period is indeed entirely flexible, ranging from 'the fulness of time' to 5,199 years (in Jean d'Outremeuse and elsewhere), to 5,025 years 'and more', later amended to 5,228 (which is common in English versions) in the Auchinleck *Life* in Middle English, 5,200 in Lutwin and 5201 in Hans Folz. Meyer in his edition of the *Vita* lists alter-

---

[66] Halford, *Illustration and Text*, plate 13. See Brian Murdoch, *The Recapitulated Fall: a Comparative Study in Medieval Literature* (Amsterdam: Rodopi, 1974), pp. 158f on the Nuremberg blockbook *Biblia Pauperum* of Hans Spoerer in 1471.

[67] Blake, *Prose*, p. 111. 'Eve was with childe er heo went from Adam. So twelve moneth heo dwellet there . . .'. Twelve angels come to assist her in most versions (sometimes fifteen, probably due to a confusion between xv and xii).

natives in his *varia*, from 5,199 years down to 6,500.[68] However, Adam spends different amounts of time in hell – 4,304 years in the English *Cursor Mundi* and 4,604 in the Vernon *Life*. The specificity of all these times is quite interesting, especially as it was clearly not fixed. The figure is not as such important, but the essence of the scene is the promise of a Redemption within a finite period, which is of course already in the past from the point of view of the receptive 'now'. The English *Canticum de Creatione*, for example, has a very detailed but not completely precise breakdown of the *aetates* of human history in numbers of years, concluding with the year of the Incarnation – *anno Domini* – in which the text itself was written.

More immediate is the problem of what happens to Adam after death. His body is usually (on angelic instruction) buried with the seeds that will become the cross, although even this can have variations. The fragmentary Auchinleck *Life* in English has Christ order the angels to inter both the unburied Abel and Adam (573–92), something which Seth and Eve observe with great curiosity because this, too, is naturally a novelty in the world, and it is presented as instruction. What happens to his soul is more complex. The handing-over of Adam's soul (and that of Abel) to Michael in the Latin *Vita* leaves the matter potentially in abeyance, but vernacular versions do vary on whether Adam's soul was sent to hell or to limbo. In the Vernon *Life* in English, Adam expresses (though it is not in the *Vita*) the 'hope yit to come to the blisse of Paradis', whilst being well aware that 'whon ich am ded I wot wel that I schal weende to helle', as indeed happens to his soul 'er the bodi were cold'. Jans Enikel explains in his German *Chronicle* that Adam was not a Christian: 'Ich wil iu bescheiden:/ Adam was ein heiden' (1660f) (Let me make this clear to you: Adam was a heathen), and therefore Adam's soul had to go to hell because of his disobedience. In the *Cursor Mundi*, Adam, although he is aware of what will happen to him, laughs out loud when he hears that although he is about to die, the oil of mercy will be granted in the fullness of time. He actually prefers hell to his weary life; 'leuer was siþen to lenger in helle/ þan langer in þis liue to dwell' (1411f).

There is variation on the point, however, in two different dramas in the same language – Cornish in this case. Adam's soul is not handed over to Michael, but dragged off to hell by gleeful demons in the *Cornish Ordinalia* (it takes both Satan and Beelzebub to bring him down to Lucifer), whilst in a slightly later and incomplete Cornish creation play called *Gwreans an Bys*, the creation of the world, the devils actually try to haul Adam's soul away, but are – to their manifest annoyance – prevented from doing so by Lucifer himself, who tells them that Adam is destined for limbo. This is, of course, seen as a form of hell – as Marlowe's Mephi-

68 *The Chester Plays*, ed. Hermann Deimling and [J.] Matthews (London: Kegan Paul, 1893–1916) (= EETS/ES 62 and 115), II, 321 ('Christ's Descent into Hell', vv. 73–80); Jansen Enikel's *Weltchronik*, ed. Philipp Strauch (Hanover: Monumenta Germaniae Historica, 1891–1900), v. 1664, p. 33 (the notes give still further references); *Das Redentiner Osterspiel*, ed. Brigitta Schottmann (Stuttgart: Reclam, 1975), p. 49 (vv. 339–572). Many relevant vernacular examples plainly follow the *Vita*. Jean d'Outremeuse refers to 5,199 years, Borgnet I, 319: 'VmIIc seul mons de années' (cinq mille deux cent moins un). Medieval wisdom texts have 5,228 years: see *Solomon and Saturn*, ed. Cross and Hill, p. 83; there is some variation even in the transmission of the *Gospel of Nicodemus*.

stopheles again was to point out so clearly – since it is still an abstraction from the face of God, but it is not the deepest pit, in which Cain, for example, has by this stage already been placed in the Cornish play.[69] Sometimes the distinction is unclear: in the Low German Fall-drama by Arnold Immessen, Adam is taken to hell when he dies, but is later on placed by a stage direction *in limbo*. On the other hand, the Irish *Saltair* (following here the pattern of the Greek and Slavonic versions of the life of Adam rather than the Latin) has the soul of Adam handed over, after pleas by the angels and purging in a lake, to Michael to be kept in Paradise in the third heaven, as in II Corinthians 12:2–4. This point is possibly the most theologically confused of those reflected in the vernacular texts, although the humanitarian urge to have the wrongdoer Cain, but not the (apocryphally) penitent Adam and the (biblically) innocent Abel, consigned to hell for longer than anyone else is understandable. If Adam is actually taken to Paradise, as in the *Saltair*, the symbol and actual progenitor of man has himself been granted grace, rather than just being told of it.

The vernacular versions of the *Vita*, the important disseminations to a wider audience of a work itself already theologically important in its increase of Old Testament typology, vary considerably in overall effect. Of course, the more often a work is transmitted or translated, the more possibility there is for plain error on a small scale. This can be to do with the increasing opacity of a given motif, such as the alternative etymology of Cain and the stalk of grass or corn, which results in the Irish lawn-mowing. Sometimes, too, errors can creep in purely for technical reasons, and only comparative work can make clear that these are indeed only errors. That the *Cursor Mundi* (Cotton text, v. 1443f, and in all the other MSS) cites in words a figure of 4,304 years from Adam's death until the Redemption is a case in point. There is no explanation of this rather odd figure, but a clue may perhaps be contained in the equally unusual figure of 4,604 in the prose *Life* in the Vernon manuscript. That manuscript writes the figure out as 'foure thousand yeer viC and four', and in manuscripts the distinction between Roman six – vi – and three – iii – is easily blurred if they are close together. If we add 4,604 to Adam's age, 930 years in the Bible, we get 5,534, which is (one is tempted to say 'of course') easily recognisable as the 5,500 years usually quoted, plus the thirty-four years of Christ's life needed until the Harrowing of Hell is possible. However abstruse, it is not unusual in terms of medieval numerology, and is in fact once again merely part of the literal method of interpretation; Odo of Morimond's *Analecta numerorum et rerum in theographyam* makes clear that numerology can be far more complicated than that,

---

[69] See Whitley Stokes, *Gwreans an bys: the Creation of the World* (London: Williams and Norgate, 1864); the most recent edition is by Paula Neuss, *The Creacion of the World: a Critical Edition and Translation* (New York and London: Garland, 1983). Neuss indicates in her introduction, p. xlv, that the handling of the Rood material is quite different in the *Ordinalia* and the later play. The *Ordinalia* was edited by Edwin Norris, *The Ancient Cornish Drama*, 2 vols (Oxford: Oxford University Press, 1859; repr. London and New York: Blom, 1968). See also the translation by Markham Harris, *The Cornish Ordinalia: a Medieval Dramatic Trilogy* (Washington: Catholic University of America Press, 1969). See for the works in general my 'Creation, Fall and After in the Cornish Mystery Play *Gwreans an bys*', *Studi Medievali* 29 (1988), 685–705.

and his Cistercian successors Theobald of Langres and William of Auberive took the mathematical-significatory aspects further still.[70]

Hans Folz's prose version of the *Vita* in German, finally, has an obscure reference in the Seth narrative to the sons of the earth, but on closer examination this is *not* a new and fascinating apocryphal element – it is just another misreading. Latin manuscripts were invariably abbreviated, and 'trium foliarum' (of three leaves) – the twig Seth takes away from Paradise – would look much like 'terrarum filiorum' (of the sons of earth), if it appeared in abbreviated form.[71] Folz himself spotted and removed this phantom motif when he reworked the text into a poem, but it is worth noting as an illustration of the way apparent variations and new motifs can occur. These are the identifiable ones; others might be less clear, and they might have crept in at any point in the extended tradition.

The vernacular extensions of the pseudepigraphic Adam tradition differ in form – although the prose/verse distinction is less significant for the Middle Ages – and in presentation. Those that show only the penance do not always point so strongly to the Redemption. The German penance versions in particular are, beside stressing the miraculous nature of events, essentially parænetic, showing Adam as a priest and stressing the necessity of penance and of recognising the devil. Placing the work into a chronicle gives a finite limit to historical time, whilst in a work like that by Lutwin and to a certain extent already in the Irish *Saltair na Rann* the human aspects of the whole can be developed: that first marital disagreement as shown to us by Lutwin stays in the mind. But the real point is always to have spelt out to Adam and mankind what appears in the Old Testament proper as prophecy.

The self-referential history of the works, the story of how these things came to be written, affords them an inner legitimisation. Not only do they tie together the two poles of the economy of history in theological terms, but they guarantee their own authenticity. In the *Vita* the story of the Fall is inscribed on tablets preserved in pillars of clay and marble, and the motif is modernised in the later Cornish play *Gwreans an bys* where Seth is shown placing large books into the two pillars. At other times, though, precisely this motif is missing: Lutwin and the *Saltair* do not have it, and since they are fixed in biblical contexts this is of interest, as the *Vita* material becomes merged completely with the biblical; after the death of Adam in Lutwin we progress to Noah before the work ends.

It is difficult to distinguish between the theological and the literary aspects of the Adamic texts, and both the *Vita* and the vernacular developments flesh out and humanise the story of Adam and Eve with respect to factual elements, with naive and false-naive questions about what really happened and what happened next. But they they also stress the soteriological aspects of the story of Adam in their supplementary Old Testament typology. This is especially clear in those vernacular works which integrate the material into the biblical narrative. By providing additional bases for typological interpretations at the same time as showing us a literal promise of the Redemption in the first generation of fallen man, they make clear

---

[70] See Evans, *Language and Logic*, pp. 59–66, and Heinz Meyer, *Die Zahlenallegorese im Mittelalter: Methode und Gebrauch* (Munich: Fink, 1975), who points out on p. 47 that Odo's unedited text is known under various titles.

[71] See Murdoch, *Hans Folz*, pp. 117f.

the hermetic nature of the divine economy. Whether or not there was ever anything approaching a pre-Christian Adamic apocryphon – which seems highly unlikely – the *Vita* in particular, especially when it is linked with the Holy Rood narrative, ties the Testaments together.

It will have become apparent from the number of different works cited in such a variety of languages that before the Reformation, and in many places afterwards, the ongoing tradition of Adamic apocrypha was massively well known, in spite of the proscription of apocryphal writings including a *Penance of Adam* – whatever was meant by that – in the so-called *Gelasian Decretal*.[72] Canon and apocrypha do not have quite the same clear distinction in the Middle Ages,[73] especially when we are dealing with texts the ultimate effect of which is to indicate to Adam's descendants that Redemption has always been promised and is indeed possible: Adam's descendants, now all very clearly *sub gratia* after the lapse of 5,500 years, have already been given the oil of mercy.

The apocryphal Adam-material expands the brief biblical story in human terms, and at the same time reinforces the identity of Adam with his descendants. It also makes very clear – in real and in typological terms – the connexion between the Fall and the Redemption, with a stress on the reality of salvation; the iron gates did not slam shut at all. These two functions make for literary, historical and spiritual interest, and this is made clear in the way the Adamic pseudepigrapha develop in versions in western vernaculars. Their derivation from the Latin branch (in the main) is not as relevant as the fact that they demonstrate the ongoing transmission, dissemination and development of the Adamic material, a development which is not cut off after the Latin *Vita*. In fact, the *Vita* and indeed other of the 'primary' Adambooks develop in chronological terms in parallel with some of the western vernacular versions. The increase in soteriological clarity culminates in the latest of the texts, such as the Breton play, which is admittedly extended and somewhat wordy. But after Eve has interrupted her penance in the river and come to Adam who recognised the devil, the devil explains his ongoing envy in terms of the single tag: *consolatio miserorum est habere pares* – misery seeks a companion. As in the *Vita*, Adam appeals to God for pity – not for a return to Paradise, but for aid against the devil in future so that he does not fall prey to despair. In reply, God tells Adam in detail of what will happen when he dies, of the growth of the cross on which the son of God will die on Calvary and harrow hell:

> Hen-nes a dioro persier ar Barados
> Ha dre he Bassion a rai d'ac'h guir repos   (1751–2)

---

[72] *Decretum Gelasianum de libris recipiendis et non recipiendis, PL* 59, 157. See Heinrich Denzinger and Clemens Bannwart, *Encheiridion Symbolorum* (Freiburg i. B.: Herder, 17th edn, 1928), p. 71, and E. Hennecke and W. Schneemelcher, trans. R. McL. Wilson, *New Testament Apocrypha I* (London: SCM, 1963), p. 46. On the acceptance or otherwise of apocrypha, however, see Schwarz, *Die neue Eva*, pp. 57–9. Schwarz recognised the importance of the apocryphal Adam-stories in the continuous tradition of interpretations of the Fall, one of the few critics to have done so.

[73] See such studies as that by Achim Masser, *Bibel, Apokryphen und Legenden: Geburt und Kindheit Jesu in der religiösen Epik des deutschen Mittelalters* (Berlin: Schmidt, 1969) (noted in Murdoch, *Saltair na Rann: Commentary*, pp. 24f), and Máire Herbert and Martin McNamara, *Irish Biblical Apocrypha* (Edinburgh: Clarke, 1989), pp. xiii–xxvi

(It is the Saviour who will open the gates of Paradise, and by His
Passion will regain eternal rest for you.)

Vernacular Adam-narratives, especially the more expansive ones, can have
other functions. They are stories of the marvellous and the miraculous (as in the
birth of Cain); they address the more mundane issues of the beginnings of agriculture[74] and, as we have seen, of clothing; there is even a drama of relationships,
exploited by writers like Lutwin, as Eve leaves her husband and goes more than a
thousand miles to the west. But overall the focus is on the grace that is actually
given to Adam, not a hope but a promise, so that from the very first, living with the
awareness of the guilt of the first Fall was made possible.

Reference to the Breton work reminds us again of the longevity of the tradition
– certainly down to the 1830s – and also of its popularity in the specific sense. The
variety of genres represented in the very large literary tradition into which the
material permeates is of as great an importance and deserves as much attention as
the examination of individual and perhaps more restricted early texts, always
bearing in mind that 'early' is a difficult term when the manuscript tradition, say,
even of something like the *Apocalypse of Moses*, is very late.[75] The vernacular
Adambooks in the west are both 'theological writings' and 'medieval literature'. In
the Middle Ages, however, that distinction is hardly a clear one. The influence of
these stories was far-reaching. Literary works, and often great ones at that, use
motifs from the expanded story of Adam, either from the apocrypha or from
exegesis of the canonical story, to support their own presentation of the Fall and the
promised Redemption that should free mankind of despair, making clear the fact
that Adam as man is already *sub gratia*. Adam and Eve tried to get back to the Paradise they had known at first hand and remembered all too well, and Adam at least
was given either a vision or a direct prediction of a future in which a return would
be possible. Seth was allowed to see through the gate, and if this is not granted to
Adam's later progeny directly, at least the audiences of the *Vita* material are
permitted to look into Paradise – and what was then the future – through Seth's
eyes.

---

[74] Moses Maimonides refers in the *Moreh nebukhim* to a sect which held that Adam himself – on this
occasion born from a man and a woman, however – wrote a book about agriculture: *The Guide of the
Perplexed*, trans. Chaim Rabin, ed. Julius Guttmann (Indianapolis: Hackett, 1995), p. 177.
[75] See Bertrand, *La Vie grecque*, pp. 41–3.

TWO

WRITTEN IN TABLETS OF STONE:
ADAM AND GREGORIUS

THE LIFE OF GREGORY, pope and saint, was well known throughout the Middle Ages.[1] The French metrical *Vie du Pape Saint Grégoire*, which may have originated in the ambit of Henry II of England and Queen Eleanor, exists in several different versions from the late twelfth and early thirteenth centuries. An edition was a desideratum for a long time, and now that we have it, with eight rhymed versions (including two critical ones based on the London and the Tours manuscripts respectively) printed in parallel columns, with a couple of late versions added as an appendix, it is one of the most cumbersome texts imaginable.[2] The saint's life is recorded in German in a fine poetic version by Hartmann von Aue, derived from a French source and written in about 1190,[3] and a Middle English strophic text, also based on a French original, came just over a century later. The modern edition of the latter again prints parallel versions from several rather different manuscripts.[4] Soon after it was composed, Hartmann's German was adapted into Latin verse by the chronicler Arnold, abbot of St John's in Lübeck, for the use of Duke Wilhelm of Lüneburg, the son of Henry the Lion and incidentally also Henry Plantagenet's grandson. Such a rendering of Gregory's life into the respectability of Latin is noteworthy of itself,[5] and later on Hartmann's

---

[1] There is an excellent schematic survey of the texts used in this chapter in Bernward Plate's edition of the late German prose texts, *Gregorius auf dem Stein* (Darmstadt: WBG, 1983), pp. 2f, and Plate also provides a good introduction to research on the story as a whole. For a general introduction see the study by A. van der Lee, 'De mirabili divina dispensatione et ortu beati Gregorii pape', *Neophilologus* 53 (1969), 30–47, 120–37 and 251–6.

[2] Hendrik B. Sol, *La Vie du Pape Saint Grégoire* (Amsterdam: Rodopi, 1977), cited unless otherwise noted from the critical text based on MS Egerton 612 in the British Library. Sol also prints a late French text in alexandrines, pp. 385–99. See Volker Mertens, *Gregorius Eremita* (Munich: Artemis, 1978), pp. 27–31 on the Angevin connexions. Mertens' highly useful survey of the different versions (with more detail than in Plate), is summarised in his entry 'Gregorius' in *Die deutsche Literatur des Mittelalters: Verfasserlexikon*, 2nd edn by K. Ruh (Berlin: de Gruyter, 1978–), III, 244–8.

[3] Hartmann von Aue, *Gregorius*, ed. Friedrich Neumann (Wiesbaden: Brockhaus, 1958); there is a more recently updated standard edition, that originally by Hermann Paul, 11th edn by Ludwig Wolff (Tübingen: Niemeyer, 1966), 13th edn by Burghart Wachinger (Tübingen: Niemeyer, 1984), with line-reference links to the French versions, but Neumann's edition is especially valuable for the notes. Over ten manuscripts are known (of), but see Horst Wenzel, 'Der "Gregorius" Hartmanns von Aue. Überlegungen zur zeitgenössischen Rezeption des Werkes', *Euphorion* 66 (1972), 323–54.

[4] *Die mittelenglische Gregoriuslegende*, ed. Carl Keller (Heidelberg and New York: Winter, 1914), cited principally from the text of the Vernon manuscript, with reference also to the Auchinleck text.

[5] Johannes Schilling, *Arnold von Lübeck, Gesta Gregorii Peccatoris: Untersuchungen und Edition* (Göttingen: Vandenhoek und Ruprecht, 1968); this replaces the edition by Gustav von Buchwald published a century earlier. Schilling indicates the value of this work for the study of the legend in general and Hartmann in particular, p. 11. The new edition by Schilling, with line-references to Hartmann, has begun to stimulate further studies in German in particular: Rainer Zäck, *Der guote sundaere und der*

poem was put into German prose and incorporated into a much augmented compilation based on the *Golden Legend* (in which our saint did not, in fact, appear)
called *Der Heiligen Leben* (Lives of the Saints). This is known from the end of the
fourteenth century in more than 150 manuscripts and over forty printed texts, and
the saint is associated there with 28 November.[6] Even the small edition by Bernward Plate of these late medieval German prose versions presents three separate
texts in parallel columns, something to which scholarship on the story seems rather
prone. It makes the works hard to read, but it does underscore their popularity and
variety. It also inclines us to select and concentrate upon the key elements and
constants of the saint's life.

By the middle of the fourteenth century a brief Latin prose version had appeared
in a well known moralising story-book, the *Gesta Romanorum*, with the story
again derived from French. Not all of the many manuscripts of the *Gesta* have the
story, or they have it in a slightly truncated form, but the *Gesta* was widely translated, and our *legenda*, with didactic pointers attached, comes via the *Gesta* or the
French original into most of the European languages, including Spanish, Italian,
Czech and Hungarian, and even Coptic.[7] An expanded German version seems to
have been turned into a *Volksbuch* in the later seventeenth century but printed
versions – and the story was still being printed in the nineteenth century – became
conflated with the earlier German prose redactions, and even with Hartmann,
whose poem had been edited by the 1830s.[8] There are independent French, Latin
and Low German versions, often heavily didactic,[9] and there is a celebrated

---

peccator precipuus (Göppingen: Kümmerle, 1989), and Jens-Peter Schröder, *Arnold von Lübecks
Gesta Gregorii Peccatoris* (Frankfurt/M: Lang, 1997). Earlier comparisons are those by Hans Schottmann, 'Gregorius und Grégoire', *Zeitschrift für deutsches Altertum* 94 (1965), 81–108, and by Peter F.
Ganz, 'Dienstmann und Abt. "Gregorius peccator" bei Hartmann von Aue und Arnold von Lübeck',
in *Festschrift für Werner Schröder* (Berlin: Schmidt, 1974), pp. 250–75. German works *were* occasionally put into Latin, and there is an early example in Ratpert's metrical Latin life of St Gall, for which
the German original has not even survived.

6   Eberhard Dorn, *Der sündige Heilige in der Legende des Mittalalters* (Munich: Fink, 1967), pp.
86–9. The earlier German prose versions are in Plate, *Gregorius*, whose bibliography has references to
later versions. On the *legendarium* version see Volker Mertens, 'Verslegende und Prosalegendar: zur
Prosafassung von Legendenromanen in "Der Heiligen Leben" ', in *Poesie und Gebrauchsliteratur in
deutschen Mittelalter*, ed. Volker Honemann (Tübingen: Niemeyer, 1979), pp. 265–89. The move from
verse narrative to prose has interesting implications for the reception of the material.

7   *Gesta Romanorum*, ed. H. Oesterly (Berlin, 1872; repr. Hildesheim: Olms, 1963), see pp. 399–409,
trans. Charles Swan, rev. Wynnard Hooper (London: Bell, 1877), pp. 141–54. On the breadth of the
story as a whole, see the interesting study by John Boswell, *The Kindness of Strangers: the Abandonment of Children in Western Europe from Late Antiquity to the Renaissance* (Harmondsworth:
Penguin, 1991), pp. 374f. See *Gregorius: a Medieval Oedipus Legend by Hartmann von Aue*, trans.
Edwin H. Zeydel and Bayard Q. Morgan (Chapel Hill: UNC Press, 1955), pp. 1–5 on the various versions.

8   See J. Elema and R. van der Wal, 'Zum Volksbuch *Eine schöne merkwürdige Historie des heiligen
Bischofs Gregorii auf dem Stein genannt*', *Euphorion* 57 (1963), 292–320. The authors compare an
eighteenth-century *Historie* printed by Christian Everaerts and the medievalist Karl Simrock's text in
the nineteenth century. Simrock would have known Hartmann's version and possibly others. Elema
and van der Wal also note, pp. 305f, the absence of the legend from a number of the *Gesta Romanorum*
manuscripts.

9   The brief but interesting Low German version is described as 'didactic and homiletic' by Olaf
Schwencke, '*Gregorius de grote sünder*: Eine erbaulich-paränetische Prosaversion der Gregoriusleg-

modern retelling by no less a writer than Thomas Mann, who first encountered it in the *Gesta Romanorum*, though he did read Hartmann's poem later on.

Medieval versions of the *vita* of this particularly worthy saint and pope stress not only its moral usefulness, as one might well imagine – though it is, as we shall see, a life that is to be wondered at rather than imitated – but also its absolute truth:

> Al of a storie ichulle ou rede
> Þat is soþ wiþ oute lesyng
> How eueri mon scholde sunne [= sin] drede
> Þat wolde come to god endyng.   (5–8)

All this is marred only somewhat by the fact that although there were several early popes called Gregory (probably five by the time the life was first composed, some of them indeed canonised), sadly this one did not actually exist, in spite of his medieval popularity and the attempt by the first editor of the French text in the 1850s to link him with Gregory the Great. The story of our literally legendary Gregory is, nevertheless, a memorable one, as the arresting title of the German chapbook makes clear: 'A fine and remarkable history of the holy bishop Gregorius on the rock'. Although we may wonder about that reference to the rock, the *most* memorable aspect of the life of Gregorius – we may keep his Latin name to distinguish him from those historical popes – is almost certainly multiple incest, as the noble hero, already born of a ducal brother and sister, later marries his mother/aunt. The tale also tells, though, how he undertook a seventeen-year-long penance chained to a rocky islet, and after that became pope. There *are* realistic elements in the story, certainly, but there are many that are plainly miraculous, and much of the tale is meant to be extreme, so that more ordinary lives can be set against it for comfort, rather than for fellowship.

It is probably not too surprising to learn that this particular Gregorius is a literary invention. What is more surprising, in view of what has been indicated of his life so far, is that in spite of everything Gregorius is a paradigm for mankind. The tale as a whole is based largely on that of the biblical and the apocryphal Adam, albeit an Adam placed under the grace of the Redemption. In fact, the equation of Gregorius with Adam makes clear the way in which the literary mediation of the Fall rests upon the identity of Adam's role as the historical progenitor who is also the beginning of salvation history; on his role as the model sinner whose actions – in the words of the real Gregory the Great in his *Moralia in Job* – we imitate every day; and at the same time upon the ongoing and ineradicable essence of mankind, the old Adam, the embodiment of man burdened with original sin. Noble birth, multiple incest, excessive penance and election to the papacy notwith-

ende', *Jahrbuch des Vereins für niederdeutsche Sprachforschung* 90 (1967), 63–88. The Dominican text is in J. Klapper, *Die Erzählungen des Mittelalters in deutscher Übersetzung und lateinischem Urtext* (Breslau: Marcus, 1914), and the (very brief) French prose was edited by P. Meyer, 'La Légende en prose de Saint Grégoire', *Romania* 33 (1904), 42–6, and see Sol, *Vie*, pp. 400–2. Wolfgang Stammler's *Spätlese des Mittelalters* I (Berlin: Schmidt, 1963), pp. 3–19 contains a Low German text stressing the penance in its title, *Van sante Gregorio vp dem mer.* Schwencke refers to other German prose versions, p. 79, nn. 13f.

standing, Gregorius is also Adam in whom *all* sinned, another unique and universal figure.[10]

An indication of the variations in this story and a hint at further problems are given in the various contrasts and emphases found in the titles, subtitles and repeated epithets. Gregorius is not only the great sinner, *Gregorius de grote sünder* in Low German (already an ambiguous adjective), but also the good sinner, *le bon pecheur, der guote sundaere*, which presents a set-piece paradox similar to the *felix culpa* of salvation history. Elsewhere Gregorius is tagged by his penance on the rock, and in other versions again – the *Gesta Romanorum* is a case in point – it is his incestuous birth that is highlighted. Finally, the subtitle of a modern translation of Hartmann's medieval German version is revealing: Edwin Zeydel and Bayard Quincy Morgan dubbed the work 'A Medieval Oedipus Legend'. The link with Oedipus, though it has engaged critical attention, is not particularly enlightening and certainly need not be pursued, even though the Greek story was known in the Middle Ages through Statius's *Thebaid*. Beyond the incest itself (which has undergone reduplication) there are otherwise few points of essential contact between the medieval religious narrative – a positive work, the keynote of which is salvation – and the Greek tragedy.[11] Gregorius is remarkable not only (and perhaps not even primarily) because of the incest and his extended penance, however. What is of major importance in the medieval world, and what removes him completely from the sphere of Greek myth, is the point underlined in the title of the version by Arnold of Lübeck: *Gesta Gregorii peccatoris ad penitenciam conversi et ad papatum promoti*, a sinner and a penitent who is elevated to the papacy (and even in the one version – that in Low German – in which he does not become pope, he is at least made a bishop). Gregorius is more than just a reflection of Adam; he takes even further the casting of Adam into the role of priest that was already visible in the *Vita Adae*, a work which, Oedipus parallels notwithstanding, has exerted a far more important influence. The setting this time, though, is all in the *sub gratia* world, so that the Adam-figure can (eventually) understand the Redemption in full, and can indeed become a priest in the proper sense. The medieval story of Gregorius is, in effect, the last stage in the presentation of the divine economy by way of a vernacular popularisation of the pseudepigraphic life of Adam and Eve. But the

---

[10] The link with Adam has been made in the context of Hartmann in most detail by Rosemary Picozzi, 'Allegory and Symbol in Hartmann's *Gregorius*', in *Essays . . . in Honor of Joyce Hallamore*, ed. M. Batts and M. Stankiewicz (Toronto: University of Toronto Press, 1968), pp. 19–33, by Frank J. Tobin, 'Fallen Man and Hartmann's *Gregorius*', *Germanic Review* 50 (1975), 85–98, and in my own paper, 'Hartmann's *Gregorius* and the Quest of Life', *New German Studies* 6 (1978), 79–100, which anticipates some of the points developed in the present study. It has been examined most fully with reference to many of the versions in the seminal work by Friedrich Ohly, *Der Verfluchte und der Erwählte*, referred to already. I cite the excellent English version by Linda Archibald, *The Damned and the Elect* (Cambridge: Cambridge University Press, 1992), in which Ohly's illustrative citations from various languages are also translated. See also Frank J. Tobin's book *'Gregorius' and 'Der arme Heinrich'* (Berne and Frankfurt/M: Lang, 1973), and Rodney Fisher, 'Hartmann's *Gregorius* and the Paradox of Sin', *Seminar* 17 (1981), 1–16. See most recently Mary V. Mills, *The Pilgrimage Motif in the Works of the Medieval German Author Hartmann von Aue* (Lewiston: Mellen, 1996).

[11] See Peter Wapnewski's handbook on *Hartmann von Aue* (Stuttgart: Metzler, 5th edn 1972), pp. 77–82, and Zeydel and Morgan's translation pp. 4–6 on Oedipus. There is a more recent prose version in Hartmann von Aue, *The Narrative Works*, trans. Rodney W. Fisher (Göppingen: Kümmerle, 1983).

tale of Gregorius goes further than the *Vita*, and takes into account not only details of the biblical Fall, but also the Pauline doctrine of the second Adam and the resolved paradox of the *peccator iustus*. The literary Gregorius represents the first Adam in many respects, but not only is he a man already fully redeemed, but he becomes *a* and then *the* representative of Christ. The Fall and the Redemption are thus mirrored in the *vita* of one man – we may retain the hagiographic term, even though critics have warned from time to time about placing the story too firmly into this generic mould.[12] The story offers an answer to the human dilemma of living with the liability to sin but, since it operates within the framework of theocentric human history, the protagonists do not understand the divine intent while it is in progress. Gregorius's birth is memorable, but he is born with the original sin that all men have, no more and no less; and yet Gregorius is a test case, showing that original sin can be discounted, and that actual sin can be atoned for.

The story of Gregorius is made up of a series of clearly defined and circumscribed incidents. A nobleman, usually the duke of Aquitaine (though he is raised to the purple in the *Gesta Romanorum*), dies, leaving a son and a daughter. His wife had died long before. He commends the daughter to the son's care, but the son, prompted by the devil, instigates an incestuous relationship – the girl's degree of acquiescence varies from text to text – and as a result a child is born. The brother at once goes on a journey of penance to the Holy Land, where he dies. The mother rules as duchess, but the penance placed upon her is one of perpetual chastity. The child is placed in a boat and put out to sea, although the mother places in the boat some expensive cloth, a sum of money and a tablet or tablets inscribed with the details of the incestuous birth and also an indication of the nobility of the parents, though without giving their name. No criticism is made of the mother for this act, incidentally.[13] The child is found by fishermen and brought to an abbot, who names the child Gregorius after himself. The child is baptized, brought up by one of the fishermen and given a monastic education. Following an incident in which he fights (details vary) with one of the fisherman's actual sons, his foster-mother curses him as a foundling. At this, Gregorius decides to leave the monastery and seek his fortune as a knight. The abbot tries to dissuade him, effectively promising him the abbacy after his death, but eventually reveals the details of the young man's birth – both the nobility and the incest – which he is now old enough to understand. Gregorius departs nevertheless, leaving the direction up to God, and finds himself in his mother's lands, where she is under siege from another nobleman who wishes to marry her. He rescues his mother – it is of major importance whether or to what extent she recognises the clothes he is wearing as made from the fine cloth she left with him as a baby – and on the advice of her counsellors, she marries him. Eventually the tablet is discovered and the pair are plunged into despair. Gregorius undertakes a penance, having himself chained to a remote rock for (in almost all versions) seventeen years, where he is kept alive by a miracle. When he goes to the rock he leaves the tablet on which his story is inscribed behind him. The pope dies,

12 The *Vita Adae* is, of course, not a saint's life either: see Dorn, *Heiliger* on the topic in general. One of the *Gregorius* poets, Hartmann von Aue, uses the generic structures and distinctive elements of the saint's life in other works, such as *Der arme Heinrich*, discussed here in Chapter 4.
13 A fact noted by Boswell, *Kindness*, p. 375.

and an angel instructs the cardinals to find Gregorius. The key to his chains is recovered miraculously and he also finds his apparently indestructible tablet. He is taken to Rome and enthroned as the new pope, and later grants absolution to his mother.

Most of what appear to be evil twists in the story are attributed in all versions quite specifically to the devil, although he does not appear in person as he does in the *Vita Adae*. Most of the points at which there is actual movement are attributed equally specifically to God, whether it be the arrival of the child in his boat, Gregorius's journey to his mother's lands, his journey of penance or his journey to Rome. The whole can be viewed, indeed, as the working out of a divine plan and a parallel to *the* divine plan. Various links with the story of Adam, either from the biblical or the apocryphal tradition, are immediately apparent. These include the casting out of a noble but sinful couple who are of one flesh from a paradisiacal situation; a quite specific birth sin; the question of recognition of diabolical activity at various points; the provision of clothing and indeed of names; the penance on a rock in water; and the inscribing of the story of the original sin on indestructible tablets.

The young Gregorius is given formal instruction by the abbot, whose name he takes, probably studying doctrine, exegesis and pastoral theology, and it is appropriate for us to do likewise and consider three statements, the first on original sin, the second a tropological interpretation of the Fall, and the third on the nature of penance. The distinction between original and actual sin is summed up admirably by another genuine medieval pope, Innocent III, in a letter to Ymbertus, archbishop of Arles, in 1201:

> peccatum est duplex: originale scilicet et actuale; originale, quod absque consensu contrahitur, et actuale, quod committitur cum consensu. Originale igitur, quod sine consensu contrahitur, sine consensu per vim remittitur sacramenti; actuale vero, quod cum consensu contrahitur, sine consensu minime relaxatur . . . Poena originalis peccati est carentia visionis Dei, actualis vero poena peccati est gehennae perpetuae cruciatus.[14]

> (sin is twofold, original or actual; original sin is contracted without consent, actual sin is committed with consent. Thus original sin, since it is contracted without consent, can be removed without consent by the force of the sacrament; actual sin, which is contracted with consent, cannot be remitted without effort . . . The penalty of original sin is the loss of the sight of God, and in truth the penalty for actual sin is the torment of everlasting hell.)

There has been much discussion about the precise nature of Gregorius's sins, and Innocent's lucid description is worth bearing in mind.

The tropological interpretation by the real Gregory the Great of the story of the Fall is of some importance in this context, and one even wonders about a possible influence on the name of the literary Gregorius. At all events, Gregory's comments on the Fall from the *Moralia in Job* became the standard moralising interpretation virtually for the entire Middle Ages. He offers a tropological reading of the story

---

14 Denzinger and Bannwart, *Enchiridion Symbolorum*, p. 180, no. 410.

which matches the homiletic didacticism claimed in nearly all the versions of the Gregorius legend:

Quatuor quippe modis peccatum perpetratur in corde, quatuor consummatur in opere. In corde namque suggestione, delectatione, consensu et defensionis audacia. Fit enim suggestio per adversarium, delectatio per carnem, consensus per spiritum, defensionis audacia per elationem . . . Nam serpens suasit, Eva delectata est, Adam consensit; qui etiam requisitus confiteri culpam per audaciam noluit. Hoc vero in humano genere quotidie agitur, quod actum in primo parente nostri generis non ignorantur. Serpens suasit; quia occultus hostis mala condibus hominum latenter suggerit. Eva delectata est; quia carnalis sensus verba serpentis mox se delectationi substernit. Assensus vero Adam mulieri praepositus praebuit; quia dum caro in delectationem rapitus, etiam a sua rectitudine, spiritus infirmatus inclinatur. Et requisitus Adam confiteri noluit culpam quia videlicet spiritus, quo peccando a veritate disiungitur, eo in ruinae suae audacia nequius obduratur.[15]

(There are four stages by which sin is perpetrated in the heart, and four in which it is actually put into practice. In the heart, these stages are: suggestion, delight, consent and brazening-it-out. In practice, the suggestion comes from the Old Enemy, delight from the flesh, consent from the spirit, and brazen self-justification from a general over-confidence in the self. . . . Now, the serpent made the persuasive suggestion, Eve delighted in it, Adam consented, and when he was called upon to confess his guilt, he brazenly denied it. And, I do assure you, all this happens with mankind every day, the very same things as were experienced by our first natural parents. The serpent did the persuading, just as now the Old Enemy secretly makes evil suggestions to mankind. Eve delighted in it, just as the sensual flesh gives way to pleasure when it hears the old serpent's words. Adam consented to what the woman put to him, just as, once the flesh has been seized with delight, the weak spirit then bends towards it. And when he was required by God to confess his guilt, Adam would not do so, just as the spirit, turned from the true path by sin, becomes – to its own ruin! – hardened by brazen audacity.)

[15] *Moralia in Job* IV, 27 (*PL* 75, 661) and see Augustine's stages in *PL* 34, 1246; see my book *The Fall of Man in the Early Middle High German Biblical Epic* (Göppingen: Kümmerle, 1972), pp. 42, 55 and 139 for a list of places where the exegesis and similar later passages in the *Moralia* are repeated. The influence of Gregory's work in general has been described by Fowler, *Bible in Early English Literature*, pp. 40–78. For a Latin poem which uses the motif, see A. G. Rigg, '*De motu et poena peccati*: a Latin Poem on the Causes and Effects of Sin', in *Literature and Religion in the Later Middle Ages (Philological Studies in Honor of Siegfried Wenzel)*, ed. Richard G. Newhauser and John A. Alford (Binghampton, NY: Medieval and Renaissance Texts and Studies, 1985), pp. 161–77. I have translated the passage of Gregory in *The Grin of the Gargoyle* (Sawtrey: Dedalus, 1995), p. 24. The importance of Gregory's *Moralia* as a tropological exposition in medieval writing (and cited indeed in versions of our story) is stressed by Rosemary Combridge in a relevant context, 'The Uses of Biblical and Other Learned Symbolism in the Narrative Works of Hartmann von Aue', in *Hartmann von Aue: Changing Perspectives*, ed. Timothy McFarland and Silvia Ranawake (Göppingen: Kümmerle, 1988), pp. 271–84 (see p. 217).

This tropology of the Fall by the principal pastoral theologian of the Middle Ages – echoing as it does earlier moral interpretations of Eve as the seducible flesh which in its turn affects the *ratio*, the rational mind, represented by Adam – is not only much quoted in subsequent exegetical writing, but is frequently echoed in medieval literature. Propensity to sin is the real effect of original sin. Augustine himself laid out a manner of coping with this (in the same way as Gregory the Great described the way in which sin occurs) and it was developed by the scholastics around the time our story was first written. Prævenient grace calls man towards goodness; the will to do the right thing and the strength to do so, *gratia operans* and *gratia cooperans* come next; and although man in Gregory's terms is prone not just to sin but to brazening it out, he is also provided with the *donum perseverantiae*, the gift of being able to persevere (in terms of Matthew 24:13 'qui usque in finem persevaverit, salvus erit'). This can lead to *gratia sanans* and *gratia remissionis*. This pattern has been worked out in some detail in studies of Hartmann, most notably by Ute Schwab in her book *Lex et gratia*, taking its title from the two elements of the interpretation of the Good Samaritan story with which Hartmann prefaces his poem, and to which reference will be made again.[16]

Actual sin, then, requires penance, and the clearest example of an actual sin in our story is incest. The *Penitential* of Theodore of Tarsus, who was archbishop of Canterbury at the end of the seventh century and whose work was used as an authority by many later writers, including Regino of Prüm in his own *Ecclesiastical Discipline*, prescribes fifteen years penance for incest, Alain of Lille thirty.[17] The comments on this particular sin in two other widely known penitentials are interesting; Regino's *Ecclesiastical Discipline* was expanded about a century after it was composed in a larger work called *The Corrector* or (significantly) the *Physician* by Burkhard I, bishop of Worms from 1000 to 1025, which later acquired the title of *The German Penitential*.[18] Burkhard also prescribed fifteen years penance for incest, but Regino's general comments to the confessor, used also by Burkhard, are of interest, and they contain clear echoes of Gregory the Great on Genesis: 'et si non vult incestum dimittere, non potes ei dare poenitentiam: si autem vult, potes' (if he will not abandon his incest, thou canst not give him penance, but if he will, thou canst). The confessor is then required to say (and remember, it is incest that he is dealing with):

> Frater, noli erubescere peccatu tua confiteri, nam et ego peccatorsum, et fortassis pejora quam tu feceris habeo facta. Haec idcirco admoneo, quia

[16] See R. S. Moxon, *The Doctrine of Sin* (London: Allen and Unwin, 1922), pp. 98f for a succinct summary of the pattern of grace. There are translations of the relevant passages in H. Bettenson, *Documents of the Christian Church* (London: Oxford University Press, 2nd edn 1963), pp. 77–9. There is a more detailed presentation in our context by Ute Schwab, *Lex et Gratia: der literarische Exkurs Gottfrieds von Strassburg und Hartmanns Gregorius* (Messina: Università, 1967), p. 74. See also Zäck, *Peccator*, pp. 222–33.

[17] McNeill and Gamer, *Penance*, p. 186. Ohly, *The Damned and the Elect*, pp. 157f.

[18] See the nineteenth book of his *Decretorum libri XX – Liber hic Corrector vocatur et Medicus* (*PL* 140, 949). The whole text is at *PL* 140, 537–1058. Regino's far shorter work is in *PL* 132, 187–400. See McNeill and Gamer, *Penance*, pp. 316 and 325f for a translation of both texts and for comments on them.

usitatum humani generis vitium est, ut beatus Gregorius dicit, et labendo peccatum committere, et commissum non confitendo prodere, sed negando defendere, atque convictum defendendo multiplicare. Et qui diaboli instigante nefanda crimina perpetrare non metuimus . . . erubescimus confiteri . . .[19]

(Brother, do not blush to confess your sins, for I also am a sinner, and have possibly committed worse sins than you. So let me warn you, since – as Gregory the Great tells us – it is a habit of the human race both to commit a sin and to fail to confess what been committed, but rather to defend it by denying it, and in denying it, to multiply the offence. We are not afraid of perpetrating wicked crimes at the devil's instigation, but we do blush to confess them . . .)

The tale of Gregorius is predicated upon the fact that since man is now *sub gratia*, any sin can be forgiven: Hartmann cites the customary negative example of Judas who did not believe this, and was thus damned. It is Hartmann, too, who, by using in his prologue the example of the Good Samaritan, underlines the idea that the sins incurred on the journey through life need not actually be *deserved*. The traveller healed of his wounds by the Samaritan is seen soteriologically as the sinner healed by Christ, but the wounds were inflicted from outside. Even saints can sin; Eberhard Dorn refers in his study of sinful saints to sexual sinners, parricides and thieves (including both St Landelinus the robber and St Peter Telonearius, the tax-official), but the sin of incest is a special case. It links – as we shall see in detail – with Adam and Eve; it is also a paradigmatically serious sin; it is one that can be committed without knowledge on the part of the sinner; and it can be committed repeatedly and with enjoyment. That such a sinner could also become a saint returns us to the idea of the *peccator iustus* or *praecipuus*, the latter word carrying the meanings 'special', 'extraordinary' and 'excellent'. There are other saints' lives in which incest plays a part – all of them, it has to be said, literary rather than historical – and both St Metro and St Albanus, plus various other eastern saints, enjoyed cult status in the Middle Ages.[20] The link with Adam is a feature of the Gregorius story, however, and direct references to Adam are introduced with cumulative effect at different key points in different versions. Sometimes, too, the proximity of the two narratives is underscored by the manuscript transmission. The English *Gregorius*-poem is found in the Edinburgh Auchinleck manuscript, which has also a metrical English version of the *Vita Adae*, while the Vernon manuscript in the Bodleian has both the *Gregorius*-poem and a life of Adam in English prose.

The first element in the story of Gregorius which links with Adam and Eve is the initial brother-sister incest. Adam and Eve are themselves of one flesh, perhaps even closer than brother and sister; in the English *Life of Adam* in the Auchinleck manuscript, Adam points out to Eve that they could not be more closely related: 'þou miʒtest be me no ner sibbe'. In a sense Adam is both father and brother to

---

[19] *PL* 140, 950f (Cap. IV). The translation is mine rather than McNeill and Gamer's.
[20] Dorn, *Heiliger*, pp. 80–9. See especially Ohly, *The Damned and the Elect*, on all these points, including in detail the example of Judas.

Eve, something which may be related to the *double* incest in *Gregorius*.[21] One medieval tradition even has Adam and Eve born under the sign of Gemini.[22] 'We ben . . .' says the son in the English version '. . . of one blod' (75), and the poet reiterates this several times, both to stress the incest and to remind us of the Adamic connexion. Furthermore, Adam is placed in a position of trust as a ruler over Eden, and he is a noble figure, made in the image of God and commanding the service of the angels. A beautiful and noble couple, then, of one flesh, are left isolated by their father in what ought to have been an ideal situation which is also one of great responsibility, and thus they match the case of the protoplasts. In our legend, too, the son is again given one single injunction, which ought to have been easy to keep: to let no harm come to his sister.[23] The English version gives this initial precept (significantly in the light of the original commandment in Genesis) in a negative form:

> Do þi suster non outrage
> And i preye þe for my sake
> Þat þou hire kepe and hold in ore
> Til heo haue a lord i take
> Sone i beseche þe of no more.   (68–72)

But the couple are *not* Adam and Eve, and the world in which their particular Paradise is set is a postlapsarian one in which concupiscence in particular can be a temptation. They are as isolated as Adam and Eve were in their noble position, and they are also prey to temptation by the devil, who is, we are told in most versions, again consumed with envy at their blessed state. *Invidia* is the reason given in most medieval sources for the devil's decision to tempt the protoplasts, the devil having been cast from heaven after his refusal to worship the image of God in the younger creation, and thereafter jealous of Adam and Eve when he saw them enjoying the delights that he had lost. He tells the story to Adam in the *Vita Adae* when Adam challenges him, and it is mirrored here. Even the briefest of the versions, such as the Low German prose or that in the *Gesta Romanorum*, make it clear that the boy was tempted by the devil, but Hartmann develops the point. He reminds us first that the devil was locked up in hell because of his original envy, then says more generally that the devil is always envious of human well-being, only to particularise again with the attack on the pair. In all of the medieval versions of *Gregorius*, though, it is the devil who persuades the brother to make his advances upon his sister.

---

[21] Adam refers to Eve in some medieval texts expressly as his sister; see the *Mystère de la Passion* of Arnoul Greban, ed. Paris and Raynaud, p. 19 (line 1280, 'ma seur'). For the *Life of Adam* in the Auchinleck manuscript, see the edition by Horstmann, v. 168.
[22] See Annette Volfing, *Heinrich von Mügeln, Der meide kranz: a Commentary* (Tübingen: Niemeyer, 1997), p. 377, where a text containing this point is cited.
[23] Variations between, say, the French and German versions here, and the supposedly more courtly injunctions in Hartmann, are not at issue here, since the basic precept, however embellished, is the same. See David A. Wells, 'Fatherly Advice: the Precepts of "Gregorius", Marke and Gurnemanz and the School Tradition of the "Disticha Catonis" ', *Frühmittelalterliche Studien* 28 (1994), 296–332, esp. pp. 308f.

Thomas Mann recognised the connexion of this part of the story with Adam and Eve. In his ironical and elaborately Gothic narrative he has the boy persuade the girl, and has the girl respond, in the words of the Old French *Mystère d'Adam*, the twelfth-century play of the Fall. He does not cite the words of the devil to Eve, however, but gives those of Eve to Adam to the boy, reversing the roles and giving a new meaning to the eating of the fruit. Try it, says the boy, and you may well like it: 'Manjue . . . Nel poez saver sin gusteras' (Eat it – you won't know until you have tasted it).[24]

Hartmann's version has fairly obvious echoes of the Adam and Eve story at this point, but they are clearer still in Arnold of Lübeck's Latin adaptation. His reference to the *invidia* of the devil and the link to the situation of mankind is more specific. Somehow, though, he still seems to place a heavier emphasis on the woman's guilt:

> Cuius invidia mors intravit mundum
> qui usque hodie genus vexat humanum
> et qui in paradiso deliciarum Adam
> seduxit per feminam,
> ipse nunc per marem
> corrumpere temptat feminam . . .   (I, 3, 17–22)[25]

(The one by whose envy death entered the world and who vexes mankind until this very day, who in the Paradise of delights seduced Adam through the woman, he now led the woman into corruption by way of the male.)

Moreover, the whole is couched in the terminology of Gregory the Great and of the tropology of the Fall: the first stage is *dyabolica suggestio* (29), which diabolical prompting is in Hartmann as well, but then Arnold refers to *titillacio carnalis* (30), to consent (36) and the overcoming of the *ratio* (39) and then the difficulty of confession. The homiletic approach to the Fall is known in other medieval writing.

---

[24] Thomas Mann, *Der Erwählte* (Frankfurt/M and Hamburg: Fischer, 1951, repr. 1967), p. 37. The English version (1952) by Mann's now widely discredited translator Helen Lowe-Porter, *The Holy Sinner* (Harmondsworth: Penguin, 1961), p. 26 is readable but inaccurate. For the text of the *Mystère*, see *Le Mystère d'Adam*, ed. Paul Studer (Manchester: Manchester University Press, 1949), and earlier Karl Grass, *Das Adamsspiel* (Halle/Saale: Niemeyer, 1928), pp. 18f. There are translations by Edward Noble Stone, *Adam* (Seattle: University of Washington Press, 1928), and by Richard Axton and John Stevens, *Medieval French Plays* (Oxford: Blackwell, 1971), pp. 1–44. Mann was given the information by Erich Auerbach, who described the passage in the French play in a memorable essay from 1946: 'Adam and Eve', in *Mimesis*, trans. Willard Trask (New York: Doubleday, 1957), pp. 124–51. See on the connexion H. J. Weigand, 'Thomas Mann's Gregorius', *Germanic Review* 27 (1952), 10–30 and 81–95. Mann's work is deliberately parodistic in parts: see Karl Stackmann, '*Der Erwählte*: Thomas Manns Mittelalterparodie', *Euphorion* 53 (1959), 61–74.

[25] There is a reference to Arnold's mention of Adam in Tobin, 'Fallen Man', p. 90, n. 26, but not to Gregory the Great, who is, however, mentioned by Schilling in his notes, p. 188. On the use of the Gregorian typology in the Vienna *Genesis*, see my *Fall of Man*, p. 131. Curiously, David Duckworth, *Gregorius: a Medieval Man's Discovery of his True Self* (Göppingen: Kümmerle, 1985) pays little attention to Gregory on Job, although his book has a frontispiece of the real Pope Gregory from a manuscript of that text.

Gregory the Great's tropology is presented in an excursus in the earliest German poem on Genesis, the so-called Vienna *Genesis*, in the eleventh century, and Arnold, too, ends on a generalised injunction: 'Nunc igitur ex animo/ renuncia dyabolo!' (56–7) (Therefore drive the devil from your soul!).

It is sometimes claimed of the *Vita Adae* that the second temptation of Eve in that work was intended to exonerate Adam from the responsibility for the Fall. This is not in fact the case, as he has by that stage already fallen, and what the second temptation is intended to demonstrate in the *Vita* is the far from simple recognisability of the devil. (The same point will be made in the equivalent in the *Gregorius*-narrative to the second temptation of Eve.) This temptation does seem to be a reversal, however. The devil selects Eve for her susceptibility to flattery for her beauty, or because she is thought to be an easier target in general terms, or because she is less intelligent. But if more orthodox medieval interpretations of Genesis might have linked *mulier* with *mollier* (the softer), here the clearly indicated *suggestio* of the devil does work upon the male in the first instance, and in many of the versions the girl resists. The incest is described with only a few words in the *Gesta Romanorum*, but the French texts and their derivatives have the girl – in French she is *trespensive et anguissuse* (170) – weigh up her private shame against calling for help and bringing public shame upon her brother and hence her family. In spite of the reversal of roles, there is no exoneration of the Eve-figure, however. Nearly all the versions signal that the hero of the tale is begotten that very night, but only in Hartmann (who is also unusual in not yet indicating who the child will be) does *delectatio* ensure, once the girl has acquiesced, that the sin is repeated with enjoyment on both sides.

> Donc fu engendrés sains Gregorie
> De qui Deu fist puis si saint home
> Que apostoile en fist de Rome   (Tours, 210–12)

> (Thus St Gregory was conceived, of whom God would later make such a saintly man that he gained the apostolic see at Rome.)

When the girl realises that she is pregnant she requires help. Even in his earliest experiences in the world after the Fall in the *Vita Adae*, Adam is given external help and advice, both on practical matters, when the Archangel Michael assists at the first birth, and on religious ones, when Seth returns with the angel's message about the Redemption. Similarly, in the Gregorius-legend both practical advice on childbirth and religious instruction are provided by an old and wise retainer, whom the now-dead father had recommended. In Hartmann's narrative the girl herself makes even before the birth the theological point that the specific sins of the father are not visited upon the child, even though this is not always as clear as might be expected in doctrine or indeed in canon law, especially in view of Exodus 20:5.[26]

In the specific case of incest, in fact, it might be worth noting that one of the

---

[26] See Christoph Cormeau, *Hartmanns von Aue 'Armer Heinrich' und 'Gregorius'* (Munich: Beck, 1966), pp. 104–7.

canons of the first Lateran council, held under Callistus II in 1123 and best known for its role in the question of lay investiture, also condemned – or reaffirmed the condemnation of – marriages between blood relatives and also of their offspring, depriving them of hereditary rights in ecclesiastical as in civil law. There has been no marriage here, however, even if the question of hereditary rights for the child does arise to an extent, and when Gregorius himself later marries his own mother this is unintentional.[27] However, within the developed context of a theology of original sin the sexual act between the brother and sister, for all that it here represents *the* original sin, is only an actual sin on their part, and need not necessarily be counted against the child. Since the child is a descendant of Adam, his birth carries original sin in any case. It may be an unusual birth, but it is still a birth, and every birth brings with it the taint of original sin, transmitted by the sexual act. The severity of the verse of Exodus is countered throughout the story of Gregorius by the spirit of Ezechiel 33:11. The sins of the father are visited upon the children, but God does not want the death of the sinner.

The complaint of the girl in the English poem recalls Eve's despair at the birth of Cain in the *Vita Adae*, though *her* pains were more literal. The word *i bounden* is also not without significance in a Middle English context:

> Heo seide what schal beo my red
> Liuere me lord out of þis pyne
> And bring me out of peynes strong
> Þat icham nou i bounden Inne
> Þat no fend in þis world long
> Ne fonde my body wiþ more sinne   (143–8)

Although the adviser is not a priest, an old and wise retainer is able to help and indeed to suggest a penance for the pair. In the *Vita* the initial penance is necessarily self-imposed, but the imposition of specific penances here by someone who is not a priest is unproblematic, although formal absolution can come only from a priest, something reserved for the very end of the story.[28] In this case the brother is to make his lands over to his sister and then undertake a pilgrimage to the Holy Land; the girl's penance is to be her ongoing chastity. Meanwhile, she will be tended secretly until the child is born, and then take up her place in the world once again.

The father/uncle of Gregorius functions as Adam in the first discrete episode in order to provide the central figure with an explicitly and clearly sinful birth. For the protoplasts the primary result of the Fall is death, and the brother does indeed soon suffer death on his pilgrimage, but he is – appropriately enough – replaced, in the symbolism of the work, by his own child, who takes over the role of Adam, as direct and indirect comments in all versions make clear.

The new-born child is placed in its boat and put out to sea, together with gold,

---

[27] The text of the canons of the first Lateran Council is in J. Mansi, *Sacrorum Conciliorum . . . collectio* (Florence etc., 1759–81), XXI, 282–4. The text of Can. 5 is also in Denzinger and Bannwart, *Enchiridion Symbolorum*, p. 167 (no. 362).

[28] In the *Gesta Romanorum* the pair do make confession before consulting the knight.

the fine cloth that will indicate its noble background, and the tablet or tablets of ivory on which the story is inscribed for the future, just as Seth inscribed the sinful tale of Adam and Eve for all of their posterity. Of course, this is a private message for Gregorius himself, but the message of (the) original sin as recorded in Genesis in reality and by Seth on tablets in the *Vita Adae* tradition is also a private message for every individual. The words placed with the child also indicate that he is to be baptized and to be given a theological education. The lady herself rules the land, still undergoing a penance which, like Eve, she will not in fact fulfil to the end.

Actuality and perception play a contrastive role throughout the story, as unshriven sinners appear to the outside world to be spiritually acceptable.[29] Nearly all the versions of the Gregorius story take the narrative to the point where the mother is besieged by a neighbouring lord, who wishes to marry her and who is frustrated to violence when he is refused; they then move back to the child, whose little boat – set out to the will of God – is found by fishermen after three days at sea in most of the texts (*feria sexta*, 'on the sixth day' in the *Gesta Romanorum*). These and other parallels with Christ – such as the role of the fishermen – now become patent and need only be indicated. The abbot Gregory baptizes the child, gives him his own name, and clothes him – clothes can play an important and complex role here,[30] signalling changes of identity at various points, and also, of course, in terms of Adam, simply covering nakedness. Names are equally significant: the brother and sister are never named except by Thomas Mann, and indeed in most versions the only name that occurs at all is Gregorius, conferred by the abbot as God's representative. Even when the child is born, where the French and English texts again name him as the future saint and pope, Hartmann speaks of him only as 'der guote sundaere' (the good sinner) (671) and by a series of other paradoxical pairings, such as 'the rich beggar'. Adam may have been given a name directly by God, but the naming principle comes in the *sub gratia* world only as part of baptism.

The childhood in the monastery is idyllic, a Paradise of innocence, but it comes to an end when Gregorius strikes his foster brother, the child of the fisherman. The child tells his mother and she curses Gregorius as a foundling. Most of the versions are unspecific on the actual incident, and it is difficult to see it as anything but an accidental acquisition of guilt. For Hartmann (and in the prose versions of his poem) the incident happens expressly 'against his [Gregorius's] will' – 'ez enkam von sînem willen niht' (1291), which Arnold renders simply as *nolens* (II, x, 22) – and afterwards he is in any case contrite, *riuwec* (1360). He strikes his foster brother with a ball by chance in the *Gesta Romanorum*, and only in the Tours version of the French poem does Gregorius play a very active role. It does not even appear to be the will of the devil at this point, and might be seen as part of God's plan, an impetus for the next stage of the narrative.

It is also the beginning of knowledge. The abbot, trying to persuade Gregorius to stay, shows him the tablet and reveals too his noble background. But Gregorius exercises his free will in deciding to leave the monastery. Various points arise: first,

---

[29] There is a reflection of this in the medieval commonplace of Lady World, beautiful to look at directly, but a mass of worms and decay behind.

[30] Again focussing upon Hartmann, see Anke Bennholdt-Thomsen, 'Die allegorischen *kleit* im *Gregorius*-Prolog', *Euphorion* 56 (1962), 174–84.

the question of Gregorius's real motivation, described by Gregorius himself in Hartmann (though not elsewhere except in Arnold's translation) as *tumpheit*, usually translated as 'stupidity', but also a youthful rebelliousness.[31] Certainly he appears to be in a state of confusion, and Hartmann's psychological insights are interesting at this point. Gregorius has discovered, or at least begun his discovery of, his participation in Adam's sin, and he cites shame as a motivating force: 'ja vertribet mich diu schande' (1426) (shame drives me away), although he also wishes to establish his own identity. These problems do not arise in some of the other versions in which the psychology is not explored and where he wishes to go to the Holy Land, or simply to pray for the sins of his parents. In terms of Adam and Eve, Gregorius's desire to establish his real homeland also harks back to the *patria paradisi* ('paradise the true home') topos:

> '. . . un jor repos n'avrai
> Desi a tant ke jo savrai
> De quel lignage jo sui nez,
> E pur quei jo sui issi getez.'   (1021–4)

(I shall have not a day's rest until I know from what lineage I come, and why I was cast up here.)

The accidental implications of *getez* are significant. In Hartmann, Gregorius hopes to find the same information specifically by God's grace, and indeed the abbot makes clear to him that he is able to exercise free will which may lead in either direction, 'ze schanden oder ze êren' (1442) (to shame or to honour). The difficulty is always in knowing which way the decision will take the individual, and one of the key features of the story as a whole is the ultimate trust which must be placed in God by the *homo viator in bivio*, the man faced with choice on his journey through life, something which Hartmann makes clearer than most of the other versions in the submission of the central figure at various points to the divine will, the overall plan of which is revealed only at its culmination.[32] 'E'n la sua volontade è nostra pace'.

The role of the abbot is ambiguous.[33] In all versions he promises Gregorius the abbacy after his death, but this may equally well be seen as an attempt to create the young man in his own image, actually to act as God. Against the many critical

---

[31] See H. B. Willson, 'Amor inordinata in Hartmann's *Gregorius*', *Speculum* 41 (1966), 86–104, see p. 94, and F. P. Pickering, 'Historical Thought and Moral Codes in Medieval Epic' (1977) in his *Essays on Medieval German Literature and Iconography* (Cambridge: Cambridge University Press, 1980), p. 145.

[32] Werner Schwarz, 'Free Will in Hartmann's *Gregorius*', *Beiträge/*Tübingen 89 (1967), 128–50, and Marianne E. Kalinke, 'Hartmann's *Gregorius*: a Lesson in the Inscrutability of God's Will', *Journal of English and Germanic Philology* 74 (1975), 486–501. See also Wolfgang Harms, *Homo viator in bivio* (Munich: Fink, 1970), pp. 35–40.

[33] There is a wealth of material on the point, with reference almost exclusively to Hartmann and to the French text of which the most useful recent study is that by Nigel Harris, 'The Presentation of Clerical Characters in Hartmann's *Gregorius* and in the *Vie du pape saint Grégoire*', *Medium Aevum* 64 (1995), 189–204, with reference to further material, esp. note 10. See also Carl Lofmark, 'The Advisor's Guilt in Courtly Literature', *German Life and Letters* 24 (1970/1), 3–13.

considerations of the guilt of the central figure there have been fewer speculations upon the guilt of the abbot, who wishes to make the young man into what he is not destined to be. There is in medieval terms a perfectly good reason, too, for Gregorius's desire to become a knight: heredity – usually seen as more powerful than environment, for all we may see it as a youthful and romantic urge toward self-assertion.

In the French versions Gregorius is now either twelve or fifteen years old and he is twenty in the Low German prose. We are not given his age in Hartmann, but we are told that he is at an age when he can distinguish between good and evil, the effect, of course, of the tree of knowledge.[34] Gregorius has acquired the knowledge of maturity, and can now understand all the implications of his foundling status, including the birth sin. Adam acquired his knowledge of good and evil suddenly, but Gregorius – like mankind – does so by the slower process of growing up.

Whatever his intent, Gregorius finds himself in his mother's lands. In the Low German prose version (which is rather different from most of the others) he has actually heard of the lady and sets out to help her, without knowing who she is; elsewhere, his arrival is a matter of apparent chance. It is interesting that while Hartmann attributes the journey to the intention of God, the Egerton French text blames the devil 'ki le volt damner' (1037) (who wants to damn him). The devil is part of the divine plan, and the Jobian testing of the central figure is stressed by this apparent contradiction. In Hartmann, incidentally, the young traveller is described here, as he was when he made his first journey as a baby, as *der ellende* (the exile) which is a phrase used regularly throughout the work for him, but equally regularly applied in medieval German to Adam, the exile from the homeland of Paradise. But what is of importance in this version is Gregorius's own submission, here and throughout, to the will of God. He asks to be sent somewhere 'dâ ich zu tuonne vunde' (1871) (where I shall find work to do). He does not know in how many senses this will be true.

Man's nature after Adam's Fall was – in the words of John Healey's seventeenth-century translation of the *De civitate dei* XIII, 3 – 'depraved into the admission of concupiscential disobedience in his members against his will', and Augustine's view that one of the results of the first sin is an inclination to concupiscence in particular, the sexuality by which sin is passed on, informs the next stage in the narrative, Gregorius's marriage to his mother after defeating her attacker and unwelcome suitor. Once again there are parallels with the *Vita Adae*, even if they are less obvious than those with the Oedipus story. On Gregorius's side the incest can only be unwitting,[35] but his mother now takes up again the role of Eve. Still undertaking her penance of chastity, she is suffering in the world in a perfectly real sense and is offered something that will make things easier, just as the devil in the *Vita* does to Eve. She fails to recognise the situation, and takes what is offered. That she is advised to marry Gregorius by her counsellors proves only that appearances

---

[34] On the links with the Fall at the point, see Willson, 'Amor inordinata', pp. 96–8.
[35] See on the point two of the best studies (with those by Ute Schwab and Frank Tobin) of the theological implications of Hartmann's poems: Cormeau, *Hartmanns von Aue*, pp. 104–17 on the notion of the sins of the father and the *culpa praecedens*, and K. Dieter Goebel, *Untersuchungen zu Aufbau und Schuldproblem in Hartmanns 'Gregorius'* (Berlin: Schmidt, 1974), pp. 118–20.

can indeed be deceptive. However, Hartmann's ironic and brief comments at this point about the positive value of marriage are an effective literary encapsulation of what Augustine took rather longer to express in the second book of his *De gratia Christi et de peccato originali.*

The recognisability of the cloth that she placed with the child and which has now been used to make his clothing is a key issue. There is considerable variation in the versions: in the *Gesta Romanorum* the potential recognition is missing entirely, but in other versions the recognisability is stressed when the mother rationalises away the possibility that the cloth could be the one she placed in the vessel with the child: 'plusurs pailes unt un semblant' (1128), she thinks, translated in the English texts as 'mony a cloþ is oþeres i liche' (832). In Hartmann she recognises it, but does not follow her thoughts through, and Hartmann, followed by Arnold, refers at this point to the fact that it is the devil who is now operating, adding that he had done the same when he tricked Eve in Paradise. Arnold does not follow Hartmann exactly, but he does retain the image of the protoplasts. The patterning of the tale of Gregorius upon Genesis and the *Vita Adae* here in Hartmann and Arnold is not exact, but the mother is tempted from her penance for the first sin, just as Eve was in the *Vita*. There is also a clear psychological dimension: she is attracted to this unknown man who reminds her of her brother/lover.[36] But she *does* wish to be more comfortable, and in realistic terms this requires a husband, penance notwithstanding. Advised too by her counsellors to marry for excellent political reasons, she chooses to follow the advice which *seems* so good, and assumes that Gregorius has been sent by God. Eve followed the advice of the devil in the *Vita Adae* to abandon her penance because she wished to do so, and she also believed that the devil was, as he claimed, an angel sent by God. Ironically, of course, Hartmann's Gregorius genuinely *has* been sent to his mother's land by God, but the German poet concludes the extract with the words: 'dâ ergie des tiuvels wille an' (2246) (now the devil's will was done). Arnold expands the idea to half a dozen lines, describing the devil's delight. The devil is frequently tricked into premature rejoicing.

The marriage is a happy one (and only Thomas Mann complicates an already impossible family tree by giving the couple children), but two sins are now involved: Gregorius and his mother are committing an actual sin regularly in their incestuous marriage; Gregorius is unaware of this, but he is aware of original sin because he equally constantly reads and weeps over the tablet on which is inscribed the story of his origins. When the wife and mother becomes aware of the tablet, the next crisis is precipitated, and with it Gregorius's next move in his own process of self-discovery (if we take a psychological view), in his journey through life (in a more general sense), and in his own and man's salvation history (if we take the broadest view). This new fall from a paradisiacal state is again provided in many of the versions with overtones of the first Fall, as the protagonists come close to despair. The devil, Hartmann tells us in his version, has had his way again.

The mother's reaction even has, in one version, an interesting echo of a tiny motif in the *Vita Adae*, one of those which perhaps points back, in fact, to a no

---

[36] Hartmann, 1939–62; Arnold II, 14; Schilling, pp. 120f.

longer comprehensible Hebrew word-play associated with one of the rivers of Eden. In the *Vita Adae* after the second temptation, Eve's colour is green when she emerges from the river: 'et caro eius erat sicut herba'. In the English *Gregorius* the mother falls down in a faint, and her colour is also like grass. The Auchinleck version tells how she

> ... wex boþe pale and grene
> Sche fel aswon on hir bed   (Auchinleck MS, 751–2)

But where in the *Vita Adae* (of which there is also an imperfect text in the Auchinleck MS) Eve's response is to go a long way from Adam, here it is the man who sets forth, again at hazard, on a journey which will lead him to his own penance on the rock in the water. This is a far more straightforward reflection of an earlier part of the *Vita*.

Virtually all the versions place in the mouth of the mother the words of Job 3:3, the wish never to have been born: it is there in the French texts, in Hartmann and his derivatives, and twice in the *Gesta Romanorum*. Only the English text omits the idea. One theme of the enormously influential biblical book of Job is the avoidance of this kind of despair. Job, of course, referred to the conception of a male child – again the genders have been turned around. The passage clearly has potential for drama, and some of the accusations to God are dramatic indeed. However, the English text has the mother acknowledge the existence of a divine plan:

> Lord þat semly sit a boue
> Þou wost hit al from ende to oþur
> Þi muchele Merci and þi loue
> May sunfol wommon helpe and froþur   (1083–6)

Hartmann's Gregorius counters the despair with a simple reference to trust in God and to genuinely contrite penance:

> niht verzwîvelt an gote:
> ir sult harte wol genesen.
> jâ hân ich einen trôst gelesen
> daz got die wâren riuwe hât
> ze buoze über alle missetât.   (2698–702)

> (Don't despair in God – you can be healed. I have read the comforting words that God will accept true contrition as penance for all misdeeds.)

In a general presentation, the semantic niceties of a foreign language cannot always be elucidated, but here we need to note that *verzwîfeln* is more than 'despair', it is to fall prey to *desperatio*, to the illusion of complete and irrevocable alienation from God. The verb *genesen* means to be redeemed, rescued, but in its basic form it means 'healed, cured'. Arnold refers here to 'our healing by the heavenly doctor', 'celestis medicus/ qui sanare nos venerat' (III, 17, 2–3) and the idea is picked up again at the very end of Hartmann's work, when we are all to hope that God will steer us – another significant choice of words, by the way – to an equally *genislich ende* (4004) (to healing at the last). Two further key words are *riuwe* (contrition – it is cognate with the English 'rue', though it is even in modern German rather more heartfelt) and *buoze* (penance as such). Hartmann also reminds us, by telling us that Gregorius has *read* about this, that his hero has had the training to be a priest, even if he is not one yet. In the French texts, too, the mother asks Gregorius what to do in very much the same way and in the same tone as Eve asks Adam after the first Fall for advice, especially on penance: 'domine mi, dic mihi quid est penitencia et qualiter peniteam':

> Dunc dist la mere: 'Amis, bels emfes,
> Pur amur Deu, kar on penses,
> Quant tu les livres as tuz liz
> E sages hoem es des escriz,
> Dunc me deis bien doctriner
> Coment me puisse demener.
> Conseille mei, pur Deu merci . . .'   (1575–81)

> (The mother said: 'My dear friend and child, for the love of God, because you have read all the books and what wise men have written, you can teach me how to behave. In God's name, give me advice . . .')

Gregorius's marriage was unintentional and, as James Boswell notes, a marriage involving an *error in personam* was automatically invalid, even though this did not justify any sexual acts that may have occurred. There is a similar case in the Middle English Romance *Sir Eglamour of Artois*, in which a son unknowingly marries his mother, but that marriage, significantly, is *not* consummated.[37] Even though the proscriptions of the first Lateran council regarding marriage itself would not apply, there has still been a repeated re-enactment of the Fall, as in the Genesis interpretation in the *Moralia in Job*. As far as Gregorius himself is concerned, though, this is his first penance, and that the form it takes is fasting for a long period on a rock makes the connexion with the apocryphal Adambooks very clear.

The familiarity in the Middle Ages of the postlapsarian narrative of the *Vita Adae* is not, incidentally, to be underestimated. Amongst the numerous small allusions to the penance of Adam in literary works there is an apposite illustration of the general awareness of the *Vita Adae* (or more specifically to the episode of it usually headed *Penitentia Adae*) in a slightly unusual source. There is a fifteenth-century parodistic version of the story of the Fall in German, a comic and frankly obscene poem which nevertheless makes a point about sexuality. This anonymous German piece was placed – almost certainly by mistake – as the first item in a compilation manuscript now in Karlsruhe; the compiler had almost certainly not read past the first dozen lines, which look orthodox. In the parody the point is made that Adam was ejected from Paradise for breaking one commandment about eating the fruit, but specifically *not* for any sexual activities. The conclusion drawn in the

---

[37] Boswell, *Kindness*, p. 375n. See *Sir Eglamour of Artois*, ed. Frances E. Richardson (London: Oxford University Press, 1965) (= EETS/OS 256).

parody is that sexual licence is therefore permitted, a conclusion which misses – or very possibly confirms – Augustine's definition of concupiscence as *poena peccati*, as one of the results of the Fall. In any case, the Council of Trent would condemn ultimately the view that concupiscence was *the* original sin. But the parodist refers to Adam as having completed a penance for his actual sin:

> Man líset, daz der Adam nye
> Keyn sünde mer begye
> Wann daz er den apffel aß.
> Víl sere jnn gerawe daz,
> Daz er buß dar uber nam
> Vnd büßet die vngehörsam . . .[38]

> (We read that Adam only sinned/ the once, and only in one thing:/ he took the apple and he bit/ and very much regretted it,/ and undertook a great penance/ to clear his disobedience . . .)

In the narrative of Gregorius, as in that of postlapsarian Adam, the penance on the rock is central. However, it provides an accumulation of motifs which incorporate in one figure the first and the second Adam.[39] Adam does his penance standing on a stone in the Jordan in the *Vita Adae*, for forty days in many versions, echoing Christ in the wilderness. Gregorius's seventeen-year penance, close as it is to Theodore's penitential sentence for incest, also has numerological significance in medieval terms as half the years of the life of Christ, who was crucified, traditionally, within His thirty-fourth year at the age of thirty-three; this makes Gregorius a model of sinful man, but also – and to the modern reader somewhat less clearly – it is an indication of the fulfilment of the Old Testament by the New, adding the seven gifts of the Holy Spirit to the Ten Commandments and thus placing the latter literally *sub gratia*. That point is actually Augustine's, in an exposition of figurative biblical interpretation in the *De doctrina Christiana*.[40] In fact there are even more complex numerological patterns in Hartmann's poem in particular, where there is a reference to 153 pieces of gold; this figure, a multiple of seventeen, is widely discussed in medieval exegesis, as it is the number of fish caught in John 21:11. Such figures would have had a resonance, and Hartmann's skilled use of them has been elucidated by Ute Schwab in her study of law and grace in his poem.[41]

---

[38] I have discussed the poem in question in an article 'Genesis and Pseudo-Genesis in Late Medieval German Poetry', *Medium Aevum* 45 (1975), 70–8, and translated it in *Grin of the Gargoyle*, pp. 25–31. The original may be found in *Codex Karlsruhe 408*, ed. Ursula Schmid (Berne and Munich: Francke, 1974), pp. 46–61. I cite lines 66–71.

[39] See Oliver Hallich, *Poetologisches, Theologisches: Studien zum Gregorius Hartmanns von Aue* (Frankfurt/M: Lang, 1995), pp. 140–221, Murdoch, 'Quest', and Mills, *Pilgrimage Motif*.

[40] Pierre Labriolle, *History and Literature of Christianity from Tertullian to Boethius*, trans. Herbert Wilson (London: Kegan, Paul, Trench, 1924), pp. 415–18. For examples, see Meyer, *Zahlenallegorese*, pp. 151, 158f, 184–6.

[41] Schwab, *Lex et gratia*, note 3, p. 66 proposes an even more complex view of the seventeen years, but Schwab herself is not persuaded by it. Her other parallels are both interesting and convincing, dealing with the increase in the money provided for the child, for example. See also Fritz Tschirch, 'Schlüsselzahlen', in *Festgabe für Leopold Magoun* (Berlin: Deutsche Akademie der Wissenschaften,

Gregorius is led to the rock by a fisherman, chained up and the key is thrown into the waves; he is fed by miraculous drops of water.[42] The rock has of course multiple connotations: of the *Vita* and the penance of Adam, of Moses, of Peter as the rock of the church. This last is reinforced when the key is miraculously recovered after seventeen years from inside a fish, another classical and folk motif of some antiquity used to good effect in a Christian context – St Peter's key via the ancient Christian ιχθoς-symbol. It is also required by Gregorius as a sign that this is not yet another diabolical ruse to persuade him to break off the penance. There are further Adamic references when the emissaries from Rome find the suffering Gregorius. In Hartmann especially he attempts to cover up his nakedness because he is ashamed, a clear enough allusion, and he is described as looking like a wild beast – no longer lord of creation, but the fallen Adam of Genesis 3. Yet his wounds, from the fetters, are like stigmata, and he is described as a living martyr. There is in Hartmann at least another allusion to the *Vita Adae*, made by Gregorius himself, which is imitated neither in Arnold nor in the prose versions, where it may not even have been recognised. In the apocryphon, Seth finds his way back to Paradise by following the track where the grass withered under the sinful feet of the ejected protoplasts. Gregorius rejects the idea of returning:

> sô hôhe sô mîn schulde stât
> sô möhte boum unde gras
> und swaz ie grünes bî mir was
> dorren von der grimme
> mîner unreinen stimme   (3522–6)

> (My guilt is so great that trees and grass and anything green
> around me would wither at the evil sound of my impure voice.)

Scholarship on the Gregorius story seems to fall into patterns. Just as the modern editions of the various texts are – with the exception of the textually fairly secure Hartmann – diverse and difficult to use, so too it has become a kind of commonplace in criticism of Hartmann's *Gregorius* not just to speculate on the precise nature of his guilt, but to preface this with increasingly lengthy Surveys of All Previous Conclusions. Elisabeth Gössmann summarised the position up to 1974 and categorised the various answers to the fairly simple question of what Gregorius's sin actually *is* into theological, theological-cum-literary, literary, and socio-historically orientated interpretations. This took her nearly forty pages. In 1985 a somewhat ponderous volume took about 450 pages to do roughly the same thing (and there have been other studies since), so that it would be otiose to try again.[43] Some critics have even seen the fact of this apparently insuperable

---

1958), pp. 30–53. K. D. Goebel sees a balance between the two halves of Hartmann's poem, the first part also taking seventeen years, though his schema is something of an oversimplification: *Aufbau und Schuldproblem*, p. 124.

[42] I have discussed this in 'Adam *sub gratia*: zur Bußszene in Hartmanns *Gregorius*', *Archiv* 227 (1990), 122–6, with reference to other possible influences.

[43] Elisabeth Gössmann, 'Typus der Heilsgeschichte oder Opfer morbider Gesellschaftsordnung?' *Euphorion* 68 (1974), 42–80. See Duckworth, *Gregorius*, passim. These provide bibliographical keys to most of the other studies.

problem as a kind of flaw not in themselves, but in Hartmann's work, although that flaw would then surely be common to all the versions. I proposed in a short paper some years ago a Gordian knot solution, and I see no reason to move away from that. Within the narrower limits of medieval German studies the matter might indeed seem complicated, but in theological terms the answer to the question of what Gregorius is doing penance *for* is a simple one. Gregorius has lived incestuously, and for this sin he does penance. There has even been debate in Hartmann studies at least as to whether or not this is in accord with the orthodox tenets of the church, although it would have been very surprising indeed for any of our writers *not* to have followed orthodox teaching.[44] Gregorius cannot be doing penance for leaving the monastery, nor indeed, in specific terms, at least, for the sins of his parents. The Jansenist proposition that one could do penance throughout one's life for original sin was refuted officially by Alexander VIII in 1690, but the single response to original sin – namely grace – was always clear. And besides, throughout the penance on the rock the one thing that Gregorius does not have with him is the tablet reminding him of original sin. This is not a chance motif. It is still there when he comes to look for it – it is indestructible – but it is not counted. Gregorius's pentitent *attitude* for the sins of his parents is, however, constant throughout the work, in his weeping over the tablet.

The apparently incidental question of the lost but indestructible tablet on which the story of Gregorius's origin is inscribed is important. That tablet not only contains the information relating to original sin, but actually *represents* original sin. Ivory – the usual substance from which it is made in the texts – is chosen for its durability; the gold and gems sometimes included are less significant, serving only to stress the importance of original sin, whilst stone would presumably have sunk the boat. Seth's tablets of clay and stone were designed to withstand fire and flood, and in Hartmann again we are told that the hut in which Gregorius left the tablet has since been burned.[45] In most texts, however, apart from the later abridged versions which sometimes ignore the tablets after Gregorius is taken from the rock, it is stressed that they are as pure and clean as when they were left behind. Original sin survives all things, and cannot ever be destroyed, though it is not in the foregound when Gregorius is completing his penance for the actual sin of incest. Penance is no help against original sin, the only answer to which is the divine grace which both keeps Gregorius alive and rescues him. Grace discounts original sin, but does not eradicate it, so that the tablets are unchanged.

The making of original sin into a physical document may derive not only from the tablets inscribed by Seth in the *Vita Adae* tradition, but may also perhaps

[44] K. C. King, 'The Mother's Guilt in Hartmann's *Gregorius*', in *Medieval German Studies Presented to F. Norman* (London: IGS, 1965), pp. 84–93.
[45] Schwab, *Lex et gratia*, p. 68 discusses the resurrection of the tablet; but it is not in fact resurrected, rather it is preserved unchanged as a reminder of the old law. Of course, the tablet is found again at periodic intervals throughout the story, and this too is significant. What Hartmann actually says is that the fisherman burned what was left of the hut after it fell down twelve weeks after Gregorius left it, and possibly Hartmann meant simply that he took the wood away. Whether the tablet actually passed through the fire is unclear. J. B. McLean thinks that it has been purged by fire, though Hartmann does not really say so: 'Hartmann von Aue's Religious Attitude and Didacticism in his *Gregorius*', *Rice Institute Pamphlets* 39 (1952), 1–17, see p. 9.

contain an echo (though no more than that) of another apocryphal motif, namely that of Adam's cheirograph. In the Slavonic Adambooks, for example, the devil makes a pact with Adam which is set down in the form of an actual document which is redeemed by Christ. The precise reason and the nature of the bargain with the devil varies between different narratives (sometimes it is for light, sometimes for food), but the motif is of very considerable antiquity and is developed by the Greek fathers in particular, linked in exegesis with the notion in Colossians 2:14,

> delens quod adversus nos erat chirographum decreti, quod erat contrarium nobis, et ipsum tulit de medio adfigens illud cruci

namely that the inscription over the cross wiped out the documents that were against man – sometimes Christ is even seen as presenting a ransom note.[46] The link with the Redemption and the cancelling by Christ as part of the process of salvation – Redemption of this pledge in the strictest sense – is a common enough motif in medieval literature:

> Qua scisso chirographo
> Adae culpae veteris
> Ovem pastor perditam
> revexit in umeris[47]

(The document of Adam's guilt of old was cut up . . . the shepherd bore the lost sheep back on his shoulders.)

In the eastern church, where more is made in general terms of the pact between Adam and the devil, relatively recent icons – Friedrich Ohly prints a nineteenth-century example from Romania – even show the baptism of Christ as he stands on a stone in the Jordan, the stone being that on which Adam has inscribed the pact with the devil.[48] Here the document as such is precisely *not* cut up, however, since this is not after all the actual document, which was destroyed at the Incarnation. After the Fall original sin is a fact which cannot be eradicated; but it can be set aside, not counted by Christ, especially when the hero is undergoing a specific penance for a specific actual sin. The dual nature of sin is at its clearest when the tablet is left outside the confessional, as it were, although in Hartmann we are told that the tablet was still on Gregorius's mind whilst he was there.

---

[46] As in *Piers Plowman* B XIV, 191: William Langland, *Piers the Plowman*, ed. Walter W. Skeat (London: Oxford University Press, 1886, repr. 1961), p. 426.

[47] *Analecta Hymnica*, XXXIX, no. 26, pp. 32f, a sequence from the thirteenth century. See also Zosimus, *De peccato originale* (*PL* 20, 693). The best study of the cheirograph in the apocryphal material and early exegesis is that by Georg Megas, 'Das Χειρόγραφον Adams', *Zeitschrift für die neutestamentliche Wissenschaft* 27 (1928), 305–20, who starts from a modern version, in fact, and it is discussed by Stone, *History*, pp. 35f. See also more recent studies such as C. W. Marx, *The Devil's Rights and the Redemption in the Literature of Medieval England* (Cambridge: D. S. Brewer, 1995).

[48] *The Damned and the Elect*, pp. 48f discusses this in some detail. Plate 5 reproduces a nineteenth-century Wallachian icon. In some medieval texts, Eve actually writes the pact down: *Fasciculus Morum*, ed. Siegfried Wenzel (University Park and London: Pennsylvania State University Press, 1989), p. 212. It is again cancelled by Christ.

Adam's fully completed penance in the river in the *Vita Adae* ends not in the return to Paradise, but with the driving away of the devil and the direct promise of divine help for mankind. So too here, Gregorius is not restored (like Job) to his previous position, but is made into a priest in the fullest sense and at the highest level, the representative of Christ amongst men. He can, as a properly ordained priest, even give absolution to his mother, and he does so in most of the versions. It is interesting, however, that in the earliest manuscripts of the *Gesta Romanorum* (and even in some of the vernacular versions) the text does not include this motif, but a voice from heaven declares the remission of the sins, 'peccata vestra vobis remitto',[49] while in the Low German prose, where the ending is slightly different in any case, with Gregorius only becoming a bishop, he and his mother petition the pope together. The notion of healing is picked up here once again in Hartmann especially, as the soteriology of the whole narrative comes to the fore.[50] Medical imagery informs Hartmann's version in any case, which is opened with and programatically introduced by an interpretation of the tale of the Good Samaritan in which the healing of the wounds of the man robbed on the way to Jericho is seen as the Redemption of all men from sin. This is a familiar exegesis; the oil and wine of Luke 10 are interpreted either as faith and hope, or as grace and the law. The latter pair are necessary for salvation, an idea picked up later by Hartmann when Gregorius as pope softens the hardness of the law by imposing lighter penances. Seth was sent by Adam in the *Vita* for the oil of mercy, which will save Adam. The whole medical side of the Samaritan story in various guises is used elsewhere in medieval literature, and in Langland, for example, the wounded man, the sinner, beaten and hurt by the world, can only be healed if he is bathed and baptized in blood, and – it sounds odd to a modern ear – 'plastred with penaunce'.[51]

Gregorius auf dem Stein: Gregorius's penance on the rock is clearly a parallel to that of Adam in the *Vita Adae*, which was itself intrinsically linked with the baptism of Christ. In the legend of Gregorius, and especially in a version such as that of Hartmann, the central scene of penance draws in a whole range of symbols

---

49 See Elema and van der Wal, 'Volksbuch', p. 306.

50 Two early medieval German poems also stress the soteriological aspect, and both are part of a wide European literary tradition in doing so, as I have shown in papers on each: 'Die sogenannte *Wârheit*', in *Akten des V. internationalen Germanistenkongresses* (Berne and Frankfurt/M: Lang, 1976), II, 404–13, and '*Trost in Verzweiflung*: an Analysis of an Early Middle High German Fragment', *Neuphilologische Mitteilungen* 96 (1995), 187–201; the last part of the latter poem expresses hope against *desperatio* in medical terms. However sinful a man is, 'er vindet einen arzât/ der im heilet sîne wunden' (142–3) (he will find a doctor to heal his wounds). Connexions were once seen between the reference to wounding in *Trost in Verzweiflung* and the interpretation of the Samaritan story in *Gregorius*, but these have now been modified to an assumption of shared motifs. The reference to the snares of the devil in *Trost in Verzweiflung* is echoed at the end of Arnold's adaptation, however. On the soteriology of *Gregorius*, see Fritz Tschirch, 'Gregorius der *heilaere*' (1964) in his *Spiegelungen* (Berlin: Schmidt, 1966), pp. 245–77.

51 See Schwab, *Lex et gratia*; the citation is from *Piers the Plowman* xvii, 90–5. On the Samaritan parable, see Werner Monselewski, *Der barmherzige Samaritaner: eine Auslegungsgeschichtliche Untersuchung zu Lukas 10, 25–37* (Tübingen: Mohr, 1967). On its use in Hartmann, see among other studies that by H. B. Willson, 'Hartmann's *Gregorius* and the Parable of the Good Samaritan', *Modern Language Review* 54 (1959), 194–203, and my 'Quest'. Christopher Frayling, *Strange Landscape* (Harmondsworth: Penguin, 1995), pp. 62–4 has interesting comments on the iconographical linking of Adam and Eve and the Samaritan in a window in Chartres cathedral.

linked both with the first and the second Adam: the rock has become the Petrine rock of the papacy and St Peter's key became a sign from God that this was no diabolical temptation away from a penance. And yet Hartmann reminded us through the behaviour of Gregorius when first encountered on the rock of the connexion with Adam, naked and ashamed. But this is Adam not just promised a Redemption, but already redeemed, and he can now be clothed with white garments, the clothing associated with the angels in much medieval exegesis. Ultimately the devil does not get his way, and the broader plan can now be seen by the protagonists and by the audience, who can then wonder at the story. The whole story, too, is inscribed for the benefit of posterity on tablets which are designed to be indestructible.

Let us return to the question of reality for a moment. Medieval hagiography is often concerned with saints who did not, as far as we can tell, actually exist, and familiar examples are those of St George and St Christopher. But as Dieter von der Nahmer, in an admirably clear presentation of the genre, points out, this does not prevent such saints acquiring a kind of meta-reality supported by relics, for example, the apparently tangible evidence of which gives rise to belief: relics ultimately become the saints' passport from story into history. There seem to be no known relics of our saint, although St Gregorius the Hermit is depicted with an iron ring around his body, has a feast-day in November (not a saint's day in the Roman calendar) and has acquired a reality by the setting of his life into a geographically realistic context – Aquitaine, Rome, – and into an at least potentially verifiable historical context, the papacy.[52] He is also apparently to be invoked against toothache, however, and there are few things more real than toothache.

Saints' lives are often *imitationes Christi*, displaying precocious learning on a saint's part, or miracles and healing. Gregorius is a prodigy, but he performs no miracles; the miraculous element is that of fortitude and his preservation on the rock (that the bells begin to ring of their own accord when he enters Rome is incidental only and happens fairly regularly in hagiography). In most of the versions, too, the great length of the penance is presented as something that is specifically unusual, although penance as the answer to sin goes back, in terms of the *Vita*, to Adam. But it must be accompanied by genuine contrition. Alain of Lille's early thirteenth-century *Penitential* refers to the fact that penances need not be as hard as they were in former times:

> olim natura humana robustior erat ut ferendum poenitentiae onera quam modo, et ideo temperanda est poenitentia[53]

> (the human constitution used to be firmer for carrying out the burdens of a penance than now, so penance should now be tempered . . .)

---

[52] Dieter von der Nahmer, *Die lateinische Heiligenvita* (Darmstadt: WBG, 1994), pp. 124–30 on fictive saints. See pp. 131–45 on the genre as such, pp. 146–52 on miracles performed, and pp. 153–69 on other topoi. For St Gregory the Hermit – who is not often included in lists of saints (Volker Mertens' book on the theme is called *Gregorius Eremita* and the term recurs) – and his attributes, see Jos. M. von Radowitz, *The Saints in Art*, trans. Christopher Benson (Rome: Victoria, 1898), p. 35. November 28 is used only for relatively minor early saints and one or two recent ones.

[53] *PL* 210, 293, cited in my paper 'Origins of Penance', p. 219.

Hartmann introduces the idea that when Gregorius is installed as pope he endorses the principle that penance should not be too hard or it might fail:

> man sol dem sündaere
> ringen sîne swaere
> mit senfter buoze,
> daz im diu riuwe suoze.
> daz reht ist alsô swaere ...   (3809–13)

> (one should take the burden from a sinner by imposing a gentle penance so that he can become contrite. The law is hard enough ...)

The same point was made in the *Vita Adae* by Adam when imposing a lighter penance upon Eve.

The legend of Gregorius has a great deal in it which links with the biblical Fall and with the *Vita Adae*, and of course both Adam and Gregorius are unusual. Adam is unique by definition, Gregorius because his case is so extreme. This, however, is the point: the pair are both memorable as examples. Adam is granted the Redemption; Gregorius, however sinful, and however much he is unable to avoid sin, is forgiven, and his sin of birth is not held against him. Both the *Vita Adae* and the legend of Gregorius, too, stress the divine plan. In the *Vita*, Seth is told of the coming Redemption; in *Gregorius*, it is worked out, and the devil – apparently victorious in getting his way – is really subordinate to God's will. Only God sees, in the words of the English *Gregorius*, 'from ende to oþur'. Of the unique case of Adam and Eve, Gregory the Great said that this 'in humano genere quotidie agitur' (happens every day), and the legend of Gregorius demonstrates this by showing the acquisition of sin in a manner which is linked constantly with Adam and Eve directly, but by people who are *not* Adam and Eve; they are born with original sin, yet are also *sub gratia*.

The real Pope Gregory was cited earlier in establishing the theology of original and actual sin, showing how the first sin can be both real and repeated, both a model and a cause, leaving a propensity on man's part to incur sin even when it is not deserved. But both original and actual sins require grace, and the literary Pope Gregorius provides an illustration of the placing of Adam *sub gratia*. And at the same time the tale of Gregorius makes clear the application of the divine economy, the foreseen plan of Fall and Redemption to the individual sinner. In the *Vita Adae* the Redemption was only promised. In this legend it has already happened, so that even though the Fall is repeated by everyone, and even though it is impossible to avoid sin at some level – and indeed quite possible to incur, without deserving to do so, the greatest of all sins – Paradise can still be regained.

THREE

STULTUS ET INSIPIENS:
ADAM, PARZIVAL AND THE KNOWLEDGE OF GOD

T HAT MEDIEVAL BIBLICAL COMMENTARY was a weighty matter might be tested fairly literally, provided one could one find a suitably accommo-dating librarian, by the simple process of weighing first a Bible, and then the collected volumes of Migne's *Patrologia* – the *Latina* alone should suffice to make the point. One might wonder, equally, whether literary works on the Fall and the Redemption do not also simply add to the weight on the wrong side of the scales. However, unlike specifically theological texts, a literary work will, in conforming to the principle of *prodesse* and *delectare*, typically use the latter to lead the audi-ence to the former; certainly it may incorporate interpretations of the Bible or more complex theological arguments, but it will equally certainly simplify them, and may indeed resolve controversies, sometimes quite major ones, in a pragmatic manner; and it will, perhaps most importantly, address the way in which basic theological ideas affect the individual, since it is of individuals that audiences are made up. The use of literature to provide a *moral* exemplar is an old established practice which is still (fortunately) recommended on a regular enough basis; the other senses of scripture – to keep to medieval terms – come into play as well, however.

In the first essentially literary expansion of the biblical Genesis, the apocryphal Adambooks place the same characters into the human world of time and death after their fall from Paradise and observe their reactions and their more immediate confrontations with the devil. Although in spite of their efforts Adam and Eve cannot return to their earthly Paradise, the Adambooks promise them – and hence mankind – a Redemption at some future time. A second literary stage is repre-sented by stories like that of Gregorius, which ostensibly involve new characters, but which contain sufficient and sufficiently close allusions to Adam and Eve for us to see in that case the saint's life as a reworking of the same theme in a world that is, however, clearly *sub gratia*. The legacy of Adam's Fall – original sin – ensures, however, that mankind repeats that Fall, and as Gregory the Great made clear, it does so daily. The literary reflection of this state of affairs throughout the Middle Ages and beyond can take many forms. Frequently the central figure in a literary work represents Adam, but the equation is rarely straightforward, and the problem is, of course, partly Romans 5:12, that Adam is also man. But Adam (and hence man) was, at least potentially, from the very moment of leaving Eden subject to the grace of God in the promise of the Redemption; Augustine makes the point clearly when combatting the Pelagians in the *De gratia Christi et de peccato originali*,[1] and it is given concrete form in the promise made directly to Seth in the *Vita Adae*.

---

[1] *PL* 44, 398.

When the figure representing Adam is placed not simply outside Paradise but into a period after the Redemption, the question of the relationship between the original Adam and his literary parallel (who is also his actual descendant) becomes even more complex. It is a problem that has a special resonance for literary critics. In a very stimulating paper on ignorance, epistemology and the Fall, themes that will become central to this chapter, Andrew Martin commented that Eden – when Adam gave the beasts their names – was the very last time that *signifiant* and *signifié* actually coincided.[2]

Medieval literature did produce direct literary allegories of the Fall and the Redemption. In the twelfth century, or perhaps at the end of the eleventh, a writer we know only as Eupolemius wrote what is usually called a Messiad, a complex Latin poem in which the good king Agatus – most characters have speaking names derived from Greek – leaves Antropus, clearly Adam, in charge of a garden, in which he is deceived by Ophites, the serpent, whose master Cacus is eventually overcome. Others are more complex, as when elements from the story of the biblical Fall are incorporated into other and larger narrative structures; the *Anticlaudianus* of Alan of Lille – the poem of the creation of the new man as a replacement for Adam – might serve as an example.[3] We may take as a shorter example, however, a passage plucked out of an extended allegorical poem of the fourteenth century, Langland's *Piers the Plowman*, in which the visionary Will is told by Wit – intelligence – about someone called Do-well:

> 'Sire Do-wel dwelleth', quod Witte, · 'nougt a day hennes,
> In a castle that Kynde made · of four kynnes thinges;
> Of erthe and eyre is it made · medled togideres,
> With wynde and with water · witterly enioyned,
> Kynde hath closed there-inne · craftily with-alle,
> A lemman that he loueth · like to hym-selue
> *Anima* she hatte · ac Enuye hir hateth,
> A proud pryker of Fraunce · *prynceps huius mundi*,
> And wolde winne hir awey · with wyles, and he migte.'[4]

Making Sir Envy, who is plainly the devil, into a haughty French knight is, admittedly, rather English, but the rest of it is clear. Sir Do-well is man, of course, living in the four elements and Adam was traditionally made of them as well. Man's body also contains the soul, *anima*, and to see that as a woman prone to the blandish-

---

[2]   Andrew Martin, 'The Genesis of Ignorance: Nescience and Omniscience in the Garden of Eden', *Philosophy and Literature* 5 (1981), 3–20. See also John Leonard, *Naming in Paradise: Milton and the Language of Adam and Eve* (Oxford: Clarendon, 1990) and (of general importance) Eric Jager, *The Tempter's Voice* (Ithaca and London: Cornell University Press, 1993).

[3]   See G. R. Evans, *Alan of Lille: the Frontiers of Theology in the Later Twelfth Century* (Cambridge: Cambridge University Press, 1983), pp. 147–65, on the complicated poem which is, nevertheless, relevant to the study of Adam and the Redemption by showing the perfect man.

[4]   Langland, *Piers the Plowman*, ed. Skeat, I, 264 = IX, 1–9 of the B text. Earth, air, *fire* and water is a more usual quartet, but Skeat is dismissive in his notes of attempts to emend *eyre* to *fyre*, II, 138f, on the grounds that this is what all the manuscripts have. His explanations otherwise are fairly obscure, however, and in spite of the manuscripts there is surely still a case for emendation. Skeat does, however, note an intrusion of national prejudice in the reference to France (II, 139).

ments of the envious devil again reflects medieval interpretations of the temptation of Eve. Langland's literary allegory draws upon a whole series of such interpretations of the Fall, including the literal tempting of Eve and the tropological seduction of the soul.

That passage makes the central figures into knights and ladies, albeit allegorical ones, and as such it serves to introduce the principal work for this chapter, the knight at the centre of which is perhaps less immediately recognisable as a literary Adam, though his kinship with and parallels to the protoplast are nevertheless strong. His tale is – I cite Christopher Brooke[5] – 'one of the great traditional stories of the Middle Ages', that of the Arthurian knight Sir Percival, Perceval or Parzival and his finding of the Holy Grail. We shall concentrate on the German version of his tale told by Wolfram von Eschenbach in a vast poetic romance from the beginning of the thirteenth century, and for this reason I shall refer to the hero as Parzival, although his name varies from version to version. Wolfram claims, famously and on two occasions in his work, to be illiterate, but without being too arrogant as critics, we need not take that claim very seriously.[6] His apparent source, the Grail story by the Frenchman Chrétien de Troyes,[7] is incomplete, and rather different, so that 'source' is actually a fairly loose term, and Wolfram himself plays games with the reader on that score. The various continuators of Chrétien[8] are not especially relevant, and the Welsh equivalent in the *Mabinogion*, *Peredur*, is a weak and ill-remembered adaptation of a French source, in which the Grail, the holiest of central symbols, has become a plate with a severed head on it. In English, the separate romance of *Sir Percyvale of Galles* lacks the spiritual dimension, and by the time we get to Malory, Sir Percival is reduced to a kind of supporter of Sir Galahad.

There are three of the various different medieval French versions, however, which do merit at least a brief glance by way of background. Robert de Boron, roughly contemporary with Chrétien at the end of the twelfth century and who was, so Pierre le Gentil tells us, 'endowed with boldness and piety but with mediocre talent', wrote a poetic history of the Grail itself, the *Roman de l'estoire dou Graal*, starting with an epitome of the Fall and the Redemption, including the Harrowing of Hell, and providing a clearly eucharistic origin for the Grail as the cup from the Last Supper. In the so-called *Didot Perceval*, a prose text from the same period, Perceval at one point finds two children in a tree beside a cross; they tell him that he

---

5   *The Medieval Idea of Marriage* (Oxford: Oxford University Press, 1989), p. 176.

6   I have cited the text from Wolfram von Eschenbach, *Werke*, ed. Karl Lachmann, 6th edn Eduard Hartl (Berlin and Leipzig: de Gruyter, 1926, repr. 1964), indicating the book from which each citation is taken; the somewhat curious verse-numbering in thirty-line sections established by Lachmann has been used in subsequent editions, and throughout Wolfram-criticism. There is a translation by A. T. Hatto, *Wolfram von Eschenbach, Parzival* (Harmondsworth: Penguin, 1980), but translations given here are my own.

7   Chrétien de Troyes, *Le Roman de Perceval*, ed. William Roach (Geneva and Paris: Droz, 1959); Chrétien, *Le Conte du Graal (Perceval)*, ed. Félix Lecoy (Paris: Champion, 1972–5). There is a translation by Ruth Harwood Cline, *Chrétien, Perceval* (New York: Pergamon, 1983), and see below, note 13.

8   Albert Wilder Thompson, 'Additions to Chrétien's *Perceval*', in Roger Sherman Loomis, ed., *Arthurian Literature in the Middle Ages* (Oxford: Clarendon, 1959), pp. 206–17.

has reached the castle of the Grail, and then vanish, leaving Perceval (and indeed us) wondering if they are phantoms. T. S. Eliot took up the motif in the *Four Quartets*. But they echo the 'child in the tree motif' in the Holy Rood legends, and at the same time may represent Adam and Eve in a state of innocence.[9] The link with the end of the *Vita Adae* and the Holy Rood is there, thirdly, in the later and somewhat rambling second section of the medieval French prose Lancelot-story that influenced Malory, the *Queste del Saint Graal*, which incorporates a curious chapter on the Tree of Life. The work, described by its most recent translator as a 'spiritual fable', has Eve take a branch from Paradise at the expulsion, and the tree which grows from it survives through the ages, rather in the manner of the Holy Rood.[10]

As far as the most famous *modern* adaptor of the story of Parzival is concerned – Wagner, that is, though there have been plenty of others in English and German particularly[11] – one might bear in mind the *Leitmotiv* 'Durch Mitleid wissend, der reine Tor' (the pure fool, knowing by sympathy). An equally appropriate motto, however, would be the opening verse of the Vulgate Psalm 13: 'dixit insipiens in corde: "non est Deus" '. Both stress the notion of the fool, and Parzival's tale is the story of a fool, although the allusion in my title is not only to the Psalm, but to another celebrated medieval work in which a fool is placed in the centre, Anselm's *Proslogion*.

One of the best known Arthurian specialists, Roger S. Loomis, made a very large claim of Wolfram's *Parzival* when he said that 'though Parzival cannot be considered a philosophical poem, it does take up the perennial problem of God's justice, and I question whether any better theodicy has been proposed by the philosophers than is found in this Arthurian romance'.[12] The claim is one that has to be taken seriously, even though what a recent translator of Chrétien said of the story as told by Wolfram's predecessor is true to an extent of Wolfram as well. Both

---

9   This rather odd motif has been analysed in connexion with T. S. Eliot's *Four Quartets* by Wallace Fowlie, *Love in Literature* (Bloomington: Indiana University Press, 1965), pp. 149–52. Fowlie's book was entitled *The Clown's Grail* when it first appeared in 1948. I understand that a performance of the Chester Plays has used small children to play Adam and Eve before the Fall, with adults replacing them afterwards, a point which is theologically not entirely sound, but an interesting solution to the dramatic problem of nakedness nevertheless.

10   Robert de Boron, *Le Roman de l'Estoire dou Graal*, ed. William A. Nitze (Paris: Champion, 1927); *The Didot Perceval*, ed. William Roach (Philadelphia: Pennsylvania State University Press, 1941), trans. Dell Skeels, *The Romance of Perceval in Prose* (Seattle: University of Washington Press, 1966); *La Queste del Saint Graal*, ed. Albert Pauphilet (Paris: Champion, 3rd edn 1965); *The Quest of the Holy Grail*, trans. P. M. Matarasso (Harmondsworth: Penguin, 1969). See Matarasso's introduction and pp. 222–35. See on Robert: Pierre le Gentil, 'The Works of Robert de Boron and the Didot Perceval', in Loomis, *Arthurian Literature*, pp. 251–62.

11   I cite two quite fortuitous examples, one in verse and one in prose. The first is by Albrecht Schaeffer, *Parzival: Ein Versroman in drei Kreisen* (Leipzig: Insel, 2nd edn 1924); that this blank verse rendering in 632 pages by a prolific and once widely-read but now virtually forgotten writer active in the first years of the twentieth century reached a second edition is itself of interest. The other, which offers a curiously hybrid spelling of the name of the central character, is by, the blurb informs us, 'a successful screenwriter, playwright and poet' from New York, and was published in what is described as a 'science fantasy' series, though the first element of that opaque term seems particularly puzzling: Richard Monaco, *Parsival or a Knight's Tale* (Glasgow: Futura, 1977). It has an endearingly dotty afterword, telling us amongst other things that the 'spiritual grail' is 'a recognition of the total field in which the individual is an inseparable waveform'.

12   Roger S. Loomis, *The Development of Arthurian Romance* (London: Hutchinson, 1963), p. 70.

poems have digressions, and both operate on several levels. 'The "meaning" of the romance', said Nigel Bryant, 'is not an appeal to get on the next boat to the Holy Land, any more than it is an appeal to get married and make confession and remember the power of the sign of the cross.'[13] And yet all these things do play an important part. Wolfram's version, moreover, is far more of a theological work than Chrétien's.

The reason given in the biblical Genesis for the breaking of the commandment is the acquisition of knowledge: but knowledge and wisdom are not the same thing, and Parzival is, like Adam and as a descendant of Adam, cast into a world he does not understand, and his lack of understanding, though material to an extent, is also spiritual. It is said of Adam in Genesis 3:7 that his eyes were opened after he had eaten the fruit, but medieval exegesis invariably balances this with a closing of the inner eyes, a loss of the knowledge of God; ignorance is one of the results of the Fall, part of original sin. Adam's actual sin caused his ejection from Paradise into a new and confusing world, from which he tried – in vain – to return to Eden. Parzival is a man, and he twice becomes an outcast from Paradise, once following his human destiny, once because of a sin. This reflects again the double burden of mankind: of original sin, and of the concomitant propensity to incur actual sin. Parzival tries to return, first to the Paradise of his childhood, and secondly to the Paradise of the Grail castle, from which he is cast out because of an error of his. Like Adam, he cannot return to the first Paradise he has known, that of his mother's lands; but Parzival, unlike Adam, is living in a world *sub gratia*, and can be saved, or in literary terms can find the Grail once again. Since his world is *sub gratia*, there are outside theological advisers to help him overcome his most serious fall, and to point the way to *his* and to *the* Redemption.

Even if the story is here epitomised from Wolfram it should be noted that this will concentrate on Parzival himself and will ignore for the most part the attendant narratives of Gawan – our Sir Gawain – who in the long and complex romance serves as a kind of (but only a kind of) secular counterpart to the spiritual hero. Parzival is the son of Herzeloyde and of Gahmuret the Angevin, a brave knight who is killed before Parzival is born. Gahmuret had previously been married to the pagan queen Belakane and had a son, Feirefiz, who plays a role in Parzival's story, whilst Herzeloyde was originally married to Castis – the name is a significant one, the chaste king – and that marriage was unconsummated. When Parzival is born he is kept from the world by his mother, and when on one occasion he asks, significantly, 'waz ist got?' (what is God?), he is told only that God is a shining being. One day the young Parzival sees some knights and, after first assuming (because they are literally in shining armour) that they are God and then finding out what they really are, he decides that he too will go out into the world and fulfil his destiny as a knight. His mother, hoping to force him back, dresses him as a fool, but also gives him various pieces of practical advice, all of which he misinterprets, thus proving the point, and incidentally causing a series of problems. Parzival is to acquire armour; to avoid crossing streams where the water is dark; to take advice

[13] Chrétien de Troyes, *Perceval: The Story of the Graal*, trans. Nigel Bryant (Cambridge: D. S. Brewer, 1982), p. xv.

from a grey-haired man; and he should gain kisses and a ring from a lady. However, he takes all of these very literally: the advice is asked for rather bluntly, the kisses and the ring are taken by force, causing some embarrassment and misunderstanding when the lady's husband returns, and the boy rides all day beside but fails to cross a shallow river that looks dark because it is overshadowed with trees. The one real sin, however, is when the advice to gain armour results in his killing a kinsman, Ither, with a javelin, followed by what is technically corpse-robbing. The callow Parzival now has some armour, but he is still very much a fool underneath. He is eventually given what we may call more advanced instruction by a knight, who persuades the young man to relinquish the fool's clothing which he has still been wearing under the stolen armour, teaches him about the mass, how to cross himself, and tells him to go to church regularly. He also tells him not to talk too much or ask questions.

Parzival meets and marries Condwiramurs, a speaking name, but leaves her to try and return to his home. On the way, however, he encounters a richly dressed fisherman and then finds himself in a mysterious castle, where he is well received, but where he sees puzzling things: the lord of the castle is ill, there is much weeping, and he sees a bleeding lance, and above all else the ceremonial bearing-in of the enigmatic Grail. Still clinging to the advice of silence, however, he asks no questions in the castle, something which Wolfram points up several times in a despairing tone, and in the morning he finds it deserted except for one page, who abuses him as he leaves, precisely for *not* asking any questions. In Chrétien the drawbridge is literally hauled up just as his horse jumps clear. Baffled, Parzival rides on, and is told first by his cousin Sigune that he has behaved badly, and later at Arthur's court he is cursed by the strange and wild figure of the Grail messenger, Cundrîe, for failing to ask the question that would have redeemed the wounded fisherman, who is also the Grail king, from his pain. His despair at what he has done – or rather, has left undone – causes Parzival to despair of God.

Parzival's sin was one of omission, but now his fall from God is real, as he becomes an outcast in the fullest sense. Not until after some years of wandering is he brought back to God – I choose the phrase carefully – in the central ninth book of the poem, when he encounters on Good Friday first Sigune again, then a pilgrim knight, and finally the hermit Trevrizent, who leads him back to God and to the church he has not visited for several years. Eventually he is able to return to the Grail castle of Munsalvaesche – linked with the German place-name Wildenberg, *mont sauvage*, but also *mons salvationis* – and ask the question referred to in German as the *Mitleidsfrage*, the expression of sympathy for the wounded king, and can become Grail king himself. His pagan half-brother Feirefiz, unable initially to see the Grail, is then baptized and becomes able to see it.

But how does all this complicated romance storytelling relate to Adam, to the nature of God, and to the notion of salvation in general? When the knight whom Parzival takes to be God – and whom indeed, anticipating later events, Parzival immediately asks for help – meets the boy, we are told that he is the most beautiful lad since Adam's day. But the references are more concealed than those in the *Gregorius* poem. Concordances to the two major versions provide only one reference, as far as I know, in Chrétien's *Li contes del graal* to Adam, and that is a simple formula about a lady who is the most beautiful woman 'since the wife of

Adam'. There are more frequent direct references in Wolfram, although some are equally formulaic. Nevertheless, in the story as told by Wolfram indirect lapsarian allusions are made, and the overall pattern of Fall and Redemption is clear.[14] In the central figure we can perceive a parallel to Adam, but also – as German critics like Walter Johannes Schröder[15] pointed out long ago – a mirror of the whole process of salvation, as the individual passes from ignorance, which is a result of the Fall, to wisdom; from a state of being lawless, *ante legem*, to one of instruction, a *sub lege* state, (though, as we are in a Christian society, the central figure is the whole time at least potentially under the grace); and then, after a lapse, a return, and a lesson, to a final state of genuine grace, of being *sub gratia*. The work, in Wolfram's version in particular, is a theodicy, however, a justification by illustration of the ways of God to men.

The poem is usually typified as a quest[16] – mirroring the progress through life – and Parzival's first move is when he leaves the Paradise of his childhood. Indeed, the Arthurian romance frequently exhibits the pattern of a transgression on the part of the individual knight which then requires expiation. Parzival is not expelled, like Adam, for a specific sin, although his failed attempt to return home might mirror Adam in the *Vita*. Other characters in the story, it is true, do see Parzival's simple act of leaving as a sin – this happens both in the French and the German versions – because it causes the death of his mother, but even this judgement is questionable. The simple soul issues from the hand of God into time already bearing the sin of the protoplasts, but the incurring of actual sins, the imitation – which Gregory the Great claimed happened every day – of Adam's actual sin, comes later. Wolfram expresses, or at least alludes to, the sinful nature of birth in an interesting manner. Of course there is no incest to underscore it, as there was in the tale of Gregorius, but there are nevertheless cross-allusions to the same point. When Parzival is born, Gahmuret is already dead, and Herzeloyde virtually quotes, albeit enigmatically, the devastating words of Gregorius's mother to her son and husband: 'ich bin iuwer muoter und iuwer wip' (*Gregorius* v. 2604: 'I am your mother and your wife') when she says of her dead husband '[ich] bin sîn muoter und sîn wîp' (II: 109, 25) (I am his mother and his wife), and afterwards she says as she holds the baby Parzival 'si dûht, si hete Gahmureten/ wider an ir arm erbeten' (II: 113, 13–14) (it was as though her prayers had brought Gahmuret back to her arms). This is only allusive, but the continuity of human kind through sexual reproduction and the

[14] At the end of the nineteenth century, Samuel Singer adduced a large number of such allusions, some of them verbal parallels with other German works: 'Zu Wolframs *Parzival*', in *Abhandlungen zur germanischen Philologie: Festgabe für Richard Heinzel* (Halle/S: Niemeyer, 1898), pp. 353–436: see pp. 347–412.

[15] *Die Soltane-Erzählung in Wolframs 'Parzival'* (Heidelberg: Winter, 1963). See also Petrus W. Tax, 'Wolfram von Eschenbach's *Parzival* in the Light of Biblical Typology', *Seminar* 9 (1973), 1–14.

[16] See Klaus M. Schmidt, 'Frauenritter oder Artusritter? Über Struktur und Gehalt von Ulrichs von Zatzikhoven *Lanzelet*', *Zeitschrift für deutsche Philologie* 98 (1979), 1–18 for observations on the usual pattern of the genre applied to a work which does not conform. On the quest in *Parzival*, see for example Friedrich Ohly, 'Die Suche in Dichtungen des Mittelalters', *Zeitschrift für deutsches Altertum* 94 (1965), 171–84 and Stephen G. Harroff, *Wolfram and his Audience* (Göppingen: Kümmerle, 1974).

attendant concupiscence is pointed up by these otherwise enigmatic comments.[17] It is of interest too that Herzeloyde, who does in some respects symbolise Eve, the mother of all, should have been linked with Castis, 'Chaste'.[18] The relationship of Adam and Eve in Eden was intended to be a chaste one – 'erat enim prius casta coniunctio masculi et feminae', said Augustine in one of his Genesis-treatises,[19] and indeed this was occasionally 'imitated' in chaste bed-sharing by male and female hermits in the practice of *conhospitio* or syneisactism, which apparently and not too surprisingly caused the twelfth-century church a certain amount of anxiety.[20] But concupiscence was, of course, a result of and a punishment for the Fall. Accordingly, Herzeloyde's *real* marriage with Gahmuret is a sexual one, and the birth of Parzival is thus a birth in original sin. And yet at the same time Wolfram provides a reminder of salvation, when Herzeloyde, suckling the infant Parzival, recalls the Virgin with the infant Jesus at her breast.

Parzival's mother sends him out into the world deliberately dressed as, and indeed still, a fool. Parzival's ignorance is a key concept in the work from now on. He is associated with the equivalent German word *tump*, ignorant, and although this is not used as a repeated formulaic epithet, the idea recurs with many variations in the first part of the book. Gregorius, incidentally, applied the same word to himself in Hartmann's version of his story, but on one occasion only, and with interesting self-reflection, when leaving the monastery. The theological significance of the consistent portrayal of Parzival as foolish or ignorant is important. It was elucidated in detail in a book by Alois Haas in 1964 with reference to a whole series of theological possibilities, some of them, as Haas makes clear,[21] both confused and confusing. *Ignorantia*, like concupiscence (with which it is identified by Hugh of St Victor), can either be the cause of the original sin, or can be a consequence of it. Isidore of Seville took the former view, whilst Peter Lombard saw *ignorantia vincibilis* as one of the results of original sin, and the question was still being considered by Kierkegaard, who merges Adam's innocence and ignorance in his attempt at the meaning of original sin in *The Concept of Dread*, and inclines to

---

[17] See my article '*Parzival* and the Theology of Fallen Man', in *A Companion to Wolfram's Parzival*, ed. Will Hasty (Columbia, SC: Camden House, 1999), pp. 143–58.

[18] Her own name, though there are questions about the precise etymology, nevertheless clearly echoes the German word for 'heartache'.

[19] *De Genesi contra Manichaeos* (*PL* 34, 187).

[20] See Giles Constable, *The Reformation of the Twelfth Century* (Cambridge: Cambridge University Press, 1996), p. 68. Adam and Eve are sometimes seen as having been, as it were, in an enclosed monastery, which made their sin greater: see the fourteenth-century *Fasciculus Morum*, ed. and trans. Wenzel, pp. 684f. On chastity in marriage in *Parzival*, see also Brooke, *Idea of Marriage*, p. 194, and Dyan Elliot, *Spiritual Marriage: Sexual Abstinence in Medieval Wedlock* (Princeton: Princeton University Press, 1993).

[21] Alois M. Haas, *Parzivals tumpheit bei Wolfram von Eschenbach* (Berlin: Schmidt, 1964). See pp. 19–37 for a fourfold medieval view of the idea of folly, with comments also on *niceté* in Chrétien. On the relationship with original sin, see pp. 264–5. In general-theological terms, see Maurice Wiles, *The Christian Fathers* (London: SCM Press, 2nd edn 1977), p. 84. Wiles refers to the difficult fourth chapter of Osee (Hoseas), which has various elements in it that might be related to Parzival's tale (ignorance of God, loss of the mother, rejection of priests). On ignorance and original sin in Parzival, see the perceptive reading of the work by Richard G. Dimler, 'Parzival's Guilt: a Theological Interpretation', *Monatshefte* 62 (1970), 123–34, especially pp. 127f.

the notion that ignorance came before the breaking of the prohibition.[22] More recent theologians have tended to see the problem as one that does not admit of a solution.[23]

The view that ignorance is a result of original sin seems to be that most relevant to the situation in Parzival; Adam was, before the Fall, in what Andrew Martin has called 'a state of primordial nescience'. But Parzival is first of all in a fallen world, and whatever its origins, is prey to *ignorantia*, which can generate sin, deserved or not. That man was condemned to ignorance at the Fall is expressed vividly in an earlier German vernacular text, the Genesis-poem from Vorau in Styria, in a passage which is close to a sermon by Bernard of Clairvaux. The devil captures Adam and Eve, we are told, and

> er warf si sâre. in sinen charcare.
> der heizet ignorancia.[24]

(He soon threw them into his dungeon, which is called ignorance.)

When Parzival leaves, his mother faints and dies, and it is this that is levelled by other characters against Parzival (and indeed Perceval) as an actual sin. However, like the abbot in *Gregorius*, Herzeloyde was trying to cheat destiny, and there is no question on this occasion of the *vita contemplativa* even as a viable alternative; her attempt was unreasonable. In the biblical Genesis, a man is supposed to leave his mother.

Sending Parzival out dressed as a fool has Adamic connotations beyond that of original sin. God provides the protoplasts with their first garments, and in medieval writing there is extensive discussion of the origins of clothing. That this is a resonance of the Fall is borne out by an interesting aside in a paper by Lorraine Stock on the way in which the episode of Daun John and the merchant's wife in Chaucer's *Shipman's Tale* can be seen as a parody of the Fall. She cites the fourteenth-century English *Book of Vices and Virtues* on what we might nowadays call the semiology of clothing:

> I holde hym a fole þat wolde be proud to weere a garnement þat were but a tokne of his fadre shame and his owene. Þis is þe riȝt tokenynge of cloþing, þat was founden for no þing but for þe synne of oure first fadre for to hyle his confusion, þat is his vndoynge and oures . . . also it falleþ ofte þat vnder riche and noble cloþinge þe soule liþ ded in synne . . .

The English text was translated from the French Dominican *Somme le Roi* of 1279,

---

[22] Søren Kierkegaard, *The Concept of Dread* [1844], trans. Walter Lowrie (Princeton: Princeton University Press, 2nd edn 1957), pp. 37–41. 'The prohibition alarms Adam . . . because the prohibition awakes in him the possibility of freedom.' Adam now possesses 'the alaming possibility of *being able*. What he is able to do, of that he has no conception . . . There is only the possibility of being able, as a higher form of ignorance . . .', p. 40. The last chapter of Kierkegaard's work uses, incidentally, the image of the young innocent in a fairytale, setting out to learn fear.
[23] See Martin, 'Genesis of Ignorance', pp. 3f, referring to Gerhard von Rad, for example.
[24] Murdoch, *Fall of Man*, pp. 77–80. The passage from St Bernard is not exact.

and there is a slightly shorter and less forceful version in Dan Michel's *Ayenbite of Inwyt*, which comes from the same source.[25]

There is a more direct allusion to Genesis and to the status of Parzival as a reflection both of Adam and of mankind in his encounter with his first major adviser, Gurnemanz. In Wolfram – though not in Chrétien – some of this knight's advice echoes Genesis, first when he tells the boy not to incur shame, 'ir sult niemer iuch verschemen' (III: 170, 16), and secondly in his injunction to the boy to cherish women. He does this in Chrétien, too, of course, and it is part of the normal chivalric code, but in Wolfram the biblical echoes are unmistakable:

> man unt wîp diu sint al ein;
> als diu sunn diu hiute schein,
> und ouch der name der heizet tac.
> der enwederz sich geschieden mac:
> si blüent ûz eime kerne gar . . .   (III: 173, 1–5)

> (Man and woman are one, undivided as the sun that shone today
> and what we call the day itself; they cannot be separated, and
> grow from the same seed . . .)

Genesis 2:24 – 'quamobrem relinquit homo patrem suum et matrem et adhaerebit uxori suae, et erunt duo in carne una' – looks both backwards and forwards. Parzival was intended to leave his mother, and marriage will be important later on, though *in extremis* Parzival will long first for the spiritual goal of the Grail and for his wife second, the priority that Adam put on things, to the annoyance of Eve, in Lutwin's version of the *Vita Adae*.

During his visit to Gurnemanz, however, what Parzival is taught is quite specifically adherence to the Church, to its laws and technicalities, such as crossing himself. It is sometimes argued in studies of *Parzival* that Wolfram somehow attempts to keep the clergy out of the picture; he does not, and that Parzival does not encounter a bishop or any higher clergy is less than relevant. From Gurnemanz he learns specifically about the externals of Church law, and more significantly he learns about the repudiation of the devil. The general usefulness of the instruction is also underlined:

> dô gienc der helt mit witzen kranc
> dâ man got und dem wirte sanc.
> der wirt zer messe in lêrte
> daz noch die saelde mêrte,

[25] Lorraine Kochanske Stock, 'The Reenacted Fall in Chaucer's *Shipman's Tale*', *Studies in Iconography* 7/8 (1981–2), 135–45. Stock makes very clear the problem in literary products of a postlapsarian world of indicating both sin and original sin at the same time. The text – cited on p. 136, and, as she indicates, a medieval topos – is from *The Book of Vices and Virtues*, ed. W. Nelson Francis (London: Oxford University Press, 1942 = EETS/OS 217), p. 286. See also *Dan Michel's Ayenbite of Inwyt I. Text*, transcr. Richard Morris, ed. Pamela Gradon (London: Oxford University Press, 1965 = EETS/OS 23), p. 258. The French *Somme le Roi*, ascribed to the Dominican and confessor to King Philip III, Lorens d'Orléans, is also the source of Caxton's *Royal Book*.

opfern und segnen sich,
und gein dem tiuvel kêrn gerich.   (III: 169, 15–20)

(The ignorant and untutored warrior went to where his host was
having a mass sung to God, and at mass his host taught him to
participate in the sacrifice and to cross himself, and in that way
to ward off the devil – this still increases one's blessings today.)

Mit witzen kranc in that passage is another of the various circumlocutions in
German for folly and ignorance.

Parzival's first chance visit to the Grail castle in Book V of Wolfram's poem is
the next high point. He is permitted to see the Grail and the other accoutrements,
which clearly have liturgical significance, whatever their origins in folklore may
be, but he does not yet understand them, any more than does the audience, which
keeps pace with the learning process of the young man. What is of particular
interest is the express connexion of the Grail already at this point with Paradise. A
lady comes in bearing the Grail on a tablet; from Wolfram we are not clear what
shape it is, or indeed precisely *what* it is, but this matters very little:

ûf einem grüenen achmardî
truoc si den wunsch von pardîs,
bêde wurzeln unde rîs.
daz was ein dinc, daz hiez der Grâl,
erden wunsches überwal.   (V: 235, 20–4)

(Upon a green silk she bore the desire of Paradise, root and
branch – a thing called 'the Graal', above all earthly desires.)

The Grail itself in *Parzival* is actually given a name by Wolfram – either *lapsit
exillis* or some variation on it, since the manuscripts differ – and this has given rise
to a great deal of scholarly speculation, not all of it entirely sane. I have cited elsewhere in this context some comments by C. S. Lewis, and cannot do better than cite
them again: 'we must not say that the Grail "is" a Celtic cauldron of plenty . . .
Within a given story any object, person or place is neither more nor less nor other
than what the story effectively shows it to be.'[26] Wolfram's Grail is a sign for Paradise as such, for the height of all desires. Certainly it may have its origins in Celtic
myth, and probably the most famous modern expositions of its nature have been in
the (now rather muddied) anthropological wake of Sir James Frazer.[27] But in
Robert de Boron it is the chalice at the Last Supper, and the liturgical overtones
become clearer later; in other versions it is a plate, and in Wolfram it is *ein dinc*, a
thing, a significantly neutral term. Since Wolfram's Grail produces food and gives

[26] C. S. Lewis, 'The Genesis of a Medieval Book', in *Studies in Medieval and Renaissance Literature*, ed. W. Hooper (Cambridge: Cambridge University Press, 1966), pp. 18–40, citation pp. 39f.
[27] The exposition by Jessie L. Weston (incidentally an early translator of *Parzival*), in *From Ritual to
Romance* (Cambridge: Cambridge University Press, 1920), which influenced T. S. Eliot, is well
known. Taking the tale of the Fisher King as a vegetation myth is perfectly possible, and may even lie
at the root of the whole tale; but Wolfram's and most, if not all, of the written versions have relocated it
into a Christian context, and it is this that we need to elucidate.

life, it also echoes the Paradise of unfallen man, an allegory of Paradise itself, sought by fallen man. When he first sees the Grail, however, Parzival, not yet *in* a state of grace, can do nothing about it, and it is only when he achieves understanding that he is able to return. His pagan half-brother, Feirefiz, at the end of the work, cannot even *see* it until he is baptized. To those who *are* baptized, the possibility of regaining Paradise is literally visible, and the Grail is therefore Paradise in itself.[28] Later on we shall hear – with Parzival – much more about the paradisiacal connexions, but it is his lack of comprehension at present that is significant. It is a mystery in every sense, and although the Grail is not in this version either a dish or a chalice – as with Robert de Boron – there are already *echoes*, at least, of the *Canon Missae* in the provision by the Grail of food and drink, and those echoes are stronger than those of the pagan cornucopia:

Accipite et bibite ex eo omnes. hic est enim calix sanguinis mei noui et aeterni testamenti mysterium . . . offerimus panem sanctum uitae aeternae et calicem salutis perpetuae . . .[29]

Parzival's failure to express pity for the Fisher King is a failure to show the love of his neighbour. It is in consequence of this – when he has been cursed and seems unable to find his way back to make amends – that, having broken the second commandment of the New Testament, he rejects God as well, thus breaking the first. The passage in Wolfram's sixth book in which Parzival, speaking to his friend Gawan, actually rejects the love of God is probably the most frequently cited of this work. It intensifies with an initial *wê* (alas) the question of innocence that he had posed to his mother at the very beginning, and it will be some time before Parzival is given an answer to the question:

Der Wâleis sprach: 'wê waz ist got?
waer der gewaldec, sölhen spot
hete er uns bêden niht gegebn,
kunde got mit kreften lebn,
ich was im diens undertân,
sît ich genâden mich versan.
nû wil i'm dienst widersagn.
hât er haz, den wil ich tragn.'   (VI: 332, 1–9)

(Parzival of Wales said: 'Alas, what is God? If he were all-powerful and could actually do something, He would not have brought us to this shameful state. I have served Him ever since I

[28] See Walter Johannes Schröder, *Der Ritter zwischen Welt und Gott* (Weimar: Böhlau, 1952), pp. 46–55 on the essentially symbolic effect of the Grail in Wolfram. Margaret J. C. Reid, *The Arthurian Legend* (Edinburgh: Oliver and Boyd, 1938) has a particularly neat overall survey of the treatments of the Grail as 'Celtic magic, Bible lore and moralising allegory', pp. 128–58.

[29] *The Missal of Robert of Jumièges*, ed. H. A. Wilson (London: Henry Bradshaw Society, 1896), p. 46. (Take and drink, this is the chalice of my blood, the mystery of my new and eternal law . . . let us offer the holy bread of life and the chalice of eternal salvation.)

first heard of grace. Now I withdraw my service. If He hates me,
then I shall put up with it.')

This is Parzival's real fall. He has now broken the two commandments of the New
Law expressed (and underlined by the injunction 'hoc fac ut vives') in Luke 10:27,
and explained by the parable of the Good Samaritan, which played such a part in
Hartmann's *Gregorius* and in other medieval works, often in the exegetical context
of the Fall.[30] Parzival's reaction is the mainspring of his continued exclusion from
the Paradise of the Grail, and it is many years before he can return. But his heartfelt
question – what is God? – represents the essence of the whole work.

Parzival's outburst against God is not, of course, an expression of atheism,
which would be unlikely at the period. Parzival – and specifically, Parzival's ignorance – has reached a state where he needs to be convinced of the nature, rather
than the existence, of God. There has been some discussion of the question of
atheism in the Middle Ages, partly because of a quite natural desire to affirm that
the rationality of the medieval mind was precisely the same as now. However, in a
very sensible paper on Anselm's *Proslogion* and the whole question of ontological
proof, John Clayton distinguished between the possibility of an emotional reaction
and that of a rational one. It would have been quite possible that 'even a model
monk, in a moment of deep distress . . . may have been tempted to deny God's existence. But it was impossible from Anselm's perspective for the non-being of God
to be conceived rationally.' Clayton goes on to cite Book III of the *Proslogion*: 'sic
ergo vere es, domine deus meus, ut nec cogitari possis non esse' (You are so truly,
O Lord, that it is impossible to think that You might not be).[31] It is this view that is
implied throughout in Wolfram's central figure. Even in his emotional state,
Parzival does not deny the existence of God, but rather he withdraws his service.
He can, he says, withstand the *ira Dei* (God's anger) but he lacks specific knowledge, rather than the basis of belief. In fact, during his travels in the next part of the
book – we only glimpse him from time to time, as a nameless wanderer referred to
only as the 'Red Knight', although Gawan does identify him for us – Parzival still
invokes God, as when he accepts the surrender of a group of defeated knights,
enquires about the Grail, then sends them to his wife with the parting blessing 'daz
iuch got bewar!' (VII: 389, 14) (may God preserve you).

Parzival does not return to God after his fall away from Him until the ninth
book, set symbolically on Good Friday. The opening, in which the spirit of the
book asks where Parzival is, echoes the direct 'ubi es?' of Genesis 3:9, which in
exegesis is usually seen as a chance for repentance offered to Adam by God; the
same voice goes on to enquire whether he has been redeemed.[32] And indeed it is

---

[30] See Monselewski, *Der barmherzige Samaritaner.*
[31] John Clayton, 'The Otherness of Anselm', *Neue Zeitschrift für systematische Theologie und Religionsphilosophie* 37 (1995), 125–43. The citation is from p. 126. There is a full study of the notion of
atheism, or rather, of the necessity for the proofs of God's existence in the period by E. Scott
Matthews, 'Rational Inquiry and Communities of Interest: Anselm's Argument and the Friars' (Ph.D.
Diss., Lancaster, 1996). I am indebted to Dr Matthews for valuable comments on the topic.
[32] See my paper *'Parzival* and the Theology of Fallen Man'. On the point that this is not divine ignorance but an admonition and a chance to repent, see Augustine's *Literal Interpretation of Genesis* (*PL*
34, 449) and Gregory the Great's *Moral Interpretations of the Book of Job* (*PL* 75, 558). Other

now, after nearly five years' wandering, that Parzival returns to God after his fall. He first encounters his cousin Sigune, who is now a kind of anchorite, and then a grey-haired knight with his daughters, all of whom are barefoot. The knight reproaches Parzival for being in armour on that day, just as God's first question to Adam is to ask why he had covered himself. These echoes of Genesis made on Good Friday again merge the ideas of Fall and Redemption. Thus far, Parzival has been actively seeking the Grail, but on the instigation of the pilgrim knight he decides that he will submit literally to the divine will,[33] and simply allows his horse to take him wherever God chooses: 'nu genc nâch der gotes kür' (IX: 452, 9) (go where God wills).

Good Friday celebrates the turning point of the divine economy of human history, and the old knight points out its paradoxical significance as a day when 'al diu werlt sich freun mac/ und dâ bî mit angest siufzec sîn' (IX: 448, 8–9) (the whole world may rejoice and at the same time be cast down with sorrow). But Parzival is now on the road to the joy of Easter. This section of the work – at the centre – is the most obvious in a set of liturgical references throughout, although Parzival himself has not been attending mass and does not know what day it is, or, apparently, its importance.[34] It is the pilgrim knight who points out its significance, after Parzival has first declared his ignorance (in this case of the date), and then told him (and reminded us) of his earlier decision to serve God no longer, having despaired of God's help:

> Ich diende eim der heizet got,
> ê daz sô lasterlîchen spot
> sîn gunst übr mich erhancte:
> mîn sin im nie gewancte,
> von dem mir helfe was gesagt,
> nû ist sîn helfe an mir verzagt.   (IX: 447, 25–30)

(I used to serve someone called 'God' before He chose to inflict vile mockery upon me; I never swerved away from Him, since His help was promised to me. Now His help is refused me.)

commentators, such as Isidore (*PL* 83, 220) refer the passage to God's offer of repentance for all sins in Ezechiel 33:11. I have enumerated some in my *Fall of Man in the Early Middle High German Biblical Epic*, pp. 119–29.

[33] The lesson learned by Parzival is shared by two of the heroes in poems by Hartmann von Aue: Gregorius, having committed incest, reacts first with a similar kind of anger to that shown by Parzival, but then does specific penance for it, submitting himself to the will of God, and parallels with *Parzival* include even the rough fisherman, who directs Parzival in the third book: see Christine Wand, *Wolfram von Eschenbach und Hartmann von Aue* (Herne: Verlag für Wissenschaft und Kunst, 1989), pp. 188–91. The central figure in Hartmann's *Der arme Heinrich* is – as we shall see in Chapter 4 – struck down with leprosy, and exhibits first despair but then submission, when he too declares: 'gotes wille müeze an mir geschehen' (let God's will take its course with me): Hartmann von Aue, *Der arme Heinrich*, ed. Hermann Paul, 16th edn by Kurt Gärtner (Tübingen: Niemeyer, 1996), v. 1276.

[34] See Hermann J. Weigand, 'Die epischen Zeitverhältnisse in den Graldichtungen Crestiens und Wolframs', *PMLA* 53 (1938), 917–50, and especially Arthur Groos, 'Time Reference and the Liturgical Calendar in Wolfram von Eschenbach's *Parzival*', *Deutsche Vierteljahresschrift* 49 (1975), 43–65. See also Petrus W. Tax, '*Felix culpa* und *lapsit exillis*: Wolframs *Parzival* und die Liturgie', *MLN* 80 (1965), 454–69.

The concept of help is central. At the very start, Parzival's first words to the knight he thought was God were to ask 'hilf got, dû maht wol helfe hân' (III: 121, 2) (help, O God, You can help me). Later, Parzival has regularly expressed longing, first for the Grail, and secondly for his wife. The latter represents earthly happiness, the former the spiritual. It is of some interest to compare Wolfram's poem at this point – bearing in mind again Loomis's judgement of *Parzival* as a masterful theodicy – with that other justification of God, Anselm of Canterbury's *Proslogion*, something which also exploits the biblical Fall and famously provided answers for the fool. Much of Anselm's poetic first chapter is relevant, particularly the early expression of what (when turned on itself) would centuries later become the notion of the *deus absconditus*:

> Quid faciet servus tuus anxius amore tui et longe proiectus a facie tua? . . .
> O durus et dirus casus ille! Heu, quid perdidit et quid invenit, quid abscessit et quid remansit . . .
> Heu publicus luctus hominum, universalis planctus filiorum Adae![35]

> (What shall Your servant do when he is eager for Your love but cast away from Your face . . . O what a hard and cruel fall. Alas, what did man lose and what did he acquire, what did he break off and what remains . . . Alas for the common sadness of men and the universal complaint of all the sons of Adam.)

Anselm also exploits the commonplace of the *patria paradisi*, the notion that mankind is now in exile, needing to regain and return to the proper homeland, which was lost through disobedience. The notion is found frequently in exegetical comments on the angelic advice in Matthew 2:12 to the Magi to return to their own country by a different route. The concept is found in commentaries and sermons from Gregory onwards, and Bede summarises it in his Gospel-commentary in this context as:

> Regio nostra est paradisus, ad quam per oboedientiam reverti debet genus humanum, quod inde per indoebedientiam expulsum est.[36]

> (Our homeland is Paradise, to which mankind may return through obedience, since it was expelled from it through disobedience.)

It is also a commonplace exploited in medieval literature that Adam is an exile, and the corresponding Middle High German word *ellend* – literally 'from the land', which comes eventually to mean 'wretched' or 'miserable' – is found regularly. In the development of the topos of the *patria paradisi*, the true homeland of fallen man is the heavenly, not the earthly Paradise. There is no return to the latter, so we

---

[35] *Sancti Anselmi Opera Omnia*, ed. F. S. Schmitt (Edinburgh and Rome: Nelson, 1938–61, repr. Stuttgart: Frommann, 1968), I, 98f. (= *Proslogion* I). There is a translation of the *Proslogion* in *The Prayers and Meditations of St Anselm*, trans. Benedicta Ward (Harmondsworth: Penguin, 1973), though translations here are my own.

[36] Commentary on Matthew, *PL* 92, 13.

must strive for the former, the promised homeland, and return there, like the Magi, *per aliam viam*, on the 'other' path of righteousness. Like Adam, Parzival has been prevented from returning to his former home but, just as Adam was given, in the *Vita Adae*, the promise of a return, Parzival has seen the new Paradise and the new homeland, though he was not yet permitted to stay. When he has completed his penance he can do so, and indeed he assumes the kingship and takes up the Grail crown at the end of the work.[37]

As critics have made clear, Wolfram exploits biblical passages in the work as a whole – the first Epistle of John on sin and the devil, and the Epistle of James on the question of unwavering perseverance and indeed on the heavenly crown – but the influence of Genesis, the Gospels and the Psalms is nevertheless at the forefront, which is precisely what one would expect, and the Psalms play a great part at the time of Parzival's recovery from his fall. The Psalms, the first book studied in the medieval schools and certainly familiar to medieval vernacular authors, either for themselves or through the claims made for them by the great authorities – Augustine in the *Confessions* is a case in point[38] – are cited frequently at the beginning of Anselm's *libellus* too, of course, in the direct requests for help: 'invitas nos: adiuva nos. Obsecro, domine, ne desperem suspirando' – (You invite us to say 'help us'. I pray, O Lord, that I might not sigh without hope). Parzival goes through the same process. Told by the pilgrim knight that Good Friday is a day of sorrow and joy, because it was the day of Christ's suffering, but also of the Redemption, he first of all recalls his feud with God and his desire to have help from Him, then recalls God as the Creator, and finally articulates the desire for that help:

> alrêrste er dô gedâhte,
> wer al die werlt volbrâhte,
> an sînen schephære,
> wie gewaltec der wære.
> er sprach: 'waz ob got helfe phligt,
> diu mînem trûren ane gesigt?
> wart ab er ie ritter holt,
> gediente ie ritter sînen solt,
> ode mac schilt unde swert
> sîner helfe sîn sô wert,
> und rehtiu manlîchiu wer,
> daz sîn helfe mich vor sorgen ner,
> ist hiute sîn helflîcher tac,
> sô helfe er, ob er helfen mac.'   (IX: 451, 9–21)

(Now he again gave a thought to the one who had made the world, his creator and how mighty He was. 'Maybe God does have the power to help overcome my sorrow?' he asked himself.

---

[37] Duckworth, *Biblical Terminology*, pp. 122–34 (appropriately enough in his ninth chapter) discusses James 2:14 in a somewhat Protestant view of the nature of good works and the formal religion from which Parzival has distanced himself.

[38] R. L. Ottley, *Studies in the Confessions of St Augustine* (London: Robert Scott, 1919), p. 90. The *locus classicus* in the *Confessions* is IX, 4, 8.

> 'If He ever looked well upon a knight, and if any knight ever
> earned His reward or if shield and sword and true manliness can
> be worthy of His help and could save me from my cares, and if
> this is His day of help, then let Him help me, if help He can.')

The reiteration of the verb *helfen* – frequently pointed out by the critics[39] – speaks for itself, and there is a clear link with Psalm 21, with the words of Christ on the Cross, and with the Good Friday liturgy:[40] 'Tu autem Domine ne elongaveris auxilium tuum a me.' (O Lord, do not withdraw your help from me.)

Divine help is needed for the fool. Even though Parzival has long since removed his fool's garments, he has remained a fool in a variety of ways, either in his failure to recognise situations, or in his rejection of God. As indicated, the fool in general terms, and especially that one referred to in the Psalm, is also the starting point of Anselm's proof of God in the *Proslogion*, and there are parallels between this work and *Parzival*. Anselm may not be a potential direct source (which has, I think, never been developed, though the general influence of a whole variety of texts on Wolfram has been postulated at different times),[41] but the *Proslogion* certainly contributed to the culture of ideas in the period, and Wolfram might well have drawn on it without necessarily being aware of the direct source of the arguments. Anselm makes the point that the fool has *something* in his understanding, but does not understand that it exists, a state which, philosophically, is precisely the case with Parzival. Anselm's chapter containing the ontological proof indicates (though this is of course rather an oversimplification of Anselm's argument) how the fool can come to understand by a picture:

> Aliud enim est rem esse in intellectu, aliud intelligere rem esse. Nam cum pictor praecogitat quae facturus est, habet quid in intellectu, sed nondum intelligit esse quod nondum fecit. Cum vero iam pinxit, et habet in intellectu et intelligit esse quod iam fecit. (II)

> (It is one thing to have something in your mind, something else again to grasp its existence. When a painter thinks up what he is going to paint, he has it in his mind, but he doesn't understand it because he hasn't made it yet. But when he has painted it, he has it in his mind and he understands it, because he has painted it.)

The image is a cogent one. Parzival – and also Wolfram's audience as it observes his physical and spiritual adventures – requires the painting to be complete to be understood, although it was there already in essence. Parzival has not denied the

---

[39] Otto Springer, 'Wolfram's *Parzival*', in Loomis, ed., *Arthurian Literature*, pp. 218–50, p. 239 with reference to other studies. See also David Duckworth, *The Influence of Biblical Terminology and Thought on Wolfram's Parzival* (Göppingen: Kümmerle, 1980), p. 280.

[40] See my '*Parzival* and the Theology of Fallen Man'. The verb *nêren* is also significant; it can mean 'heal' or 'cure', and is applied also to Christ. The vocabulary of soteriology is used regularly in this context.

[41] In such texts as Schröder, *Ritter zwischen Welt und Gott*, and Peter Wapnewski, *Wolframs Parzival: Studien zur Religiosität und Form* (Heidelberg: Winter, 1955); Duckworth, *Biblical Terminology*.

existence of God, and incidentally characters elsewhere in Wolfram's writing, such as the Saracen king Terramer in his *Willehalm*, for example, are dubbed fools for doing just that. But Parzival is certainly not reasoning. Anselm refers in his third *capitulum* to Psalm 13:

> Cur itaque 'dixit inspiens in core suo: non est deus', cum tam in promptu sit rationali menti te maxime omnium esse? Cur, nisi quia stultus et insipiens? (III)

> (Why therefore has the fool said in his heart 'there is no God' when according to the rational mind, You, O Lord, exist most fully of all things? Why, except that he is indeed stupid and foolish?)

Whether or not Wolfram did know any of this material directly, the response to Anselm on behalf of the fool by Gaunilo is equally relevant.[42] Gaunilo wondered how reason would cope with the postulation of the perfect, but lost island, the *insula perdita*, and there are echoes of Gaunilo's lost land in Parzival's search for the Grail castle. Gaunilo said of his island that someone would be a fool for imagining it,

> nisi prius ipsam praestantiam eius solummodo sicut rem vere atque indubie existentem nec ullatenus sicut falsum aut incertum aliquid in intellectu meo esse docuerit.[43]

> (unless he first shows to my understanding that the island's excellence exists as a true and indisputable thing and is in no way uncertain or false.)

Parzival's lost land, however, *does* exist because he has been there, although he did not at the time understand it. It is as if his recovery from his fall away from God encompasses a scholastic exposition of the existence of God which takes into account (as Anselm did in *his* answer to Gaunilo) the objection of the perfect island. It is an additional *literary* irony that the lost land of the Grail is one that *is in fact* only imagined – by Wolfram and his fellow writers.[44] The lost country may have been seen by Parzival, but he himself is a subcreation of Wolfram; but Wolfram also portrays himself as a fool.

The notion of help to overcome folly is part of the philosophical realisation of God, and the help for which Parzival asks is again frequently found in the Psalms. The assistance of grace is also the *adiutorium sine qua non* of Augustine's theology, without which man could not persevere of his free choice. Moving

---

[42] Medieval vernacular writers do make direct poetic attempts to counter the fool of the Psalms as well. Thus in the fourteenth century William of Shoreham opened his important poem on the Trinity and the Creation with the same quotation – *per nys no gode* – and attempted to justify the existence of the deity in cosmic terms before moving on to the biblical story of the Fall: *William of Shoreham*, ed. Konrath, pp. 130–60.

[43] Gaunilo, *Pro insipiente* vi, in Schmitt, *Anselmi Opera*, I, 128.

[44] See the introductory comments by Peter Lamarque in 'Fiction and Reality', in *Philosophy and Fiction: Essays in Literary Aesthetics*, ed. Peter Lamarque (Aberdeen: Aberdeen University Press, 1983), pp. 52–72.

chronologically beyond Wolfram, but summing up his figure of Parzival very neatly, it is worth quoting not Augustine, but rather his far later successor Aquinas:

> Homo autem variabilis est et de malo in bonum et de bono in malum. Ad hoc igitur quod immobiliter perseveret in bono, quod est perseverare, indiget auxilio divino.[45]

> (For man wavers from bad to good and from good to bad. And so that he may strive unwaveringly for the good, that is, persevere, he requires divine help.)

Again there is an echo of Matthew 24:13. Parzival is directed for that help to the hermit Trevrizent, who is not a priest, although he has before him an altar stripped (in accordance with the Easter rite) of its cloth, and Parzival addresses him with the *peccavi* formula: 'ich bin ein man der sünde hât' (IX: 456, 30) (I am a man who has sinned). Before Parzival even tells his story, Trevrizent assures him that God's help is always available, but then continues to explain that God is perfection and indeed truth: 'got heizt und ist diu wârheit' (IX: 462, 25) (God is called, and is, the truth),[46] adding a little later that

> swer iuch gein im in hazze siht,
> der hât iuch an den witzen krank.   (IX: 463, 1–2)

> (If anyone saw you expressing this hatred for God, he'd think you a fool.)

Trevrizent also points out, in another echo of Anselm, how God comes into man's mind. He is the one 'der durch gedanke vert' (IX: 466, 15) (who comes into thoughts), even though man tries to resist. As a simplification of the ontological argument, and indeed even with a resolution of Gaunilo's objections, the passage is of some interest. Anselm's third *capitulum* of the *Proslogion* is entitled *Quod non possit cogitari non esse* (What it is impossible to think of as not existing), and it is as if Wolfram is countering Gaunilo by saying that, yes, the perfect place can exist, albeit as a picture painted not by an artist, but by a poet.

The hermit is able to explain to Parzival the human condition, and at the heart of his presentation of the nature of man's estate is an exposition of the theology of the Fall. The passage is frequently cited:

> Von Adâmes künne
> huop sich riwe unde wünne,
> sît er uns sippe lougent niht,
> den ieslîch engel ob im siht,
> unt daz diu sippe ist sünden wagen,
> sô daz wir sünde müezen tragen.   (IX: 465, 1–6)

---

[45] Thomas Aquinas, *Summa contra gentiles* III, clv (Quod homo indiget divino auxilio ad perseverandum in bono), cited from the edition published in Turin: Marinetti, 1922, p. 407. On Augustine (the citation is from the *De correptione et gratia*) see Bettenson's collection of Augustinian statements on grace: *Documents of the Christian Church*, p. 78.

[46] One manuscript of *Parzival* has *ein wârheit*, 'a truth'.

(From Adam's race there arose both sorrow and joy, since on the
one hand He whom all angels see above them does not deny
kinship with us, and on the other hand that this kinship is the
vehicle of sin, so that we have to bear sin.)

Parzival, part of Adam's race, has fallen from God so completely that his recovery
necessitated a renewal of the knowledge of God. The ignorance that is one of the
results of the Fall has to be overcome in detail before he can achieve the place
planned for him, the Grail crown, which might also be seen as a heavenly crown to
be received in a regained Paradise. Paradise *can* be regained, though it is not the
earthly Paradise that Parzival first left behind him: his mother is dead and there can
be no return that way, any more than Adam could ever actually return to Eden.

Parzival's specific sins are recounted and categorised, and Parzival does during
his wanderings make amends for some of his misdemeanours. Everything goes
back, however, to the sin of birth, the original sin passed on through his parents,
which he can do nothing about as such, and which has led to his ignorance, his
status as a fool. This in turn has led him to incur and to commit further sins, failing
to show sympathy with his neighbour, and especially the actual sin of having
lapsed from God so far as to reject Him.

To return briefly to an early Christian work which addresses the notion of a
lapse of faith and which was also widely known throughout the Middle Ages, the
De lapsis of Cyprian of Carthage from the third century tries to clarify the problem
of those who had willingly or otherwise abandoned the faith during the Decian
persecutions in his own time, and who then wished to return, although it has
general implications too, which accounts for its survival. It also contains the notion
of testing and – appropriately for Parzival – condemns the idea of anger against
God. Cyprian's work is comforting in that it does permit the return of the lapsed,
and indicates that they, too, can receive the heavenly crown. For Parzival, that
crown is a real one, that of the Grail kingship, and Trevrizent also explains to
Parzival the whole nature of the Grail in a passage that calls strongly to mind the
Unde et memores portion of the mass. The liturgical overtones are now very clear;
the elevation of the chalice and the subsequent references to Melchisedec and to
the carrying of the sacrifice to heaven by the angel all have echoes in what Trevrizent tells Parzival.[47]

How is Parzival to return to the Grail? He has lapsed, and although the visit to
Trevrizent has made him aware again of his sinfulness – of original and actual sin –
as well as of the nature of God, Parzival requires absolution, and here lies one of
the real narrative problems shared by Wolfram and Chrétien. Trevrizent gives
Parzival a kind of absolution, not in completely formal terms, but simply by saying
'gip mir dîn sünde her' (IX: 502, 25) (give me your sins) at the very end of the ninth
book. He offers to guarantee before God Parzival's change of heart so long as
Parzival follows the advice he has given him. It is important to examine just what

---

[47] See again *The Missal of Robert of Jumièges*, Wilson, p. 46. The passage is of course still in the
Roman service.

95

that is: to lament his mother's death and to do penance for his other major sin, the unlawful killing of the Red Knight. 'Sô solte', says Trevrizent, 'im wandel drumbe gebn' (IX: 499, 18) (atone to Him [God] for this), a line very close to the Baptist's injunction μετανοεῖτε[48] in Matthew 3:2 and 4:17. Indeed, a little later Trevrizent tells Parzival to do penance: *nim buoze* (IX: 499, 27). The question of Trevrizent taking on his sins, however, is a little problematic in technical terms, since he is a layman, but Trevrizent is not offering formal absolution; he is simply echoing words like those of Cyprian to the lapsed:

Quaeso vos, fratres, adquiescite salubribus remediis, consiliis oboedite melioribus; cum lacrimis nostris vestras lacrimas iungite, cum nostro gemitu vestros gemitus copulate. Rogamus vos ut pro vobis Deus rogare possimus . . .

(Brethren, submit, I beg you, to these wholesome remedies; yield to better counsels, join your tears to ours, add your sorrow to our sorrow. We appeal to you, so as to be able to appeal to God for you . . .)[49]

The advisers that Parzival has had so far are all outside orthodox religion, and this is something again made (over)much of in criticism. It is true that it is not difficult to find statements from Ambrose's *De Poenitentia* onwards[50] and certainly after say, Chalcedon, restricting absolution to the priesthood. Leo the Great wrote to one of his bishops in 452 stressing that grace came to fallen men not only through baptism, but *per poenitentiae medicinam*, yet he still noted that absolution came only from a priest: 'indulgentia Dei nisi supplicationibus sacerdotum nequeat obtineri'.[51] However, while there may be a deliberate attempt on Wolfram's part, as has been suggested, to stay outside orthodox religion, lay confession was not necessarily condemned even in the twelfth century,[52] and a purely sacramental conception of penance does indeed take a time to establish. Trevrizent does not, on the other hand, grant formal absolution anyway, and may with his statement wish simply to guarantee that what he has said is true, that Parzival must give the appropriate satisfaction. Charles Williams,[53] writing of his

[48] Dimler, 'Parzival's Guilt', p. 131 speaks of a necessary *metanoia* to overcome the renunciation of God. Dimler does not go on to explore how Parzival comes to (re)learn about God, however. On a different German text, see David Duckworth, 'Heinrich and the Knowledge of God in Hartmann's Poem', *Mediaevistik* 5 (1992), 57–70.
[49] Cyprian, *De lapsis* 32, in *De lapsis and De ecclesiae catholicae unitate*, ed. and trans. Maurice Bénevot (Oxford: Clarendon, 1971), p. 49.
[50] George D. Smith, *The Teaching of the Catholic Church* (London: Burns Oates and Washbourne, 1948), II, 960.
[51] Letter 108 (*PL* 54, 1011).
[52] See Wapnewski, *Wolframs Parzival*, pp. 179–81 (with reference also to the corresponding passage in Chrétien), and P. B. Wessels, 'Wolfram zwichen Dogma und Legende' (1955) in Heinz Rupp, ed., *Wolfram von Eschenbach* (Darmstadt: WBG, 1966), pp. 232–60, esp. pp. 234–6. I refer to the case of Adam as layman/priest in the *Vita Adae* in 'The Origins of Penance'.
[53] 'The Way of Exchange' (1941), reprinted in his *Selected Writings*, ed. Ann Ridler (London: Oxford University Press, 1961), p. 127. See on the idea of substitution (with reference to Anselm) C. S. Lewis, *Arthurian Torso* (Oxford: Clarendon, 1948), pp. 123–5. I am indebted to Mrs J. Forster for the pointer towards Williams' idea.

own theory of substitution in 1941, cited the words of one of the desert fathers, and those comments (together with Williams' own on the membership of the Church) are pertinent here as well:

> A certain old man used to say: 'It is right for a man to take up the burden of those who are akin (or near) to him, whatsoever it may be . . . and finally the matter must be accounted by him as if he himself had put on the actual body of his neighbour, and as if he had acquired his countenance and soul . . . he must suffer for him as he would for himself.'

However confusing the statement may be that Trevrizent will take on the sins, it is of greater importance that he also directs Parzival towards the establishment of the Church, towards a priest. The advice of Gurnemanz earlier on, teaching him to cross himself to keep the devil at bay, comes back to mind, and the satisfaction theology of Anselm's *Cur deus homo* is perhaps echoed as well:

> 'du muost zen pfaffen haben muot.
> swaz dîn ouge ûf erden siht,
> daz glîchet sich dem priester niht.
> sîn munt die marter sprichet,
> diu unser flust zebrichet:
> ouch grîfet sîn gewîhtiu hant
> an daz hoeheste pfant
> daz ie für schult gesetzet wart.'   (IX: 502, 12–18)

> ('You must put your trust in priests; nothing you see on earth is like a priest. It is from his mouth that we hear about the Passion that cancels out our loss. His consecrated hand takes the highest pledge that was ever set against a debt.')

What Trevrizent has done overall is to enable Parzival to understand – *intellegere* – but the initial submission to renewed belief after the encounter with the grey-haired knight had to come first. It is almost as if this is a working-out of the pattern of *credo ut intelligam*, the concept that links Anselm and Augustine.[54] The literary context has simplified a theological argument by showing us how it works out in a practical situation.

It is less than usual, perhaps, to draw an interpretation to a close when we are only finishing the ninth book out of sixteen, although for many years the German Reclam-series of popular and cheap classics had an abridged *Parzival* with sixty-plus pages up to Book IX and fewer than ten pages for the rest of the work.[55] But

54 For two separate but complementary views by rather different historians, see G. G. Coulton, *Studies in Medieval Thought* (London and Edinburgh: Nelson, 1940), p. 101, referring to John Scot's variation; and David Knowles, *The Evolution of Medieval Thought* (London: Longmans, 1962), pp. 101f. Knowles refers also to Isaiah 7:9 in the Septuagint version. See also James Bowen, *A History of Western Education II* (London: Methuen, 1975), pp. 48f. Anselm develops the idea in the *De fide Trinitatis (PL* 158, 272).
55 Wolfram von Eschenbach, *Parzival: Eine Auswahl*, trans. Wilhelm Hertz, ed. W. Hofstaetter (Stuttgart: Reclam, 1959).

Parzival has been given the answer and can now actually return to Paradise, the new Paradise, the Grail castle and his birthright, rather than the Paradise of childhood to which he now finds he cannot return. This is part of the divine plan, the individual reaching his destined goal after perseverance, at the time appointed. In the later parts of the work, too, much of the action is concerned with Gawan, Parzival's counterpart in the strictly Arthurian sphere, and we need not be detained by the stories of Gawan's chivalric service for various ladies, ranging from the charming comedy of his championing of Obilôt, who is about eight, to Antikonîe, who is an adult and, in modern terms, frankly over-sexed. Gawan's major adventure, however, does demand attention. This is his liberation of a large number of prisoners (Christian and otherwise, including a large number of maidens) held in Schastel Marveile (a speaking name not unlike Munsalvaesche) by Clinschor, whom Wolfram's translator, A. T. Hatto, describes succinctly as 'a castrated sorceror', and in whom Wagner was particularly interested. Castrated because of adultery, the magician-knight Clinschor both imprisons people and makes them unhappy. Impotent himself, then, and spreading gloom, he is a devil-figure, and we are told expressly that only with God's help can he be defeated. Gawan's rescue of his prisoners is a kind of Harrowing of Hell, and there are elements which are parallel to Parzival's own story. Though brave, Gawan has to submit his actions to the will of God, and when he enters the enchanted castle

> er . . . liez es walten
> den der helfe hât behalten,
> und den der helfe nie verdrôz . . .   (XI: 568, 1–3)
>
> (he left things up to God, who is able to help, and who is never averse to helping . . .)

'Da quod iubes, et iube quod vis.' The passage also continues the notion of help at some length, although one cannot push the analogy with the Harrowing too far, since Gawan is in most respects no Christ-figure. However, Malory spotted the parallel in his version. 'The Castell of Maydyns', he says, 'betokenyth the good soulys that were in preson before the Incarnacion of Oure Lorde Jesu Cryste.'[56] The adventure might also provide a reminder that no one need now remain a prisoner of the devil. It is also the representation of a deed by a secular knight which, as Hugh Sacker says, 'demonstrates the dependence of Arthurian society on God', and the episode is unusual – and therefore important – as a Gawan-story in its insistence both on the help of God and the necessity of confidence in that help.[57]

It is virtually at the close of the whole that Parzival's half-brother, the pagan Feirefiz, also the son of Gahmuret, is baptized, and the position right at the end of the work is not without significance. There has been some criticism of this scene as

---

[56] *The Works of Sir Thomas Malory*, ed. Eugène Vinaver, 3rd edn rev. P. J. C. Field (Oxford: Clarendon, 1990), II, 892.
[57] See Hugh Sacker, *An Introduction to Wolfram's Parzival* (Cambridge: Cambridge University Press, 1963), pp. 143–6 for a particularly clear description of the whole episode, without, however, a parallel with the Harrowing.

hasty, even flippant, since Feirefiz's motivation for baptism looks at first glance as if it is purely a passport to marriage into the Grail family.[58] But Wolfram uses the passage to explain, through a venerable priest, and at the very end of the story, the nature of the Trinity and then of the capacity of baptism to wash away the sin of Adam and rob the devil:

> dâ stuont ein grâwer priester alt,
> der ûz heidenschaft manc kindelîn
> och gestôzen hête drîn.
> der sprach: 'ir sult gelouben,
> iwerr sêle den tiuvel rouben . . .
> ime wazzer er ze toufe gienc,
> von dem Adâm antlütze enpfienc.
> von wazzer boume sind gesaft.
> wazzer früht al die geschaft
> der man vür crêatiure giht.
> mit dem wazzer man gesiht.
> wazzer gît maneger sêle schîn,
> daz die engl niht liehter dorften sîn.'   (XVI: 817, 8–30)

(A venerable old priest stood there, a man who had already baptized many a heathen child . . . He said: 'you should believe and rob the devil of your soul . . . The one in whose image Adam was made entered the water of baptism. Water gives sap to the trees and brings to fruit everything that we call "creature". We see by water, and water gives to many souls a glory that is not less than that of the angels.')

Both Adam and Christ, linked by the baptism idea, are present, as is the notion of baptism opening the eyes. One of the effects of the Fall is that although the pair had their eyes open when they ate the fruit in Genesis 3:7 this is usually interpreted as the opening of the eyes of the flesh, with a corresponding closing of the inner eyes, which are opened only with baptism. Here, too, Feirefiz now sees the Grail. The lengthy description of the water of baptism is entirely in accord with medieval liturgical blessings of the font, as spoken by the priest at the renewal of baptism on Holy Saturday, in other blessings of the water, and in the baptism service *ad caticuminum faciendum* as such.[59] Parzival was born a Christian, and we did not see his baptism; the baptism of Feirefiz, whilst showing the unity of Creation,[60] is also a reminder in completely orthodox terms of the sacrament without which Parzival

---

[58] See Sacker, *Wolfram's Parzival*, p. 164, who nevertheless seems to think that shallowness is acceptable in Feirefiz.

[59] The *Missal* of Robert of Jumièges again has various clear examples of blessings of the water, ed. Wilson, pp. 97–8, 276.

[60] Wolfram's views on religious tolerance have been much discussed. See for a summary Neil Thomas, 'The Ecumenical Ideal in Wolfram von Eschenbach Revisited', *Amsterdamer Beiträge zur älteren Germanistik* 50 (1998), 111–29.

could not even have seen the Grail, which he then attains through the other sacrament of penance.

Parzival is the representative of the old Adam, placed into the world in ignorance. He moves from lawlessness (*ante legem*) to formal instruction (*sub lege*) and then to the grace that was always there potentially, as the Adam-figure is saved by Church and Christ, and there are clear parallels with Adam throughout. But Parzival's actual sins are those against the laws of the New Testament: the failure to love God and his neighbour. The one, born of the ignorance that is part of original sin, requires grace to cover it; the other requires satisfaction in the general sense, and Parzival atones both for the death of the Red Knight and, by the penance of an extended pilgrimage, for his initial apparent lack of sympathy for the Grail king. The *Vita Adae* expanded the story of the Fall to show us the Redemption during the lifetime of the original characters. The Gregorius-legends showed the workings of original sin and the repeated Fall fairly directly, but already in a world that is *sub gratia*. The tale of Parzival goes further, showing us a lapse from God by another son of Adam and Eve. But this time, before the Redemption can be shown to us in the allegorisation of the story, the nature of God has to be made clear to the lapsed hero. We may be in a *sub gratia* world, but the passing of time has taken mankind further away from that obvious relationship between God and man that was there when Adam spoke directly to his creator. Here an explanation of God at the turning point in the whole narrative is necessary, as Wolfram, the *soi-disant* illiterate, shows us a fool who is the simple soul issuing from the hand of God into the hands of time – to cite T. S. Eliot once again – and having to learn for himself about the necessity of divine aid.

We may end with the plea by Adam himself in a medieval French play, which virtually offers a concise summary of Parzival's tale. In the twelfth-century *Mystère d'Adam*, Adam is in despair when he realises how he has fallen, and, like Parzival, despairs specifically of God's help. But he does know that there is only one source of help anyway, although it is perhaps expressed anachronistically (in a way that will appear in later drama too), for all that the situation of Adam when he makes the comments immediately after he has eaten the fruit is still outside real time:

> Por queil nomai?
> Il m'aidera? Corocié l'ai.
> Ne me ferat ja nul aïe,
> For le filz qu'istra de Marie.
> Ne sai de nul prendre conrei,
> Quant a deu ne portames fei.
> Or en seit tot a deu plaisir . . .[61]

(Why did I name God? Will He help me? I've made Him angry. There will be no help for me now except the son who shall come

---

[61] *Le Mystère d'Adam*, ed. Studer, vv. 379–85, pp. 19f. The passage is cited by Erich Auerbach in his perceptive study of the fall in the Anglo-Norman work in *Mimesis*, p. 137.

from Mary. I can turn to no one since we broke faith with God.
So let it be now according to God's will.)

Adam spoke directly to God. Gregorius never gave up his faith. But Parzival goes
through despair and a different kind of fall before he comes to an awareness of help
and submission to the divine will. Since Parzival is Adam *sub gratia* he *can* be
redeemed, and the ignorance that results from original sin can be and is overcome
in his own lifetime, even when that ignorance extends to a failure to understand or
to accept any longer the nature of God.

FOUR

INNOCENT BLOOD: REDEMPTION AND THE LEPER

WHEN THE UNNAMED TRAVELLER is set upon on the way to Jericho, the Good Samaritan treats his wounds with oil and wine. In allegorical literature, however, the wounds require rather more than that. In Langland's *Vision of Piers the Plowman*, once again, even Faith and Hope – which is what the oil and the wine are usually taken as representing – have fled from the wounded traveller, and the Samaritan is left to explain the situation:

> 'Haue hem excused', quod he · 'her help may litel auaille;
> May no medcyn on molde · the man to hele brynge,
> Neither Feith ne fyn Hope · so festred ben his woundis,
> With-out the blode of a barn · borne of a mayde
> And he be bathed in that blode · baptised, as it were,
> and then plastred with penaunce · and passioun of that babi'.[1]

A more vivid representation of the medicinal nature of Christ's blood is provided iconographically in the cathedral at Spoleto, where there is a painting by Alberto di Sozio dated 1187, depicting Christ on the Cross with the Virgin and St John. Beneath the Cross and buried deep in the hills – we look down towards it through a black opening – is a skull, a reminder of the name Golgotha, and traditionally the skull of Adam; into its open mouth flows the blood from Christ's feet in a memorable symbol of the soteriology implicit in the eucharist, curing death itself. Sometimes it flows into a chalice in iconographical representations.[2] Langland, of course, had compressed the soteriology further by referring not to Christ on the Cross, but to the infant Christ.

In literature, the innocent blood that can redeem the descendants of Adam is sometimes other than that of Christ. On occasion the blood of any innocent child may be prescribed as an actual, rather than an allegorical, medical cure, and for a specific disease: leprosy. The curing by bathing in or being anointed with any innocent blood – the modalities vary – will always carry echoes of the salvation, and just as clearly the appalling but above all else highly visible disease of leprosy can be interpreted as a sign of punishment for a committed sin. The idea that it can be used by God as a test, as with Job's equally disfiguring disease, is an alternative. It is easy in allegorical terms to link the curing of leprosy with the cleansing of

---

[1] Langland, *Piers the Plowman*, ed. Skeat, B XVIII, 81–95. See Hugh White, *Nature and Salvation in Piers Plowman* (Cambridge: D. S. Brewer, 1988), pp. 101–10, and in general D. W. Robertson and Bernard F. Huppé, *Piers Plowman and Scriptural Tradition* (Princeton: Princeton University Press, 1951).
[2] The work is illustrated and described in Juan Ainaud, *Romanesque Painting*, trans. Jean Stewart (London: Weidenfeld and Nicolson, 1963), plates 43 and 44. See also Barbara C. Raw, *Anglo-Saxon Crucifixion Iconography* (Cambridge: Cambridge University Press, 1990).

baptism – Elisha and Naaman provide the Old Testament parallel here – and Christ Himself heals *leproi* in Mark 1:40–5 (Matthew 8:2–4 and Luke 5:12–15), although biblical criticism has wondered about the precise nature of the disease in these cases.[3] Christ heals, however, by means of a miracle, and God eventually heals Job in the same way.

The notion that leprosy can be healed by bathing in the blood of children or, sometimes, of a virgin is a familiar motif in medieval writing, but two things need to be stressed right away: first, that the leprosy itself is very rarely described in any detail; secondly, and far more importantly, that this supposed cure, though prescribed, is very rarely seen as actually being put into practice. It is, in fact, almost always an allegory in the last analysis, though the distinction in medieval literature is sometimes hard to make. Whether the use of innocent blood was ever an actual medical prescription rather than a purely literary motif is more than just doubtful. McEdward Leach, in a relentlessly anthropological introduction to one of the medieval literary works involving such a cure by human blood does, it is true, tell us firmly that 'child sacrifice has been practised by every people at some time in their development',[4] and a century earlier Friedrich von der Hagen had referred to possible practices in ancient China;[5] but the evidence for its use in the treatment of leprosy at all, let alone in the twelfth century and after, is extremely slight. In a discussion of another case of literary leprosy, in Robert Henryson's *Testament of Cresseid*, in which the central figure is *not* cured because leprosy precisely *is a seiknes incurabill*, Douglas Gray draws the sensible conclusion that all supposed medical cures, especially drastic ones, would quickly have been established as pointless. Gray cites what is by comparison a fairly mild example, a concoction of adders baked with leeks, and makes clear that it was only literature (which includes the Bible) that was able to offer any cures at all.[6] The question of innocent blood as a cure for leprosy was considered, too, in a far-ranging study of the disease in literature by Paul Remy, who cites a report – that is, second-hand evidence only – of a single incident in a sixteenth-century chronicle; suggestions are made from time to time that blood *might* be a remedy, but no actual cases seem to be identifiable. Remy notes, indeed, that Louis XI, 'se croyant lépreux, se contentera d'un remède moins cruel: du sang de tortue'. Less cruel indeed, although hardly for the tortoise.[7] The supposed use of human blood was also seen in medieval literature as a 'Jewish remedy', probably to add fuel to medieval anti-Semitism in general.

It is true that ancient and medieval recipes for a variety of diseases, especially those of a particularly intractable but at the same time visible nature, such as epilepsy or leprosy, vie with one another in the eccentricity of their ingredients. On

---

3 See Stanley G. Browne, *Leprosy in the Bible* (London: Christian Medical Fellowship, n.d. [c.1970]).
4 *Amis and Amiloun*, ed. McEdward Leach (London: Oxford University Press, 1937, repr. 1960 = EETS/OS 203), p. xlix.
5 Friedrich von der Hagen, *Gesammtabenteuer* (Stuttgart and Tübingen, 1850, repr. Darmstadt: WBG, 1961), III, clii.
6 Douglas Gray, *Robert Henryson* (Leiden: Brill, 1979), p. 195.
7 Paul Remy, 'La lèpre, thème littéraire au moyen âge', *Le Moyen Age* 52 (1946), 195–242. See pp. 222f.

the whole, those designed to counter epilepsy are worse; a relatively recent recipe (it was collected in Scotland in the nineteenth century) calls for part of the corpse of an executed malefactor. In the case of leprosy, the Middle English *Liber de diversis medicinis* suggests as palliatives, not as a cure, an ointment of grease, watercress, nettles and quicksilver, and elsewhere one made of eggs and brimstone: 'if a leprous man be anoynt þer-with, it will do hym mekill gude & mekill ese'. Yet another leech-book prescribes woad, hemlock, butter and honey, presumably also as an ointment.[8] Both epilepsy and leprosy, on the other hand, have long been afforded non-medical attributes. Epilepsy, in classical terms the sacred disease, continued to be seen as a form of possession, but although very noticeable and indeed frightening, a fit is at least temporary. Leprosy, which in the Middle Ages meant not just Hansen's disease, but a whole range of disfiguring skin ailments, was equally visible, but was both longer-term and in the literal sense repulsive. It is not surprising, then, that it came to be seen as something inflicted as a punishment, something that rightly cut the sufferer off from the rest of the world. The best known and highly informative study of the disease in literature, that by Saul Brody, is actually entitled *The Disease of the Soul*, and Brody makes clear how the medieval view of the leper as a pariah shapes the literary view of the leper as someone 'whose body bears the stain of his spiritual corruption'. A rather large and more recent German study of the metaphors of sin in medieval Latin and German by Meinolf Schumacher considers leprosy in the whole context of the *maculae carnis* as a sign of sin.[9] Sometimes it was seen as the punishment for sins of the flesh, and in the case of Henryson's Cresseid the disease is clearly a warning, but in other literary cases of leprosy things are rarely as specific as that.

Leper-houses were familiar enough in the Middle Ages, but actual descriptions of the disease are rare in literature. Henryson's picture of the unfortunate Cresseid after her rejection both of Troilus and of Diomede is one of the few, but even there the point is the contrast with what she was before:

> scho was sa deformait
> with bylis blak ouirspred in hir visage
> and hir fair colour faidit and alterait . . .

whilst her voice, which had become 'rawk as ruik, full hiddeous hoir and hace' (rough as a rook's, and hideously harsh and hoarse) – apparently a genuine

---

[8] *The Liber de Diversis Medicinis in the Thornton Manuscript*, ed. Margaret Sinclair Ogden (London: Oxford University Press, 1938 = EETS/OS 207) has the first remedies on pp. 39 and 65. See also O. Cockayne, *Leechdoms, Wortcunning and Starcraft of Early England* (London: Rolls Series, 1864–6), II/i, 79 for the third. On the various cures for epilepsy, see my paper '*Peri hieres nousou*: Approaches to the Old High German Medical Charms', in *Mit regulu bithuungan*, ed. J. Flood (Göppingen: Kümmerle, 1988), pp. 142–60.

[9] Saul Nathaniel Brody, *The Disease of the Soul: Leprosy in Medieval Literature* (Ithaca and London: Cornell University Press, 1974); see especially chapter IV; the quotation is on p. 146. Meinolf Schumacher, *Sündenschmutz und Herzensreinheit: Studien zur Metaphorik der Sünde in lateinischer und deutscher Literatur des Mittelalters* (Munich: Fink, 1996). In his study of one of the texts to be discussed in this chapter, David Duckworth looks at the specific sins associated with what he refers to as 'spiritual leprosy', *The Leper and the Maiden in Hartmann's Der arme Heinrich* (Göppingen: Kümmerle, 1996).

symptom – used to be clear and beautiful in her courtly singing.[10] In the Occitan Arthurian romance of *Jaufré* we get a slightly longer and particularly horrible description of a leper,[11] again including some genuine symptoms, but that, too, is part of a contrastive picture, since the leper in question has captured an especially beautiful girl, and the anonymous late twelfth-century poet is aiming at a beauty-and-the-beast effect. A leper in *Jaufré* also collects the blood of children so that it can be used as a medicine.[12]

There are several medieval literary texts that develop in more detail the literalisation of Langland's allegory, that the blood of an innocent can cure leprosy. Even in literature, however, the cure is, for a variety of reasons, very rarely put into practice; and on the rare occasions when it *is* used, it is usually countered by a miracle. Indeed, in those medieval works where leprosy plays a prominent role, its cure is rarely the real issue; the implicit or explicit soteriology of the cure is of greater importance.

Medieval narratives in which leprosy is cured by the death of another person though the use of their blood, then, are unusual. In the later prose stories of the search for the Holy Grail, in the *Queste del Saint Graal* and in Malory, Galahad, Bors and Percival come upon a castle in which a leprous girl can be cured by blood from a maiden who is a virgin both in fact and in intent – that is, we may exclude child-murder, where the innocence is, at it were, accidental – and such a 'clene virgyne in wylle and in worke, and a kynges daughter' comes forward in the form of Percival's sister and does indeed sacrifice herself for the other maiden. Percival's sister is presented as a martyr, and there are aspects of this curious and brief episode in the lengthy Grail quest which will be of relevance later.[13] There is also a brief narrative in the *Gesta Romanorum* in which a girl is cured of leprosy by the royal blood of a king, who therefore gives his life for her. The victim there is not an innocent, but the regality provides equal support for a soteriological reading. These are very rare cases, however.

---

[10] Robert Henryson, *The Testament of Cresseid*, ed. Denton Fox (London: Nelson, 1968), vv. 394–6 and 443–5. See Fox's introduction and also Gray, *Henryson*, p. 194 n. 67 for medical references. In 1961 Sanford V. Larkey offered Henryson's description of Cresseid to medical historians: 'Leprosy in Medieval Romance', *Bulletin of the History of Medicine* 35 (1961), 77–80. There is a wealth of material in Peter Richards, *The Medieval Leper and his Northern Heirs* (Cambridge: D. S. Brewer, 1977). See also Gretchen Mieszkowski, 'The Reputation of Criseyde', *Transactions of the Connecticut Academy of Arts and Sciences* 43 (1971), 71–153.

[11] Remy, 'La lèpre', pp. 203f cites the relevant passage from the Occitan romance, which is edited by C. Brunel, *Jaufré* (Paris: SATF, 1943), vv. 2312–33. The leprosy theme is incidental in the lengthy Arthurian romance. See Paul Remy, '*Jaufré*', in Loomis, *Arthurian Literature*, pp. 400–5.

[12] See in general Danielle Jacquart and Claude Thomasset, *Sexuality and Medicine in the Middle Ages* (Princeton: Princeton University Press, 1988). Sexual behaviour can seem to be both cause and effect with leprosy; the supposedly exaggerated lustfulness of lepers is indicated in *Jaufré* in the rape scene, and plays a slightly more complex role in the story of Tristan and Isolde, where in Béroul's version at least Yseult is thrown to the lepers to satisfy their lust. But Tristan also has to disguise himself as a leper in some versions, a symbol too of his role as an outcast from the social milieu because of his adulterous affair with the queen.

[13] See the translation by Matarasso of *The Quest of the Holy Grail*, pp. 249f and the edition by Vinaver of Malory, II, 1002f (Book VII = Caxton's XVII, 11); see also the convenient Everyman edition of *Le Morte d'Arthur of Sir Thomas Malory* (London and Toronto: Dent, 1906), II, 253. The hero manages to prevent a literal bloodbath in *Jaufré*, and the motif is not there in the *Testament of Cresseid*.

The first group of works in which innocent blood cures leprosy in a clearly miraculous context but without (ultimately) the death of the innocent is the very widespread story of *Amicus and Amelius*, which is, as might be guessed from the first name, a friendship story. In fact the names vary somewhat, and occasionally are replaced altogether – in a German version by Konrad von Würzburg the two friends are renamed Engelhard and Dietrich, for example – but the outline of what has been described as a 'self-consciously confusing plot' remains pretty well constant.[14] The story has been linked on the one hand with medieval tales of friendship without the leprosy element, and on the other with the very different tale of Constantine, where there is no question of any friendship motif. The connexions with the former group of narratives are far stronger, and the leprosy-motif in the *Amicus and Amelius* group of stories is very much secondary to the main theme of the tale, although there are elements in it that can be related to the soteriological presentations of the disease and its literary cure.

The *Amicus and Amelius* narrative – there are approaching forty distinct versions in a variety of languages, but we may keep the Latin names – displays in its various forms a greater or lesser religious tone, sometimes even making the two principal protagonists into saints. Indeed, a distinction has been made and is frequently cited, between 'romantic' and 'hagiographic' versions. The story is known in Latin prose and verse, and indeed the earliest known version is a metrical summary by Radulfus Tortarius of Fleury from the late eleventh century. It became widespread in the thirteenth century through the much-translated *Speculum Historiale* of Vincent of Beauvais, and then later still through the tales of the *Seven Sages of Rome*, where the names are again different. In English we have a long strophic romance, in French a *chanson de geste*, other verse and prose texts and finally a miracle play, plus a poem in Anglo-Norman; German, Italian, Dutch and Icelandic metrical and prose texts exist, and a version in Welsh prose in the *Red Book of Hergest*.[15]

Amicus and Amelius are close friends from birth and virtually identical to look at. Amicus is (falsely) challenged to a fight to save the honour of a lady; Amelius

---

[14] Thus the entry on the French *chanson de geste*, *Ami et Amile* in the *New Oxford Companion to Literature in French*, ed. Peter France (Oxford: Clarendon, 1995).

[15] Leach, *Amis and Amiloun* has a lengthy introduction in which he distinguishes between the romantic and the hagiographic versions; that introduction has to be used with caution, since it is not without error. However, he lists seven 'romantic' and no fewer than twenty-seven 'hagiographic' versions, all with bibliographic details, pp. ix–xiv. Leach does not mention Konrad von Würzburg's *Engelhard*, though he seems to know it, though he confuses it with Hartmann's *Der arme Heinrich*, to which he refers, but with which he is very clearly unfamiliar. It would be no inconsiderable task to catalogue all the various text editions, some of which are tucked away in appendices to other editions. Line references to the Middle English text are to this edition. Brody, *Disease*, discusses many of the texts, and there is a very useful earlier edition by Eugen Kölbing, *Amis and Amiloun* (Heilbronn: Henninger, 1884), which includes the Anglo-Norman poem (in different versions), Latin prose and verse texts, and an Icelandic strophic version. For further texts and congeners, see Mary Brockington, 'Tristan and Amelius: False and True Repentance', *Modern Language Review* 93 (1998), 305–20. Leach's text is based on that in the fourteenth-century Auchinleck manuscript, which contains both *Gregorius* and the metrical *Life of Adam* in English, but versions in other manuscripts vary considerably. See on the story A. K. Krappe, 'The Legend of Amicus and Amelius', *Modern Language Review* 18 (1923), 152–61.

leaves his own wife to stand in for him, and wins the battle. But he has had to swear an oath that he has never made advances to the lady (which is technically true, since he is not the person he is taken to be), but he also has to pretend (in some cases actually to go through with a) marriage to the lady. Amicus then replaces him, and has two children. But Amelius had been warned by a voice that if he went through with the deceit he would be punished with leprosy after three years. This happens, and his own wife drives him away. Eventually he is told by doctors that the sole cure is the blood of innocent children. After a dream in which an angel tells Amicus that his children's blood can effect the cure, Amicus agrees to this, usually against the wishes of his friend and anguished both at the idea of killing the children and at the acquisition of sin. Their friendship is stronger than the children, who are duly killed so that their blood can cure Amelius. However, in all the versions the children are miraculously brought back to life. The point of the extremely well known story is not really the cure as such, but the testing of the friendship. The actual killing of the children is treated curiously lightly, and it is clear that this is not a realistic motif. In the English version, for example, an angel tells Amis (the equivalent of Amicus) to kill the children on Christmas morning – the soteriological connexion is already there – and, as Brody has pointed out, there is no indication from the angel that Amis (any more than Abraham in the parallel biblical story) would be committing a sin, although he himself is predictably appalled by the idea. His wife is, on the other hand, surprisingly unconcerned:

'O lef liif' she seyd þo
'God may sende us childer mo' (2392–3)[16]

That line will be used again as an argument from outside in a rather different work. In the French *Chanson de geste*, even the children agree, and their awareness of their own innocence as something that will take them to Paradise will also reappear with a rather different resonance later:

'Biax tres douz peres', dist l'anfes erramment,
'Quant vos compains avra garissement
Se de nos sans a sor soi lavement,
Noz sommez vostre, de vostre engenrement,
Faire en poéz del tout a vo talent.
Or noz copéz les chiés isnellement,
Car Dex de gloire noz avra en present
En Paradis en irommez chantant
Et proierommez Jhesu, cui tout apent
Que dou pechié voz face tensement . . .'[17]

('Most sweet father', said the child firmly, 'since your friend

---

[16] On the passage and on the didactic nature of the English text in general, see W. R. J. Barron, *English Medieval Romance* (London: Longman, 1987), p. 202.

[17] *Ami et Amile: Chanson de geste*, ed. Peter F. Dembowski (Paris: Champion, 1969), *laisse* 154, vv. 3000–6. There is a translation into modern French by Joël Blanchard and Michel Quereuil, *Ami et Amile* (Paris: Champion, 1987).

will be cured by bathing in our blood, we are yours, born of you,
do what you can, cut off our heads quickly, for God will take us,
and we shall go singing to Paradise, and pray to Jesus, who
knows all, that He may ease your sin . . .')

Once again the message has come from an angel 'que m'envoia Jhesus de majesté'
(2900) (sent by Jesus in His majesty), but the anguish is still present, even though
the compliant child promises to pray in Paradise for forgiveness for the pair. The
pathos of the section is clear, and the father is racked with *moult grans pitiés* (3013)
until the children are restored a very short while later. The miracle is rapid in most
versions, to mitigate the element of horror.

The different literary possibilities of the situation are exploited in various ways.
In Vincent of Beauvais, for example, the reluctance of the friend to ask for this
impossible cure is stressed, and that, too, will become a key theme in other leprosy
stories. That God does restore the children so swiftly, however, makes their killing
more of a test of friendship or of loyalty, a fulfilled reflection of the would-be sacrifice of Isaac, one of the more difficult stories of Genesis, and one that also becomes
a type of the Crucifixion.[18] The concluding comments of Radulfus's Latin version
explain that the restoration of the children demonstrates *tanta fides purae prestat
amicitiae*, how great was the loyalty of this pure friendship.[19] The distinction
between what Leach called the romantic and hagiographic versions is not always
as clear-cut as he implies,[20] but the full title of the French dramatisation, which is
one of the later versions of the story, is significant: here the story is placed into a
cycle of Marian miracles, since she restores the infants to life:

Un miracle de Nostre Dame d'Ami et d'Amille, lequel Amille tua ses deux
enfans pour gairir Amis son compaignon, qui estoit mesel: et depuis les
resuscita Nostre Dame.[21]

(A miracle of Our Lady about Ami and Amille, in which Amille killed his
two children to cure Ami his friend who had leprosy; and then they were
revived by Our Lady.)

The leprosy cure is, in effect, added onto the friendship story in this case, and
serves primarily to indicate the miraculous powers of God. Thus in Konrad von
Würzburg's *Engelhard* the whole leprosy incident comes very close to the end of
the work, while the restoration of the children is repeatedly stressed as a miracle
performed by Christ. 'Nû prüevet grôzez wunder . . .', says the narrator, almost as
soon as the blood has been used – 'Now here's a miracle!' It is interesting that the

[18] The point is developed very clearly by Timothy R. Jackson in a highly relevant brief paper, which
takes account of the Fall parallels too in *Gregorius* and *Parzival*, at least *en passant*, in the context of
the *felix culpa*: 'Abraham and Engelhard: Immoral Means and Moral Ends', in *Connections: Essays in
Honour of Eda Sagarra*, ed. Peter Skrine et al. (Stuttgart: Heinz, 1993), pp. 117–26.
[19] Leach, *Amis and Amiloun*, p. xxix, citing Radulfus of Fleury, whose version he gives in translation,
pp. 101–5.
[20] So too Brody, *Disease*, p. 173.
[21] *Miracles de Nostre Dame*, ed. Gaston Paris and Ulysse Robert (Paris: Didot, 1876–93), IV (1979),
1–67 (= Play XXII).

two friends are, after the cure, 'beide trûric unde frô' (both happy and sad), the same juxtaposition of emotions that the Easter story imposes on characters in medieval narratives.[22]

The first clear link between the leprosy cure and the full pattern of sin and Redemption comes not in one of the friendship tales, however, but in the case of an emperor, Constantine, who can afford to command the best cure possible. Leprosy is an *extreme* disease, and in the case of the emperor's affliction the whole case is an extreme one; and yet once again the situations with which we are presented in literature are intended to have a general validity, underlining the human condition in a memorable manner.

Constantine the Great was a real emperor, and the saint who effects his miraculous cure from leprosy, Silvester I, was, unlike Gregorius, for example, a perfectly genuine fourth-century pope. Their relationship to one another was, however, developed through the Middle Ages in a fanciful *vita* for the saint according to which it was the curing of Constantine's leprosy by Silvester that brought Christianity to the Roman empire and, indeed, put Constantine much more firmly into the debt of the Church, rather than his independent vision at the Milvian Bridge, the story known to us through Eusebius and others. Links have been made to the legend of Abgar of Edessa, supposedly cured of leprosy (or occasionally of the more prosaic gout) by baptism, but the *Vita Silvestri*, found independently in a number of Latin versions, had a far-reaching influence.[23] It was much used in the Byzantine chronicles of the eleventh to the thirteenth centuries, and in the west the lengthy entry on Silvester in the seventh-century papal chronicle, the *Liber pontificalis*, begins with a brief reference to the saint's exile, his return in glory, and his baptism of the emperor, whom Christ then cured of leprosy. The bulk of the entry records a large number of gifts to the Church during Silvester's pontificate, amongst them the font, made of porphyry and completely encased in silver, in which Constantine was baptized; it is described as being embellished with a picture of John the Baptist and carrying as an inscription the words of the *Agnus Dei*.[24] The words *qui tollis peccata mundi* (who taketh away the sins of the world)

---

[22] Konrad von Würzburg, *Engelhard*, ed. Paul Gereke, 3rd edn Ingo Reiffenstein (Tübingen: Niemeyer, 1982). The edition also includes a late medieval German prose text of the Amicus and Amelius story. Lines cited are 6375 and 6355 respectively. On the use of leprosy as a punishment (and on the comparison with Job, which points always to testing) see Peter Kesting, '*Diu rehte warheit*: zu Konrads von Würzburg *Engelhard*', *Zeitschrift für deutsches Altertum* 99 (1970), 246–59.

[23] For a brief and admirably clear summary of the background of the Silvester story, see Timothy R. Jackson, *The Legends of Konrad von Würzburg* (Erlangen: Palm und Enke, 1983), pp. 29–31, as well as the earlier study of the sources of the German *Kaiserchronik* by Ernst Friedrich Ohly, *Sage und Legende in der Kaiserchronik* (Münster i. W., 1940, repr. Darmstadt: WBG, 1968), pp. 165–71. See the earlier work by G. Prochnow, 'Mittelhochdeutsche Silvesterlegenden und ihre Quellen', *Zeitschrift für deutsche Philologie* 33 (1901), 145–212. Ohly provides a large number of additional references to primary and secondary sources.

[24] See the translation by Raymond Davis, *The Book of Pontiffs* (Liverpool: Liverpool University Press, 1989), pp. 14–26. The original may be found in Theodor Mommsen's edition for the *Monumenta Germaniae Historica* of the first (and only) part of the *Gestorum Pontificum Romanorum I: Liber pontificalis* (Berlin, 1898). There is also a text in *PL* 127–8. The Sylvester entry with the cure of Constantine from leprosy speaks of the joint consulship of Constantine and Volusianus; it may be noted that there is a separate legend of Tiberius being cured of leprosy by the vernicle, with Volusianus

109

on the font are thus set against the *in hoc signo vinces* (in this sign shalt thou conquer) on the labarum. More important still was the inclusion of this leprosy story in the so-called *Donation of Constantine*, a celebrated and historically important forgery of the eighth or ninth century, from which we may epitomise the legend.[25] According to the *Donation* (which was exposed as a fraud in 1440 by the Humanist Lorenzo Valla), Constantine, having voluntarily rejected a proposed cure involving the blood of children after an appeal from their mothers, was sent a dream of Saints Peter and Paul by Christ. Silvester, who had been in hiding on Mount Serapte (or Syraptim or Soracte), is summoned, and he baptizes and heals the emperor, converting his empire with him. Constantine himself then leads Silvester to the papal palace and confers on him the primacy over other bishops, and establishes a tithe for the Church. A rather splendid thirteenth-century fresco in the oratory of the Church of the Four Crowned Martyrs in Rome shows the emperor leading the saint into the city; the pope is riding, the emperor is on foot.[26] The supposed donation was exploited politically as if it were historical by Leo IX as early as 1054.

The *vita* of Saint Silvester contains other elements: there are details of his early life, and after the conversion he not only deals with a dragon, but disputes with twelve learned Jews on the nature of Christianity, defeating them by argument and indeed ultimately by another miracle. However, the curing of the leprosy and the baptism belong as much to the legend of Constantine as of Silvester, whose role in that part of the story is paradigmatic for a saint's life, namely the imitation of an act of Christ. Other saints, such as Crescentia, heal lepers, but here the emperor's change of heart takes centre stage. The part played by baptism is also important. Other acts of Silvester's are more individual, but in the leprosy story, the saint functions simply as an intermediary between the emperor and Christ, and the sickness and healing of the emperor, and thus of the whole empire, can be viewed as a soteriological paradigm as well as an historical event. There are links between this story and that of Amicus and Amelius, but other influences come into play, too, including Herod's massacre of the children, and the liturgical proximity of the feast of the Holy Innocents to that of St Silvester is also material.

The story of Constantine's cure is just as widespread as the story of Amicus and Amelius. Beside the Latin texts and the Byzantine chronicles there are early metrical versions of the story in French and in German. It is included in a lengthy chronicle of emperors and popes called the *Kaiserchronik*, the *Imperial Chronicle*, with an independent text, the Trier *Silvester*, based upon it, and the tale crops up later in other German chronicles. The primary disseminator in the later Middle

as a mediator. That legend, associated with the death of Pilate, also comes into vernacular literature: see my 'The *Mors Pilati* in the Cornish *Resurrexio Domini*', *Celtica* 23 (1999), 211–26.

[25] See H. Grauert, 'Die konstantinische Schenkung', *Historisches Jahrbuch* 3 (1882), 3–30 and H. Fuhrmann, 'Konstantinische Schenkung und Silvesterlegende in neuer Sicht', *Deutsches Archiv für Erforschung des Mittelalters* 15 (1959), 523–40. There is an abridged translation in Bettenson, *Documents of the Christian Church*, pp. 135–40. Lorenzo Valla's *De falso credita et ementita Constantini Donatione declamatio* was an important attack on the papacy.

[26] Maria Giulia Barberini, *I Santi Quattro Coronati a Roma* (Rome: Palombi, 1989). Some of the pictures are included in Ainaud, *Romanesque Painting*, plates 30–3. There are other iconographical representations, some of them from the tenth century. Of course, there are also paintings of the alternative story of Constantine's conversion.

Ages, though, was James of Voragine, archbishop of Genoa in the thirteenth century, whose *Legenda Aurea* was translated or adapted into a number of European languages in a variety of forms; relevant texts of our legend include direct versions in prose or verse in various vernaculars, a poem by Konrad von Würzburg in the thirteenth century, sermons such as that of John Mirk – significantly for the feast of the Holy Innocents – in his *Festial*, and the exploitation of the story in broader-based works like John Gower's *Confessio Amantis* in English in the late fourteenth century. Both Mirk's and Gower's use of the *Golden Legend* on Silvester are of particular relevance, since both of them extract the leprosy narrative and isolate it to illustrate a point. Finally, the *Golden Legend* influenced the drama, and in this medium all the elements in the Silvester story (including the fight with the dragon) gained a visual impact even stronger than that in iconography. The two principal versions are plays in French and, less well known, in Cornish, although, to add a little extra confusion to the picture, an apparently promisingly titled fifteenth-century German *Spiel vom Kaiser Constantin* presents only Silvester's debate with the Jews, while Constantine merely looks on, presumably having been cured of leprosy well before the play started.[27]

In the narrative of the curing of Constantine various questions arise. The first, which is treated by different writers in different ways, is to do with the character of Constantine and why he is struck down with leprosy. The next stage is the proposal of the cure – involving the blood of up to three thousand innocent children in a clear parallel with the massacre of the innocents – and how Constantine prepares for it. Constantine is rich, and has power over life and death. A third point is Constantine's motivation in giving way to the misery of the mothers, and the nature of his dream, leading to the actual cure and the baptism of the emperor and indeed of his empire.

The *Donation of Constantine* purports to come from Constantine himself, so does not discuss the reasons for his leprosy, and mentions only that he was advised to have the blood of many children. The tears of the mothers move him, and he sends the children back, after which Christ sends the dream that will lead him to Silvester. Silvester imposes penance and then triple immersion (there is an echo of the sevenfold immersion of Naaman in IV Reg. 5), and he rises from the baptism cleansed of the leprosy. He also comes to understand the mystery of Christianity, and the other elements of the Donation as such follow. The parallel between the cleansing of sin by baptism and the removal of leprosy is implicit throughout; the leprosy is seen as a filth that can literally be washed away, not by the blood of the innocent children, but by the water of baptism, something to which the emperor could only be directed after he had shown the virtue of charity.

Even the earliest vernacular adaptations develop individual elements. That in the German *Kaiserchronik*[28] is brief, but the emperor is presented in a positive

---

27 The play is no. 106 in Adelbert von Keller's collection of *Fastnachtspiele aus dem 15. Jahrhundert* (Tübingen: Stuttgarter lit. Verein, 1853, repr. Darmstadt: WBG, 1965). See David Brett-Evans, *Von Hrotsvit bis Folz und Gengenbach* (Berlin: Schmidt, 1975), II, 16–18.
28 The text cited is that of Eduard Schröder, *Die Kaiserchronik eines Regensburger Geistlichen* (Hanover: Monumenta Germaniae Historica, 1892), cited by line number. That edition takes account of the independent poem from Trier which derives from it, ed. M. Roediger, 'Trierer Bruchstücke III:

light, even though he is not a Christian, and the sickness, whilst making him repulsive to all men, is not seen expressly as a punishment. He is advised to take the
blood of children, and the parallel with Herod and the innocents in Matthew 2:16 is
made clear in that these have to be under two years of age. Moved by the mothers,
Constantine undergoes a change of heart: 'ich enwil diu kindelîn niht haizen
slahen' (7833) (I will not have these little children killed). The dream comes to
him, but there is no reference to his having banished Silvester, even though when
the latter is sent for he thinks that he is going to be martyred. His discussion with
Constantine, however, is very clearly soteriological – the word *arzat* (doctor)
appears repeatedly – and the pope first of all protests that he is not a doctor, or at
least has never practised *werltlîche erzenîe* (7894) (worldly medicine), a significant distinction. Hearing of the dream, he realises that he can indeed heal Constantine, and after the threefold immersion the emperor is cured. The equation of the
leprosy (which is never really described) with the sinfulness of heathendom is
made very clear in the description of the scene:

> Als [Constantine] ûz der toufe gie,
> die hût im elliu ab viel,
> jâ wart im der lîp sîn
> als ein niwe gebornez chindelîn;
> er wart hail und gesunt.
> er rief an der stunt
> daz got von himel waere
> ain wârer hailaere.   (7944–51)

(When Constantine rose from the baptism all his skin fell off,
and his body became like that of a new born child, and he was
healed and healthy. He cried out at once that God in heaven is a
true healer.)

The play on 'saviour' and 'healer' is present in German, and in this version the
leprosy is functional rather than realistic. Instead of killing little children, the
emperor has become as one, and Constantine *sub gratia* has not out-Heroded but
de-Heroded Herod. In one of the few criticisms of the emperor in the text we are
then told that the erstwhile wolf became a sheep, and that Rome had to relinquish
its false gods. As in the *Donation*, of course, the grateful emperor takes Silvester
by the hand and grants him great powers; indeed, here we are told how the pope
takes up the role of priest and formally crowns Constantine.

The *Legenda Aurea* stabilises the story.[29] James of Voragine's narrative for 31

Silvester', *Zeitschrift für deutsches Altertum* 22 (1878), 145–209. Jansen Enikel's *Weltchronik*, ed.
Strauch, also contains the story of the leprosy cure (with another tale of Constantine) in lines
25129–520. There is an early French text (twelfth-century) edited by Paul Meyer, 'La vie de Saint
Silvestre en vers français', *Romania* 28 (1899), 280–6.

[29] *Jacobi a Voragine Legenda Aurea*, ed. Theodor Graesse (Leipzig, 2nd edn 1850, repr. Osnabrück:
Zeller, 1969), pp. 70–9. The most celebrated English version is that by Caxton, which has been much
reprinted. See the modern translation by William Granger Ryan, *The Golden Legend of Jacobus de
Voragine* (New York: Arno, 1969), pp. 72–82.

December is concise: Constantine persecutes the Christians and for this he is punished. Three thousand children are required for the bloodbath, but the spectacle of the mothers makes him relent, with a splendid rhetorical speech about the virtue of pity and the fact that Rome cannot be seen to be so barbarian. After the dream, Silvester is sent for and again he fears martyrdom, but instead baptizes the emperor after imposing a fast of seven days. Constantine declares that whilst being baptized he has seen Christ, a conflation with Eusebius's story of the vision of the Cross.[30]

Of the various continental versions of the Silvester story adapted from the *Golden Legend*, one of the fullest is the German poem by Konrad von Würzburg (who had also treated the Amicus story, which he clearly perceived as rather different, in his *Engelhard*).[31] The Constantine episode takes up only a part of the narrative, and the emperor is presented several times as *der rîche keiser* (the rich emperor), who nevertheless persecutes the Christians, and it is again for this that God exacts a revenge upon him:

> des kêrte zuo dem mâle
> got ûf in diu râche sîn.
> er tet an im vil harte schîn
> daz er ie was gewaltec
> und daz vil manecvaltec
> ist sîn êre und sîn genuht.
> er sluoc in mit der miselsucht . . .   (890–7)

(For that, God turned His vengeance upon him, and made him a severe illustration of how powerful He is, and how his works are manifold. He struck him down with leprosy.)

The possible cure is dwelt upon in great detail. A bath, a *piscine*, is to be filled with the blood of children, and Constantine calls for again three thousand innocent children – words like *rein* (pure) and *schuldelôs* (innocent) are used of them repeatedly – to be brought to Rome. The mothers of the children weep and tear their garments, and Konrad stresses, perhaps slightly oddly, that their naked beauty strikes Constantine. Told who they are, he undergoes a change of heart quite literally, as 'er erschrac in sînem herzen' (1015) (he shuddered in his heart) and realises that if he has the children killed, he will 'so mange schulde tragen . . . vor gotes ougen' (1025) (carry such guilt in the eyes of God). It is an unusual comment for a pagan, but in this version he has effectively already come to acknowledge God. He weeps for the children – a sign of contrition – and gives his new commands in God's name. If he has the children killed he will lose all hope of salvation and will die eternally. The vocabulary and the tone are entirely Christian, and now he is described not only as the rich but also as the virtuous emperor. In the dream of

---

[30] *Life of Constantine*, i. 28f. The passage is frequently cited and translated: see Henry Melvill Gwatkin, *Selections from Early Christian Writers* (London: Macmillan, 1902). There Constantine also has a dream, of course, leading to the conversion.

[31] Konrad von Würzburg, *Die Legenden I.*, ed. Paul Gereke (Halle/Saale: Niemeyer, 1925). Other German versions (there are several) based on the *Golden Legend* include the text of the rhymed *Passional*, which was put into prose in the fifteenth-century *Der Heiligen Leben*.

Peter and Paul he is told quite specifically that Silvester will baptize him, or rather, that Silvester will explain *die piscînen/ der gotheit* (1508f) (the baths of divinity). The surface fact of curing the leprosy is already firmly linked with the spiritual cleansing, and this is developed when Silvester, after his initial fear that Constantine wishes to have him killed, finally meets the emperor. He instructs him in the faith, continuing the motif of the *piscîne*, and explaining that

> der touf ist ein piscîne,
> die vröude und ein gesundez leben
> lîb und der sêle mac gegeben.   (1534–6)

(baptism is a bath that can give body and soul joy and a healthy life.)

Constantine is instructed to put aside his imperial garments as these are a sign of sin, to fast, and then to undergo baptism. Konrad stresses the general importance of all this throughout the passage:

> got aleine si
> gewaltic und gewârhaft,
> der einem wazzer gît die kraft
> daz ez die sêle reinet
> und dem lîbe erscheinet
> vil guoter arzenie . . .   (1604–9)

(God alone is powerful and good enough to give water such potency that it can purify the soul and appear to the body as good medicine.)

We may note that the implications of baptism have taken precedence over the cure for leprosy and that, as far as any realism is concerned, the actual leprosy is indeed curable only by God. Konrad does not describe the disease in any case. The strength of the water of baptism is later on generalised as a remedy for any misfortunes, and Constantine is healed *von süntlichem meine* (1721) (from the spotting of sin). This narrative is about the baptism of the sinner, the formal placing under grace of fallen man, and the liturgical and soteriological tone is unmistakable.

Two English versions of the story, a century later than Konrad, concentrate on Constantine almost to the exclusion of any real role for Silvester. John Mirk's *Festial*, a collection of sermons written perhaps around or just before 1400, includes in the sermon for Holy Innocents what he calls an example which he found in the life of Saint Silvester. He has in fact just told the tale of the Innocents, explaining that their death implied a baptism to be equated with baptism by water; he adds that Herod afterwards committed suicide by stabbing himself and thus shed his own blood. This leads the Shropshire prior at once to the story of Constantine as a direct contrast, since the latter *did* show mercy. The story is told in the barest outlines, which in itself makes clear that the basic pattern of sin–mercy–baptism–salvation is the essence of the narrative. The wailing of the mothers leads Constantine to consider that he is just one man but that many of the children may become worthy men in the future. His next comment is of interest,

114

however: he becomes aware that his leprosy is a punishment, though Mirk does not tell us what for:

'Nay!' quod he, 'I woll not so, let hom goo hom aȝayn, and I wyll take þe penaunce þat ye ordeynet for me.'

Presumably it is God who has ordained leprosy as a penance, for He now sends the dream. There is no reference to the persecution of Silvester, who is barely mentioned here, but the saint does baptize the emperor, whom God heals because he showed compassion towards the children. In the water of baptism – the contrast between the supposed bath of blood and that in the water is not exploited – the leprosy falls from him and he again becomes as clean as any of the children *þat he delyuerd before.*[32] Constantine, having first become aware of God's penance, then becomes an innocent himself, and often there is a reluctance to vilify the emperor even before his conversion.

John Gower, writing at roughly the same time as Mirk, uses the Constantine story as an example of charity at the end of the second book of the *Confessio Amantis* as a counter to the discussion of envy. He tells the story in only about 400 lines, but several elements are of interest.[33] Constantine is introduced to us as 'the worthi Emperour of Rome', and is struck down with leprosy in his prime, 'whan he was in his lusti age', although we are again not told why. The blood of children is again prescribed, the English text specifying that they should this time be under seven. The Latin marginal summary refers to male children, bringing it closer to the narrative of the Innocents. Hearing the mothers, and on this occasion also the children, crying, Constantine undergoes a change of heart 'as if he had awoken from a sleep', and addresses the *divine pourveance* which has ordered all things, saying that no one should try to avoid what nature has imposed upon them. After a discourse on providence which is both worthy and relatively lengthy, he sends the children home and – as in other versions, too – gives them great gifts into the bargain, from his own treasury. Gower then adopts a device not unlike that of Konrad in his *Engelhard*, by marking a somewhat abrupt peripeteia: 'But now hierafter thou schalt hiere', he says, 'What God hath wroght in this matiere . . .' (II, 3325). Only after the dream and the arrival of Silvester do we hear that the emperor, whose stoical speech came close to Christianity, has been in the past an enemy of the Christians. Silvester now begins

> with al his wit
> To techen upon holi writ,
> Ferst how mankinde was forlore,
> And how the hihe god therefore
> His Sone sende from above . . .   (II, 3385–9)

---

[32] *Mirk's Festial: a Collection of Homilies, I,* ed. Theodor Erbe (London: Kegan Paul, Trench, 1905 = EETS/ES 96), pp. 36f. John Mirk (Myrk, Myrc etc.) was prior of the canons regular of Lilleshall in Shropshire. The details of the three thousand children indicate knowledge of the *Golden Legend* version, though the retelling is very brief.

[33] *The English Works of John Gower,* ed. G. C. Macaulay (London: Oxford University Press, 1900–2, repr. 1957 = EETS/OS 81–2), I, 214–25, lines 3174–530.

What we have in those few lines is a highly compressed *summa theologiae*, making very clear the parallels between the salvation story and the idea of baptism. The actual act of baptism is made much of: the vessel that had been prepared for the blood is again, as it was in Konrad, used for water, a light shines as the emperor is immersed, and his leprosy falls away like fish scales until body and soul are cleansed. The implications are quite clear in Gower.

Two plays present the story in visual form. The fifteenth-century *Miracle de Saint Sevestre* does so fairly briefly, showing first the exiled Silvester in hiding from Constantine, then the leprous emperor – he simply tells us that this is the case – is informed that the blood of 'biaucop d'enfans petiz' (139) (many small children) will cure him. Much of the action which now follows shows the taking of the children and the objections of their parents, an action that is dealt with in rather greater detail, of course, in plays of the Holy Innocents in the English cycles or in such lively and rather different works as the Digby Herod-play.[34] The appeal of one of the mothers arouses the pity of the emperor, however, who once again condemns this proposed barbarism in a lengthy speech. God Himself appears in the work, sending the two saints quite literally to the emperor, who in turn sends for Silvester. Again terrified at first, Silvester explains that Saints Peter and Paul are not themselves gods, but instructs Constantine in the basic tenets of the faith. Here again the work is essentially about the baptism of the emperor and his nation, and apart from a reference once more to the cure of Naaman, the actual leprosy motif plays a very small role.[35]

In England the story was dramatised at about the same time in Cornish, as part of the only non-biblical saint's play known in medieval England. The two-day drama cycle from Camborne, *Beunans Meriasek*, the life of the Breton saint Mereadoc, who had a Cornish cult as Meriasek, interweaves scenes from the life of the barely known Meriasek with parallel scenes from that of Silvester and indeed with another legend of the Virgin.[36] Two Silvester episodes appear, the second being his fight with the dragon, but the Constantine story is also told. In this case, the emperor is shown initially as a monster, egging his soldiers on to murder the Christians. He is shown as a standard medieval pagan – this is unusual, but makes his conversion even clearer, of course – worshipping Mahound (Mohammed), Jove and Apollo, the usual curious mixture of Islamic and Roman beliefs. Medieval Cornish drama, which was performed in an open-air playing-place like an amphitheatre, often indulges in vigorous scenes with bullying soldiers and torturers, and again the parallels are with works like the Digby Herod-play.

---

[34] *The Digby Plays*, ed. F. J. Furnivall (London: Oxford University Press, 1896 = EETS/ES 70), pp. 1–23. The play is distinguished by the bragging of Watkyn and is rather different from those in, say, the Chester or Townely cycles.

[35] Paris and Robert, *Miracles de Nostre Dame*, play no. 20, vol. III (1878), pp. 187–240.

[36] The best edition (with a translation) is by Myrna Combellack-Harris, 'A Critical Edition of Beunans Meriasek' (Ph.D. Diss., Exeter, 1985). I cite the older, but accessible, edition by Whitley Stokes, *The Life of St Meriasek* (London: Trübner, 1872). There is a prose translation by Markham Harris, *The Life of Meriasek* (Washington: Catholic University of America Press, 1978) and one into verse by Myrna Combellack, *The Camborne Play* (Redruth: Truran, 1988). The latter separates the various parts of the play into sections, and the Silvester passages may easily be located. The unity of the play depends upon the interlinking of themes, however. I have discussed this in detail in *Cornish Literature* (Cambridge: D. S. Brewer, 1993), pp. 99–126.

But Constantine is struck with leprosy. The text we have is a prompt-copy, and the stage directions are in English, so that we know there was 'a vysour aredy apon Constantyn ys face'. At once he becomes aware of the reason for his disfigurement, that he was overly cruel to the Christians. Nevertheless, he turns to his pagan 'bishops' to cure him, and after much stage business involving urine samples and failed potions, the blood of three thousand babies is called for. He sends out his soldiers to gather up any children under three years, and there is again much play on the soldiers efforts and indeed on their relish. In *Beunans Meriasek*, the whole proceeding has a well drawn gradual effect on the emperor, who first expresses general unease with the situation in terms of kingly duty and Roman law about unlawful killing. In a kind of parodistic counter to the wife's comments in the English *Amis and Amiloun* that she can have more children, one of the torturers even comments that he will happily engender replacements. But Constantine relents, and the grateful mothers wish him health, something for which he offers his whole kingdom.

Christ sends the saints in a dream to tell him where Silvester can be found, and penance and baptism follow on stage, with Constantine visibly made clean ('ye vysour away'). The notion that Constantine actually sees Christ is realised here, as Christ himself explains on stage that it is on account of his pity for the children that he is healed. The notion of penance also comes to the fore:

> Penys purguir yv ov luyst
> ha creya pup vr war crist
>   mercy rag ov fehosov
> then guan ha tus omthevas
> in dewelyans am pehas
>   manneff ry alesonov   (1824–9)

> (To do penance is all I want, and to call on Christ at all times for mercy for my sins. To the weak and to orphans, in atonement for my sins, I shall give alms.)

The link with the massacre of the innocents by Herod is not quite typological, but an event which took place at least before the sacrifice of Christ has been reworked in this story in a positive manner. Constantine is struck down with leprosy as a punishment, the hope of a cure by the blood of the innocents tests him, and he is saved in fact by his acts, first of charity, and then of submission to the divine will. The cure has not been invoked, and since Constantine and his empire are in historical terms under the grace, there was no need in any case of a second massacre.

We have come a stage further in our progression. In *Jaufré* we heard simply of children being used to provide the innocent blood that will cure lepers. Sir Perceval's sister was perceived as a martyr, laying down her life for another as a kind of *imitatio*. In the friendship story of *Amicus and Amelius*, the children are also actually killed for the sake of their blood but are restored by a miracle. In Constantine's story, the sacrifice was averted and baptism replaced it, and so the shedding of blood was unnecessary even on a temporary basis. The ongoing paradox is, of course, that leprosy, since as a disease it was until recently quite untreatable, can

117

only function as an allegory of sin. It betokens usually a broad sinfulness which can only be cured by grace. The actually ineffectual bath of blood is therefore replaced with baptism, because the innocent blood has already been shed by Christ.

All this is taken a stage further in a final text, another work by the author of the German *Gregorius*, the late twelfth-century writer Hartmann von Aue. His short verse novella, *Der arme Heinrich* (Heinrich the Unfortunate), was admired both by Dante Gabriel Rossetti and by Longfellow, and it has been imitated by various modern German writers as well.[37] Although there are few extant manuscripts of the work, it was certainly well known, well enough for the name of the hero to be attached (more or less gratuitously) to a Latin charm against the plague written down in the first decade of the sixteenth century as *Pauperis Heinrici praeservativum ab epidemia*.[38] The story has also been linked with the Amicus and Amelius story (though less often with that of Constantine, to which it is far closer); McEdward Leach, in fact, in his introduction to the English *Amis and Amiloun* for the Early English Text Society, clearly forgot the advice of Martin Routh of Magdalen College, Oxford, to a young scholar: always verify your references. He gives a confident and detailed plot summary, allegedly of Hartmann's poem, but it is, alas, more or less that of Konrad's *Engelhard*. One suspects he looked at neither.[39] The point of Hartmann's brief exemplary work, however, is very simply to show that man, however good, can fall into sin, and that God can and will punish that sin. The allegorical sickness of sin is inevitable, but man has already been cured of the effects of sin, at least potentially, by the one person since Adam who was born without original sin. There has already been one sacrifice, one blood-letting, and there need not be another.

Hartmann's story is of a lord called Heinrich, who is presented as being both popular and rich and indeed idealised in all kinds of ways. Hartmann spends a good part of his opening building up the picture of the young lord as a figure admired by all the world for his accomplishments and indeed for his good deeds. The admira-

---

[37] The most recent standard text is that edited by Gärtner, *Hartmann von Aue, Der arme Heinrich*, and see the English translation in Fisher, *Hartmann von Aue*. For modern German texts (not always by major authors) based on the work, see Fred Wagner, 'Heinrich und die Folgen', in *German Narrative Literature of the Twelfth and Thirteenth Centuries: Studies Presented to Roy Wisbey*, ed. Volker Honemann et al. (Tübingen: Niemeyer, 1994), pp. 261–74. There is an enormous amount of secondary literature on the work, only a little of which can be mentioned here. For good general discussions, see H. Bernard Willson, 'Symbol and Reality in Der arme Heinrich', *Modern Language Review* 53 (1958), 526–36, and Leslie Seiffert, 'The Maiden's Heart', *Deutsche Vierteljahresschrift* 37 (1963), 384–405. Kurt Ruh presents an interesting comparison of the Amicus, Silvester and Grail stories with Hartmann's work, adumbrating a number of parallels without pursuing them in detail or indeed contrasting them: 'Hartmanns Armer Heinrich: Erzählmodell und theologische Implikation', in *Medievalia Litteraria: Festschrift für Helmut de Boor zum 80. Geburtstag*, ed. Ursula Hennig and Herbert Kolb (Munich: Beck, 1971), pp. 315–29.

[38] Gerhard Eis, 'Der Seuchenspruch des armen Heinrichs', *Forschungen und Fortschritte* 25 (1949), 10–12. 'Henry the Unfortunate's charm against plague.'

[39] Leach, *Amis and Amiloun*, pp. xlvii–xlviii. The connexion with Hartmann as such had been made, however, in the early nineteenth century: the modern German translation of *Der arme Heinrich* by Karl Simrock (Berlin: Laue, 1830) contains a translation of the Amicus story from Vincent de Beauvais, for example, pp. 60–76.

tion of the *world* is the crucial point, however, and the idea of worldliness is stressed as much as the goodness of the man. He is then struck down with leprosy, with a disease that precisely cuts him off from the world. His response is in the first instance that of Constantine – he seeks cures, confident that he can afford anything. However, a doctor tells him that he is both curable and incurable, and this is the key to the whole leprosy imagery. He needs innocent blood, this time from the heart of a virgin of marriageable age who is willing to die specifically for him. The point, expressed by the scientific doctor – who is not characterised, but beautifully drawn as the voice of worldly, but *only* of worldly, reason – is that this is completely impossible, *unless God decides to act as the doctor*, 'got enwelle der arzât wesen' (204). The proviso is a crucial one. Heinrich agrees that this is impossible, expressing it as an absolute, however, rather than referring it to himself. He thinks

> daz daz waere unmügelich,
> daz iemen den erwürbe
> der gerne vür in stürbe   (234–6)

> (that it would be impossible for anyone to find someone who would be willing to die for him.)

He becomes, the poet tells us, completely despondent, robbed of any comfort, like Job in the early stages, and allusions to Job continue throughout the work.

Heinrich withdraws to the estate of a yeoman farmer (who is not, incidentally, a peasant, as he is sometimes termed in English) who is a tenant of his, and here he encounters the young daughter – she is eight years old – of the farmer, who is the one person who does not shun him. We are told that she has been given a *süezer geist* (348) by God, a sweetness, *dulcedo*,[40] of spirit that makes Heinrich appear pure to her, and she simply does not recognise the disfigurement that he suffers. A close bond is forged between Heinrich and the little girl, and over the years Heinrich comes to realise the reason for his leprosy. It is a visible punishment for sin; he had succumbed to the pride of not acknowledging that all his good things came from God:

> 'ich hân den schämelîchen spot
> vil wol gedienet umbe got.
> . . .
> Daz herze mir dô alsô stuont,
> als alle welttôren tuont
> den daz raetet ir muot,
> daz si êre unde guot
> âne got mügen hân . . .'   (383–99)

> ('I thoroughly deserved this shameful mockery that God has put upon me . . . my heart was like that of all worldly fools, who think that they can gain esteem and belongings without God's help . . .')

---

[40] See Friedrich Ohly, *Süsse Nägel der Passion* (Baden-Baden: Loerner, 1989), on the use and semantics of *dulcis* in theological thought.

Accepting all the worldly benefits as if they were his of right, rather than acknowledging that they all came from God, is perhaps a sin of omission, but it is a serious one, and it is a sin of ignorance yet again, the ignorance that comes with original sin and is part of the human condition. In spite of the regular comparisons with Job (whose strength God is testing), Heinrich, although also – as we shall see – being tested by God, is clearly guilty, even though some critics have denied this, largely by confusing ignorance with innocence, and failing to notice both the doctrine of original sin and the distinction between what is known and what ought reasonably to be known.[41] At the other extreme it is regularly claimed that his sin is that of *superbia*, but even if the sin is as specific as that, it stems from the distancing from God that man's fallen state implies. Heinrich speaks of his *tumber wân* (400), his 'foolish thoughts', and refers to himself as a fool several times. The fool has again not denied but has ignored or failed to understand the workings of God. Heinrich achieves a partial understanding, but does not fully grasp the implications; rather, he has reached an awareness of sin without yet realising the possibility of salvation, and now desires (like Job) only that God send him a speedy end. But he now begins to learn about salvation. In brief, the girl, hearing of the sole and apparently impossible cure, decides to offer herself.

Hartmann's presentation of the would-be provider of the innocent blood combines the two types that we have seen already: she is a child when we first meet her, but reaches the age of knowledge and consent, so that she can make her decision rationally.[42] She is a virgin, and we are also told that, although the daughter of a farmer, she is beautiful enough to be the child of an emperor. Hartmann's unnamed girl has attracted a considerable amount of attention in critical writing, and one could easily list a whole sequence of contradictions: she is a passive victim not only of potential murder but also of voyeurism, for example, in some recent studies, whilst in others she is presented as a selfish adolescent, parroting the words of her elders and concerned only with gaining her own heavenly crown.[43] The more extreme views were set firmly aside in 1988 in a sensible paper by Martin Jones,[44] but what remains striking is the way in which those interpretations,

---

[41] See Ronald Finch, 'Guilt and Innocence in Hartmann's *Der arme Heinrich*', *Neuphilologische Mitteilungen* 73 (1972), 642–52 (on Heinrich and the girl), and also (stressing the *superbia*) Leslie Badanes, 'Heinrich's Leprosy: Punishment or Test?' *Modern Language Studies* 10 (1980), 88–92. Those who argue that Heinrich is not really guilty include Cormeau, '*Armer Heinrich*' *und* '*Gregorius*', R. Endres, 'Heinrichs *hôchvart*', *Euphorion* 61 (1967), 267–94 and R. D. Haage, 'Der "mystische Dreischritt" und der "Märchenschluß" im *Armen Heinrich*', *Leuvense Bijdragen* 73 (1984), 145–62. All are discussed and competently refuted by David Duckworth, 'Heinrich and the Godless Life in Hartmann's Poem', *Mediaevistik* 3 (1990), 71–90 (with references also to *Parzival* and *Gregorius*, but not to original sin). See also Duckworth's specific argument against Endres in 'Heinrich and the Knowledge of God', *Mediaevistik* 5 (1995), 57–70. There are elements of the fairy-story here too, in which self-immolation can also play a part.

[42] See H. B. Willson, ' "Marriageable" in *Der arme Heinrich*', *Modern Philology* 64 (1966), 95–102.

[43] Ernst Rose, 'Problems of Medieval Psychology as Presented in the 'klein gemahel' of Heinrich the Unfortunate', *Germanic Review* 22 (1947), 182–7 is a good example.

[44] 'Changing Perspectives on the Maiden in *Der arme Heinrich*', in *Hartmann von Aue, Changing Perspectives*, ed. T. McFarland and Silvia Ranawake (Göppingen: Kümmerle, 1988), pp. 211–31. Jones' article is probably the clearest view of the girl offered thus far.

certainly those more extreme ones, regularly ignore the evidence of the principal witness, Hartmann himself. Hartmann as narrator never names her (though she is characterised charmingly when a child), and this might well place her in a special position as a functional, rather than an actual, character.[45] Equally, however, not only does the narrator never criticise her, but every single statement that the narrator-voice makes about her is positive: she has an angelic nature, and the word is not used lightly: she shares in *der engel güete* (465) (angelic goodness).

The girl expresses first to her parents her willingness to die for Heinrich. She does this for three nights, washing her parents' feet with her tears and echoing thereby the Magdalen. The parents, not unnaturally, try to dissuade her. What stands out, however, is not the argumentation as such, but the way in which it is done. The girl – remember that she is of marriageable age, which means that she is about twelve – presents a rhetorically balanced argument which employs all the *colores* of medieval rhetorical training. She preaches what is in effect a *contemptus mundi* sermon, beautifully balanced with the devices of anaphora, careful antitheses, images and examples, crowned with a paradisiacal topos in which she rejects the possibilities open to her in a continued worldly existence in favour of marriage to a *frîer bûman* (775) (a free yeoman farmer), Christ, whose farm is perfect in every way. She gives, indeed, a *locus amoenus* description of Paradise. Her age, her sex and her class all make such a speech entirely impossible in realistic terms. The parents realise this, as must the audience, and draw the conclusion that it must be the Holy Spirit speaking through her, and indeed, this is an entirely reasonable conclusion within the fictionality of the story. Hartmann allows the parents, indeed, to recognise it as a hagiographical motif. Nor may her actual reasoning be criticised in any way. Hartmann's concern is to undertake the difficult task of making the impossible acceptable, of showing us, in a fallen world, a case where someone genuinely *is* prepared to go further than shunning the world to become a bride of Christ (much of the speech made by the girl could be applied to someone about to cut themselves off from their family by entering the cloister) and actually to sacrifice herself, to join Christ in a quite literal sense. The parents agree, and so, after much consideration, does Heinrich.

The final part of the story – still told with economy – is full of memorable incidents. The pair travel to Salerno to the doctor, who quizzes the girl in detail on whether or not she has genuinely reached this decision on her own; he does so in a scientific spirit, since the cure will not work if this is not the case.[46] The girl shows then the strength that she has acquired by asserting that she is a woman, and has the power to suffer this. Hartmann pushes the suspense of the audience to the limits. The doctor prepares for the operation, excluding Heinrich from the room, and making the girl undress. He has already warned her that she must be naked, and has

---

[45] Marianne Wynn considers this point in her paper 'Heroine without a Name: the Unnamed Girl in Hartmann's Story', in *German Narrative Literature*, ed. Honemann et al., pp. 245–59. Wynn's thoughtful paper does, however, place the girl on an equal footing with Heinrich himself.

[46] There is a wealth of information on the realities of this scene in a paper by Gerhard Eis which has been reprinted several times: 'Salernitanisches und Unsalernitanisches im "Armen Heinrich" des Hartmann von Aue', *Forschungen und Fortschritte* 31 (1957), 77–81.

said that she will be ashamed, but when it comes to the point, the girl (quite unlike Hartmann's other figure, Gregorius, when found on his rock) is *not* ashamed:

> [the girl] wart nacket unde blôz;
> si enschamte sich niht eins hâres grôz . . .   (1195–6)

(she was quite naked and was not ashamed in the slightest.)

The statement is a striking one: how can she possibly be naked and unashamed, since to be so would imply that she is without original sin, like Eve before the Fall.[47] The only person since that time devoid of original sin is Christ, who is also stripped of his garments at the Crucifixion. The doctrine of the Immaculate Conception of the Virgin, though not promulgated officially until *Ineffabilis Deus* in 1854, was under discussion in the twelfth century,[48] and will have played a role here too, but the girl at this point also represents Christ, free of original sin, ready to die for a sinner. One of the problems with criticism of this work, and indeed when teaching it (since it is a basic text in classes on medieval German), is to explain that the unnamed girl exists on three levels. She is a real child and young woman, conscious of her ability to decide to die for someone else and a contrast to the innocent but also uncomprehending children in the Constantine story. She is a being possessed by the Holy Spirit in order to put her point across and indeed to act as one devoid of original sin within the hagiographic fictionality of the work, the *imitatio Christi* that is a feature of saints' lives. She is an allegorical figure, an imitation of Christ. Within the fictional mode there is an interesting parallel with *Jaufré*, in which the hero rescues a beautiful woman from a leper with a knife who is after her blood: here the leper himself effects the rescue, this time from a doctor with a knife, by a change of heart.[49]

Hartmann plays with his audience again as he has the doctor sharpen his knife for the unfortunate Heinrich (and for us) to hear. Heinrich observes the beauty of the girl through a crack in the wall – there seems little need to interpret this scene as voyeurism,[50] though eroticism need not be a negative feature – and his first

---

[47]   David N. Yeandle considers the use of the word 'shame' in Hartmann, but although he mentions the Genesis-parallel in noting this (and the nakedness of Gregorius as well) he does not draw any parallels with original sin: '*Schame* in the Works of Hartmann von Aue', in *German Narrative Literature*, ed. Honemann et al., pp. 193–228.

[48]   See Marina Warner, *Alone of All Her Sex* (London: Weidenfeld and Nicolson, 1976), chapter 16.

[49]   That Hartmann's story could be a type of the beauty-and-the-beast tale, as suggested by Seiffert, 'Maiden's Heart', p. 400, has been refuted by David Blamires, 'Fairytale Analogues to *Der arme Heinrich*', in *Hartmann, Perspectives*, ed. McFarland and Ranawake, pp. 187–98, although the happy-ever-after ending has fairytale parallels, as Blamires makes clear.

[50]   As for example in Ann Snow, 'Heinrich and Mark, Two Medieval Voyeurs', *Euphorion* 66 (1972), 113–27; John Margetts, 'Observations on the Representation of Female Attractiveness in the Works of Hartmann von Aue', in *Hartmann, Perspectives*, ed. McFarland and Ranawake, pp. 199–210; and as an extreme case, Kerry Shea's 'The H(i)men Under the Kn(eye)fe: Erotic Violence in Hartmann's *Der arme Heinrich*', *Exemplaria* 6 (1994), 385–403. The heavy-handed and really rather silly title still manages to remain almost completely opaque, and the paper lays great stress on 'gender identity' and on the social and sexual dominance of the male (an obvious enough assessment for the twelfth century), but has a somewhat cavalier dismissal of the critical emphasis on the religious aspects of the miracle, which is, for all that, the main point of the story, and one in which a woman is elevated to a

thought, realistically enough, perhaps, is that he will regret not seeing her beauty again. Almost immediately, however, he undergoes a clearly marked change – the German word *verkêren* is used – and he behaves much as Constantine had when he saw the children: 'ich enwil des kindes tôt niht sehen' (1256) (I do not wish to see the death of this child). But the girl is clearly more than a child: she is, in her willingness to become one with Christ (and we recall that the children in the French *Ami et Amile* thought about the fact that they would go straight to Paradise), almost a Christ-figure herself. Now Heinrich, too, has moved from self-love to altruism, and is no longer thinking of himself: the forced objectivisation of the situation, which he is able to observe at first hand, is initially self-reflective, then turns outward, and he acknowledges his folly:

> dû hâst einen tumben gedanc,
> daz dû sunder sînen danc
> gerst ze lebenne einen tac
> wider den nieman niht enmac.
> dû enweist ouch rechte was dû tuost.   (1243–7)

(You are a fool to think that you can live without depending even for a single day on the one who is all-powerful. You know not what you do.)

The echo of Christ's words of forgiveness on the Cross, remembered and integrated into Heinrich's own experience, is unmistakable. Heinrich now reaches the conclusion that Job reached: accept what God has laid upon you. Like Wolfram's Parzival, the central figure of *Der arme Heinrich* had moved after a fall in despair and frustration away from God, but it was still only through the leprosy and his enforced isolation that he could come to realise the fact that he deserved his illness because he did not think sufficiently of God; but he did not at once think further that God can help him. To have the lesson brought home to him fully he required not only to be tested by the disease, but to have placed before him the image (though not in the event the reality) of an innocent sacrifice, in fact, of Christ's sacrifice for man. The novella itself places it in front of us, the audience. Only when he has seen this does Heinrich realise that he is living *sub gratia*, that, indeed, one such sacrifice was enough. Like Constantine, like Parzival, like Gregorius, and for that matter like Job, Heinrich too submits to the divine will with a verbal 'thy will be done' – 'gotes wille müeze an mir geschehen' (1276) (may God's will be done with me).

It can be argued that the doctor's role in the work is to show that Heinrich's cure is impossible, and that the girl's role is to show that it is not, and as a corollary of this, that neither is important enough to have a name. The girl *is* an instrument, but even though she is unnamed, she is, in the most specific sense, an image of Christ. This notion – it was put by H. B. Willson – has been criticised, but it must be stated clearly: the girl is an image of Christ as a willing sacrifice, here without original

parallel for Christ. Less odd, but curiously unenlightening, is Peter Meister's *The Healing Female in the German Courtly Romance* (Göppingen: Kümmerle, 1990), see chapter 4.

sin, stripped naked for her immolation. All kinds of verbal and physical allusions point to this. She is not equal to Christ, but she *is* a parallel, a postfigurative type in exactly the same way as Isaac is used in Christian exegesis as a prefigurative type.[51]

Heinrich is the representative, the observer, whilst the girl is the object-lesson. Having submitted himself to the divine will, he forces the doctor to stop the proceedings, and at this point the girl herself undergoes a change, tearing her hair and protesting that she has lost the heavenly crown that was clearly in store for her. There are some difficulties with the character of the girl, who is occasionally seen as self-centred, concerned as she apparently is (especially at this point) so much with her own salvation. But to judge her in this manner misses two crucial points: that she has been up to now willing to die *for someone else*, hardly a light decision, and also a good work entirely in accord with the teaching of the church, literalising the notion of the girl's becoming a bride of Christ; and secondly, that she has not, thus far, been entirely her own person, which is not to deny that her choice was freely made. Even her parents recognised, though, that she was aided by the Holy Spirit when she made her speech. Now that she has been returned abruptly to the world, she curses Heinrich roundly.

It is at this point that God recognises her fidelity and indeed her suffering (the possessive adjective used here in German might apply to both of them, since *ir* can mean either 'her' or 'their', but it seems likely from what goes before that it is the girl who is referred to);[52] God is seen as *cordis speculator* (the one who sees into hearts), an irony since the girl's was to have been cut out. God therefore effects the healing miracle, and Heinrich becomes a twenty-year-old, like the literary Adam. This can then lead to the fairy-tale conclusion, the marriage of the girl to Heinrich. One thing she did claim was that she could gain a heavenly crown even though she was of low rank, and this comment comes back to mind when she marries her over-lord; her crown is in the world, rather than in heaven.

The whole episode, however, is the working out of a divine plan; we are told that the whole thing is a *suezer list*, a 'sweet strategy' on God's part, and as such it is a mirror of the divine plan as a whole. We may need to remind ourselves, too, that God already foresees the ending, whilst leaving the choice up to the individuals. Heinrich has fallen, his sin is made visible, but it can be healed by the workings of grace. The sin was, in a sense, inevitable, however good in basic moral terms he might be; original sin has distanced man from God and this is apparent in Heinrich. Of course he is worldly: mankind has been cast out, away from God into the world, and the visible punishment inflicted upon Heinrich forces him into a reverse *contemptus mundi* because the world now holds *him* in contempt. What he has to learn, however, is first of all that he was guilty and what was the nature of his sin, then that sufficient grace has already been provided as part of a divine plan.

[51] H. B. Willson, '*Ordo* and the Portrayal of the Maid in *Der arme Heinrich*', *Germanic Review* 44 (1969), 83–94. I would also argue against Winder McConnell (to whom I am nonetheless grateful for his paper and his comments) in '*Sacrificium* in Hartmann von Aue's *Der arme Heinrich*', *Neuphilologische Mitteilungen* 84 (1983), 21–8, which, in placing emphasis on 'pre-Christian, pre-scientific superstition', perhaps interprets the cure for leprosy too literally.
[52] See Hilda Swinburne, 'The Miracle in *Der arme Heinrich*', *German Life and Letters* NS 22 (1969), 205–9.

Some of the interpretative confusion that has arisen with those readings of *Der arme Heinrich* which deny any actual guilt, or do not see the leprosy as a spiritual problem, arises from the failure to see in this and other leprosy texts first of all the fact that the motif of a physical cure by innocent blood is at root typological. That is, the basic idea is the New Testament narrative in which the innocent and willing victim sheds blood as σωτηρ to heal the intrinsically, but not irredeemably, sinful. The realised soteriology is especially clear in the baptismal element in the Constantine story, especially in those texts where the vessel originally intended for the blood of the innocents is used for the water of baptism. The story of Heinrich is more complex, but Hartmann gives enough pointers to the doctrine of original sin at one end of the divine economy and to the Passion at the other to make clear the message that man's presence in the world, rather than in Paradise, is unfortunate, and that, however inwardly good, sinfulness is inevitable unless one is Christ. The spared children in the Constantine story remind us of the biblical Holy Innocents, with Constantine's compassion pointing to a reworking that is already Christian. The girl in Hartmann's poem is a reminder for Heinrich and for the audience of the sacrifice of Christ himself. It is interrupted, as it has to be, because that sacrifice has already taken place. Heinrich sees and takes the point of the image, a literary learning process within a work of literature.

The girl, naked and unashamed, was a figure of Christ, but she is also Eve, and that the work should end in a real marriage in the real world goes beyond the fairy-tale. The paradox of the *felix culpa* is very clearly put in Hartmann's little poem – it is not much more than 1500 lines long – by the one person who seems to stand outside the theology of it all, the doctor, and in giving him the key to the whole, Hartmann seems to be telling us that this supposedly medical idea is no such thing, but is a soteriological allegory. The doctor told the leprous hero at the start

> ein seltsaene maere
> das er genislich waere
> und waere doch iemer ungenesen.   (185–7)

> (a strange tale of how he was curable, but yet would always remain unhealed.)

But it was that same doctor, we may recall, who also gave Heinrich, a little later, the answer to this paradox. Healing *is* impossible, 'got enwelle der arzât wesen' (204) (unless God is the doctor). When God *does* act as the doctor, the resolution of the paradox becomes clear: in becoming a new man, something which the girl has eventuated, even though not in the way she had in mind, Heinrich is not only cured physically but inwardly as well, so that he and his wife can, after a long and sweet life – 'sweet' is a key word in the text – enter at the last the heavenly Paradise, 'daz ewige rîche' (1516) (the eternal kingdom). The opening of Hartmann's work provided a deliberately distanced framework, in which we heard of a knight called Hartmann who wanted to tell a story that was entertaining but which also was of religious significance. It is up to the reader or listener, as well as the protagonist, to interpret the leprosy in its spiritual sense. Leprosy is a physical disease. But it is also sinfulness as such, and the message is precisely that one should not despair; the answer has been provided already, and Adam is now *sub gratia*.

125

FIVE

PROMISES TO ADAM:
THE FALL, THE REDEMPTION AND MEDIEVAL DRAMA

A T THE START OF A PLAY written in 1527 and performed before King John
III of Portugal and Queen Catherine in Almeira, and entitled (without undue
modesty) *Breve sumário da história de Deus*,[1] a brief summary of the divine plan,
the Spanish/Portuguese dramatist Gil Vicente announced his theme:

> E porque o tenor
> da resurreição de nosso Senhor
> tem as raizes naquele pomar,
> ao pé, d'aquela árvore que ouvistes contar,
> onde Adão se fez pecador,
> convém se lembrar.

> (It is well to remember why the essence of our Lord's resurrec-
> tion has its roots in the same orchard, at the foot of the tree from
> which, as you have heard tell, Adam became a sinner.)

More extensive medieval literary representations of Genesis in prose or verse
usually indicate the promise of a Redemption, and medieval Gospel-poems often
begin with a reference, sometimes quite a detailed one, to the Fall. Such references
to the Redemption at the time of the Fall are sometimes made intrinsically, that is,
not as an authorial aside, but within the time-frame of the action – by God himself
to Adam, for example. The possibility of authorial comment is always there,
however, sometimes as a comforting reminder of Old Testament typology.

The simultaneity of the divine economy in a *sub gratia* world and the causal and
allegorical parallelism of the Fall and the Redemption are more difficult to demonstrate and comment upon in visual forms like iconography or the drama. However,
one illustration of the double effect is provided by the late medieval *Biblia
Pauperum*, the pictorial and allegorical Bible.[2] The pattern of these works – and
there are various of them extant – is, in the later stages after the middle of the
fifteenth century, dramatic of itself. Each page presents us with three scenes,
framed in a kind of proscenium. In the middle is a scene from the Gospel, the antitype, and it is flanked on either side by Old Testament prefigurations, the types.
Surrounding the central picture are four prophets whose words point onward

---

[1] Gil Vicente, *Obras Completas*, ed. Marques Braga (Lisbon: Da Costa, 4th edn 1968), II, 171–215.
[2] On the *Biblia Pauperum*, see such general studies as Henrik Cornell, *Biblia Pauperum* (Stockholm:
Thule-Tryck, 1925), Gerhard Schmidt, *Die Armenbibeln des XIV Jahrhunderts* (Graz: Böhlau, 2nd
edn 1969), Ute von Bloh, *Die illustrierten Historienbibeln* (Bern: Lang, 1993), the last on the
creation-illustrations in German texts. There is also a very useful introduction to these and similar
iconographical texts in Rosemond Tuve, *A Reading of George Herbert* (London: Faber, 1952).

towards the New Testament scene. In some versions of the *Biblia Pauperum* there are full commentaries in Latin or in the vernacular, with Latin titles for the Old Testament scenes and an indication at least of the names of the prophets, with the relevant citation next to them. In one illuminating example – on a parchment roll from the collection in the Topkapi Seraglio and probably made in Venice in about 1450 – the writing is minimal; illustration 10 has a central scene with Christ being tempted by the devil to turn the stones into bread. On the right we have the Fall, with Eve taking the fruit from the serpent, and the caption summarises: 'historia primorum parentum coeptatorum a serpente. Genesis 2o. co.' (the story of the protoplasts taken by the serpent, Genesis 2 [sic]). To the left is an illustration of Esau selling his birthright to Jacob for food, captioned 'historia esau coeptati de lenticula per fame Genesis 25o co' (Esau taken by hunger . . .). There are no other comments, nor any indication of the names of the prophets who are placed, as it were, in theatre boxes observing the pattern of type and antitype. In fact these are David (who wears a crown) and Isaiah at the top, and Nahum and Job below. They are not actually portrayed as watching the New Testament events which they themselves have prophesied, but they seem at least to be standing in windows observing the juxtaposed scenes, as they might have done for a medieval play.[3]

It might be thought that the *Biblia Pauperum* is a medium 'to educate the general populace in the articles of the faith'. In fact it requires detailed knowledge to make it coherent, and the medieval medium most suited to that end, and the one to which Stanley Kahrl's comment was really applied, is the drama.[4] We may ask whether and how dramas manage to imply the simultaneity of the Fall and the Redemption within the divine economy in a non-static genre. There are plays devoted largely to Adam and Eve – the earliest is the Anglo-Norman *Ordo Representationis Adae*, the *Mystère d'Adam* – and similarly restricted narratives continue as folk-plays virtually into modern times. The story of Adam and Eve can also be part of a loose sequence of dramas which may or may not have been created as a whole; the Old French *Mistére du Viel Testament* is such a loose collection, while the biblical sequences of the great Corpus Christi cycles in English and the two-, three- or four-day pageants in continental Europe, or indeed in Cornish, are examples of a more structured approach in which the Redemption is linked dramatically with the Fall in physical terms, although this may or may not be made explicit. It may also be made clear in a spoken preface in which the whole plot is outlined, as happens in the great French *Mystères*, for example. Finally, the Passion

---

3 *Die Armenbibel des Serai, Rotulus Seragliensis no. 52*, ed. Adolf Deissmann and Hans Wegener (Berlin and Leipzig: de Gruyter, 1934). See in general Cornell, *Biblia Pauperum*, and for further examples the *Biblia Pauperum. Deutsche Ausgabe von 1471*, ed. R. Ehwald (Weimar: Gesellschaft der Bibliophilen, 1906), the *Biblia Pauperum: Facsimile of the Forty-leaf Blockbook in the Library of Esztergom Cathedral*, ed. Elisabeth Soltész (Budapest: Corvina, 1967) and Avril Henry, *Biblia Pauperum* (London: Scolar Press, 1987). There are other facsimile editions. On the well established connexion between iconography, especially in churches, and the drama, see such standard studies as M. D. Anderson, *Drama and Imagery in English Medieval Churches* (Cambridge: Cambridge University Press, 1963).
4 Stanley J. Kahrl, 'Secular Life and Popular Piety in English Medieval Drama', in *The Popular Literature of Medieval England*, ed. Thomas J. Heffernan (Knoxville: University of Tennessee Press, 1985), pp. 85–107, quoted p. 103.

play as such may well have a prefatory scene indicating the Fall as the reason for the Passion.

'There is a dialectic in Christian sacred art', said Dorothy Sayers in 1943 in the important introduction to her own mystery play, *The Man Born to be King*, 'which impels it to stress, from time to time, now the eternal, and now the temporal elements in the Divine drama.'[5] Early theological expressions of the simultaneity of Fall and Redemption are found in exegetical interpretations of the protevangelical verse, Genesis 3:15, and in the apocryphal Adam-texts, especially the full versions of the *Vita Adae et Evae* with the Sethite quest, shading into the legends of the Rood and taking in the promise of a Redemption in five thousand or so years referred to by Seth in the *Decensus* portion of the *Gospel of Nicodemus*. Elements from the *Vita*, most notably the penance of Adam and Eve, with the quest of Seth for the oil of mercy and the seeds of the Cross, are sometimes, though not often, dramatised. However, the interpretation of Genesis 3:15 and the expansion of the promise that the woman shall bruise the serpent's head are even less frequently indicated in medieval drama, even in those plays which contain what we might now think of as undramatic explanatory passages. Of the earliest texts, the *Mystère d'Adam* in the twelfth century[6] does point up the protevangelical verse at least briefly: God curses the serpent and stresses that the woman shall be its enemy

> Ocur raïz de lui istra
> Qui tes vertuz tost confundra,   (490)

> (until a root comes from her that will confound your cunning)

The *Mystère*, as Lynnette Muir made clear in her study of the work, handles the theology of atonement and the linking of the Old and New Covenants with particular skill, but Muir too (rightly) cites Dorothy Sayers' introduction on dramatisations of the Passion overall; Sayers commented that 'any theology that will stand the rigorous pulling and hauling of the dramatist is pretty tough in its texture'.[7]

Usually, however, medieval dramatists did not develop the protevangelical aspects of Genesis 3:15 at all (although those in the Reformation would do so to a greater extent), choosing to offer simply the idea that there will be enmity between the serpent and the woman, even when the serpent is clearly seen as the devil-tempter. Thus God addresses the serpent in its biblical place in an Italian example, in the Bologna cycle of mystery plays in the early fifteenth century:[8] 'fra ti e la donna sempre serà guerra/ Tu serai suo tentatore duro e forte . . .'(310f) (there shall be enmity between you and the woman, you will be her hard and severe tempter). The complex exegetical history of Genesis 3:15 from Augustine onwards is rarely

5 Dorothy L. Sayers, *The Man Born to be King* (London: Gollancz, 1943), p. 17.
6 Text cited from *Le Mystère d'Adam*, ed. Studer.
7 Lynnette R. Muir, *Liturgy and Drama in the Anglo-Norman Adam* (Oxford: Blackwell, 1973), see pp. 114–17. The importance of Sayers' introduction to *The Man Born to be King*, pp. 17–42 for the understanding of medieval drama needs to be restressed.
8 *Laude drammatiche e rappresentazioni sacre*, ed. Vincenzo de Bartholomaeis (Florence: Le Monnier, 1943), III, 191–291.

developed in medieval drama, and frequently it is omitted entirely. The textual crux
in it of whether the woman (and hence the Virgin) or the woman's seed shall bruise
the serpent's head – a point that weighed so heavily in the Bull *Ineffabilis Deus* in
1854 – is not particularly susceptible of dramatisation in any case.[9] For all that,
later Protestant scholarship, which insisted that the second part of the verse refers
back not to *mulier* but to *semen*, allowing for a more clearly Christological reading,
sometimes *is* echoed in Protestant plays.[10]

In medieval drama, if the verse is rendered at all, the point is made into a
specific promise: that man will be redeemed, or that the oil of mercy will be given
(this may be interpreted in its own right as Christ). Otherwise the promise is treated
rather more pragmatically, in that the seed is not of the woman, but quite literally of
the original tree and hence, at the same time, the Cross and the Redemption. Brief
comments like that in the Bologna play about the general conflict between the
woman (or sometimes all mankind) and the serpent are common, although later on
the Bologna Play does introduce material from the *Vita Adae*, and hence the
dramatist probably did not feel the need for an essentially undramatic explanation
at this point. In English, the Wakefield and York plays pass over the verse, and only
the N-Town play of the Fall[11] expands Genesis 3:15 to make the point; here the
serpent is to be cursed

> tyl a mayden in medyl-erth be born
> þou ffende I warn þe beforn
> throwe here þi hed xal be to-torn.   (345–7)

Even this somewhat unspecific, though clearly Marian, comment is expanded by
the angel with the flaming sword who expels Adam and Eve from Paradise, telling
them that they will not be let in again:

> Tyl a chylde of a mayd be born
> and vpon the rode rent and torn
> to saue all þat ȝe haue forlorn
> ȝour welth for to restore.   (374–7)

9   See on the early exegesis my *Fall of Man in the Early Middle High German Biblical Epic*, pp.
140–54. Further bibliography on the interpretation of the verse is extensive: see M. Flunk, 'Das Prote-
vangelium (Gen. 3. 15) und seine Beziehung zum Dogma der unbefleckten Empfängnis Marias',
Zeitschrift für katholische Theologie 28 (1904), 642–63, F. Drewniak, *Die mariologische Deutung von
Gen. 3. 15 in der Väterzeit* (Breslau: Nischkowsky, 1934) and D. J. Unger, *The First-Gospel* (St
Bonaventure, NY: Franciscan Institute, 1954), especially pp. 535–621.
10 Luther devoted considerable space to a discussion of the verse in his lectures on Genesis: see the
Weimar edition of *D. Martin Luthers Werke: kritische Gesamtausgabe* (Weimar: Böhlau, 1883–),
XLII, 141–7. There is a translation by George V. Schick, *Luther's Works* (St Louis: Concordia, 1958–),
I, 188–98.
11 *Ludus Coventriae or the Plaie called Corpus Christi*, ed. K. S. Block (London: Oxford University
Press, 1922 = EETS/ES 120). This passage is discussed by Rosemary Woolf, *The English Mystery
Plays* (Berkeley and Los Angeles: University of California Press, 1980), p. 121; her additional
comments that scenes like this might have been supported by visual images of the Redemption as are
found sometimes in manuscripts (she cites the Holkham Bible Picture Book) are speculative, however.
Woolf does indicate the unusual nature of the N-Town play at this point.

This of course takes us from the woman of Genesis 3:15 to the child, her seed, though no further details are given. Even where the Bible is followed closely, then, little need be made of the protevangelical nature of the verse.

There are occasional (sometimes slightly odd) Trinitarian reminders even in the scene in which God judges the protoplasts. That scene is a brief one, for example, in the so-called Vienna Passion play,[12] a thirteenth-century fragment in a mixture of German and Latin, probably originating from the Rhineland. In response to God's challenge, Adam replies by asking for grace and addressing God as the son:

> Gnâde, hêrre Ihesu Crist!
> wie wol mir waz, sô wê mir ist!

> (Mercy, Lord Jesus Christ, I am as unhappy now as I was fortunate before.)

Even whilst still in Paradise, and thus – as in the example just given – also outside time, Adam referred to the Incarnation in the French *Mystère d'Adam*, but an even more unusual indication of the Redemption *after* the expulsion into the world of human time is found in another brief Genesis play, this time from fifteenth-century Provence.[13] The presentation is more or less biblical, and the protoplasts are driven from Paradise by St Michael, but the final words of the play are directed at God by Eve. She acknowledges God as creator, confesses her own sin, and asks for pardon on behalf of herself and of all those who are condemned to eternal pain until

> ton filh prengua passiou
> Per fayre la redemptio
> Del gran peccat que ieu iey comes   (294–6)

> ([until] your son undergoes the Passion to carry out the Redemption for the great sin which I committed)

Eve's unusually specific, sudden and quite unbiblical comments on what will happen are her first words *in the world*, as well as the last in the play, and serve simply to remind (rather than instruct) the audience of the simultaneity inherent in the notion of a divine economy. Medieval drama is more complex than is often suspected, and in a case like this – there are clearer examples in the Cornish mystery plays – historical and extra-historical time can co-exist, allowing Eve to 'know' about Christ.

The majority of the cycle plays present the Fall and the Redemption as separate scenes within a continuous sequence. There are sometimes reflections, however, of the earliest writings to develop a fuller indication of the promise of Redemption at the time of the Fall, namely the Adambooks, although the reflection need only be

---

[12] The *Wiener Passionsspiel* is in Richard Froning, *Das Drama des Mittelalters* (Stuttgart: DNL, 1891), I, 302–24.

[13] *Les Mystères provençaux du XVe siècle*, ed. A. Jeanroy and H. Teulié (Toulouse: Privat, 1893), pp. 1–12.

slight and does not always refer to the Redemption aspects. This is true of the English N-Town play of the Fall, in which Eve asks for death since she has been the cause of the Fall. This happens in the *Vita Adae*, but in the drama Eve is very specific; none of the versions of the *Vita* actually has Eve specify a method by which Adam is to kill her, although she does ask for death:

> Wrythe on to my necke bon
> with hardness of þin honde

His response is the biblical reminder that she is of his own flesh, but this is repeated at this point in the *Vita*:

> I wyl not sle fflescly of my fflesch
> Ffor of my flesch · þi fflesch was wrought.   (389–94)

A rather longer indication of knowledge of the Latin *Vita* tradition occurs in the Chester *Creation*, where there *is* a hint of the Redemption. The play (which goes down to the death of Cain) renders the protevangelical verse of Genesis more or less literally, but as soon as Cain and Abel are born, Adam gives them (rather than Seth) a long account of his apocalyptic vision, in which Michael had told him how God will dwell with men, and of the destructions by fire and water. This is close to the first part of the *Vita Adae*, although there Adam's words are addressed to Seth, and Adam has not heard it in a dream but directly from Michael. In the Chester plays, Adam tells his sons that

> god will come from heaven hie
> to overcome the devill so slie

so that eventually

> a new law then shall begin.   (450–4)

This is a clear link to the New Testament, but the play now moves on to the tale of Cain and Abel, without further echoes of the *Vita*.

Only a few dramas contain the full episode of the penance in the river, which ends with an expressly soteriological promise of aid against the devil. The Italian cyclic play from Bologna *does* contain this rare element in medieval drama, but the ending is abrupt, and God gives in the Italian play the instructions to the protoplasts to go forth and multiply and till the earth, without further indication of forgiveness. The scene is followed by the so-called *processio prophetarum*, the sequence of prophets – like those in the *Biblia Pauperum* – whose words point onwards to Christ.[14] The *processio* is essentially a bridge passage, and it appears as early as in the *Mystère d'Adam* and in works such as the far later Low German play of the Fall by Arnold Immessen, which will be examined in more detail later. It is,

---

[14] Muir, *Liturgy and Drama*, p. 117 is unhappy about the presentation of these scenes, and her final comments, though not developed, bear further thought (referring to C. S. Lewis on the final part of *Paradise Lost*).

of course, not particularly promising in dramatic terms, and indeed, it works rather better in other genres, most notably in poetry, where it is frequently encountered.

The fullest of the dramatisations of the *Vita Adae* material is probably that found in the Breton cycle play, recorded in a manuscript of the early nineteenth century, but clearly some centuries older. It may have had a French origin, but there are no precise equivalents in French to the use in Breton of material from the *Vita*. It was published with a French translation by Father Eugène Bernard in the first decade of the present century. The fourth act of this work (on the first of the two days over which it was played) contains the penance in the river, and is clearly derived from a version of the *Vita*, although at the end of the episode God promises Adam the salvation in what is clearly a concise version of the Holy Rood legend. God tells Adam in very specific terms what will happen when he dies, referring to the three seeds which will grow into the Cross:

> Da composin eur groas da pean da holl gles,
> Pehinin vo savet voar lein mene Calvar,
> Da laquat map Doue.   Neuse e teui d'ar gloar.   (1746–8)

> (they will make a cross which will pay all debts, which will rise up on the top of mount Calvary, and on it the son of God. So you will enter the glory.)

The development of the Latin *Vita* at this point is significant; sometimes a promise is made at the expulsion from Paradise that Adam will one day receive the oil of mercy, and the information about the Rood is elsewhere given to Seth at his father's death. That God refers here to the 'Saviour who will open the gates of Paradise' is striking, since even in the *Vita* God merely drives away the devil.

Late folk-plays display a soteriology that is principally expressed through contextual juxtaposition, even when they, too, depend to some extent upon the *Vita*. The Christmas play from Obergrund in Silesia, for example, which is far briefer than the Breton drama, but which is also of at least sixteenth-century origins, is entitled in its early nineteenth-century manuscript: *Die Erschaffung der Welt sammt der Menschwerdung Jesu Christi* (The Creation of the World with the Incarnation of Jesus Christ), and those two elements are closely juxtaposed in the relatively short play. After the Fall there is no development of the protevangelical verse; instead we have a debate between justice and mercy, not as part of the broader debate between the four daughters of God, which regularly forms part of medieval and later drama, developed from St Bernard's allegory of the *litigatio sororum* based on Psalm 84, but placed immediately before God's judgement.[15] For justice, Adam is to be expelled from Paradise, but an angel now makes clear in verse (up to now we have been in prose) that God will in one of the persons of the Trinity show mercy and suffer for man. It is hard to tell how old the original of the work is precisely, although some of the rhymes point to the end of the Middle Ages. This is a folk-play and the words of the angel are splendidly blunt:

[15] See Almut Agnes Meyer, *Heilsgewißheit und Endzeiterwartung im deutschen Drama des 16. Jahrhunderts* (Heidelberg: Winter, 1976), pp. 58–72 and earlier Hope Traver, *The Four Daughters of God* (Bryn Mawr, Penn.: Bryn Mawr College Monographs, 1907).

> Dass ihr verschonet seid davon [from eternal death]
> Das sollt ihr danken Gottes Sohn,
> Der nehmen wird die Menschheit an,
> Dass er für euch genug leiden kann
> Verfolgung, Marter, Hohn und Spott,
> Ja endlich gar den bittern Tod.
> Dann wird er wieder auferstehn
> Und glorreich in den Himmel geh'n.
> Nun obschon dies für euch geschicht
> So ist's euch gar geschenket nicht;
> Es soll in Elend, Angst und Not
> Adam erbaun das liebe Brot,
> Und Eva soll mit Schmerz und Pein
> Gebären ihre Kinderlein.
> Verhalt't euch stets nach Gottes Verweis'
> Und packt euch aus dem Paradeis.

An attempt to imitate here the (rough and rustic) rhymes may be useful in providing an indication of that memorability – necessary to amateur performance – which is familiar from so much medieval drama in different languages:

> That from death's grip you have been won
> is thanks only to God's own son,
> who'll take the likeness of a man,
> and suffer for you all he can
> of spite and pain, and sneering too,
> and in the end he'll die for you.
> Now, though Redemption's what you'll get
> there's not much in it for you yet.
> In wretchedness and sweat and dust
> Adam will have to earn a crust,
> Eve's pains and tears will drive her wild
> whenever she has another child.
> So keep God's law, the pair of you
> and clear off out of Eden, shoo!

That the Obergrund play includes the penance in the river is itself a sign of antiquity, but it is ended somewhat abruptly (and in contrast to the Breton work) before Adam is given any answer to his plea that God should help him against the enemy. Instead the Annunciation follows, as a nice counter to the temptations of Eve in an intensified form of the Eva-*Ave* reversal that is so familiar in medieval writing.

How is the simultaneity to be made clear, then, in the drama? In addition to the development of the protevangelical verse, which is, as we have seen, less than dramatic, the addition of material from the *Vita Adae* is another possibility, although if it does not go on to the Holy Rood legends, and stays, for example, at the penance in the river (itself hard enough to produce dramatically, though perhaps not as bad as the parting of the Red Sea, which also appears from time to time), the problem is similarly undramatic, in that God simply explains to Adam what will happen in the future. Different dramatists make the leap from the Fall to the Redemption in different ways. To offer a broad sweep, as the cyclic plays do, is one way of expressing the interrelatedness of Fall and Redemption, since between the two actual events come the Old Testament narratives which foreshadow the second polar event. To lay emphasis therefore on such Old Testament stories reinforces the point.[16] Thus in the fourth of the Chester plays – the sacrifice of Isaac, a familiar type of Christ – an expositor underscores the point clearly and firmly:

> Lordings, this significacion
> of this deed of devotion,
> and you will, you wit mon,
> may turne you to much good.
>
> This deed you se done in this place,
> In example of Ihesu done yt was,
> that for to wyn mankinde grace
> was sacrifised on the rode.   (IV, 461–8)

Or *will be* sacrificed. The time-references in this brief passage point both at a dramatic present in spatial and chronological terms ('you se done in this place') and at an already achieved act of salvation by Christ which indicates the present as experienced by the audience.

It is of interest to examine how that bridge between the two poles of salvation history is constructed in the shorter medieval plays, either of the Fall or of the Passion. Here, incidentally, the term 'medieval' is again a treacherous one, since the tradition of continental drama at least is discontinuous; thus the Breton play is far older than the written form still being performed in the first decades of the nineteenth century, and it is equally hard to date other plays. Many of the German folk-plays of Adam and Eve, for example, derive even in Catholic areas from a play by the Protestant Hans Sachs. Some of their solutions to the bridging problem, however, are ingenious, and two such folkplays are worth considering in addition to the one looked at already from Obergrund in Silesia. All three overlap to an extent, but there are differences in presentation.[17]

The Laufen play from the border of Bavaria and Austria was taken down from oral sources in the 1860s but probably dates back to the sixteenth century and is known from other towns as well.[18] As with the other German folk-plays, the devil first appears as himself, and announces that he will disguise himself as a snake for the purpose of temptation. At the scene in which God passes judgement on the

---

[16] The best study of this in English drama is by Woolf, *English Mystery Plays*, pp. 132–58. Of importance, too, is her paper 'The Effect of Typology on the English Medieval Plays', originally in *Speculum* 34 (1957), 805–25 and reprinted in *Art and Doctrine: Essays on Medieval Literature*, ed. Heather O'Donoghue (London: Hambledon, 1986), pp. 49–75.

[17] See on these and other folk-plays of Adam and Eve: Klimke, *Paradiesspiel*, and also Schwarz, *Die neue Eva*, with reference to folklore and to folktales in general.

[18] A. Hartmann, *Volksschauspiele in Bayern und Österreich-Ungarn gesammelt* (Leipzig: Breitkopf und Härtl, 1880, repr. Walluf: Sändig, 1972), 39–50, cited by line number. The inclusion of songs is a late feature, as is the loss of any debate between Justice, Mercy and God.

protoplasts and the serpent after the Fall, however, he is clearly a devil again, and a jubilant one at that, whom it is difficult to resist quoting (and imitating) as he is shown literally looking forward to stoking the fires of hell in readiness for the human race:

> Ich will mein Höll ganz tapfer hitzen
> Sie müaßen mit mir zugleich schwitzen.
> Ich will sie führen in mein Reich;
> Sie müaßen mit mir brinnä-r- und braten zugleich . . .   (178–81)

Once again the style is vigorous and memorable:

> I'll get the fires stoked well today.
> If I've to sweat, then so will they!
> I'll lead them down into my hell –
> they'll have to bake and roast as well.

However, God reminds us that he is still in the form of a serpent, and the *interpretatio literalis* of the serpent as the instrument of the devil is taken a stage further as God condemns what He Himself calls a *Höllenhund* (a hellhound), to crawl on his belly. The animal-imagery may be confused, but the interpretation of Genesis is clear enough. And yet, although the judgement upon Adam is biblical, there is no indication of the protevangelical verse; instead there is a far less complicated exchange in which Eve begs for mercy and is told by an angel:

> Eva, du sollst kein Zweifel fassen!
> Ehr deinen Mann, erzieh dein Kind!
> So verzeiht dir Gott all deine Sünd.   (209–11)

> (Eve, do not despair, honour your husband and bring up your children and God will forgive you all your sins.)

The Wildalpen Paradise play from Styria,[19] also in Austria, copied in 1905 from an earlier manuscript, seems in some of its elements to be older than the Laufen play, although the texts overlap considerably. It resembles the Obergrund play, too, in that it contains the debate between God, Justice and Mercy. Where the Obergrund play followed that debate and the decision that God's son should come to save man with the more dramatic penance in the river, the Wildalpen play does not have the *Vita* material. Instead, after Christ's agreement to suffer on behalf of Adam, and a song of praise by an angel in the name of the Trinity, the judgement scene is close to that in the Laufen play. However, the debate between God and the devil, whilst using some of the same dialogue, is developed more seriously. An angel pleads directly for assistance from God, and when the devil repeats a line that he has used already, stressing that no one can reclaim those he has imprisoned, God replies in the words of Ezechiel 33:11:

---

19 Oskar Pausch, *Das Wildalpener Paradeisspiel mit einem Postludium Vom Jüngling und dem Teufel* (Vienna: Böhlau, 1981).

So wahr ich leb und bin auch Gott
So will ich nit des Sünders Tod
Sondern daß er sich bekehr ...   (645–7)

(As truly as I am God I do not want the death of a sinner, but that
he repent.)

The devil is banished to hell, and although there has been no direct indication of the
protevangelical verse, on this occasion an angelic song takes us again to the Virgin
(with a temporal disjunction in the reference to the liturgical feast):

Maria lag verborgen
Bis auf den Lichtmeß Morgen ...   (660–1)

(Mary was hidden until the feast of Candlemas.)

The angel then describes in a concluding speech that Christ will die on the Cross to
provide mankind's *Läschi-Geld* (bail money).

Just as Adam and Eve plays frequently close with a look to the future, independent plays whose central focus is the Passion may also begin with a presentation of the Fall. This happens with medieval metrical Gospels on a regular basis,
and there is indeed often an overlap between the drama and such writings, as is the
case with the English *Stanzaic Life of Christ*, the Cornish *Pascon agan Arluth* and
the German *Erlösung*.[20] Not every Passion play starts that way, of course, nor
indeed is this necessary, since Gospel-based plays may (and do) refer throughout
to the resolution of the Old Testament events in the context of their New Testament
antitypes, at a time, therefore, in the action where they are being or have just been
rendered invalid by the Gospel events. Thus the Sainte-Geneviève *Passion nostre
Seigneur*,[21] probably of the fourteenth century, is an extensive work on the Passion
as such, but it refers to Adam at significant points. At the Crucifixion the angels
sum up the Fall and Redemption:

Par Adam, qui pecha jadis
Tous estoient en enfer mené,
Mais la mort Jhesu ramené
Vous a trestous a sauvement   (2946–9)

(Through Adam, who once sinned, everyone was put into hell,
but the death of Jesus has redeemed and saved you all.)

Here, as in other plays too, we are later shown Adam and Eve being rescued from
hell, and reference is made there to the Fall once again, and also to the sacrifice
which has, in the dramatic present, only just happened. The Harrowing of Hell
scene also permits a reminder of the Fall as the reason for the Redemption. In a

[20] See my paper, 'Various Gospels', *Studi Medievali* 3/36 (1995), 776–96.
[21] Edward Joseph Gallagher, *A Critical Edition of La Passion Nostre Seigneur from manuscript 1131
from the Bibliothèque Sainte-Geneviève, Paris* (Chapel Hill, NC: UNC, 1976). The manuscript
contains other Gospel-plays and hagiography.

rather later Middle Low German work, the fifteenth-century Easter play from a manuscript from Redentin, near Wismar on the Baltic coast, but probably composed in Lübeck, we are shown not only Adam and Eve in hell but also Seth, who recounts the story of the quest for the oil of mercy known in the *Vita Adae* and the legends of the Holy Rood (probably from a Low German version of the latter). Seth tells the audience of how Michael had refused him the oil of mercy, but had promised that the Redemption would come by way of the Virgin's child after – in this case – 5,600 years. Much of this may derive from the Harrowing of Hell section of a version of the *Gospel of Nicodemus*. Other prophets give their typological statements, as in works like the *Mystère d'Adam*, but here they have become retrospective, since the dramatic work begins *after* the Crucifixion with a scene in which the Jews ask Pilate to ensure that the grave is guarded.[22] A further illustration of the simultaneity and of the interrelationship of the two Testaments is provided by the so-called Innsbruck Easter play, a fourteenth-century High German text probably composed in Brixen, but contained in a manuscript now in Innsbruck. The same manuscript also contains a heavily exegetical Corpus Christi play from a different area which does begin with Adam and Eve and then shows us the prophets and apostles. In the Easter play, however, the Harrowing has no mention of Seth, but the dialogue between Christ and the protoplasts echoes very clearly the judgement of God in Genesis. Christ questions Adam first as to why he sinned, and he explains that the devil came to Eve disguised as a serpent; Eve herself then tells how she took the fruit, as a result of which she and all women were cursed. The pair are redeemed, but Lucifer has to remain in hell, and now bewails his own Fall. What we have is a reverse run-through of the beginnings of the history of salvation placed into a *sub gratia* context, a reminder of the Fall while the Redemption is actually manifesting itself in its most dramatic way, just after the Latin stage-direction 'et sich Ihesus frangit tartarum'[23] (and thus Jesus breaks open hell).

Sometimes a play will offer no more than a brief introductory passage on the Fall as a reminder of the need for the Passion. Moving back to Low German or Dutch, the fragmentary fourteenth-century Easter play from Maastricht[24] has a brief scene of the Creation and Fall – the entire fall of the angels occupies about 35 lines, for example, and the Fall itself not much more, although a part of it is missing from the manuscript. In the judgement scene there is no reference to the enmity between the woman and the serpent (God simply says that everyone will fear and

---

[22] *Das Redentiner Osterspiel*, ed. and trans. Schottmann, see lines 339–62. There is a similar and very concise use of the prophets and their comments in the Middle English poem of the *Devils' Parliament*, in which each of seven Old Testament figures plus St John has a two-line statement at the Harrowing. Abraham, for example, greets God 'þat sauede my sone fro bittir bande' – which restores to reality the incident that is customarily seen as a prefiguration: see Marx, *Devils' Parliament* (B version, 366), pp. 78f. There is an older edition of this text (from one manuscript only) in *Hymns to the Virgin and Christ*, ed. Frederick J. Furnivall (London: Trübner, 1868 = EETS/OS 24), pp. 52f.

[23] *Das Innsbrucker Osterspiel. Das Osterspiel von Muri*, ed. and trans. Rudolf Meier (Stuttgart: Reclam, 1962), pp. 28–31 (lines 317–36).

[24] Julius Zacher, 'Mittelniederländisches Osterspiel', *Zeitschrift für deutsches Altertum* 2 (1842), 302–57; the play, although defective, is of considerable interest, and has been insufficiently studied. See Brett-Evans, *Von Hrotsvit bis Folz und Gegenbach*, I, 157–9.

despise him: the serpent is clearly taken literally here), but immediately after Adam and Eve are expelled from the garden, God asks his daughter Mercy to make clear to the audience that there will be a Redemption. The play then presents various Old Testament prophecies pointing on to the sacrifice of Christ, and even one by the *Heiden man Vergilis* (the pagan Vergil) – presumably a reference to the standard medieval interpretation of the Fourth Eclogue – and then moves at once into the Annunciation. All this introductory material will only have occupied about a tenth of the play as a whole, although, as indicated, the manuscript is defective.

A somewhat late, but striking, example of the prefacing of a Passion play with a brief reminder of the Fall is provided in a reduced form in a familiar place, in the Oberammergau Passion play. In fact the addition is relatively late. Faced in the 1630s with a vow to present a Passion play, Oberammergau first used a late medieval text borrowed from Augsburg, then a somewhat operatic piece specially written by Ferdinand Rosner, a monk from Ettal. In its turn his work was supplanted in the first years of the nineteenth century by a more completely biblical text by another Ettal monk, Othmar Weiss. He was the last one, in fact, since when the monastery was secularised in 1803 he remained there alone. Weiss kept one innovation of Rosner's, the use of *tableaux vivants* of Old Testament scenes with introductory verses, the first of which is of the expulsion from Paradise. These tableaux were retained in the next revision (the one still in use) by Alois Daisenberger, Weiss's pupil. The tableau – the German uses the word *Vorbild* (prefiguration) – shows Adam and Eve, described in the text as *die Menschheit* (mankind) expelled from Eden and from the tree of life, which is contrasted at once with the tree of the Cross. With that, however, we move directly into the New Testament narrative.[25]

Plays which aim for a coherence in the divine economy can also make their point by a deliberately close juxtaposition of the two elements. The *Vienna Passion*, for example, written down in the form we have it in a mixture of Latin and German in about 1330 but of thirteenth-century origin and one of the earliest of the Passion plays, provides, although it is again incomplete, a good example of how brief scenes may be put together to form a coherent whole, covering in a short space the fall of the angels and then of man, with a bridging passage on sinners in hell, which moves neatly towards the redeeming of a specific sinner, Mary Magdalene (merged here with the woman taken in adultery in John 2).[26] The final part of the play as we have it offers the beginning of the Last Supper. A lot is left out, even in the Fall scene, where there is, for example, only the briefest of judgements. Nevertheless, there are some concealed pointers; immediately after the fruit has been eaten, the *persona Dominica*, the representation of God, accompanied by two angels, asks Adam not where he is (although He does do so in a German speech later), but what he has done:

25 On the history of the work, see James Bentley, *Oberammergau and the Passion Play* (Harmondsworth: Penguin, 1984), pp. 20–3. For the text, see *Das Oberammergauer Passionsspiel 1960* (Oberammergau: Gemeinde Oberammergau, 1960), p. 13. See also the translation by Eric Lane and Ian Brenson (London: Dedalus, 1984), p. 37.
26 Brett-Evans, *Von Hrotsvit bis Folz*, I, 154–6 discusses the play in some detail. It is linked with the Passion play from Benediktbeuren in the famous Codex Burana. See also Anke Roeder, *Die Gebärde im Drama des Mittelalters* (Munich: Beck, 1974), pp. 150f.

Adam, Adam, quid fecisti?
Quare stolam amisisti,
qua indutus immortalis
angelis eras aequalis?

(Adam, what have you done? Why have you thrown away the
robe of immortality that you wore; you used to be the equal of
the angels.)

That slightly odd-looking addition of a reference to a robe of immortality in an
otherwise laconic presentation rests upon a whole sequence of exegetical interpretations, not of Genesis but of the Gospels, specifically of the *stola prima* given to
the returning prodigal in Luke 15:22. This is normally interpreted as the giving
back of grace to man by Christ after its loss by Adam.[27] Here the exegetical point is
made in a very concise manner; how Adam and Eve were *actually* portrayed in the
play up to this point is unclear, but certainly after eating the fruit they are instructed
in the stage direction to make aprons. The exegetical idea that Adam and Eve were
clad before the Fall in garments of any sort, especially angelic ones, is a useful one
for drama, which has to face up to the problem of naked innocence in a post-Fall
world rather more pragmatically than other genres. Even modern films tend to use
distance shots and long grass; more seriously, a medieval Cornish play has them
wearing white leather garments before the Fall.

It would be impossible to look at the whole range of medieval biblical plays
(and even less so their modern counterparts) to see how they cope with the link
between Adam and Eve and Christ.[28] Special attention is demanded for those
dramatic works, however, which stress the coherence of the divine economy of Fall
and Redemption by utilising the intrinsic links between the Fall and the Redemption established in the promises and visions of the *Vita Adae*, or made concrete in
the early history of the Cross.

All of the great Passion plays of fifteenth- and early sixteenth-century France
contained Old Testament material and all are long: the *Passion de Semur* filled two
days, the Arras *Passion* of Eustache Mercadé and that of Arnoul Greban four days,
while Jean Michel's extension of Greban, if played in full, would have occupied
the better part of a week. Of course, they were sometimes revised and cut for
performance, or only selected days were shown, and even different manuscripts
differ in length. Arnoul Greban, the choirmaster of Nôtre Dame in Paris and later
canon in Le Mans in the middle of the fifteenth century, was a learned author; there
is an anecdote about him that he was allowed the key to the Nôtre Dame theo-

---

27 I have examined this widespread exegetical motif in 'The Garments of Paradise.'

28 It is interesting to note how modern dramatists such as John Bowen have taken the English
medieval cycles, which were made up of discrete individual pageants, and adapted them into a single
play. Bowen's work, which draws on all the English medieval cycles and was first published in 1968, is
actually called *The Fall and Redemption of Man* (London: Faber, 1968), and moves from the story of
Adam and Eve and Cain and Abel directly to God's decision that the time has now come for the
Redemption in the middle of the first of its two acts. Bowen's play was written for the London
Academy of Dramatic Art, but Bowen makes clear in his extremely informative introduction the links
with the medieval plays.

logical library, but only if he paid for having it cut himself.[29] His work – long enough as it stands – also contains a prologue of nearly two thousand lines, summarising events down to the death of Adam, and this includes Seth's quest to find the oil of mercy. The source is unclear: the writer may have known the end of a version of the *Vita*, perhaps the *Decensus* portion of the *Gospel of Nicodemus* (seen in its historical place, so to speak, as at the beginning of the Redentin play), or a version of the Holy Rood legend. The Cherub first of all promises the actual Redemption in 5,500 years time – this might just point to a *Vita Adae* recension, but is more likely to indicate knowledge of the Nicodemus Gospel – and then refers to the three seeds given to Seth to plant, which, together with the fact that he travels apparently alone to Paradise and has no vision of the child in the tree, might rather indicate a Holy Rood story as source. All this, however, is only in the prologue; the play proper begins with Adam in limbo, which is followed by an extended heavenly debate which leads to the Redemption. In the action for the third day, just before the actual Crucifixion, Adam and Eve make brief speeches from limbo once again, but the Holy Rood idea is never developed in the context of the play as a whole. There is a rather more extensive presentation of the Sethite quest in a slightly later and more disjointed late fifteenth-century French cycle of plays, too, those grouped together as the *Mistére du Viel Testament*.[30] Here at the death of Adam (who is in this case unusually predeceased by Eve) Seth is sent to Paradise alone, and his arrival there is preceded by a reprise of the debate between Justice and Mercy, the *Procès de Paradis*. Seth is not shown Paradise and he receives only the three seeds. Moreover, when he explains to Adam what he has been given, the whole point remains opaque to Adam and to the audience alike: he has been given the three seeds and told

> Que, quant on fera vostre couche
> En terre, dedans vostre bouche
> Ceste semence soit plantée,
> Car point ne sera rechaptée
> Nature, tant qu'elle ayt produit
> Arbre qui portera ung fruit,
> Du quel une huylle descendra
> Vierge, qui santé vous rendra.   (4166–73)

(that, when we make your resting-place in the earth, these seeds should be planted in your mouth, for nothing will be redeemed

---

[29] Greban, *Mystère de la Passion*, and see on the background and on comparable plays Grace Frank, *The Medieval French Drama* (Oxford: Clarendon, 1954), pp. 176–89. It is interesting that Gustave Cohen adapted the great scope of Greban and Michel into a manageable size in his modernised *Mystère de la Passion des Théophiliens* (Paris: Richard-Masse, 1950) and concentrated entirely on the Passion.

[30] *Le Mistére du Viel Testament*, ed. James de Rothschild (Paris: Didot, 1878–91, repr. New York: Johnson, 1966), I, 160. Rothschild divides the work into sections, and notes, I, p. lxxiv, that later sections of the work do not develop the story of the Rood. There is a partial edition of the first part of the *Mistere* (thus the title, without the acute accent) by Barbara M. Craig, *La Créacion, La Transgression and l'Expulsion of the Mistere du Viel Testament* (Lawrence, Kansas: University of Kansas, n.d.) with an interesting introduction.

until it has produced a fruit from which there will come a Virgin
oil which will heal you.)

The modern editor of that French text, James de Rothschild, expressed his
regret that 'on ne trouve dans le *Viel Testament* le développement complet de la
légende', which he refers to somewhat confusingly as the *Pénitence d'Adam*, a
term that applies rather to the *Vita* than to the Holy Rood material. He does,
however, comment that the story is developed more fully by a writer called Arnold
Immessen (the Marianism of whose work is actually far closer to the *Mistére*, and
indeed to Greban's massive play, than Rothschild implies), who wrote in about
1480 a play which is usually known by a High German editorial title as *Der
Sündenfall* (The Fall). However, it is not only in Low German, but is actually about
the Fall and the Redemption, although it ends not with Christ, nor even with the
Virgin, but this time with St Anne.

Immessen's portrayal of the fall of the angels and their enormously vigorous
language, especially Lucifer's, makes the work a much underestimated analogue
of Milton.[31] Lucifer bewails his new position and swears vengeance on anything
that might worship God – Adam has not yet been created. He then curses God
formally and solemnly at first, his speech developing to an increasing frenzy which
culminates in a fourteenfold anaphoric '*Vorvloket si . . .*' (Accursed be . . .)
including (Job-like) the day of his own creation. 'Eck vorvloke hir den groten god',
he begins solemnly (Here I curse God almighty), but he ends with the resounding

> Vorvloket syn de veer element,
> Vorvloket syn sterne vnde firmament,
> Vorvloket sy myn egen stad,
> Vorvloket sy, de mi gescapen had.   (612–29)

> (Accursed be the four elements, accursed all the stars and firma-
> ment, accursed be the place where I must be, accursed be He
> who created me.)

This curse on the creation that we have only just heard of makes the scene even
more effective. Adam is created, and falls after Lucifer disguises himself as a
serpent with a woman's face – a relatively late motif which becomes common in
iconography – and tempts Eve. The biblical *ubi es?* is repeated, somewhat unusually, and the biblical judgement on the serpent and the protoplasts is followed
closely, with a clearly Marian view of the protevangelical verse. 'Eyn vrauwe scal
totreden dyn houet' (1076), says God (a woman shall crush your head). There is no
further indication of any promise at this point, and the story of Cain and Abel
follows, but the death of Adam brings in the Sethite material. In this case the material is from a known Holy Rood source, the Middle Dutch *Boec van den houte*
(Book of the Cross), which Immessen seems to have known in a Middle Low
German version.[32] Seth is sent to Paradise with the instruction to follow the burnt

---

[31] See Kirkconnell, *Celestial Cycle*, p. 540. Few studies of Milton mention the work. Kirkconnell was
not aware of the edition by Friedrich Krage.
[32] See the *Boec van den Houte*, ed. Hermodsson, on the position of Immessen. See also Robert

footprints of Adam and Eve, but is to ask not for the oil of mercy as such, but rather 'Wu lange dat ick sculle myssen/ Des olyes der entfermenissen' (1335–6) (How long I shall have to be without the oil of mercy?). That 'how long' becomes a recurrent motif. We hear later that Adam was promised the oil when he left Paradise, and the answer made to Seth here takes the form of the vision of Paradise with the tree with the roots in hell (where he sees his brother Abel), with a serpent around it, and in which there is the new born child. The Cherub explains the significance of this to Seth, explaining (with an echo of the Magnificat and the Eve/Mary typology) that the child is the Redeemer:

> By dussem kindeken cleyne
> Scal de sulue maget alleyne
> Wedder vinden de gnade,
> De Adam van der maget rade
> Vorloß in vnhorsamicheyden. (1467–71)

> (By this tiny child that very maiden will find grace, the grace that Adam lost in his disobedience, on the advice of the other maiden.)

That Mary will *find* grace here does not provide, in fact, very sound support for the doctrine of the Immaculate Conception. However, the oil of mercy will be given to Adam only then. The child, the Cherub explains, must shed its holy blood, but the wood on which it will do this has to grow from three seeds from the same tree as Adam ate from in Paradise. The angel explains further that Seth is to plant the seeds in Adam's mouth, and that they will grow into three separate trees, in token of the Trinity. This concludes the use of the Holy Rood motif in the play; although Moses appears, as does Solomon later, the story of the Cross is not developed. We are given at one point – about the halfway point – a view of Adam in limbo, however, and he is allowed to voice the *De profundis* in an appeal for mercy, reminding us of the promised oil of mercy, even though the fullness of time has clearly not yet come. We are not shown the Harrowing, as we were in the Redentin play, but we are instead reminded of the need for it. There is also a reminder of what happened at the Fall towards the end of the play when God speaks to the principal prophet, Isaiah, when he too asks for mercy for suffering humanity. Adam's utterance of Psalm 129 is repeated twice, and the theme of mercy is sustained throughout the play. Just when it seems that the promised mercy will not be forthcoming, Lucifer makes a triumphant speech to Adam, the representative of all men:

> God hefft diner clegeliken wort
> Nicht getweden oder gehort.
> Swich stille vnde hebbe vngeuelle,
> Du blifft myt vs hyr in der helle. (3464–7)

Miller's *German and Dutch Versions of the Legend of the Wood of the Cross*, pp. 272–84. Miller's useful work refers to a great number of other Dutch and Low German texts. He discusses also the Redentin play and refers to the less significant Villinger Passion.

(God has not heard or listened to your words of complaint, so be quiet and suffer your misfortune – you will be staying with us here in hell.)

But a promise is a promise, and this is Lucifer's final speech in the play; immediately after we see Joachim and Anna on stage, while Adam and David complain again from limbo, and after the interventions of Justice and Mercy, God sends Gabriel to Anna to announce the birth of the Virgin, whose child will redeem Adam's guilt.

The play is unusual for a variety of reasons. It uses the Holy Rood material, but does not develop the story of the Cross itself; rather it uses the promise of the oil of mercy and, instead of showing us the concrete aspect, takes us towards the working out of the protevangelium by showing us the seed of the woman, not Mary herself, but her mother. The sustained cry *de profundis* of 'How long O Lord?' and the figure of Adam in limbo remind us throughout the play of the promise and its necessity, and it comes at the last to the mockery of Lucifer, who thinks that *he* has triumphed. We are not shown the Harrowing, but we know now that Adam will not have to remain in hell. As an attempt to show the whole of the divine economy by taking us at least to the turning point, to the birth of the Virgin, the play is impressive. Where Arnoul Greban's preface only mentioned the promise, Immessen develops and sustains it.

A glance at the useful chart in E. K. Chambers' monumental history of the English stage, which shows in tabular form which elements appear in which mystery cycles in England, makes clear that the *Vita Adae* or Holy Rood material is almost always absent;[33] indeed, the only reason that the Sethite quest appears in the table at all is that it does play a very significant part indeed in two plays written in England, although not in English. It is absent too from the Welsh material, and only in Cornish[34] do we find a dramatisation of the Holy Rood material used consistently to link Fall and Redemption with a concrete image, and indeed to make clear throughout the plays the importance of seeing, understanding and believing. This happens not only in the three-day play cycle of the late fourteenth century known as the *Ordinalia*, written probably at Penryn and performed in an open-air playing place, but also in a later play, probably from the next century, which has the English title *The Creacion of the World* in the incomplete manuscript which survives.

---

[33] E. K. Chambers, *The Medieval Stage* (Oxford: Oxford University Press, 1903), II, 321–3.

[34] The three plays are still most conveniently found in Norris's *Ancient Cornish Drama*, in the original and with a translation (the former is followed here, though I have adapted the translation); line-numbers refer to the Latin names given to the three plays: O[rigo] M[undi], P[assio] D[omini] and R[esurrexio] D[omini]. See also Markham Harris's translation, *The Cornish Ordinalia*, for a prose version of the three plays. For the later play see Whitley Stokes, *Gwreans an bys* (cited) and Neuss, *The Creacion of the World*. There is a text in modern 'Unified' Cornish (with a translation) by R. Morton Nance and A. S. D. Smith, *Gwryans an bys* (Padstow: FOCS, 1959, revised ed. by E. G. R. Hooper, Redruth: Truran, 1985). On the performance aspect in a round, rather than from pageant waggons, see R. Morton Nance, 'The Plen an Gwary or Cornish Playing Place', *Journal of the Royal Institution of Cornwall* 24 (1935), 190–217. A highly speculative recent attempt by Gloria J. Betcher to locate the plays to Bodmin, 'A Reassessment of the Date and Provenance of the Cornish Ordinalia', *Comparative Drama* 29 (1995–6), 436–53, is unconvincing.

The Cornish *Ordinalia*, then, is a dramatic rarity in the Middle Ages in using this set of motifs to show us the working-out of the divine economy. The presentation of the Fall in the first play of the *Ordinalia* is relatively brief, although there are odd motifs – Eve claims that she heard an angel singing in a tree, urging her to take the fruit, although we have seen that it was the devil disguising himself as a serpent. Adam eats so as not to upset Eve, even though he does not really want to. The condemnation by God, however, is unusual, especially in the judgement on the devil. Where in Genesis the serpent is not interrogated, here God asks the devil why he tempted Eve, and receives the answer that is given *in extenso* in the *Vita Adae* tradition directly by the devil to Adam – namely that he was jealous of the pair because they were now enjoying what he had lost:

> My a leuer thy's an cas
> rag bos thethe ioy mar vras
> ha my pup vr ow lesky
> rag henna my a's temptyas
> the behe may fe ellas
> aga han kepar ha my   (OM 305–10)

> (I will tell you why: because they had great joy and every hour I burned, therefore I tempted them to sin, so that they might sing 'alas' as I do.)

The serpent *qua* serpent is then simply told that it will be the most accursed of the beasts, although the condemnation that it is to crawl is omitted. Genesis 3:15 is cited, however, albeit briefly, simply noting that the seed of the two shall be enemies, woman and serpent. When the protoplasts are expelled from Paradise, Adam is told first of all that he cannot blame the whole thing on his wife, and that a thousand generations to come will also be blamed. He asks, however, already at this point for the oil of mercy (named in an English loan-form as *oyl a versy*, as a matter of fact, which is probably a source indication), and receives a promise that this will come *yn dyweth a'n beys* (OM 328) (at the end of the world). Adam does not know yet – as Eve seemed to in the Provençal play – precisely what will happen.

When Adam is driven out, the earth initially protests when Adam digs into it, so that he negotiates – 'haggles' is probably the better word – and eventually persuades God to allow him not just a full spade's length, but as much as he wants.[35] The Holy Rood material proper is picked up, however, at the death of Adam. Seth is sent to Paradise following the withered footprints once again, to ask – and the phrase is a circumspect one – for the 'guyroneth a'n oyl . . . a versy' (OM 740f) (the truth about the oil of mercy). The Cherub permits him to look three times into Eden and he tells us, the audience, in a neat teichoscopy, what he sees. This follows the *Legende* version of the Holy Rood story. Seth sees the fountains of Paradise and a tree that is dry in the upper part and whose roots reach down to hell; then he sees a serpent in the tree, and finally the child in the upper part. He is told

---

[35] See my *Cornish Literature*, pp. 49f on this point.

that the child is the Son of God, who is also the promised oil of mercy. Seth is also given three seeds to place under the tongue of the dead Adam, although it is still not clear what their function is, merely that they will grow into three trees. Seth buries them with Adam, and we are shown how devils drag Adam's soul to hell to join that of Abel.

Unlike other medieval works, the Cornish play develops the Holy Rood material beyond Adam and Eve as a structuring element.[36] The work remains episodic to an extent – we are shown Noah, Abraham and Isaac, and the early part of the life of Moses – but the inherent simultaneity of Fall and Redemption is indicated in small ways. Japhet, for example, refers unbiblically to an altar being placed on Mount Calvary (OM 1180). Moses eventually finds on a mountain the three stems or rods which, having escaped the flood, have grown from the seeds given to Seth, and blesses them as an expression of the Trinity. Still close to the Holy Rood narrative, we are shown incidents illustrating the healing power of the trees (when kissed by the sick), which Moses replants on Mount Tabor, in some traditions the scene of the Transfiguration. The soteriology is clear in this Old Testament drama and it is continued, as in the legends, with the discovery of the rods by David. First God speaks to Gabriel (and the audience) about the need for the Rood to be found as it will provide the Cross for Christ, but Gabriel brings David a dream of the three rods, telling him to bring them to Jerusalem:

> y feth othom annethe
>   the gvnde mab den defry
> may fo rys vn deyth a due
>   guthyl crous annethe y   (OM 1949–52)

(They will truly be needed to make for the Son of Man a cross one day.)

When David finds them they are again used soteriologically (in the literal sense), to heal the blind, the lame and the deaf, as in the Rood-legends. The dramatist does, it is true, introduce a comic interlude with a butler who is placed on guard over the rods, but his somewhat bawdy speech to his companion (he offers to find him a woman to help while away the time) leads into the David and Bathsheba narrative, passed over in the Holy Rood material simply as David's 'heavy sin'.

Next, King Solomon's carpenters find the rods, now grown into a single tree, and wish to incorporate it into the new temple at Jerusalem, but they find that it is impossible to fit it anywhere. We have nearly reached the end of the first day's action, and the *Origo Mundi* play concludes with one of the most interesting

---

[36] See C. Fudge, 'Aspects of Form in the Cornish Ordinalia', *Old Cornwall* 8 (1973–9), 457–64 and 491–8. On the use in the plays of the 'traditional language of Redemption without, however, invoking any sophisticated theories of ransom or sacrifice', see C. W. Marx, 'The Problems of the Doctrine of the Redemption in the ME Mystery Plays and the Cornish *Ordinalia*', *Medium Aevum* 54 (1985), 20–32. In the *Ordinalia* it is not really a problem. The whole Holy Rood section was extracted and presented (unjustifiably) as a separate item by F. E. Halliday, *The Legend of the Rood* (London: Duckworth, 1955). For a forthright set of comments on the artistry of the play, see Neville Denny, 'Arena Staging and Dramatic Quality in the Cornish Passion Play', in *Medieval Drama*, ed. Neville Denny (London: Arnold, 1973), pp. 124–54.

sections of the Holy Rood legends, the episode of Max(im)illa, who enters the temple and sits on the wood, causing her clothes to burst into flames so that she invokes Christ (displaying a prescience rather like that of Eve in the Provençal play), for which she is martyred as a blasphemer and worshipper of an unknown god. Maximilla's prophecy when she is taken prisoner recalls the original comments on the rods as a symbol of the Trinity, though the rods have now become one, underlining the point further. The martyrdom of Maximilla for naming Christ is a high point on which to end the first day's play, because her story not only has in the middle of it the literal and physical wood of the Cross, but her fate also prefigures that of Christ and of events that will happen in worldly time, but which are already there in eternity. The lives of saints often imitate Christ, of course, but usually *after* the events. Here we have a kind of hagiographic typology in the death of Maximilla because of the Rood and her invocation of Christ *before* the Incarnation. She is taken away by a group of torturers – these loom large in the Cornish plays, and in performance presumably were the same people as later carry off Christ himself. The wood of the future Cross, which has caused the whole incident, is removed to Bethsaida, and the pool (noted in John 5:4) acquires healing powers; it is then taken to Cedron, where it is used, appropriately, as a bridge. The motif looks backwards and forwards.

The Holy Rood narrative recurs in the second play of the *Ordinalia*, the *Passio Domini*, at the time of the Crucifixion, when it is recalled that the wood is still at Cedron. The dramatist does, admittedly, now interpolate another legend sometimes found in juxtaposition with the Rood legends in medieval writings, that of the nails of the Cross, and this legend is also noteworthy in soteriological terms as a reversal of the normal healing miracles through Christ. The smith asked to make the nails is perceived to have diseased hands when he in fact does not.[37] That the smith has his forge, incidentally, in Market Jew (that is, *marghas yow*, literally and rather oddly on Good Friday, 'Thursday Market') – in Cornwall – underlines yet again the simultaneity of events; the actual audience becomes the crowd watching the Crucifixion, and the nails have come from not far away. There are other Cornish place-names in the *Ordinalia*.

The final play of the Cornish trilogy is of the Resurrection, and this time we are again shown the breaking of the gates of hell. Seth does not appear again, but after the Harrowing, Adam sums up the Redemption:

> An luef a'm gruk me a wel
> ha'y odor whekke ys mel
> ow bos warnaf
> dre ov fegh ty a'm collas
> he gans the wos a'm prennas
> merci pysaf.   (RD 143–8)

> (I see the hand that made me and the smell is sweeter than honey over me; through my sin I was lost to you, by your blood I am redeemed. I pray mercy.)

---

[37] See my '*Pascon agan Arluth*: the Literary Position of the Cornish Poem of the Passion', *Studi Medievali* 22 (1981), 822–36.

The oil of mercy has been dispensed.

The slightly later Cornish play known as *Gwreans an bys*, the Creation of the World, but which has an English title in the manuscript, is similar in some respects to the *Ordinalia*, but differs in details and hence in sources. Adam's plea at the expulsion from Eden for the oil of mercy is answered with the promise of the Redemption, but only after the biblical reference to hardship. Adam accepts God's justice, but looks foward to the promised Redemption. There is in *Gwreans an bys* no bargaining for land, and the introduction of the morality figure of Death indicates its lateness.

Gwreans an bys uses a different version of the Holy Rood legend to that in the *Ordinalia*. In addition, some motifs are present which are found neither in the earlier trilogy nor always in the Holy Rood *Legende* itself. The announcement that the oil of mercy will come in 5,500 years time *is* there, as in the Redentin play, and it may have come from the *Gospel of Nicodemus*, the *Vita Adae*, or even the *Golden Legend* story of the Invention of the Cross. That Seth here records the whole tale might be associated with the *Vita Adae*, although it is possible that the dramatist was using a version of Ranulph Higden's *Polychronicon*.[38] *Gwreans an bys* is quite distinctive, however, when Seth reaches Paradise. He sees a tree, but in its crown is the Virgin with the child, and in the roots he sees Cain rather than Abel. This is logical: in *Gwreans an bys* we have just been shown the death of Cain at the hands of Lamech, which is dramatically rare[39] and is not present in the *Ordinalia*, where Cain is presumably still alive when Seth goes to Paradise. The most important element, however, is the Virgin with a child. In the earlier play Seth sees the tree, the serpent round it (rather than on top of it), and the child (but not the mother). Moreover, the English stage-direction of *Gwreans an bys* even refers to two trees, a tree of knowledge *and* the tree of life, and this is very unusual:

> Ther he vyseth all thingys, and seeth two trees: and in the one tree sytteth
> Mary the Virgyn, and in her lappe her sonn Jesus, in the tope of the Tree of
> Lyf, and, in the other tree, the Serpent which caused Eva to eat the appell.
>
> (At 1804)

The presence of the Virgin ties in more clearly with Marian interpretations of the protevangelical verse, but this is one of only a few Marian points in the work. Seth is again given three seeds, but they are to be placed in Adam's mouth and nostrils this time, and from them a single tree (rather than the three rods of the *Ordinalia*) will grow. The vision of the Virgin with the child has a parallel of sorts in the exclusively English 'Arundel group', of *Vita Adae* manuscripts, in which Seth sees a *pietà*, the Virgin with the crucified Christ in her lap.[40] That might have strengthened the Redemption aspects, but the later Cornish dramatist does seem to have known a different source of the Sethite material from that used by the dramatist of the *Ordinalia*.

---

[38] Fowler, *Bible in Early English Literature*, pp. 218f.

[39] I have discussed the point in 'Creation, Fall and After', with a bibliography.

[40] See Murdoch, 'Holy Rood in Cornish Drama', for comments on the Arundel-class manuscripts. The manuscripts are discussed with bibliographical details by Halford, 'The Apocryphal *Vita Adae et Evae*'.

The angel who gives Seth the seeds explains what will happen, including the promise of Redemption. The angel's words are elliptical for Adam and Seth, but clear enough in a *sub gratia* context:

> Hag a tyf a'n keth sprus-na
> un wedhen wosa hemma
> na borth dowt, a vyth pur dek
> dhe dhon an Oyl a Vercy.
> Pan vo pymp myl ha pymp cans
> a vledhynnow cler passyes,
> y'n ur-na gwaytyens dewhans
> warlergh Oyl Mercy pupprys,
> ha Salvador yn tefry
> a'n doro mes a baynys.   (1855–66)

(And when [the tree] is fully grown it shall be always ready to bear the oil of mercy when 5,500 years have all gone – after that, let [Adam] expect the oil of mercy at any time and a saviour who will release him from his pains.)

In *Gwreans an bys* both Abel and later Adam are consigned to limbo, rather than hell. Adam is told that this is

> tha remaynya rag season
> pan deffa an oyle a vercy
> te a vith kerrys then ioye
> than nef vghall a vghan   (2075–8)

(where you must remain, until the oil of mercy comes and takes you into joy in high heaven.)

Cain is clearly in hell, but Adam, in limbo, cannot be tormented the same way as Cain. Lucifer himself points out to the other demons that this is all to do with repentance: Cain not only refused to repent and gave no thought to God's mercy, but he even rejoiced. He will suffer, but Adam and those who, while not yet *sub gratia*, repented thoroughly do not suffer the greater pains of hell; and even if limbo seems to be a part of hell, it is an angel who carries Adam there. The motif links with the *Vita Adae* tradition in which an angel takes Adam's soul at his death, charged by God to keep it in custody until judgement day. In the nearly contemporary *Historia de Deus* of Gil Vicente, Abel is also sent to limbo and joined there by Adam.

It is unlikely that the full story of the Rood would have been presented in *Gwreans an bys*, of which we have only the first day. It is possible that the poet's source was a version of the *Vita Adae* without the rest of the Rood narrative, but in any case there is no room for the story of the Rood in full. What we do have of the play has the same function of pointing onward that we saw in Immessen's work. At all events, the existing first day ends with an injunction to the audience to come back on the next day to see *ha redempsion grantys* (2544), so that the second day

148

may have been devoted entirely to the granting of the Redemption. It is in the elder of the two Cornish biblical plays, the *Ordinalia*, that we have preserved, uniquely in European literature, a substantial visualisation of that concrete simultaneity underscored in the traditions of the *Vita Adae* and of the Holy Rood.

'Come back tomorrow,' says the later Cornish play, and 'you shall see great matters.' The same kind of formula is used at the end of the first two of the *Ordinalia* plays, and the *Passio Domini* invites the audience to see on the following day how Christ rose out of the tomb. The concluding lines of the first play, spoken out of role by Solomon, are significant:

> a tus vas why re welas
> fetel formyas dev an tas
>> neh ha nor war lergh y vrys . . .
> ha ta welas an passyon
>> a jhesus hep gorholeth
> a worthevys crys ragon
>> a-vorow derg a dermyn . . .   (OM 2825–43)

(Good people, you have seen how God the father created heaven and earth according to His judgement . . . and to see the Passion right away which Jesus Christ suffered for us, tomorrow come in good time.)

Again, as in so much medieval drama, the audience becomes the contemporary crowd, and the verb *gweles* (to see) is much in evidence – a point that needs to be made about medieval drama of the Fall and the Redemption. The simultaneity in the divine perspective of the Fall and the Redemption may be expressed in the drama by various means: by verbal comment from an outside narrator; more usually by direct comment from God to Adam, which the audience then perceives as part of the action; or indeed by the extended use of the story of the Rood as a physical item visible on the stage. The audience is watching a play, but it is also watching divine – and human – history at the same time, history that is made immediate to the audience not only by the performance, but by details such as the use of local names in the case of the Cornish works. In the later Cornish play, immediately after the Fall, the figure of Death reminds us that Adam and Eve were deceived by the devil 'as you have all seen here' (CW 1004). Once again the immediacy and the conflating of time-references are clear.

Medieval drama used several physical variations on what in German is referred to as the *Simultanbühne*, the parallel presentation of heaven, hell and events on earth; events in heaven and hell are of course outside time, but the real difficulty is conveying to the audience the sense that the events of the divine economy are at once part of the eternal view and also are happening in time. It is impossible in this context to expand upon the already extensive critical discussion of the mimetic dimension in medieval drama as a whole, although O. B. Hardison's concept of identification in medieval drama, and the view that the actors become, rather than impersonate, the real protagonists, is clearly an important one. The time of the plays is also significant – the 'today' of the play (frequently referred to) might well also be the 'today' of a liturgical feast. The reality of the temporal events is always

149

immanent.[41] Typically, however, medieval dramatists make clear the importance of what is being observed, since the real Fall and Redemption have now happened, and the audience is therefore *sub gratia*. The comprehension of the perceiving audience should be more than that of the participants, more too even than that of the prophets who we saw in the *Biblia Pauperum* looking at events, as it were, from their vantage points, but who are nevertheless unable, perhaps, to see the *whole* stage. The Cornish plays, especially the *Ordinalia*, underscore very clearly the importance of seeing (and believing in consequence of what has been seen) in a number of separate scenes. Indeed, some biblical passages lend themselves particularly well to this. Echoing John 19:26, 'Mulier ecce filius tuus', emphasis is placed, for example, on the Virgin observing what is actually going on – this is a very early element in medieval drama in any case.[42] The centurion too, sees and believes, and the story of Longinus, cured of blindness by the blood of Christ, is highlighted in the *Ordinalia* Passion play by a striking speech after his eyes are literally opened. The familiar story of St Thomas, the most obvious instance of seeing and believing, is told in the English cycles too, most notably in the York plays. But the Cornish *Ordinalia* is once again both unique and extremely interesting in showing us the obduracy of Pilate and his apocryphal fate. Pilate has *seen* Christ, has observed the action in historical reality. Furthermore, he later on experiences Christ's power at first hand when he is taken to Rome to appear before the emperor and protects himself by wearing Christ's seamless coat. While he is wearing the coat he is unassailable, but in spite of all this visual and empirical evidence, Pilate still chooses to deny the importance of the events observed when he is brought to justice. Eventually he commits suicide – a death which betokens *desperatio*, and which parallels that of Judas – and later still his post-mortem activities become a parody of the Resurrection. Christ rose again, but after the suicide the earth rejects Pilate's corpse, which then is cast into water, just like the Cross at Bethsaida, although this time the water promptly becomes poisonous, and causes death to a traveller, rather than offering healing to the sick.[43]

We may conclude with an image that is again to do with observation, even if it takes us beyond the Middle Ages. The famous baroque statue by Bernini of St Theresa in ecstasy in St Peter's in Rome attracts a great number of visitors who

---

[41] O. B. Hardison, *Christian Rite and Christian Drama in the Middle Ages* (Baltimore and London: Johns Hopkins Press, 1965), see pp. 32f. See on this and earlier alternative views of impersonation Roeder, *Gebärde*, p. 96, who provides a neat summary of the debate. There is an interesting chapter 'Of History and Time', in Stanley J. Kahrl, *Traditions of Medieval English Drama* (London: Hutchinson, 1974), pp. 121–35. On the time of the plays, see Rainer Warning, *Funktion und Struktur* (Munich: Fink, 1974), pp. 66f.

[42] See Sandro Sticca, *The Planctus Mariae in the Dramatic Tradition of the Middle Ages*, trans. Joseph R. Berrigan (Athens, GA, and London: University of Georgia Press, 1988). On the use of biblical verses in the drama, see Peter Meredith, 'The Direct and Indirect Use of the Bible in Medieval English Drama', *Bulletin of the John Rylands Library* 77 (1995), 61–77.

[43] See Murdoch, *Cornish Literature*, pp. 69–73 on Thomas and on Pilate. A full study of the presentation of Pilate in Cornish and the apocryphal literature relating to his fate is in press ('*Mors Pilati*'). There is a contrast of course with St Veronica, part of whose legend is involved here, although there are various apocryphal writings concerned with Pilate. On Thomas and his function, see Eleanor Prosser, *Drama and Religion in the English Mystery Plays* (Stanford, CA: Stanford University Press, 1961), pp. 147–78.

stand and admire the plastic representation of the saint being struck with the arrow of divinity by the angel. They may, indeed, interpret it in different ways; people *have* done so. Even when the church is closed to visitors, however, and perhaps *especially* then, the scene represented in the round is still being observed, this time with clear admiration, by a group of watchers, in that it was provided with an audience from the beginnings, carved in relief and watching with reverence from a series of panels surrounding the statue. This baroque metaphor is important as a dramatic principle. Drama is watched, but more important than just watching is the idea of watching properly and receiving a specific message. That the message might not be understood clearly enough is always a danger with such an immediate art as the drama, and with biblical drama we might at best have a failure to comprehend; at worst, however, the wrong sympathies might occur. Medieval dramatists made every effort to ensure that the complex message of the simultaneity of Fall and Redemption, and of dramatic and historical present – the realisation, in short, of the unity implied in Romans 5:12 – was *not* misunderstood.

SIX

BY THE SCRIPTURES ALONE?
PLAYING ADAM IN THE REFORMATION AND BEYOND

W E MAY BEGIN this chapter with an unusual literary image from a period
well before the Reformation. A seventh-century bishop is being addressed
by a well-dressed and well-preserved anonymous, but apparently ancient, corpse
found in St Paul's cathedral. When conjured to do so by Saint Erkenwald,[1] the
corpse explains that Christ had somehow neglected to redeem his soul at the time
of the Harrowing. As a result the corpse has had to remain

> Dwynande in þe derke deth, þat dyȝte vs oure fader,
> Adam, oure alder, þat ete of þat appull,
> Þat mony a plyȝtles pepul has poysned for euer.   (294–6)

However, the corpse goes on to explain, Erkenwald is in far better case than he is,
because although also born in guilt, Erkenwald lives *sub gratia*:

> Ye were entouchid wyt his tethe & take in þe glotte,
> Bot mended wyt a medecyne, ȝe are made for to lyuye
> Þat is fulloght in fonte, wyt faitheful bileue,
> & þat han we myste alle merciles, myself & my soule.   (297–300)

In fact, Erkenwald does now baptize the corpse, which promptly decays into loath-
some fungus while the soul of the dead man is redeemed. The picture is a complicated one: the sinfulness of man is stressed, and original sin is clear, as indeed is the
corruptible nature of the human form. Luther would have approved the imagery,
for all that he referred to *Legende* as *Lügende*, legends as lying. Baptism, the sacrament that Luther retained, is enough to save this lost soul even such a long time
after death. The corpse was that of a wise, though unnamed, law-giver, it tells us,
and Erkenwald performs his dramatic act before a large and admiring audience,
which appears before us in the final lines as the bells all ring of their own accord,
something which happens, as we have seen, from time to time in medieval hagiography:

---

[1]   There is a text in C. Horstmann, *Altenglische Legenden: Neue Folge* (Heilbronn: Henninger, 1881),
pp. 265–74 and another (laid out in stanzas) ed. by Henry L. Savage, *St Erkenwald* (New Haven: Yale
University Press, 1926); it is cited here from the more recent edition, set out as in the manuscript, by
Ruth Morse, *St Erkenwald* (Cambridge: D. S. Brewer, 1975); there is a modern (rather free) English
translation in *The Owl and the Nightingale. Cleanness. St Erkenwald*, by Brian Stone (Harmondsworth: Penguin, 1971), pp. 28–43; *plyȝtles* (296) means, for example, 'unpledged, not part of the
covenant'. The poem dates from about 1386, and there are no real grounds for attributing it to the
Gawain-poem. See Savage's and Morse's introductions on the theme, and in general Paul Binski,
Medieval Death (London: British Museum, 1996). Binski refers on p. 97 to a twelfth-century bishop of
Paris who was buried with a note saying that he believed he would be resurrected at the end of the
world.

152

Þai passyd forthe in procession, & alle þe pepull folowid,
And alle þe belles in þe burghe beryd at ones.   (351–2)

We, the listeners or readers, are of course part of that audience and we have observed the miracle and we have heard the bells.

After C. S. Lewis's celebrated inaugural lecture in the 1950s on literary periodisation,[2] nobody would insist very strongly these days on a rigid temporal division between the Middle Ages and the Renaissance and Reformation, certainly as far as literature is concerned, and although in some aspects of theology the Reformation is a fairly visible watershed, those aspects are not always quite so clear-cut once they have been adapted into popular culture and expression. Indeed, R. W. Scribner's admirable little survey of the German reformation has encouraged us to question all kinds of aspects of supposed uniformity there as well.[3] At all events, it is very difficult to know where medieval biblical drama in particular ends. German folk-plays of the Fall, for example, some of them attested in Catholic territory such as Silesia or Austria in manuscript only from the nineteenth century, contain both very early material – even elements from the *Vita Adae* – and equally often a text based in part on the Adam and Eve play of the Protestant Hans Sachs. The dating of the Cornish mystery plays, too, is difficult, and the later play of the Creation, *Gwreans an bys*, in which Adam is consigned to limbo, was possibly composed during the Reformation and was certainly written down in 1611; the Reformation, even the English one, was by no means an instant event. Even as late as the 1480s Hans Folz in Nuremberg was translating, adapting into verse and publishing the *Vita Adae*, so that it was clearly known and accessible.[4]

Isolating the Reformation dramas of Adam and Eve is probably less appropriate than trying to place those dramas into the continuous context of religious drama as a whole, drama, that is, which not only places Adam and Eve on the stage, but which uses their story as a basis for an allegorical narrative. We may consider the way the Fall and the Redemption appear in the drama of the Reformation period, and look at some of the differences imparted by the thinking of the Reformation and the Renaissance. The Renaissance biblical-textual studies of Lorenza Valla and others are intrinsically linked with the Reformation insistence on the Scriptures as such. The period, of course, has additional difficulties for the comparative approach – an approach necessary with a fundamental theme such as that of the Fall – in the varying rates at which national drama developed in different countries. 'English drama progressed' – I cite Derek van Abbé – 'almost at a bound, from Passion play and interlude to Shakespeare.' Other cultures were less swift, and all this distorts any chronological approach as well.[5] Of course it is possible to sum up

---

2   'De descriptione temporum', reprinted in *They Asked for a Paper*, pp. 9–25.
3   R. W. Scribner, *The German Reformation* (London: Macmillan, 1986).
4   Murdoch, *Hans Folz*. In reality, of course, the distinction between the Reformers and those dismissed as 'obscure men' was frequently blurred; there is an indicative brief piece to this end by Leonard Forster, 'From the *Schwabenspiegel* to Pfefferkorn: a Study in *Makulatur*', in *Medieval German Studies Presented to Frederick Norman* (London: Institute of Germanic Studies, 1965), pp. 282–95.
5   Derek van Abbé, *Drama in Renaissance Germany and Switzerland* (Melbourne: Melbourne University Press, 1961). Van Abbé uses the term 'Renaissance' to include the writings of the Reformers.

the Protestant drama (and I am aware that I am using a sixteenth-century political term as a form of shorthand) by stressing – as Barbara Könneker has done – that it distanced itself from medieval drama by moving away from the direct representation of scriptural truth in favour of exemplary presentations of how personal salvation might be realised. It is true that Luther, in a famous sermon of 1519 on the contemplation of the events of the Passion, also distanced himself from the Passion play, but this was not necessarily programmatic, and there is in all the countries chiefly involved in the Reformation an ongoing tradition precisely of biblical plays presenting scriptural matter, admittedly with a fairly clear either/or message and a good deal of contemporary polemic.[6] A brief but sharp reminder of the problems of mixing that kind of polemic with an urge to adhere to the word of the Scriptures is found in John Bale's interlude *The Temptation of Our Lord* of 1538, a dramatisation of the temptation in the wilderness, in the course of which the devil claims that he has the Vicar of Rome on his side.[7]

In the earlier medieval dramas of the Fall the inherent simultaneity of the divine economy is made clear sometimes by a direct promise to Adam, but more forcefully by the use of the Holy Rood material with a heavy emphasis on the role of Seth, whose role as an intermediary between Adam and Paradise is there even without a full presentation of the Holy Rood matter. The interpretation of the protevangelical verse, which provides a possibility of linking the Fall and the Redemption, plays, on the other hand, less of a role in medieval drama, and sometimes it is omitted. We might well expect – and indeed shall find – a greater emphasis upon it in an age where the Reformers lay such great stress upon faith, grace and the scriptural word. That last point, the insistence on *sola scriptura* as a basis for that faith, coupled with the fruits of Renaissance textual criticism, will also make for differences of approach in the dramatisation of the Fall. Medieval portrayals not only included apocryphal material relating to Adam and sometimes Pilate, but also expanded the simple equation of devil and serpent to give us a whole host of devils, for example, or added fairly freely what we might call logical but non-biblical characters, such as named wives for Cain and Abel.

The aim in this chapter is to do two things: to show the dramatic and in some respects the theological continuity in the scenic representation of the Fall and the Redemption; and at the same time to indicate the differences – and they are principally ones of emphasis – in specifically Reformation dramatisations. For those writers who were directly concerned with the reforming movement in those countries most affected I shall concentrate especially on a few roughly contemporary representatives, writing in the vernacular between the 1530s and the 1570s. This more or less pragmatic choice means ignoring for the most part neo-Latin writers on both sides of the Reformation controversy, such as Sixt Birck, Georg Langhvelt (Macropedius), or Hieronymus Ziegler. Of those I *should* like to consider, the

---

[6] See Thomas I. Bacon, *Martin Luther and the Drama* (Amsterdam: Rodopi, 1976), pp. 42f with reference to his sermon of 1519. I refer also to Barbara Könneker, *Die deutsche Literatur der Reformationszeit* (Munich: Winkler, 1975), p. 57. See also the various papers in *Zugänge zu Martin Luther (Festschrift für Dietrich von Heymann)*, edd. Reinhard Wunderlich and Bernd Feininger (Frankfurt/M: Lang, 1997).
[7] For Bale, see below, note 16.

German dramatist Valten Voith, from Magdeburg, is admittedly not well known, but Hans Sachs, who was personally much influenced by Luther, at least is a familiar name. The Englishman John Bale, sent to Ireland as a bishop, and who moved in and out of England as he tried to stay alive through the age of the Tudors, is an interesting dramatist, far politer in that genre than as a controversialist. In Switzerland Jacob Ruf is in some respects – but only some, even though the one full-length study of Ruf refers to his most relevant play as 'stark mittelalterlich'[8] – a late representative and (already in the Protestant world) of the writers of medieval mystery-cycles, like Greban or Jean Michel, even though his place of work, Zurich, was a kind of forcing-house of Reformation theology in the 1550s and he knew and was influenced directly by Zwingli. The Netherlands, finally, may be represented by Huig de Groot's Latin play of Adam's exile and by Joost van Vondel's related work on the same theme at the end of the seventeenth century.

Even before the Reformation, in a Middle English Creation-play, the second piece in the Chester cycle, Adam gives a warning to his children about the destruction of the world by water and by fire. Adam tells his children, and indeed us, how he was in a vision taken into heaven and shown 'thinges that shall befall', and his words are admonitory:

> To make yow ware of comberous case,
> and let yow for to doe trespas,
> some I will tell before your face,
> but I will not tell all.
>
> . . .
>
> Water or fire as witterlie
> all this worlde shall destroy;
> for men shall sin so horably
> and do full muche amisse.
>
> Therefore that you may escape that noy [distress]
> doe well and beware me bye.   (448–62)

Adam's children are to pass this on: 'your childer this tale yow may tell'. In fact it is a good Reformation principle, but Adam's vision does not accord with the Bible text, and we might expect in the Reformation period that what you see is what you have in the Bible. Certainly in earlier medieval plays the precept of *sola scriptura* was not followed, at least, not if *scriptura* was defined in the way the Reformers chose to take it.

Our questions, then, when we come to look at plays of Adam and Eve in the period of the Renaissance and Reformation (and not just those by Reformers), are not only how or whether the express simultaneity of the divine economy is maintained, but also how or if the justification by faith and grace alone, supported by the Scriptures alone, is stressed in the presentation of the Fall. In the medieval dramas

---

8 'Strongly medieval'. Thus Robert Wildhaber, *Jakob Ruf. Ein Zürcher Dramatiker des 16. Jahrhunderts* (St Gallen: Wildhaber, 1929), p. 82. The play is studied on pp. 80–90 of Wildhaber's Basel dissertation.

(and bearing in mind that that is a flexible term) it was noticeable that the so-called protevangelium of Genesis 3:15 was treated fairly briefly, if it was included at all, and usually in very specific terms. God promised to Adam that a redeemer would come, or that the oil of mercy, this interpreted as Christ, would be given within a specific time-scale. Sometimes there is a stress on the Virgin, who will crush the devil's head (this depending on the reading of the subject, rendered as a feminine *ipsa* in the second part of the Vulgate version of the text). In the most concrete form of the divine promise, the seeds of the Cross from the *Vita Adae*/Holy Rood legends were planted with Adam, and – as in the Cornish *Ordinalia* – it was made clear that the Redemption was always present as a possibility. Indeed Adam (not fully comprehendingly), and certainly Moses, David and the unbiblical Maximilla, made the eventual fulfilment clear, not as oblique prophecy or typological act, but as straightforward knowledge. In the Reformation period there is a shift. The apocryphal legends disappear with the new (and Humanist-based) insistence on a canon and a text of the Bible from which they were excluded. Indeed, the notion of an actual penance – such as that in the river – as a means to obtaining grace by one's own effort is impossible. The state of mind – as Luther made so clear in *Von der Freiheit eines Christen Menschen* (On the Freedom of a Christian) – is what matters.

A good example of a Reformation Adam-play which still retains medieval features and which also continues to underline the need for expressing the simultaneity of Fall and Redemption is provided by a relatively little-known German dramatist in the early years of the Reformation. We know very little about Valten Voith – as is customary with German dramatists of this period, even the spelling of his name varies – but he was born in Chemnitz in 1487, studied at Wittenberg, and then worked in Magdeburg and produced school-dramas. His Adam-play[9] has a significantly detailed title:

> Ein schoen Lieblich Spiel/ von der herlichen ursprung: Betruebtem Fal. Gnediger widerbrengunge. Mueseligem leben/ Seligem Ende/ vnd ewiger Freudt des Menschen aus den Historien heiliger schrifft gezogen ganz Troestlich.

> (A very fine play about the noble origins, wretched Fall, merciful Redemption, burdensome life, virtuous end and eternal delights of Man, drawn in a most comforting manner from the histories in the Scriptures.)

As Almut Agnes Meyer, one of the few critics to devote attention to the play, has pointed out, the work seems to have been based on an allegorical painting; she also makes clear that various elements in the work match very closely the late medieval

---

[9] Hugo Holstein, *Die Dramen von Ackermann und Voith* (Tübingen: Stuttgart literarischer Verein, 1884), pp. 207–316. The best study of it – indeed, almost the only study, but a full and clear analysis nevertheless – is that by Almut Agnes Meyer, *Heilsgewißheit*, pp. 14–57. Usually Voith is dismissed fairly curtly by the critics: Auguste Brieger commented in 1934 that 'Voith doziert, ohne darzustellen' (Voith lectures rather than presents), and contrasted Voith's use of the stage as a pulpit with the drama of Jacob Ruf: *Kain und Abel in der deutschen Dichtung* (Berlin and Leipzig: de Gruyter, 1934), pp. 18f.

drama, and indeed that it contains elements found in earlier plays as well, such as Lucifer's own narrative of his Fall, which is here briefly told. There is no proliferation of devils, but Lucifer and Satan both appear, as in far earlier plays. Indeed, Adam's opening words refer to his creation by the Trinity, a motif common in medieval writings.

Some new motifs – or at least, variations and new emphases – appear in the context of the Fall itself. When Adam and Eve realise their nakedness, this realisation is articulated rather more originally than as straightforward shame. They are aware of a quite specific and quite new propensity to sexual lust, which Adam even describes as a *böse lust* (202) (a 'wicked lustfulness'). Seeing Eve naked he is aware of a change in his feelings and so is she:

> Du gefelst mir anders dann vor,
> Das sag ich dir auch gantz vorwor,
> Mich thut itzt noch dir vorlangen.

To which she replies:

> Mit lust mein hertz ist gefangen   (203–6)

> ('You appeal to me rather differently than before, I am telling you the truth, I desire you.' And Eve: 'My heart is captivated with lustfulness.')

We may note that the German uses passive/objective formulations: these effects happen to the protoplasts. It is at this point, too, that the four enemies of Adam appear, three of them allegorical personifications – Justice, Death, Sin and Satan – looking for Adam even before God does. Figures like these develop in the morality play, and the introduction of Death as a figure from another visual cycle, the fifteenth-century *Dance of Death*, is probably most familiar dramatically at the start of the sixteenth century in the play of *Everyman*.[10] Death himself is already present in at least one of the English mysteries, standing behind Herod in the Hegge plays, and he comes to play a part in later Adam and Eve dramas, literally appearing when the idea of death comes into existence. Thus he is there in the later of the Cornish mysteries, the *Creation of the World*, though not in the *Ordinalia*, and has a brief but significant part, warning the audience directly about sin. In Gil Vicente, too, he appears at the moment of the Fall.[11] Other, rather different, allegorical figures have appeared before, of course: Justice and Mercy are there in the paradisiacal debate scenes in early dramas. But although they are not strictly part of the Scriptures, they are implicit in the exegesis of the Fall and the Redemption. Death as a neutral entity, and projections of human character points, like sinfulness, will play a developing part in drama, as biblical revelation gives way to the morality in dramatic terms.

[10] Binski, *Death*, pp. 153–9. See pp. 159–63 on the serpent as death.
[11] J. M. R. Margeson, *The Origins of English Tragedy* (Oxford: Clarendon, 1967), p. 33. *Everyman*, edited by A. C. Cawley (Manchester: Manchester University Press, 1961) has a frontispiece with a contemporary woodcut of the Death figure and Everyman. The standard work on the Dance of Death is Hellmut Rosenfeld, *Der mittelalterliche Todestanz* (Cologne and Graz: Böhlau, 3rd edn, 1974).

When God comes to look for Adam (following the biblical Genesis 3:9) Valten Voith adapts a well known and long-established exegetical tradition. The attempted avoidance of blame by the protoplasts is seen thoughout medieval exegesis as the indirect attempt to blame God.[12] This line of argument is also in accord with Reformation notions of man's corrupt nature, however, and Voith unusually develops it as a conscious plot on Eve's part. Hearing the voice of God, Eve – *nota bene* – actually suggests that they should both try to pass on the blame, and that in that way

> So bleiben wir beide unvorletzt,
> So wert Gott auch mehr schulde han
> Dann wir so wöln wir ihm entgan . . .   (322–4)

> (We will both get away with it, God will get more of the blame
> than us, and we'll escape from him.)

The passage is followed by a biblically exact version of the judgement, which does, however, make clear grammatically in the rendering of Genesis 3:15 that it is the *seed* of the woman rather than the woman herself, an implicit *ipse*, that will crush the serpent. Although medieval plays do not necessarily develop the *ipsa* of the Old Latin and Vulgate reading in any case, the new biblical scholarship of the Renaissance demands the reading. Since that reading was also accepted within a fairly short time elsewhere, it is unlikely that later drama of any colour will place the same emphasis on the Virgin that we find with the interpretation of the verse in Marianic works like Immessen's Low German play of the Fall. By the 1670s the Dominican church historian Noël Alexandre was referring to the *ipse* reading as *melius et congruentius*, and citing Jerome's *Questions on the Hebrew Genesis* in support.[13] In Voith's play, the protevangelical implications are realised, however, and put into words by Satan himself, possibly because[14] the dramatist does not wish to attribute to God material that is not actually in the Bible. The point is entirely Christological:

> Von eim weib sol geporn werden
> Der heilandt aller auf erden
> Sal mir auch mein kopff zu tretten.   (393–5)

> (The Saviour of the world shall be born of a woman, who shall
> crush my head.)

This also has the effect of removing the application of the prophecy from the serpent and reapplying it interpretatively to the devil. After the expulsion Adam also indicates his understanding of this:

---

[12] Murdoch, *Fall of Man in the Early Middle High German Biblical Epic*, pp. 130–9 with reference to the *Moralia in Job* of Gregory the Great (*PL* 75, 661). It remained current throughout the Middle Ages as an exegetical commonplace.

[13] Natalis Alexander (Noël Alexandre, 1639–1724), *Dissertationum ecclesiasticarum trias* (Paris: Dezallier, 1679), p. 310.

[14] As noted by Meyer, *Heilsgewißheit*, pp. 34f.

Das merck, Eva, frw und spat

Das von dir sal geporen werden
Aller mensch heiland auff erden,
Der sol erwürgen unser veind . . .   (470–3)

(Note, Eve, and remember at all times that from you shall be
born the Saviour of all men who shall strangle our enemy.)

There is an echo here of New Testament references to the destruction of the old
serpent. Adam develops his interpretation later on in the course of a debate with
Justice, Sin, Death and Satan. He is clear on the Redemption, even if this context is
not biblical:

Es wert komen inn lezten tagen,
Ein sam des weibes sal er seyn,
Doch warer Gott, den ich auch mein,
Der wert ghen inn meiner gestalt,
Gantz elent, arm, an al gewalt,
. . .
Wie wol er stirbt gantz willig dar . . .   (692–702)

(In the last days the seed of the woman will come, who is also
truly God, who will come in my form, poor and powerless . . .
and will die willingly . . .)

Adam makes the point repeatedly, underlining not just the simultaneity, but the
need for faith on man's part. The belief which has to sustain man, and faith in
general, are both emphasised throughout the play, which now takes us through
Abraham (by way of the faith of the aged Sara) to the story of Isaac. Told to sacrifice Isaac, Abraham comments that he had hoped Isaac would be the seed from
which the Redeemer would come, an interesting version of the normal typological
interpretation by which Isaac *represents* Christ. The demonstration of Abraham's
complete faith is thus a reminder of the typology. After a scene with David –
unusually in drama the story of David and Bathsheba[15] – the point of which is (as
Nathan points out) that David has repented and can therefore be forgiven, Christ
himself appears and overcomes man's enemies.

Voith's play puts an increased emphasis on faith and the commandment of God,
and the concrete evidence provided in the Rood legend has been replaced by the
repeated injunction to believe in what you have been told. In the same year as Voith
wrote his drama, a comparable work (with an equally detailed title) appeared by a
prominent English Protestant, John Bale, who started out as a friar – one might
even say 'started life', since he was despatched at a very early age, and largely for
reasons to do with family finances, to join the Carmelites – but who converted in
1530, left the Whitefriars, and eventually became the Protestant bishop of Ossory

---

[15] This does appear in the Cornish *Ordinalia*, but it is rare until the seventeenth century: see Inga-
Stina Ewbank, 'The House of David in Renaissance Drama', *Renaissance Drama* 8 (1965), 3–40.

in Ireland, not the most comfortable of appointments in any Tudor reign, and especially not in one as brief as that of Edward VI. Under Mary he went to Switzerland, and returned when Elizabeth became queen. He was traditionally (there is not a great deal of evidence) a member of Jesus College, Cambridge,[16] and we may accept or reject the view that – according to the edition of *Dodsley's Old English Plays* by William Carew Hazlitt, the grandson of the essayist – was apparently 'insinuated by Bishop Nicolson', that Bale's conversion depended upon a dislike of celibacy. It is hard to prove or disprove that at such a distance, even if he was certainly scornful in his controversialist writings about celibates of various sorts. At all events, Bale was a vigorous propagandist, and that much is clear too from his small number of surviving plays, these offering – I cite Glynn Wickham – 'a signpost to Redemption from a strictly Protestant viewpoint'. In dramatic terms they are, in comparison with the medieval texts, fairly spare, adhering far more than did Voith to the principle of *sola scriptura*. But again, this does not preclude interpretation.

Bale's interlude, written in 1538 and known usually and appropriately by its short title as *God's Promises*, he actually called 'A Tragedye or enterlude manyfesting the chefe promyses of God unto man by all ages in the Old Law from the Fall of Adam to the Incarnacyon of the Lorde Jesus Christ'. This could summarise any of the earlier mysteries, of course: the Cornish *Ordinalia* would fit admirably. Indeed, the whole notion of the *aetates* is medieval.[17] But this is – apart from its relative brevity – a very different piece. The play is divided into seven acts, each devoted to a dialogue between God as *Pater Coelestis* and various Old Testament figures (more than in Voith) and finally John the Baptist. There is not a great deal of action (a stricture made by some critics about Voith, but which applies better here) and again there are no devils and even fewer opportunities for stage business. Bale himself as Prologue sets the whole in context and says precisely what God's promises are, stressing at the same time the need for all men to know the Gospel story or be lost. There is no suspense: 'after that Adam bewaileth here his Fall/ God will show mercy to every generation' (Prologue). This could be part of a medieval play, especially since it comes from an outside speaker, the Prologue.

The first act shows Adam after the Fall – as we have seen before – pleading for

---

[16] For a good brief sketch of his life, see the admirable summary by Peter Happé (who has himself edited Bale's plays, 1985–6), 'John Bale, 1495–1563', *Jesus College, Cambridge Report* 93 (1997), 18–22. Reference here is to the interlude *The Chief Promises of God unto Man*, although there is material of interest also in *The Temptation of Our Lord* (both 1538). See Happé's edition, *The Complete Plays of John Bale* (Cambridge: D. S. Brewer, 1985–6), both plays being in vol. II; the text of the former is in Robert Dodsley, *A Select Collection of Old English Plays*, 4th edn by W. Carew Hazlitt (London: Reeves and Turner, 1874), I, pp. 277–322, and of the latter in Glynne Wickham, *English Moral Interludes* (London: Dent, 1976), pp. 127–142. I have cited from the introductory material to both. C. S. Lewis refers to Bale and his English prose polemics as 'the most vitriolic of the Protestant controversialists', but the plays, of course, have a different target audience, and are more generally didactic. Certainly Bale made vicious attacks on Roman (and indeed other) celibates, however, some of which Lewis quotes in *English Literature in the Sixteenth Century* (Oxford: Clarendon, 1954), pp. 296f. See also James C. Bryant, *Tudor Drama and Religious Controversy* (Mercer: Mercer University Press, 1984), p. 45 on the polemics in his *King John*.

[17] There is a good brief summary of the idea of the ages in medieval theological thought in *The Irish Sex Aetates Mundi*, ed. Dáibhí Ó Cróinín (Dublin: DIAS, 1983), pp. 1–10.

mercy for one single crime, and that committed because he had free will. God asks Adam at this point whether that means that Adam is actually blaming God, although Adam quickly denies this. It is not done in such detail as in Voith, but although the point is made in medieval exegesis and finds its way into vernacular writing too – an eleventh-century German poem comments sternly that this was worse than the actual Fall – it is rare in the drama before a period when the real stress is on the change of heart enjoined in Matthew 4:17 as μετανοεῖτε. Luther himself, concerned to take emphasis away from actual works, changed in his successive Bibles the translation of the verb from *thut pusz*, meaning 'do penance', to *bessert euch*, 'improve', and only changed back in 1545, perhaps feeling that the point had by then established itself.[18] Here, however, Adam does admit his guilt, and although God cannot commute the punishment of death, Adam is able to repent fully, and God agrees that He will grant mercy after all. It is not until this point – well after the expulsion – that Bale allows God to voice the biblical punishment on the serpent. God's covenant, the first chief promise to Adam and his successors, is that there shall be hatred between the serpent and the seed of the woman.

The biblical order is not followed. Adam is enjoined to combat the serpent's wiles from the start, to 'slay his suggestions and his whole power confound'. Gregory the Great referred in his *Morals on the Book of Job* to the attack on the devil's *suggestio*, the first stage of sin, which must be attacked if the later stages of *consensus, consuetudo* and *defensio* are to be avoided, and he was much quoted by later exegetes. But this is the first promise, and if Adam grasps it, all will be well:

> Fold it in thy faith with full hope day and hour
> And thy salvation it will be at the last.

Faith alone will save Adam, something which he cannot earn: 'Of thy mere goodness, and not of my deserving'. It will require faith alone and grace alone, although the saving will come from the seed of the woman. But by *sola scriptura* all that is meant here is that nothing is added; the order and the selectivity are not biblical. Adam voices his trust in grace alone in the words of the Prayerbook, and the sure and certain hope of the resurrection. In the other acts of the play there are frequent references to this scene: Noah talks of the relief given to Adam and Eve, and, just as in Voith, Abraham also speaks of the promise of the woman's seed, which now becames Abraham's seed too.

The enormously prolific Nuremberg poet and dramatist Hans Sachs – who, after his conversion to Luther's cause, produced a more subtle range of polemical dialogues than those of his near-contemporary, Bale – treated the Fall and Redemption on several occasions in poems and as a play.[19] The *Tragedia von*

---

[18] See *Martin Luther: Selections*, ed. Lewis Jillings and Brian Murdoch (Hull: NGS, repr. 1980), p. 39.

[19] See my 'Schöpfung, fal und erlösung: Hans Sachs and Genesis 1–3', in *Hans Sachs and Folk Theatre in the Late Middle Ages*, ed. R. Aylett and P. Skrine (Lewiston: Mellen, 1995), pp. 63–80. The poems date from 1545 (*Schöpfung, fal und erlösung Adam, Eva und gantzes menschlichen geschlechts*) and 1568 (*Gottes schopfung aller creatur im anfang, auch unser eltern Adam und Eva schweren fal und austreibung aus dem paradeis*) ('Creation, Fall and Redemption of Adam, Eve and

schöpfung, fal und außtreibung Ade aus dem paradeyß (A Tragedy of the Creation, Fall and Expulsion of Adam from Paradise) of 1548 in fact adapts freely (and actually cuts by half) a slightly earlier Latin work by Hieronymus Ziegler written in 1545.[20] As a vernacular text, Sachs's German play took on a completely independent existence and was widely copied or drawn upon in the folk-play, blurring the Protestant/Catholic distinction. This would happen again when the Passion of the Swiss Protestant Jacob Ruf was adopted in Catholic territories.

Protestant solifidianism is still very clear in all the versions of the Fall offered by Sachs, but Sachs's Paradise play does not necessarily follow the precept of a rigid adherence to the Scriptures. Since in this case only the first chapters of Genesis down to the expulsion are included, the play should therefore involve only God, the protoplasts, the serpent and the Cherub of Genesis 3:26, who is also the Prologue and Epilogue. Sachs increases this to eleven members of the cast by adding three archangels and three devils, Lucifer, Belial and Sathan. There are other small non-biblical points; the old interpretation of *malum* that makes the fruit an apple is still here (and later in Ruf), presumably out of tradition and in spite of Luther's Bible, though Voith and Bale are unspecific. The notion of a diabolical plurality is a standard feature of medieval plays, and certainly Jacob Ruf keeps the idea. Sachs's play is more modest, but there are still three non-biblical devils discussing the possibility of the Fall. In Sachs's third act there is a positively medieval scene in which the three devils dance and rejoice, in contrast to a scene in heaven, in which the angels express their sorrow. We are still, therefore, with the medieval *Simultanbühne*.

In the trial scene, although Adam tries hard to place the blame on the woman, the idea of an implicit or indeed explicit blame on God is not developed, and all are condemned, but the interpretation and use of the protevangelium is again of some significance, and it is dealt with twice. Sachs has God pronounce judgement on the serpent in biblical terms, saying that the seed of the woman will crush the head of the serpent's seed, but God reiterates the judgement as a prophecy, and this is more in line with the medieval plays: however, the prophecy is not yet entirely specific:

> Doch wirt ein sam kummen von dir,
> Welcher wirt dieser schlangen schir
> Den kopff zertretten und zerknischen . . .
> Als denn so wird ich euch begnaden.   (KG I, 46, 20–4)

(A seed will come from you that will soon crush this serpent's head . . . then I shall pardon – grant grace to – you.)

all of mankind' and 'God's creation of all things at the beginning, and also the disastrous Fall and expulsion from Paradise of our first parents, Adam and Eve'). Sachs also wrote *Meistergesänge* on the theme in 1540, 1544 and 1555.
20 The *Tragedia* of 1548 is cited from A. von Keller and E. Goetze, *Hans Sachs: Werke* (Tübingen: Stuttgart literarischer Verein, 1870–1908) [referred to as KG], I, 19–52. The longer poems are in KG I, 174–7 and KG XXIII, 425f respectively. On the source of the *Tragedia* (with extracts from Ziegler and a comparison of the two works in some detail) see Klimke, *Paradiesspiel*, pp. 45–55. Hieronymus Ziegler's *Protoplastus: Drama Comicotragicum in memoriam humanae conditionis* was published in Augsburg in 1545, and there is a summary in Kirkconnell, *Cycle*, pp. 552f. On Sachs as a mediator of theological ideas, see Dorothea Klein, *Bildung und Belehrung* (Stuttgart: Heinz, 1988), pp. 278f.

Adam's final words in a play that does not actually show us the Redemption do point to the possibility of salvation, and although the oil of mercy is not mentioned, one might wonder from the choice of words whether it was not perhaps in Sachs's mind:

> Got kan das machen wol ein end!
> Wenn er sein barmung zu uns wend.   (KG I, 49, 27–8)

> (God can make an end when He applies His mercy to us.)

The force of the protevangelium is clearer in Sachs's longer poems on the theme, and more especially in his play on the 'unequal children of Eve'[21] of 1553, originally a parable by Philipp Melanchthon and again adapted by Sachs in various different ways, even with more than one dramatic version. This story, in which God visits Eve when only half of her children have been washed, and in which the clean ones know their catechism and the dirty ones do not, is not biblical drama. However, at the end of Sach's 1553 version a herald anticipates for the audience the arrival of the Redeemer:

> Ach gott, sendt uns dein heyland her!
> Nach deym verheissen du uns tröst!
> Uns auß deiner ungnad erlöst.   (KG XI, 388, 27–9)

> (God, send us your saviour according to your promise to save us
> from your anger.)

In that same play, God himself reminds the protoplasts of the terms of the promise, explaining that the one who will crush the head of the serpent and bring Redemption is Christ who will suffer on the Cross.

Sachs does not in his Paradise play proper go on to show us the Redemption, but rather leaves the audience with the need to hope for grace and to have faith that it will come. It is a move away from the expression of complete simultaneity. The Swiss writer Jacob Ruf, too, does not show us the actual Redemption. Ruf's title – in contrast with that of Voith, for example – refers simply to his having produced *Ein nüw und lustig spil von der erschaffung Adams und Heva, auch irer beider fal im paradyß* (A New and Lively Play about the Creation of Adam and Eve and their Fall from Paradise). His printed text (in this case like Voith's) contained biblical concordances, however, marginals with biblical references. His play of Adam and Eve, whilst very clearly a Protestant version of the story, is also in many respects akin to the large-scale medieval mystery, performed as it was over two days with an enormous cast outside the cathedral.[22] The cathedral in question, though, was the

---

21 See my 'Hans Sachs and Genesis 1–3' for details of the versions of the 'unequal children' poems and plays. The various versions by Hans Sachs of Melanchthon's parable of *Die ungleichen Kinder Eve* appear in Theo Schumacher, *Hans Sachs: Fastnachtspiele* (Tübingen: Niemeyer, 1957); see Maria S. Müller, *Der Poet der Moralität: Untersuchungen zu Hans Sachs* (Berne, Frankfurt/M, New York: Peter Lang, 1985), pp. 100–12. Xystus Betuleius (Sixt Birck, of Augsburg) wrote a dramatic version in 1547. Those by Sachs date from 1547–1558.
22 I have discussed the play in two papers: 'Jacob Ruf's *Adam und Heva* and the Protestant Paradise-

163

Minster in Protestant Zurich, and when it was put on, on the 9th and 10th of June –
Corpus Christi – 1550, Zwingli himself had been dead for less than twenty years.
Jacob Ruf (whose name can be spelt more ways that ought to be possible for a
monosyllable) was very much part of the intellectual hothouse of sixteenth-
century Zurich. Beside Zwingli he knew the zoologist Conrad Gesner, and
although he produced a number of biblical plays beside the Adam and Eve drama,
his other books are on gynaecology and obstetrics; he ended his days as town
surgeon-general in 1558, dying in the same year as Voith.

Ruf's play forms a bridge between the Middle Ages and the Reformation as a
good illustration of Lewis's strictures against rigid periodisation. The play took
two days to perform, has a cast of over a hundred, not counting the animals named
individually by Adam – it is impossible to tell from the printed text whether they
actually appeared or not – and even given that the action goes as far as the Flood, a
glance at the relevant eight short chapters of Genesis might cause one to wonder
how Ruf's expansion of a couple of pages at most to a two-day-long drama
matches the idea of *sola scriptura*.

In many ways it does not. Noticeable first of all are the devils. Voith had two,
Sachs had three, but Ruf has a whole host of them. Myriads clearly fell with
Lucifer, but where even that impressive list provided by Milton in the first book of
Paradise Lost contains only (as it were) grown-up devils, Ruf's pandemonium
(like some earlier medieval mysteries) contains also a selection of *jung tüfeli* (wee
devils), if we may imitate the specifically Swiss form, one of whom complains of
having been a little angel previously. The printed texts have some of the parts
involving additional devils added on, and perhaps they were written in later.[23]
Clearly they were good comic value, however, and they establish a language of
what sounds rather like jolly blasphemy in which they actually avoid the name of
God with a euphemism, as with the exclamation 'botz hosenlatz und nestelglimpf',
which I have translated elsewhere as 'odds codpieces and dangly bits', the strictly
lexical meaning of *nestelglimpf* being the pointed end of a belt. In fact there is a
serious and technically skilful underlay to all this nonsense, as Ruf allows this
mode of speech to be adopted by groups of characters he wishes to signal as bad,
such as the revellers before the Flood, or earlier the wicked Cainites, who contrast
with the markedly *bibelfest* Sethites.[24] On the other hand, although he has supernatural characters, as it were, they do at least have biblical authority, even if not
always from Genesis, where there are of course no devils. Like Bale and Sachs,
Ruf has no allegorical figures, not even Death.

Of course there is no indication here of material from, say, the *Vita Adae*, and for
two reasons: the genuinely apocryphal writings were pronounced anathema by the

Play', *Modern Language Review* 86 (1991), 109–25, and 'Dos piezas dramáticas en verso del Génesis,
una germana y una celta, de finales de la Edad Media', *Acta Poetica* (Medieval German/Celtic
number) 16 (1995), 349–68. The latter paper compares Ruf with the (Catholic) Cornish *Gwreans an
bys*. The basic text is that edited by Hermann Marcus Kottinger, *Jacob Ruffs Adam und Heva* (Quedlinburg and Leipzig: Basse, 1848).

[23] For information on contemporary printed editions I am indebted to Janice Whitelaw, who has
completed a new edition: 'Jacob Ruff's *Adam and Heva*' (Ph.D. Diss. Stirling, 1998).

[24] There is a translation of some of the relevant portions of the play in my *Grin of the Gargoyle*, pp.
144–54. (The date is there given in error as 1555 rather than 1550.)

reformers, and as far as Adam's and Eve's penance in the river is concerned, faith is what mattered, not works, even those of an act of penance. However, assumed biblical characters do appear, even when the Bible does not mention them. There are long parts for Delbora and Calmana, for example, the wives of Abel and Cain, and later on new and not strictly biblical roles are created for Enoch and Noah. There is, as indicated, a detailed naming of the animals, and this long scene allows Adam to impart for each animal a certain amount of detailed information, or, since this is Adam doing it at the beginning of time, it might better be referred to as predictive and exegetical zoology. In spite of Gesner's more scientific *Historia Animalium*, which began to appear in 1551, and about which Ruf will have known, Ruf's Adam offers us a wonderful mixture of genuine zoology (the chamois will live up in the high mountains) and folk-wisdom (squirrels will use their tails as sails, just as they do in *Squirrel Nutkin*, whilst the cry of the peacock will drive away poisonous serpents).[25] Many of Adam's comments stress the usefulness of the beasts, however, and some are actively exegetical: the unicorn is referred to in terms of the Abelardian Trinity-formula, and the serpent is exposed even before the Fall as the one who will bring misfortune. It might even be argued that Ruf's desire to adhere to the text of the Bible actually leads him into complexities for which he has to find new solutions.[26] Thus, although we have no quest of Seth to Paradise, we do have a full treatment of the Sethite and Cainite lines in Genesis, and while recent criticism has seen these name-lists as variant versions of ancient material, Ruf, like Zwingli and the Zurich Protestants, took the two genealogies at face value and kept them well apart. In the period of the Reformation he was of course only too keen to draw sharp distinctions between one sort of believer and another, one clearly good, the other just as clearly vilified. Ruf carefully separates the good Lamech, descended from Seth, for example, from the proto-bigamist and Cainite Lemech, keeping the tiny distinction of name-form which is present in the Zurich Bible of 1531 but not in Luther's. Ruf even voices a kind of antediluvian Luddism by having his good characters express criticism of the technological expertise developed by the bigamist's children (including Naamah as the inventor of weaving, a traditional notion that is not biblical anyway and offers us yet another of the many versions of the origins of tailoring). Technology simply leads to *luxuria* and is therefore reprehensible. Ruf's play is extreme in this respect, however; else-where a set of woodcuts from 1530 with verses provided by Hans Sachs go so far as to shunt 'Lamech' the bigamous Cainite and his inventive children quietly into the Sethite line, supplanting Noah's worthy, but less interesting, proper father.[27]

Ruf treats the protevangelical verse fairly literally, although it is augmented by a brief marker that man is not doomed. In place of any penance, the notion is stressed

[25] Murdoch, 'Ruf', analyses the passage, pp. 115–17. See H. W. Hanson, *Apes and Ape Lore in the Middle Ages and the Renaissance* (London: Warburg Institute, 1952), pp. 107–44 on the beasts and the naming scene in art. See also the generally interesting study of the iconography of the Fall as a whole in Diane Kelsey McColley, *A Gust for Paradise: Milton's Eden and the Visual Arts* (Urbana and Chicago: University of Illinois Press, 1993). The study also covers material well before Milton.

[26] I have considered the point in medieval writings other than drama in 'Sethites and Cainites: Narrative Problems in the Early Middle High German Genesis Poems', in *Festschrift for R. A. Wisbey*, ed. A. Stevens et al. (Berlin: Schmidt, 1994), pp. 83–97.

[27] Murdoch, 'Ruf', pp. 120f.

that man will be redeemed if he only has faith. While Ruf is the most medieval of the Protestant dramatists in overall structure and in some detail, he is in terms of argument more Protestant than Voith, Bale or Sachs. Even at the creation of Adam (and thus before the Fall), God stresses the distinction between the corruptible body and the immortal soul, the same kind of distinction that Luther had again developed in *Von der Freiheit eines Christen Menschen*, and there is a consistent and express emphasis after the Fall on the necessity of pure belief, *sola fide*, in the power of God's grace alone, *sola gratia*. Relevant passages appear throughout the work, but Mathusalah sums it up:

> so zwyfl ich nit, bin deß vertröst
> wir werdind allesampt erlöst
> uß lutrer gnad, barmherzigkeit   (3719–21)

> (I have no doubts and am comforted by the fact that we shall be redeemed, all of us, by grace alone, by mercy.)

The last part of the play is at once Protestant ethos and Protestant historical polemic, but to achieve his effect Ruf provides for Noah, and indeed for Enoch, roles which make them faintly reminiscent of the procession of prophets in the medieval mysteries. But Noah is merged with Jeremiah rather than Isaiah, and their views are not prophetic of the Redemption, but admonitory of the Flood. The wicked city, completely preoccupied by merrymaking (as in Matthew 23:38) and presumably intended as a picture of Rome, refuses to listen to Enoch or to Noah when they both become Protestant preachers, protestant, that is, in the precise sense, protesting against evil and 'using biblical promises of grace to all men to urge repentance upon a corrupt generation'.[28] Both try to persuade the citizens to change their ways. Ruf, as chary as Luther, renders the μετανοεῖτε of Matthew 4:17 as *bekeerend üch* in Enoch's mouth and *besseren üch* in Noah's, 'change', 'improve yourselves', even 'convert', rather than as anything to do with an *act* of penance, but he is ignored. The contrast between the just man – the biblical Noah – and the corruption of humanity in general, is effective.

Two final points need to be made about Ruf's play: the Flood ends the whole work – a good dramatic spectacular in any terms, although one wonders how it was produced there on the Münsterplatz in 1550; and we are not actually shown the Redemption. Nor, indeed, do we see Noah's survival, and the ending is apocalyptic. We have to believe in the possibility of a Redemption in the face of all this when we are told about it, rather than through seeing it. Ruf did, in fact, also write a Passion play – one that was, curiously enough, also played in Catholic territories, with the author's identity suppressed[29] – but there is one final feature about his Paradise play that bears mentioning. When Enoch and Noah preach their warnings, they are, it is true, ignored or abused by the revellers, but some of the people take notice, and these are the watchers within the play, the parallel to the audience.

---

[28] Murdoch, 'Ruf', p. 125.

[29] Barbara Thoran, *Studien zu den österlichen Spielen des deutschen Mittelalters* (Göppingen: Kümmerle, 2nd edn, 1976), p. 20. Thoran has also edited the work as *Das Züricher Passionsspiel* (Bochum: Brockmeyer, 1984).

These draw inwards the external audience to make even clearer not just the message of the play, but the need to heed it, as much at the time of the performance as within the play itself. Those most concerned within Ruf's play are the soldiers in the wicked city, the guards; we may recall that for a Protestant audience in sixteenth-century Zurich the wickedest of cities was Rome, and that in 1550 in that city, as now, the guards, instituted by Julius II some forty years earlier, were Swiss.

The distortion of time that allowed Eve, cast out of Paradise, to refer in a Provençal mystery to the sacrifice of the Virgin's son when the Cherub with the flaming sword was just closing the gates behind her would no longer be possible. In Ruf, her prayer is far simpler, though liturgical:

> mitteil din gnad allzyt uns armen.
> unser herr, gott! thuo dich erbarmen,
> blyb unser herr, ouch unser gott
> gib gnad uns, z'halten din gebott   (1865–8)

> (Give us wretches your grace at all times, O Lord our God! Have mercy upon us, remain our Lord and God, give us grace to keep your commandments.)

The action of the Genesis story is kept within its own logic, but the herald who opens and closes the play is in the world of the present. He concludes the first day with a summary to the effect that God will nevertheless forgive Adam, as the Scriptures have made clear, and *uss lutrer sin'r barmhertzigkeit* (from His mercy alone) (2718). Adam's children are to hope for the advent of Christ who will break the doors of hell. No further details are given, and the ending of the first day is very similar to the close of the first day in the Cornish *Gwreans an bys* in that the minstrels are told to play and the people are sent home. But there is a major difference: the next day will not show the audience the Redemption, but the Flood, which is the punishment for sin. In spite of structural similarities between Ruf's play and the medieval mysteries, where the Cornish play ended its first day with Noah and promised the Redemption on the next, Ruf's Flood is the climax for the whole play. This leaves the inner and outer audience pondering on how to cope with the results of the Fall by faith, rather than having been shown the answer. But the audience is in the post-Fall and also by now post-Redemption world. Protestant solifidianism has been placed into an historical context, which is therefore an enhanced warning of how to behave; it is paraenetic, and manifests an intellectualisation of the simultaneity of the medieval play.

As indicated, when treating the protevangelical verse, the Swiss dramatist makes clear that it is the seed of the woman that will be victorious over the serpent. All the Protestant writers examined make clear that their reading would be *ipse*, referring back to seed, rather than *ipsa*, referring to the woman, and this is especially so in the Latin play of Adam's exile by the Dutch Jurist and Protestant theologian and also friend of Milton, Hugo Grotius – Huig de Groot – in 1601, where (and this is another feature of the Protestant Adam-play) the protevangelical verse is developed at the conclusion of the work: there the voice of God passes judgement on the serpent, and develops in full the salvation aspects of the verse. Enmity

167

is set between the serpent and the woman, the point sometimes put very briefly in medieval plays. Here, however, the voice continues:

> Lucis antiquae favillam, quase salutis praevia est,
> mente in humana fovebo, nec sinam cinere obrui . . .

and explains further

> Ipse veniet, ipse carnem sumet humanam Deus,
> Non viro genitus, sed uno femina ex semine,
> Virginali natus alvo, generis humani Salus,
> Qui triumphator superbum conteret tibi verticem . . .   (1904–18)

> (I shall encourage sparks of ancient light as presagings of Redemption in the human mind, and shall not dampen them down with ashes . . . then He shall come, God will take on human flesh, not born of man, but from the seed of the woman, born of the Virgin, the saviour of mankind who as victor will crush your proud head . . .)

Later still, in 1664, another Netherlander, Joost van Vondel, also ended his play *Adam in Ballingschap* (Adam in Exile) – which derives, Vondel tells us in a preface, in part from Grotius – with the judgement upon the couple, passed by the archangel Uriël, and citing the protevangelical verse. Vondel treated the passage literally; Adam and Eve leave Paradise with the mercy of God in the provision of clothing, and the only crumb of comfort is that 'the Highest has placed mercy (or grace) above justice'. The one line describing this,

> Hoe d'opperste het recht beneên genade stel,   (1677)

is a final reduction of the conflict of Justice and Mercy in the medieval dramas, allegorisations which continue in the Paradise plays of Catholic countries. *Merci passith riʒtwisnes*, however, already in an English dialogue-poem of the fifteenth century.[30]

The early Protestant Paradise-plays were being performed at the same time as, in France, for example, the *Mistére du Viel Testament*, or the later cyclic plays of the Passion such as those in the tradition of Greban and Michel, whose plays were merged and adapted for another century at least. There is much detail available on such a version of the Passion played at Valenciennes in 1547, for example,[31] and

---

[30] Grotius's *Adamus Exsul* appeared in 1601, and there is a text and translation in Kirkconnell, *Celestial Cycle*, pp. 96–220. I have used my own prose rather than Kirkconnell's excellent verse translations, however. See Kirkconnell, pp. 583–5 on the poet, although the comments on the debt of Milton to Grotius indicate that such debts are also slight, even though Milton knew and stayed with Grotius in 1638 in Paris. On Grotius's text was based Joost van Vondel's *Adam in Ballingschap* of 1664: see Kirkconnell, pp. 635f. Kirkconnell provides a translation of that work, too, pp. 434–79, as an appropriate ending to his own selection of Adam and Eve texts. The original is cited from J. v. Vondel, *Adam in Ballingschap*, ed. B. H. G. Molkenboer (Zwolle: Willink, 1947). The English dialogue poem (in MS Lambeth 853) is in Furnivall's *Hymns to the Virgin and Christ*, pp. 95–100.

[31] Frank, *Medieval French Drama*, pp. 171f and 188f.

some of these later redactions seem to have lasted for anything between six days and three weeks (though in the latter case it is not entirely clear *how*). In Brittany the Creation play with material from the *Vita Adae* would be known for several centuries longer, and the folk-play of Adam and Eve established itself in the Catholic southern and south-eastern parts of the German-speaking world, drawing upon Hans Sachs's *Tragedia* as it did so.[32] It is fair to note that dramatic developments affect the drama in later times in Catholic areas. There is an increasing, though by no means complete, reluctance to have God on stage – something which starts to make itself felt far later than the Reformation period, in which it is frequently placed[33] – and the increase in the appearance of allegorical figures linked with mankind is also visible here.

Some of the elements that emerge in the Protestant plays are simply part of a different, but ongoing dramatic development. For example, Death is introduced as a character, and plays a role in Voith's play, and also plays his part in the Catholic tradition. Gil Vicente's *Historia de Deus* dates from 1527, of course, but Vicente, whose play includes plenty of devils, does not include God in the Creation scene, although Christ himself defeats the devil at the end. Vicente includes not only Death but also Time and the World. The Spaniard Juan Caxes, less than a century later, in 1610, has even more allegorical parts in his *Auto de los dos primeros hermanos*, and it is Guilt and Envy that do the tempting in the garden, not even Satan, Lucifer or the serpent.[34] Another contemporary, Luis Vélez de Guevara, includes Death in his *Creación del Mundo*.[35] In Italy, Giambattista Andreini includes in *L'Adamo* of 1613 the Seven Deadly Sins (who appear as a masque, of course, in Marlowe's *Faustus*), as well as the World, the Flesh, Vain Glory (who helps Satan seduce Eve, and to whom I shall return) and others, whilst the Franciscan Serafino della Salandra provided in his *Adamo Caduto* of 1647 more allegorical roles than human, heavenly and infernal ones put together, with speaking parts for Innocence, Simplicity and Guile as well as Sin and Death, although Calmana and Delbora do appear once again, even if Seth does not. At the end of Salandra's play – a curious work, which emerged briefly and temporarily from obscurity when it, like Andreini's better-known play, was extravagantly, but (again as with Andreini's work) erroneously, thought to have been plundered by Milton for *Paradise Lost* – Sin, Death and Guile are confronted by Mercy, and in the concluding scene God proclaims the Resurrection. In this, in fact, Salandra contrasts with Andreini, the final scene of whose intrinsically far more interesting play, a work which focusses only on Adam and Eve, ends with Michael exhorting the protoplasts to a penitent life.[36]

One work by a more famous writer is a little different. Lope de Vega's three-day

---

[32] See Klimke, *Paradiesspiel*, p. 54.

[33] Meyer, *Heilsgewißheit*, p. 241.

[34] Kirckconnell, *Cycle*, pp. 591f.

[35] Luis Vélez de Guevara y Dueñas, *La Creación del Mundo*, ed. Henryk Ziomek and Robert White Linker (Athens, GA: University of Georgia Press, 1974).

[36] Kirckconnell, *Cycle*, has an abridged translation of the works by Andreini (pp. 227–67) and Salandra (pp. 290–349). See pp. 597–9 on the relatively important Andreini, and pp. 621–5 on Salandra and the history of the supposed influence on Milton of what Kirkconnell describes concisely, if bluntly, as 'an obscure fifth-rate Italian poet with whom he had no known contact'.

comedia famosa of *La creacion del mundo y primera culpa del hombre* of 1624[37] has a cast where all the characters conform to the biblical Genesis except Michael (Miguel) and Lucifer (Luzbel) as representatives of heaven and hell. There, too, Michael confirms at the conclusion that man, who has free will (*siendo libre*), can be saved by obedience and, if he loves God, can enter the glory. Michael makes the point to Lucifer, and to the audience of course, but Adam has not been given details of the Redemption. Apart from that stress on free will, which, of course, is closer to Erasmus in the *De libero arbitrio* than to Luther's response *De servo arbitrio* in the famous controversy of 1524–5, there is a stronger connexion between this work and, say, Ruf's *Adam und Heva* than might be expected. For Erasmus, free will meant seizing the chance to believe, whereas for Luther man was incapable of doing anything at all but for the workings of God's grace. What has been called 'Luther's problematic mind' on the subject was almost certainly too much for any dramatist aiming at a popular audience, and thus, although Ruf might not have mentioned free will in quite the way that Lope de Vega did, they are not so far apart.[38]

The question of characters in Lope de Vega is, finally, of some interest. God no longer appears here, but we need an angel to represent Him. This is almost the last indication of the medieval *Simultanbühne*, something which still worked in the Reformation to an extent, albeit not in works like Bale's *Promises*. In the medieval play we have God, operating in the eternal, with man below, after the Fall at least placed into a history that has, in the time of the performance, already gone through its second event. The devils – who remain in force in most plays – are both eternal and necessary to interact with mankind, and Michael is the intermediary in Lope de Vega as he was in the Adambooks.

These works, Protestant and Catholic alike, are all bound to the biblical text to a greater or lesser extent, but I have already overlapped with the morality in a reference to Everyman, and even though it necessitates retracing our steps a little, we can move directly from the dramas of the Fall and Redemption to the morality and, as far as English goes, to its immediate successor, the moral interlude of the Tudor period, the distinction between the two kinds of drama being in any case far from clear, although the five English moralities are sometimes treated as a separate unit.[39] Allardyce Nicoll's much-reprinted and still useful survey of British drama commented on how difficult it is to trace the steps from the medieval mystery to the morality play, and saw the Norwich Play of the Fall as a bridging piece.[40] Nor of course does the morality fit well into pre- and post-Reformation theological categories, especially the English ones. The medieval morality, and indeed also many Tudor interludes, is, however, closely linked with the Fall. J. M. R. Margeson

---

[37] The text is in Lope Félix de Vega Carpio, *Obras Escogidas*, ed. Federico Carlos Sainz de Robles, vol. III (*Teatro*) (Madrid: Aguilar, 3rd edn, 1967), pp. 81–100.

[38] See the useful translation of *Erasmus – Luther: Discourse on Free Will*, ed. Ernst F. Winter (New York: Ungar, 1961). The citation is from p. xi.

[39] As is done, for example, consciously and for necessary technical reasons, by Pamela M. King in her chapter on the morality in *The Cambridge Companion to Medieval English Theatre*, ed. Richard Beadle (Cambridge: Cambridge University Press, 1994), pp. 240–64.

[40] Allardyce Nicoll, *British Drama: an Historical Survey* (London: Harrap, 4th. edn, 1947), p. 41.

referred to the earliest examples as 'Temptation and Fall' moralities, pointing out that 'Adam is the first Everyman or Mankind, standing for the whole race of men and representative also in his proneness to sin.'[41] The link between Adam and Everyman is clear, of course, expressed, however the verse is read, in Romans 5:12, and as far as the moralities are concerned, all three of the plays in the late fifteenth-century manuscript once belonging to Cox Macro and still bearing his name, for example, are relevant – *The Castle of Perseverance*, *Wisdom* and *Mankind*. All show the Fall into sin and the chance of Redemption for a representative figure, who might be called Mankind or *Humanum Genus*, or might be separated into man's powers (Mind, Will and Understanding in the play of *Wisdom*).[42]

In dramatic terms it is possible to trace a shift in English drama at least from plays with the biblical Adam as the central role to morality plays with a generalised central figure. All these figures relate to Adam's situation in the world: Everyman has to face death, Mankind, in the play of that name, begins with Adam's need to labour, and the equivalent figure in the play of *Wisdom* has to cope with temptation to sin. The Macro play of *Wisdom* allows Christ to state in terms of Romans 5:12

> For euery creatur þat hath ben, or xall
>> Was in natur of þe fyrst man, Adame,
> Off hym takynge þe fylthe of synne orygynall,
>> For of hym all creaturis cam.   (109–12)

In the play of *Mankind*, too, it is Mercy who provides for the Redemption, and echoes have been heard here of Psalm 84 (85) and the medieval debate of the daughters of God in Paradise.

Of the early English moralities, the Macro *Castle of Perseverance* is of great interest in terms of descent from the Adam-plays. Humanum Genus, the representative, comes into the world equipped with good and bad angels – versions of the angels and devils of the Paradise plays, but now with a different role – but he is still Adam's child, and we meet him on the day of his birth into a world that we have already seen personified as Mundus:

> aftyr oure forme faderis kende
>> þis nyth I was of my moder born.
>
> . . .
>
> I am nakyd of lym & lende
>> as mankynde is schapyn & schorn;
> I not wedyr to gon me to lende,

---

41 *Origins of English Tragedy*, p. 31.
42 *The Macro Plays* are available in the editions prepared for the Early English Text Society by F. J. Furnivall and Alfred W. Pollard (London: Trübner, 1904 = EETS/ES 91: cited) and by Mark Eccles (London: Oxford University Press, 1969 = EETS/OS 262). There is a convenient edition of some of the relevant plays edited by Edgar T. Schell and J. D. Schuchter, *English Morality Plays and Moral Interludes* (New York: Holt, Rinehart and Winston, 1969). There is a good introduction in *Four Tudor Interludes*, ed. J. A. B. Somerset (London: Athlone, 1974), which includes both the Macro *Mankind* and *Lusty Juventus*. Mary Philippa Coogan, *An Interpretation of the Moral Play 'Mankind'* (Washington, DC: Catholic University of America Press, 1947), sees Mercy as a priest.

    to helpe my-self mydday nyn morne:
      for schame I stonde and schende . . .   (275–83)

The good angel tells him to follow Christ and the bad angel counters, offering the delights of all the sins. He enters the castle of perseverance and is dragged out again, the notion of a castle under siege going back perhaps to another work (partly) to do with Genesis, Robert Grosseteste's *Chasteau d'Amour*, which is known in various versions in English as well as the Anglo-Norman original and which is based too on the debate of the four daughters of God for the soul of man.[43]

    The struggle for man's soul goes on in the play until Justice and Mercy – again figures from the Adam-plays – rescue him with a reference to the *felix culpa*. Misericordia addresses Christ with the words:

    Ne had Adam synnyd here be-fore
    & þi hestis in paradys had offent
    Neuere of þi moder þou schuldyst a be bore   (3341–3)

Justice debates with Mercy, and at the conclusion man is shown as redeemed, as Adam was promised, since in the time of the play the Redemption has already happened. Man is taken to God's seat in the play, and the judgement of the good and the wicked concludes the work.

    Closely related to this work, and perhaps bridging the gap between the early moralities and the later plays in which Adam's representative is more advanced in the world, is the Tudor moral interlude *Mundus et Infans* (*The World and the Child*), printed by Wynkyn de Worde in 1522 and linked with an earlier English poem called *The Mirror of the Periods of Man's Life*.[44] Here the child representing man is introduced naked into the world, but we then see its various stages and indeed hear its different names as it progresses through 'Lust-and-Liking' to 'Manhood'. In this case, Perseverance is a character who teaches mankind (who by now has reached Age) the need for repentance. Having been a castle earlier and clearly male here (he is addressed as sir), it is of incidental interest that in a French work contemporary with the Macro plays Perseverance is female, Dame Parseverance; the work, *Le Lyon Coronné*, which seems to defy generic designa-

---

43 The standard edition of the (four) Middle English translations is that published by Kari Sajavaara, *The Middle English Translations of Robert Grosseteste's Chateau d'Amour* (Helsinki: Société Néophilologique, 1967), texts pp. 259–371. One of the four texts is called, indeed, *Foure Doughters*, and another *King and Four Daughters*. There is a text of one of the English metrical versions in Horstmann, *Legenden: Neue Folge*, pp. 349–54, and others in Carl Horstmann, *The Minor Poems of the Vernon Manuscript I* (London: Trübner, 1892 = EETS/OS 98), pp. 355–406 (*The Castle of Love*) and 407–42 (*The Myrour of Lewed Men*). The Anglo-Norman text is in the dissertation by Jessie Murray, '*Le Château d'Amour de Robert Grosseteste, évêque de Lincoln*' (Paris: Diss. 1918).

44 There is a convenient text in Schell and Schuchter, *English Morality Plays*, pp. 167–98. See on the relationship with the printed calendars of the early sixteenth century Eamon Duffy, *The Stripping of the Altars* (New Haven and London: Yale University Press, 1992), pp. 51f. The *Periods* poem is in Furnivall, *Hymns*, pp. 58–78. See also G. A. Lester, *Three Late Medieval Morality Plays* (London: Benn, 1981) on the source of *Mundus*. Earlier, in Gower's *Mirour de l'Omme*, the estates all blame each other: see the translation by William B. Wilson, rev. ed. Nancy Wilson van Baak (East Lansing: Colleagues Press, 1992), pp. 348f.

tion, is a moral debate between allegorical figures in which Parseverance defeats Envie.[45]

The development from the morality and the moral interlude continues, but it still keeps Adam and his Fall in sight. Having moved from Adam himself to the biblically typical, or (depending now upon the *reading* of Romans 5:12) causally connected, Everyman-Mankind-*Infans* figure, there then come more specialised roles, with single aspects of humanity placed in the forefront – *Lusty Juventus* (which contains a character called 'God's Merciful Promises'), for example – and from these we progress to the individual who is not the *tabula rasa* Adam of the morality plays. This final stage places in the centre the genuine individual who can, as the progeny of Adam, fall into any sin. The trappings may still be there: the devils may plot in hell as they did before the temptation of Eve, but the blandishments offered may be increasingly spectacular, if, indeed, one can have a temptation more spectacular than the promise that 'ye shall be as gods'. Accordingly, the stage may now be occupied by the increasingly wicked, including as early examples a renegade bishop, more than one university lecturer gone to the bad, and even, *horribile dictu*, a lady pope. Theophilus, Dr Faustus, Cendoxus, the Doctor from Paris and Pope Joan are all the subject of what remain on the individual-level plays of temptation and fall. The earlier ones, indeed, contain an individual Redemption, sometimes coming at the eleventh hour, or in some cases even later; but if Frau Jutta, in the play of Pope Joan, or the medieval Theophilus were redeemed from their pacts with the devil – we might recall the old motif of the cheirograph and the legal agreement on the Fall of man – even after death on the intervention of the Virgin and the saints, Adam himself was, after all, actually rescued from hell.[46]

Not all of these individuals, these latter-day Adams, are redeemed. Yet they are still Adam, faced with the problem that was voiced already in the *Vita Adae*, namely of how to recognise the force of evil and how to utilise the gift of free will properly – the fine distinctions of Erasmus versus Luther on the subject have by now been blurred. Let us end with our two academics, both damned. Faustus, pulled each way by his good and his bad angel in Marlowe's version (although in other ways he is less medieval than Goethe, in whose work the *Simultanbühne* has

---

[45] *Le Lyon Coronné*, ed. Kenneth Urwin (Geneva and Paris: Droz/Minard, 1958).

[46] The earliest relevant version of the play of Theophilus is that by Rutebeuf, *Le Miracle de Théophile*, ed. Grace Frank (Paris: Champion, 1970); transl. in my *Grin of the Gargoyle*, pp. 207–28. There is an interesting and rather different late medieval Low German play, edited by Ludwig Ettmüller as *Theophilus, der Faust des Mittelalters* (Quedlinburg and Leipzig: Basse, 1849). The work is very strongly Marian. The German play of Pope Joan, ed. Manfred Lemmer, *Dietrich Schernberg: Ein schoen Spiel von Frau Jutten* (Berlin: Schmidt, 1971), was written in 1480, but was printed in 1565 by the Protestants as a propagandistic indication of the wickedness of the papacy, although there is a seemingly perennial interest in the notion of a female pope. The play is headed *Apotheosis Johannis VIII Pontificis Romani*. Salvation is even possible a long time after death in some circumstances: see the Middle English *Trentalle Sancti Gregorii, eine mittelenglische Legende*, ed. Albert Kaufmann (Erlangen and Leipzig, 1889, repr. Amsterdam: Rodopi, 1970). In the introduction to an earlier edition in *Political, Religious and Love Poems*, ed. Frederick J. Furnivall (London: Oxford University Press, 1866 = EETS/OS 15), pp. 114–22, the liturgist Daniel Rock is cited (pp. xvf) as having commented that the sinful woman who is at the centre of that work would certainly have been damned already. In the fiction, however, she is not; her son, another unidentified Pope Gregory, prays for her and she is forgiven.

a last flicker of life in the *Prolog im Himmel*), makes the wrong decision, or rather, fails to understand the limitations imposed upon him by God, just as Adam had failed to see the limits of what was permitted. And in Marlowe, at the last, 'time runs, the clock will strike, the devil will come, and Faustus must be dammed'.[47] A rather clearer, if less well known, last example is provided, however, by a Latin play by a Jesuit of the Counter-Reformation, Jacob Bidermann, who was born in Ulm in southern Germany in 1578, and who died in 1639 in Rome as Censor of Books to the Society of Jesus. His legend of *Cenodoxus*, when it was performed in Munich in 1609, caused fear and trembling, and, apparently, a number of retreats into the cloistered life, including that of the actor who played the lead, who was so shocked by the play that he became a Jesuit himself. The work is linked, still, with the story of the Fall, the Redemption, and the Harrowing of Hell.

A diabolical council discusses the fall of the central figure, the learned doctor of the university of Paris known by the generalised but speaking name of Cenodoxus, vainglory, κενοδοξια. Vainglory is one of the three sins, incidentally, attributed to Adam in early exegesis, the others being greed and avarice. Adam ate the fruit, wanted knowledge, and desired to be as God; these are the sins countered by Christ in the temptation in the wilderness. The character Cenodoxus is another grown-up Adam, but his temptation is the same as before. The play is dramatically subtle in that the personified wicked characters, like Hypocrisy and Self-Love, whilst presented on stage, are visible only to Cenodoxus himself, making the work into an early psychological drama. Self-love, incidentally, was, with vainglory, the major sin highlighted by Hans Sachs at the end of his Adam and Eve play.[48] Devils may plot his fall, as in the Paradise plays, but the recognition question is always at the forefront. The diabolical figures adopt the guise of angels, just as they do to confuse Eve in the *Vita Adae*, but this motif is given a neat twist by Bidermann when Cenodoxus's guardian angel forces the devil to appear to Cenodoxus in his *proper* form in a dream to make clear the reality of hell. However, even this fails to make the waking Cenodoxus repent. The particular devil charged with his personal downfall (anticipating the *Screwtape Letters*, incidentally, by several centuries) then somewhat more traditionally disguises himself as an angel and summons a choir of devils to do likewise, and they allay the fears of the trembling Cenodoxus:

> Desine vultum perdere fletu;
> Supera dudum Numen ab aula
> Faciles votis praestitit aures;
> Nemo te adibit certius Astra.[49]

---

[47] Christopher Marlowe, *Plays and Poems*, ed. M. R. Ridley (London: Dent, 1955). See the sensible comments by Walter Stein, 'Christianity and the Common Pursuit', *Northern Miscellany* 1 (1953), 47–64, rightly countering the view that Marlowe's Faustus represents the progressive and adventurous impulse of the new age condemned by the medieval heritage of fear and superstition, something which decontextualises Marlowe completely. The rather later Dutch Faust-play is thoroughly specific in its title, *De Hellevaart van Dokter Joan Faustus* ('Dr Faustus Goes to Hell'): see *Das niederländische Faustspiel des 17. Jahrhunderts*, ed. E. F. Kossmann (The Hague: Nijhoff, 1910).

[48] See Winfried Theiß, *Exemplarische Allegorik: Untersuchungen zu einem literar-historischen Phänomen bei Hans Sachs* (Munich: Fink, 1968), pp. 145f.

[49] Jacob Bidermann, *Cenodoxus*, ed. and trans. D. G. Dyer with Cecily Longrigg (Edinburgh: Edin-

(Cease disfiguring your face with tears, the Deity has now heard
from His high court and listened to your prayers; no one is as
sure of entering Heaven as you are.)

The devil sometimes appears as an angel even in Paradise plays. Eve claims that
she was talking to an angel in the Cornish *Creation*, and she is given a virtually
identical promise to this in the *Vita Adae*, when Satan transformed himself into an
angel to interrupt her penance and assured her:

de cetero non plores, iam cessa de tristitia et gemitu ... audivit dominus deus
gemitum vestrum ... et nos omnes angeli rogavimus pro vobis.

(Cease weeping, leave your sadness and trembling, God has heard your
prayers and we angels have all prayed for you.)

Eve thought she would be let back into Paradise; Cenodoxus thought that he was
sure of a place in heaven; neither was right. Adam and Eve may have been released
from hell, but this is not the fate of Cenodoxus, who does not even gain Redemption well after the eleventh hour, as Theophilus does in some versions. Cenoxodus
is damned.

How do we know? Let us return to the opening image, to Erkenwald at St Paul's,
amongst the crowd watching the miracle. St Erkenwald was faced with a speaking
corpse, and so are we in *Cenodoxus*. When the Doctor from Paris dies, the extent of
his massive self-love and presumption is unknown to all his friends, who assume
that entry into heaven for this good man is assured. We, the audience, have seen
that his charity operates only when someone is watching, and we have heard the
voices of Hypocrisy whispering to him. The play is not over, however, and the final
part operates on various levels. We are shown the spirit of Cenodoxus on trial in
heaven for its eternal life. The pleading for Adam's soul by Justice and Mercy has
changed, because the situation has changed. The outcome of that debate in heaven
was that there should be a Redemption, but now this has happened, and it is Christ
who sits in judgement. Unlike Erkenwald's anonymous corpse, a poor relic who
had missed the benefit of baptism, Cenodoxus already lives *sub gratia*, and that has
responsibilities. In spite of the pleadings of his good angel, there is no help for him.
The trial in heaven is intercalated with scenes on earth as Cenodoxus's friends wait
by his body, which on successive days announces first that it stands accused (*accu-
satus sum*), then that it is judged (*iudicatus sum*) and finally: *justo Dei judicio
damnatus sum* (2072) (By God's justice I am damned).

But unlike Marlowe's *Faustus*, this is not the conclusion, and we may return not
only to St Erkenwald, but to one of the essential points of (medieval) religious
drama, which is of course being played in a post-Fall world: that it is played and

burgh University Press, 1975). The prose translation is mine. The work, which was not published until
after Bidermann's death in 1639, was, however, adapted into German by Joachim Meichel and this
appeared in 1635; see the edition by Rolf Tarot (Stuttgart: Reclam, 1963). I have discussed the play in
detail and tried to place it into a dramatic context in 'Devils, Vices and the Fall: Dramatic Patterns from
the Medieval Mystery to Bidermann's *Cenodoxus*', *Maske und Kothurn* 23 (1977), 15–30. See p. 1 of
Dyer's edition for details of the first performances and their results.

observed at the same time. The end of Bidermann's play is not with the distressed spirit of the Doctor himself, but with his friends, and there is a shift of perspective. The vision of the corpse is observed on stage by Bruno, who undergoes such a conversion that he and his friends seek out a life of penance, and thus the Carthusian order is founded. Thus the events on stage; I have already commented on contemporary reports of the effect on both the lead actor and the audience. Seeing, in the last analysis, has to be believing. Cenodoxus is not Adam, but even in Zurich in the Minster square in 1550 there was an inner and an outer audience of Swiss observers; and with St Erkenwald we all joined the procession.

This is a permanent problem with representations of Adam and of representations (in drama or other literature) of analogues of Adam. We are in the poem and the play as well as part of the outer audience, and so too, Adam, mankind, the role and the imitator, are all interlocked. The drama shows perhaps more clearly than any other genre how Adam and his progeny have a different and increasingly difficult role to play in a world which is already *sub gratia*.

BIBLIOGRAPHY

All biblical references are to the Vulgate, with books referred to by the standard abbreviations. So too the usual abbreviations *PL* and *CSEL* have been used for Migne's *Patrologia Latina* and the Vienna *Corpus scriptorum ecclesiasticorum latinorum* respectively, and individual texts in those collections are not listed separately here. EETS/OS and ES refers to the Ordinary and Extra Series of the Early English Text Society. In the bibliography of primary texts, the (few) modern works looked at in the introductory material have not been separated from the medieval texts on which the study is principally based; it is hoped that this will underscore once again the continuity of the motifs.

Primary Texts

Bertus Aafjes, *In den beginne* (Amsterdam: Querido, 1949)

[*Adambuch*, verse] Friedrich von der Hagen, *Gesammtabenteuer* (Stuttgart and Tübingen, 1850, repr. Darmstadt: WBG, 1961), I, 1–16

[*Adambuch*, prose] Hans Vollmer, *Ein deutsches Adambuch* (Hamburg: Lütke und Wolff, 1908)

Natalis Alexander [Noel Alexandre], *Dissertationum ecclesiasticarum trias* (Paris: Dezallier, 1679)

Ami et Amile. Chanson de geste, ed. Peter F. Dembowski (Paris: Champion, 1969); trans. into modern French, Joël Blanchard and Michel Quereuil, *Ami et Amile* (Paris: Champion, 1987)

Amis and Amiloun, ed. McEdward Leach (London: Oxford University Press, 1937, repr. 1960 = EETS/OS 203); Eugen Kölbing, *Amis und Amiloun* (Heilbronn: Henninger, 1884)

Analecta Hymnica Medii Aevi, ed. Clemens Blume and Guido Dreves (Leipzig: Reisland, 1886–)

Gary A. Anderson and Michael E. Stone, *Synopsis of the Books of Adam and Eve* (Atlanta: Scholar's Press, 1994)

[Anselm of Canterbury] *Sancti Anselmi Opera Omnia*, ed. F. S. Schmitt (Edinburgh and Rome: Nelson, 1938–61, repr. Stuttgart: Frommann, 1968) – this includes the reply by Gaunilo.

[Anselm of Canterbury] *The Prayers and Meditations of St Anselm*, trans. Benedicta Ward (Harmondsworth: Penguin, 1973)

Peter Anton, *Volksthümliches aus Österreich-Schlesien I* (Troppau: publisher not known, 1865)

[*Apocalypsis Mosis*] *La vie grecque d'Adam et Ève*, ed. Daniel A. Bertrand (Paris: Maisonneuve, 1987)

Aquinas: see Thomas Aquinas

177

Arnold von Lübeck, *Gesta Gregorii Peccatoris*, ed. Johannes Schilling (Göttingen: Vandenhoek und Ruprecht, 1968)

The Auchinleck Manuscript. National Library of Scotland Advocates' MS 19.2.1, ed. Derek Pearsall and I. C. Cunningham (London: Scolar Press, 1977)

Ayenbite of Inwyt: see [Dan] Michel

[John Bale] Peter Happé, ed., *The Complete Plays of John Bale* (Cambridge: D. S. Brewer, 1985–6)

Vincenzo de Bartholomaeis, ed, *Laude drammatiche e rappresentazioni sacre* (Florence: Le Monnier, 1943)

Monika Beisner, *Von fliegenden und sprechenden Bäumen* (Munich: Hanser, 1994)

Henry Bettenson, *Documents of the Christian Church* (London: Oxford University Press, 2nd edn, 1963)

[*Beunans Meriasek*] Myrna Combellack-Harris, 'A Critical Edition of Beunans Meriasek' (Ph.D. Diss., Exeter, 1985); Whitley Stokes, *The Life of St Meriasek* (London: Trübner, 1872); trans. Markham Harris, *The Life of Meriasek* (Washington: Catholic University of America Press, 1978) and Myrna Combellack, *The Camborne Play* (Redruth: Truran, 1988)

[*Biblia pauperum*] *Die Armenbibel des Serai, Rotulus Seragliensis no. 52*, ed. Adolf Deissmann and Hans Wegener (Berlin and Leipzig: de Gruyter, 1934); *Biblia Pauperum. Deutsche Ausgabe von 1471*, ed. R. Ehwald (Weimar: Gesellschaft der Bibliophilen, 1906); *Biblia Pauperum: Facsimile of the Forty-leaf Blockbook in the Library of Esztergom Cathedral*, ed. Elisabeth Soltész, trans. Lili Halapy, rev. Elizabeth West (Budapest: Corvina, 1967); Avril Henry, *Biblia Pauperum* (London: Scolar Press, 1987)

Jacob Bidermann, *Cenodoxus*, ed. and trans. D. G. Dyer with Cecily Longrigg (Edinburgh: Edinburgh University Press 1975); trans. Joachim Meichel (1635), ed. Rolf Tarot (Stuttgart: Reclam, 1963)

Giovanni Boccaccio, *Concerning Famous Women*, trans. Guido A. Guarino (New Brunswick, NJ: Rutgers University Press, 1963)

Dat boec van den houte, ed. Lars Hermodsson (Uppsala: Lundequist, 1959)

[Bologna Play] *Laude drammatiche e rappresentazioni sacre III*, ed. Vincenzo de Bartholomaeis (Florence: le Monnier, 1943)

Book of Pontiffs: see *Liber pontificalis*

The Book of Vices and Virtues, ed. W. Nelson Francis (London: Oxford University Press, 1942 = EETS/OS 217)

Robert de Boron, *Le Roman de l'Estoire dou Graal*, ed. William A. Nitze (Paris: Champion, 1927)

John Bowen, *The Fall and Redemption of Man* (London: Faber, 1968)

Breton Creation-Play: see *Creation ar bet*

Carleton Brown, ed., *Religious Lyrics of the XVth Century* (Oxford: Clarendon, 1939)

Georg Büchner, *Werke und Briefe*, ed. Fritz Bergemann (Wiesbaden: Insel, 1958)

Hugh Burnett, *Adam and Eve* (London: Merlin, 1963)

[*Canticum de creatione*] C. Horstmann, 'Canticum de creatione', *Anglia* 1 (1878), 287–331

[Josef and Karel Čapek] The Brothers Čapek, *R.U.R. and The Insect Play*, trans. P. Selver (London: Oxford University Press, 1961)

E. K. Chambers and F. Sidgwick, *Early English Lyrics* ([1907] London: Sidgwick and Jackson, 1947)

R. H. Charles, ed., *Apocrypha and Pseudepigrapha of the Old Testament, II: Pseudepigrapha* (Oxford: Clarendon, 1913, repr. 1963)

James H. Charlesworth, ed., *The Old Testament Pseudepigrapha* (London: Longman and Todd, 1983–5)

The Chester Plays, ed. Hermann Deimling and [J.] Matthews (London: Kegan Paul, 1893–1916 = EETS/ES 62 and 115)

Chrétien de Troyes, *Le Roman de Perceval*, ed. William Roach (Geneva and Paris: Droz, 1959); Chrétien, *Le Conte du Graal (Perceval)*, ed. Félix Lecoy (Paris: Champion, 1972–5); trans. as Chrétien de Troyes, *Perceval: The Story of the Graal*, trans. Nigel Bryant (Cambridge: D. S. Brewer, 1982), Ruth Harwood Cline, Chrétien, *Perceval* (New York: Pergamon, 1983)

O. Cockayne, *Leechdoms, Wortcunning and Starcraft of Early England* (London: Rolls Series, 1864–6)

Gustave Cohen, *Mystère de la Passion des Théophiliens* (Paris: Richard-Masse, 1950)

Cornish drama: see *Gwreans an bys*; *Ordinalia*

Creacion of the World: see *Gwreans an bys*

[*Creation ar bet*] Eugène Bernard, 'La Création du Monde: Mystère Breton', *Revue Celtique* 9 (1888), 149–207 and 322–53; 10 (1889), 102–211 and 411–55; 11 (1890), 254–317; and Noel Hamilton, 'A Fragment of La Création', *Celtica* 12 (1977) 50–74

Cursor Mundi, ed. Richard Morris (London: Oxford University Press, 1874–93, repr. 1961–6 = EETS/OS 57–68)

Cyprian of Carthage, *De lapsis and De ecclesiae catholicae unitate*, ed. and trans. Maurice Bénevot (Oxford: Clarendon, 1971)

Heinrich Denzinger and Clemens Bannwart, *Encheiridion Symbolorum* (Freiburg i. B.: Herder), 16th and 17th edn by J.-B. Umberg (Freiburg/Br.: Herder, 1928)

The Devils' Parliament and The Harrowing of Hell and Destruction of Jerusalem, ed. C. W. Marx (Heidelberg: Winter, 1993)

The Didot Perceval, ed. William Roach (Philadelphia: Penn State University Press, 1941), trans. Dell Skeels, *The Romance of Perceval in Prose* (Seattle: University of Washington Press, 1966)

The Digby Plays, ed. F. J. Furnivall (London: Oxford University Press, 1896 = EETS/ES 70)

Robert Dodsley, *A Select Collection of Old English Plays*, 4th edn by W. Carew Hazlitt (London: Reeves and Turner, 1874)

John Earle, *Microcosmography, or a Piece of the World Discovered in Essays and Characters* (1628) (London: Dent, 1934)

Eglamour: see *Sir Eglamour*

Enikel: see Jansen Enikel

[Desiderius Erasmus] *Erasmus – Luther: Discourse on Free Will*, ed. Ernst F. Winter (New York: Ungar, 1961)

Everyman, ed. A. C. Cawley (Manchester: Manchester University Press, 1961)

Fasciculus Morum, ed. Siegfried Wenzel (University Park and London: Penn State University Press, 1989)

Penelope Farmer, *Eve: Her Story* (London: Gollancz, 1985)

[Faust-play, Dutch] *Das niederländische Faustspiel des 17. Jahrhunderts*, ed. E. F. Kossmann (The Hague: Nijhoff, 1910)

[Hans Folz] Brian Murdoch, *Hans Folz and the Adam Legends: Texts and Studies* (Amsterdam: Rodopi, 1977)

Richard Froning, *Das Drama des Mittelalters* (Stuttgart: DNL, 1891)

Frederick J. Furnivall, ed., *Political, Religious and Love Poems* (London: Oxford University Press, 1866 = EETS/OS 15)

Frederick J. Furnivall, ed., *Hymns to the Virgin and Christ* (London: Trübner, 1868 = EETS/OS 24)

Gaunilo: see Anselm of Canterbury

[Geoffrey of Vinsauf] Margaret F. Nims, *Poetria Nova of Geoffrey of Vinsauf* (Toronto: Pontifical Institute, 1967)

Gesta Romanorum, ed. H. Oesterly (Berlin, 1872, repr. Hildesheim: Olms, 1963); and trans. Charles Swan, rev. Wynnard Hooper (London: Bell, 1877)

Eugen Gömringer, ed., *Konkrete Poesie* (Stuttgart: Reclam, 1972)

[John Gower] *The English Works of John Gower*, ed. G. C. Macaulay (London: Oxford University Press, 1900–2, repr. 1957 = EETS/OS 81–2); *Mirour de l'Omme*, trans. William B. Wilson, rev. edn Nancy Wilson van Baak (East Lansing: Colloquium, 1992)

Arnoul Greban, *Mystère de la Passion*, ed. Gaston Paris and Gaston Raynaud (Paris: Vieweg, 1878)

[*Gregorius* (English)] *Die mittelenglische Gregoriuslegende*, ed. Carl Keller (Heidelberg and New York: Winter, 1914)

[*Gregorius*, French prose] P. Meyer, 'La légende en prose de Saint Grégoire', *Romania* 33 (1904), 42–6

Gregorius, French verse: see *Vie du Pape Saint Grégoire*

[*Gregorius*, Low German] Olaf Schwencke, '*Gregorius de grote sünder*: eine erbaulich-paränetische Prosaversion der Gregoriuslegende', *Jahrbuch des Vereins für niederdeutsche Sprachforschung* 90 (1967), 63–88; *Van sante Gregorio vp dem mer*, in Wolfgang Stammler, *Spätlese des Mittelalters*, I (Berlin: Schmidt, 1963), pp. 3–19

Gregorius auf dem Stein, ed. Bernward Plate (Darmstadt: WBG, 1983)

Grosseteste: see Robert Grosseteste

Henry Melvill Gwatkin, *Selections from Early Christian Writers* (London: Macmillan, 1902)

[*Gwreans an bys*] Whitley Stokes, *Gwreans an bys: The Creation of the World* (London: Williams and Norgate, 1864); Paula Neuss, *The Creacion of the World: a Critical Edition and Translation* (Ph.D. Diss., Toronto, 1970; New York and London: Garland, 1983); R. Morton Nance and A. S. D. Smith, *Gwryans an bys* (Padstow: FOCS, 1959), rev. edn E. G. R. Hooper (Redruth: Truran, 1985)

Friedrich von der Hagen, *Gesammtabenteuer* (Stuttgart and Tübingen, 1850, repr. Darmstadt: WBG, 1961)

E. Hammershaimb, Johannes Munck et al. *De gammeltestamentlige Pseudepigrafer* (Copenhagen: Gads, 1953–73)

Hartmann von Aue, *Gregorius*, ed. Friedrich Neumann (Wiesbaden: Brockhaus, 1958); ed. Hermann Paul, 11th edn rev. by Ludwig Wolff (Tübingen: Niemeyer, 1966), 13th edn by Burghart Wachinger (Tübingen: Niemeyer, 1984); trans. Edwin

H. Zeydel and Bayard Q. Morgan, *Gregorius: a Medieval Oedipus Legend by Hartmann von Aue* (Chapel Hill: University of North Carolina Press, 1955)

Hartmann von Aue, *Der arme Heinrich*, ed. Hermann Paul, 16th edn by Kurt Gärtner (Tübingen: Niemeyer, 1996); *Der arme Heinrich* ed. Karl Simrock (Berlin: Laue, 1830)

Hartmann von Aue, *The Narrative Works*, trans. Rodney W. Fisher (Göppingen: Kümmerle, 1983)

A. Hartmann, *Volksschauspiele in Bayern und Österreich-Ungarn gesammelt* (Leipzig: Breitkopf und Härtl, 1880, repr. Walluf: Sändig, 1972)

De Hellevaart van Dokter Joan Faustus: see [Faust-play, Dutch]

E. Hennecke and W. Schneemelcher, trans. R. McL. Wilson, *New Testament Apocrypha I* (London: SCM, 1963)

Robert Henryson, *The Testament of Cresseid*, ed. Denton Fox (London: Nelson, 1968)

Máire Herbert and Martin McNamara, *Irish Biblical Apocrypha* (Edinburgh: Clarke, 1989)

[*Historienbibel*] J. F. L. Theodor Merzdorf, *Die deutschen Historienbibeln des Mittelalters* (Stuttgart, 1870: repr. Hildesheim: Olms, 1963)

[Holy Rood Legends] Wilhelm Meyer, 'Die Geschichte des Kreuzholzes vor Christi', *Abhandlungen der bayerischen Akademie* (München), philos.-philol. Kl. 16/ii (1882), 101–66

[Holy Rood Legends] J. R. Mozley, 'A New Text of the Story of the Cross', *Journal of Theological Studies* 31 (1930), 113–27

[Holy Rood Legends] Richard Morris, *Legends of the Holy Rood* (London: Oxford University Press, 1871 = EETS/OS 46)

[Holy Rood Legends] Arthur S. Napier, *History of the Holy Rood-Tree* (London: Kegan Paul, 1894 = EETS/OS 103)

Carl Horstmann, *Sammlung altenglischer Legenden* (Heilbronn: Henninger, 1878)

Carl Horstmann, *Altenglische Legenden: Neue Folge* (Heilbronn: Henninger, 1881)

Carl Horstmann, *The Minor Poems of the Vernon Manuscript I* (London: Trübner, 1892 = EETS/OS 98)

Hugo von Montfort [Works], ed. Karl Bartsch (Tübingen: Stuttgarter lit. Verein, 1871)

Arnold Immessen, *Der Sündenfall*, ed. Friedrich Krage (Heidelberg: Winter, 1913)

Das Innsbrucker Osterspiel: das Osterspiel von Muri, ed. and trans. Rudolf Meier (Stuttgart: Reclam, 1962)

Montague Rhodes James, *The Apocryphal New Testament* (Oxford: Clarendon, 1924, repr. 1975)

[James of Voragine] *Jacobi a Voragine Legenda aurea*, ed. Theodor Graesse (Leipzig, 2nd edn, 1850, repr. Osnabrück: Zeller, 1969); trans. William Granger Ryan, *The Golden Legend of Jacobus de Voragine* (New York: Arno, 1969)

Jansen Enikel, *Weltchronik*, ed. Philipp Strauch (Hanover: Monumenta Germaniae Historica, 1891–1900)

Jaufré, ed. C. Brunel (Paris: SATF, 1943)

Jean des Preis, *Chronique de Jean des Preis dit d'Outremeuse*, ed. A. Borgnet (Brussels: Academie, 1864)

A. Jeanroy and H. Teulié, eds, *Les Mystères provençaux du XVe siècle* (Toulouse: Privat, 1893)

[Josephus] *Works of Flavius Josephus*, trans. William Whiston, with Whiston's *Dissertations* (Halifax: Milner and Sowerby, 1859)

Juttaspiel: see Schernberg

Die Kaiserchronik eines Regensburger Geistlichen, ed. Eduard Schröder (Hanover: Monumenta Germaniae Historica, 1892)

Codex Karlsruhe 408, ed. Ursula Schmid (Berne and Munich: Francke, 1974)

Adelbert von Keller, *Fastnachtspiele aus dem 15. Jahrhundert* (Tübingen: Stuttgarter lit. Verein, 1853, repr. Darmstadt: WBG, 1965)

Søren Kierkegaard, *The Concept of Dread* [1844], trans. Walter Lowrie (Princeton: Princeton University Press, 2nd edn, 1957)

J. Klapper, *Die Erzählungen des Mittelalters in deutscher Übersetzung und lateinischem Urtext* (Breslau: Marcus, 1914)

Konrad von Würzburg, *Engelhard*, ed. Paul Gereke, 3rd edn Ingo Reiffenstein (Tübingen: Niemeyer, 1982)

Konrad von Würzburg, *Die Legenden I.*, ed. Paul Gereke (Halle/Saale: Niemeyer, 1925)

Horst Kusch, *Einführung in das lateinische Mittelalter* (Berlin: Verlag der Wissenschaften, 1957)

William Langland, *The Vision of William Concerning Piers the Plowman*, ed. Walter W. Skeat (London: Oxford University Press, 1886, repr. 1961)

Legenda Aurea: see James of Voragine

G. A. Lester, *Three Late Medieval Morality Plays* (London: Benn, 1981)

C. S. Lewis, *Perelandra* (London: Bodley Head, 1943), also as *Voyage to Venus* (London: Pan, 1953)

The Liber de Diversis Medicinis in the Thornton Manuscript, ed. Margaret Sinclair Ogden (London: Oxford University Press, 1938 = EETS/OS 207)

[*Liber pontificalis*] Raymond Davis, *The Book of Pontiffs* (Liverpool: Liverpool University Press, 1989); ed. Theodor Mommsen, *Gestorum Pontificum Romanorum I: Liber pontificalis* (Berlin: Monumenta Germaniae Historica, 1898)

[Life of Adam, Auchinleck] *A Penni worth of Witte*, ed. David Laing (Abbotsford Club, 1857), pp. 49–75

[Life of Adam, Auchinleck] C. Horstmann, *Sammlung altenglischer Legenden* (Heilbronn: Henninger, 1878), pp. 138–47.

[Life of Adam, Bodleian prose] Carl Horstmann, 'Nachträge zu den Legenden 3: The lyfe of Adam', *Archiv* 74 (1885), 345–65

[Life of Adam, Vernon prose] N. F. Blake, *Middle English Religious Prose* (London, Arnold, 1972), pp. 103–18

[Life of Adam, Wheatley prose] Mabel Day, *The Wheatley Manuscript* (London: Oxford University Press = EETS/OS 21, 1921), pp. 76–99

Federico García Lorca, *Obras Completas*, ed. Arturo del Hoyo (Madrid: Aguilar, 1971); anthology with translations: *Lorca*, ed. J. L. Gill (Harmondsworth: Penguin, 1960)

Giovanni Francesco Loredano, *The Life of Adam*, trans. T.S. in 1659, ed. Roy C. Flannagan and John Arthos (Gainesville, Florida: Scholar's Facsimiles, 1967)

Lusty Juventus: see Somerset

[Martin Luther] *D. Martin Luthers Werke: kritische Gesamtausgabe* (Weimar: Böhlau, 1883–); trans. and ed. Jaroslav Pelikan, *Luther's Works* (St Louis: Concordia,

1958–); *Martin Luther: Selections*, ed. Lewis Jillings and Brian Murdoch (Hull: NGS, repr. 1980)

[Lutwin] Mary-Bess Halford, *Lutwin's Eva und Adam: Study, Text, Translation* (Göppingen: Kümmerle, 1984)

Le Lyon Coronné, ed. Kenneth Urwin (Geneva and Paris: Droz/Minard, 1958)

[Maastricht Play] Julius Zacher, 'Mittelniederländisches Osterspiel', *Zeitschrift für deutsches Altertum* 2 (1842), 302–57

The Macro Plays, ed. F. J. Furnivall and Alfred W. Pollard (London: Trübner, 1904 = EETS/ES 91) and ed. Mark Eccles (London: Oxford University Press, 1969 = EETS/OS 262); ed. Edgar T. Schell and J. D. Schuchter, *English Morality Plays and Moral Interludes* (New York: Holt, Rinehart and Winston, 1969)

Moses Maimonides, *The Guide of the Perplexed*, trans. Chaim Rabin, ed. Julius Guttmann (Indianapolis: Hackett, 1995)

[Malory] *The Works of Sir Thomas Malory*, ed. Eugène Vinaver, 3rd edn rev. P. J. C. Field (Oxford: Clarendon, 1990); *Le Morte d'Arthur of Sir Thomas Malory* (London and Toronto: Dent, 1906)

Thomas Mann, *Der Erwählte* (Frankfurt/M and Hamburg: Fischer, 1951, repr. 1967), trans. Helen Lowe-Porter, *The Holy Sinner* (Harmondsworth: Penguin, 1961)

J. Mansi, *Sacrorum Conciliorum . . . collectio* (Florence etc., 1759–81)

Christopher Marlowe, *Plays and Poems*, ed. M. R. Ridley (London: Dent, 1955)

Friedrich Maurer, *Die religiösen Dichtungen des 11. und 12. Jahrhunderts* (Tübingen: Niemeyer, 1964–6)

John T. McNeill and Helena M. Gamer, *Medieval Handbooks of Penance* (New York: Columbia University Press, 1938, repr. 1990)

Meriasek: see *Beunans Meriasek*

Dan Michel's Ayenbite of Inwyt I: Text, transcr. Richard Morris, ed. Pamela Gradon (London: Oxford University Press, 1965 = EETS/OS 23)

Miracles de Nostre Dame, ed. Gaston Paris and Ulysse Robert (Paris: Didot, 1876–93)

[John Mirk] *Mirk's Festial: a Collection of Homilies, I*, ed. Theodor Erbe (London: Kegan Paul, Trench, 1905 = EETS/ES 96)

John Milton, *The Prose Works*, ed. J. A. St John and Charles R. Sumner (London: Bohn, 18[48]–64); *The Works of John Milton*, ed. Frank Allen Patterson (New York: Columbia University Press, 1931–8)

The Missal of Robert of Jumièges, ed. H. A. Wilson (London: Henry Bradshaw Society, 1896)

Le Mistére du Viel Testament, ed. James de Rothschild (Paris: Didot, 1878–91, repr. New York: Johnson, 1966); partial edn of first part by Barbara M. Craig, *La Créacion, La Transgression and l'Expulsion of the Mistere du Viel Testament* (Lawrence, Kansas: University of Kansas, n.d.)

Richard Monaco, *Parsival or a Knight's Tale* (Glasgow: Futura, 1977)

Hugo von Montfort: see Hugo

Moses Maimonides, ben Maimon: see [Moses] Maimonides

Brian Murdoch, *The Grin of the Gargoyle* (Sawtrey: Dedalus, 1995)

Le Mystère d'Adam, ed. Paul Studer (Manchester: Manchester University Press, 1949); ed. Karl Grass, *Das Adamsspiel* (Halle/Saale: Niemeyer, 1928); trans. Edward Noble Stone, *Adam* (Seattle: University of Washington Press, 1928); and Richard

Axton and John Stevens, *Medieval French Plays* (Oxford: Blackwell, 1971), pp. 1–44

[N-Town Plays] *Ludus Coventriae or the Plaie called Corpus Christi*, ed. K. S. Block (London: Oxford University Press, 1922 = EETS/ES 120)

Das Oberammergauer Passionsspiel 1960 (Oberammergau: Gemeinde Oberammergau, 1960); trans. Eric Lane and Ian Brenson (London: Dedalus, 1984)

[*Ordinalia*] Edwin Norris, *The Ancient Cornish Drama*, 2 vols (Oxford: Oxford University Press, 1859, repr. London and New York: Blom, 1968); trans. Markham Harris, *The Cornish Ordinalia: a Medieval Dramatic Trilogy* (Washington: Catholic University of America Press, 1969); extracts in F. E. Halliday, *The Legend of the Rood* (London: Duckworth, 1955)

[Passion Nostre Seigneur/St Genevieve] Edward Joseph Gallagher, *A Critical Edition of La Passion Nostre Seigneur from Manuscript 1131 from the Bibliothèque Sainte-Geneviève, Paris* (Chapel Hill, NC: University of North Carolina Press, 1976)

Parzival: see Wolfram

Peniarth 53, ed. E. Stanton Roberts and Henry Lewis (Cardiff: University of Wales Press, 1927)

[*Penitence d'Adam*] Esther C. Quinn and M. Dufau, *The Penitence of Adam: a Study of the Andrius MS* (University, Mississippi: Romance Monographs Inc., 1980)

Pirkê de Rabbi Eliezer, trans. Gerald Friedlander (London: Kegan Paul, Trench, 1916)

Pope Joan, Play of: see Schernberg

Terry Pratchett and Neil Gaiman, *Good Omens* (London: Gollancz, 1990)

La Queste del Saint Graal, ed. Albert Pauphilet (Paris: Champion, 3rd edn, 1965), trans. P. M. Matarasso, *The Quest of the Holy Grail* (Harmondsworth: Penguin, 1969)

Das Redentiner Osterspiel, ed. Brigitta Schottmann (Stuttgart: Reclam, 1975)

[Robert Grosseteste] Kari Sajavaara, *The Middle English Translations of Robert Grosseteste's Chateau d'Amour* (Helsinki: Société Néophilologique, 1967); Jessie Murray, 'Le Château d'Amour de Robert Grosseteste, évêque de Lincoln' (Paris: Diss., 1918)

Robert of Jumièges: see *Missal*

[Jacob Ruf] Hermann Marcus Kottinger, *Jacob Ruffs Adam und Heva* (Quedlinburg and Leipzig: Basse, 1848); Janice Whitelaw, 'Jacob Ruff's *Adam und Heva*' (Ph.D. Diss. Stirling, 1998); Barbara Thoran, ed., *Das Züricher Passionsspiel* (Bochum: Brockmeyer, 1984)

Rutebeuf, *Le Miracle de Théophile*, ed. Grace Frank (Paris: Champion, 1970); trans. Murdoch, *Grin of the Gargoyle*, pp. 207–28

Hans Sachs, *Werke*, ed. A. von Keller and E. Goetze (Tübingen: Stuttgarter lit. Verein, 1870–1908); Theo Schumacher, *Hans Sachs: Fastnachtspiele* (Tübingen: Niemeyer, 1957)

[*St Erkenwald*] Henry L. Savage, *St Erkenwald* (New Haven: Yale University Press, 1926); Ruth Morse, *St Erkenwald* (Cambridge: D. S. Brewer, 1975); modern trans. in *The Owl and the Nightingale. Cleanness. St Erkenwald*, trans. Brian Stone (Harmondsworth: Penguin, 1971)

[Salernitan Questions] Brian Lawn, *The Prose Salernitan Questions* (London: British Academy, 1979)

[*Saltair na Rann*] *The Irish Adam and Eve story from Saltair na Rann*, I, ed. and trans.

David Greene and Fergus Kelly; II, *Commentary* by Brian Murdoch (Dublin: IAS, 1976)

Dorothy L. Sayers, *The Man Born to be King* (London: Gollancz, 1943)

Albrecht Schaeffer, *Parzival: ein Versroman in drei Kreisen* (Leipzig: Insel, 2nd edn, 1924)

[Dietrich Schernberg] Manfred Lemmer, *Dietrich Schernberg: ein schoen Spiel von Frau Jutten* (Berlin: Schmidt, 1971)

A. F. Scot, *Adam and Lilith* (London: Burleigh, 1899)

Alexander Scott, *Cantrips* (Preston: Akros, 1968)

Tom Scott, *The Tree* (Dunfermline: Borderline Press, 1977)

[*Sex aetates mundi*] *The Irish Sex Aetates Mundi*, ed. Dáibhí Ó Cróinín (Dublin: DIAS, 1983)

Theodore Silverstein, *Medieval English Lyrics* (London: Arnold, 1971)

Sir Eglamour of Artois, ed. Frances E. Richardson (London: Oxford University Press, 1965 = EETS/OS 256)

[*Solomon and Saturn*] James E. Cross and Thomas D. Hill, *The Prose Solomon and Saturn* (Toronto: University of Toronto Press, 1982)

J. A. B. Somerset, *Four Tudor Interludes* (London: Athlone, 1974)

H. F. D. Sparks, *The Apocryphal Old Testament* (Oxford: Clarendon, 1984)

Edmund Spenser, *Poetical Works*, ed. J. C. Smith and E. de Selincourt (London: Oxford University Press, 1912 and reprints)

H. de Vere Stacpoole, *The Blue Lagoon* (London: Dent, [1908])

Joseph Szövérffy, *Hymns of the Holy Cross* (Brookline and Leiden: Brill, 1976)

Emma Tennant, *Sisters and Strangers* (London: Grafton, 1990)

Théophile: see Rutebeuf

Theophilus, der Faust des Mittelalters, ed. Ludwig Ettmüller (Quedlinburg and Leipzig: Basse, 1849)

Thomas Aquinas, *Summa contra gentiles* (Turin: Marinetti, 1922)

Trentalle Sancti Gregorii, eine mittelenglische Legende, ed. Albert Kaufmann (Erlangen and Leipzig, 1889, repr. Amsterdam: Rodopi, 1970)

[Trier *Silvester*] M. Roediger, 'Trierer Bruchstücke III: Silvester', *Zeitschrift für deutsches Altertum* 22 (1878), 145–209

Mark Twain, *Extracts from Adam's Diary* (London and New York: Harper, 1904)

[Valten Voith] Hugo Holstein, *Die Dramen von Ackermann und Voith* (Tübingen: Stuttgart lit. Verein, 1884)

Lope Félix de Vega Carpio, *Obras Escogidas*, ed. Federico Carlos Sainz de Robles, vol. III (*Teatro*) (Madrid: Aguilar, 3rd edn, 1967)

Luis Vélez de Guevara y Dueñas, *La Creación del Mundo*, ed. Henryk Ziomek and Robert White Linker (Athens, GA: University of Georgia Press, 1974)

Gil Vicente, *Obras Completas*, ed. Marques Braga (Lisbon: Da Costa, 4th edn, 1968)

La Vie du Pape Saint Grégoire, ed. Hendrik B. Sol (Amsterdam: Rodopi, 1977)

[*Vie de Saint Silvestre*] Paul Meyer, 'La vie de Saint Silvestre en vers français', *Romania* 28 (1899), 280–6

[*Vita Adae et Evae*] Gerhard Eis, *Beiträge zur mittelhochdeutschen Legende und Mystik* (Berlin: Akademie, 1935)

[*Vita Adae et Evae*] Carl Horstmann, 'Nachträge zu den Legenden 10: Vita prothoplausti Ade', *Archiv* 79 (1887), 459–70

[*Vita Adae et Evae*] Wilhelm Meyer, *Vita Adae et Evae*, in the *Abhandlungen der bayerischen Akademie* (Munich), philos.-philol. Kl. 14/iii (1879), pp. 185–250

[*Vita Adae et Evae*] J. Mozley, 'The Vita Adae', *Journal of Theological Studies* 30 (1929), 121–47

[*Vita Adae et Evae*] S. Harrison Thomson, 'A Fifth Recension of the Latin *Vita Adae et Evae*', *Studi Medievali* NS 6 (1933), 271–8

Joost van Vondel, *Adam in Ballingschap*, ed. B. H. G. Molkenboer (Zwolle: Willink, 1947)

Glynne Wickham, *English Moral Interludes* (London: Dent, 1976)

Das Wildalpener Paradeisspiel mit einem Postludium Vom Jüngling und dem Teufel, ed. Oskar Pausch (Vienna: Böhlau, 1981)

[William of Shoreham] *The Poems of William of Shoreham*, ed. M. Konrath (London: Kegan Paul, 1902 = EETS/ES 86)

Wolfram von Eschenbach, *Werke*, ed. Karl Lachmann, 6th edn Eduard Hartl (Berlin and Leipzig: de Gruyter, 1926, repr. 1964); trans. of *Parzival* by A. T. Hatto, *Wolfram von Eschenbach: Parzival* (Harmondsworth, Penguin, 1980); *Parzival: eine Auswahl*, trans. Wilhelm Hertz, ed. W. Hofstaetter (Stuttgart: Reclam, 1959)

Secondary Literature

Derek van Abbé, *Drama in Renaissance Germany and Switzerland* (Melbourne: Melbourne University Press, 1961)

Juan Ainaud, *Romanesque Painting*, trans. Jean Stewart (London: Weidenfeld and Nicolson, 1963)

M. D. Anderson, *Drama and Imagery in English Medieval Churches* (Cambridge: Cambridge University Press, 1963)

F. Assensio, '¿Tradición sobre un peccado sexual en el Paraíso?' *Gregorianum* 30 (1949), 490–520; 31 (1950), 35–62, 163–91, 362–90

Erich Auerbach, *Mimesis*, trans. Willard Trask (New York: Doubleday, 1957)

Friedrich Bachmann, *Die beiden versionen des mittelenglischen Canticum de creatione* (Hamburg: Lütke und Wolff, 1891)

Thomas I. Bacon, *Martin Luther and the Drama* (Amsterdam: Rodopi, 1976)

Leslie Badanes, 'Heinrich's Leprosy: Punishment or Test?' *Modern Language Studies* 10 (1980), 88–92

Maria Giulia Barberini, *I Santi Quattro Coronati a Roma* (Rome: Palombi, 1989)

J. Barron, *English Medieval Romance* (London: Longman, 1987)

Anke Bennholdt-Thomsen, 'Die allegorischen *kleit* im *Gregorius*-Prolog', *Euphorion* 56 (1962), 174–84

James Bentley, *Oberammergau and the Passion Play* (Harmondsworth: Penguin, 1984)

Dorothy Bethurum, *Critical Approaches to Medieval Literature* (New York: Columbia University Press, 1960)

U. Bianchi, 'La Rédemption dans les livres d'Adam', *Numen* 18 (1971), 1–8

Paul Binski, *Medieval Death* (London: British Museum, 1996)

David Blamires, 'Fairytale Analogues to *Der arme Heinrich*', in *Hartmann von Aue:*

Changing Perspectives, ed. Timothy McFarland and Silvia Ranawake (Göppingen: Kümmerle, 1988), pp. 187–98

Ute von Bloh, *Die illustrierten Historienbibeln* (Bern: Lang, 1993)

John Boswell, *The Kindness of Strangers: the Abandonment of Children in Western Europe from Late Antiquity to the Renaissance* (Harmondsworth: Penguin, 1991)

Maud Bodkin, *Archetypal Patterns in Poetry* (London: Oxford University Press, 1934)

James Bowen, *A History of Western Education II* (London: Methuen, 1975)

C. M. Bowra, *From Virgil to Milton* (London: Macmillan, 1945)

David Brett-Evans, *Von Hrotsvit bis Folz und Gengenbach* (Berlin: Schmidt, 1975)

Auguste Brieger, *Kain und Abel in der deutschen Dichtung* (Berlin and Leipzig: de Gruyter, 1934)

Mary Brockington, 'Tristan and Amelius: False and True Repentance', *Modern Language Review* 93 (1998), 305–20

Saul Nathaniel Brody, *The Disease of the Soul: Leprosy in Medieval Literature* (Ithaca and London: Cornell University Press, 1974)

Christopher Brooke, *The Medieval Idea of Marriage* (Oxford: Oxford University Press, 1989)

Stanley G. Browne, *Leprosy in the Bible* (London: Christian Medical Fellowship, n.d. [c.1970])

James C. Bryant, *Tudor Drama and Religious Controversy* (Mercer: Mercer University Press, 1984)

Colin C. Campbell, 'The Transformation of Biblical Myth: Macleish's Use of the Adam and Job Stories', in *Myth and Symbol*, ed. Bernice Slote (Lincoln, Neb: University of Nebraska Press, 1953), pp. 79–88

E. K. Chambers, *The Medieval Stage* (Oxford: Oxford University Press, 1903)

James Hamilton Charlesworth, *The Old Testament Pseudepigrapha and the New Testament* (Cambridge: Cambridge University Press, 1985)

Glenn T. Chesnut, *The First Christian Histories* (Macon, CA: Mercer University Press, 2nd rev. edn, 1986)

John Clayton, 'The Otherness of Anselm', *Neue Zeitschrift für systematische Theologie und Religionsphilosophie* 37 (1995), 125–43

Rosemary Combridge, 'The Uses of Biblical and Other Learned Symbolism in the Narrative Works of Hartmann von Aue', in *Hartmann von Aue: Changing Perspectives*, ed. Timothy McFarland and Silvia Ranawake (Göppingen: Kümmerle, 1988), pp. 271–84

Giles Constable, *The Reformation of the Twelfth Century* (Cambridge: Cambridge University Press, 1996)

Mary Philippa Coogan, *An Interpretation of the Moral Play 'Mankind'* (Washington, DC: Catholic University of America Press, 1947)

Roger Cook, *The Tree of Life: Symbol of the Centre* (London: Thames and Hudson, 1974)

Christoph Cormeau, *Hartmanns von Aue 'Armer Heinrich' und 'Gregorius'* (Munich: Beck, 1966)

Henrik Cornell, *Biblia Pauperum* (Stockholm: Thule-Tryck, 1925)

G. G. Coulton, *Studies in Medieval Thought* (London and Edinburgh: Nelson, 1940)

John Crosbie, *A lo divino Lyric Poetry: an Alternative View* (Durham: DMLS, 1989)

Ingrid G. Daemmrich, *Enigmatic Bliss: the Paradise Motif in Literature* (Frankfurt/M: Lang, 1997)

James R. Davila, 'Enoch in Cyberspace: the Internet meets the Old Testament Pseudepigrapha', *Computers and Texts* 15 (August, 1977), 8–10

Neville Denny, 'Arena Staging and Dramatic Quality in the Cornish Passion Play', in *Medieval Drama*, ed. Neville Denny (London: Arnold, 1973)

Peter Diehl, *The Medieval European Religious Lyric* (Berkeley etc.: University of California Press, 1985)

Myles Dillon, 'Scéal Saltrach na Rann', *Celtica* 4 (1958), 1–4

Richard G. Dimler, 'Parzival's Guilt: a Theological Interpretation', *Monatshefte* 62 (1970), 123–34

Eberhard Dorn, *Der sündige Heilige in der Legende des Mittalalters* (Munich: Fink, 1967)

F. Drewniak, *Die mariologische Deutung von Gen. 3. 15 in der Väterzeit* (Breslau: Nischkowsky, 1934)

Peter Dronke, *The Medieval Lyric* (London: Hutchinson, 1968)

David Duckworth, *The Influence of Biblical Terminology and Thought on Wolfram's Parzival* (Göppingen: Kümmerle, 1980)

David Duckworth, *Gregorius: a Medieval Man's Discovery of his True Self* (Göppingen: Kümmerle, 1985)

David Duckworth, 'Heinrich and the Godless Life in Hartmann's Poem', *Mediaevistik* 3 (1990), 71–90

David Duckworth, 'Heinrich and the Knowledge of God in Hartmann's Poem', *Mediaevistik* 5 (1992), 57–70

David Duckworth, 'Heinrich and the Knowledge of God', *Mediaevistik* 5 (1995), 57–70

David Duckworth, *The Leper and the Maiden in Hartmann's Der arme Heinrich* (Göppingen: Kümmerle, 1996)

Eamon Duffy, *The Stripping of the Altars* (New Haven and London: Yale University Press, 1992)

Raymond Graeme Dunphy, *Daz was ein michel wunder: the Presentation of Old Testament Material in Jans Enikel's 'Weltchronik'* (Göppingen: Kümmerle, 1998)

A. C. Dunstan, 'Lutwin's Latin Source', in *German Studies presented to H. G. Fiedler* (London, 1938, repr. New York: Books for Libraries, 1969), pp. 160–73

A. C. Dunstan, 'The Middle English *Canticum de Creatione* and the Latin *Vita Adae et Evae*', *Anglia* 55 (1931), 431–42

Gerhard Eis, 'Der Seuchenspruch des armen Heinrichs', *Forschungen und Fortschritte* 25 (1949), 10–12

Gerhard Eis, 'Salernitanisches und Unsalernitanisches im 'Armen Heinrich' des Hartmann von Aue', *Forschungen und Fortschritte* 31 (1957), 77–81

J. Elema and R. van der Wal, 'Zum Volksbuch *Eine schöne merkwürdige Historie des heiligen Bischofs Gregorii auf dem Stein genannt*', *Euphorion* 57 (1963), 292–320

Dyan Elliot, *Spiritual Marriage: Sexual Abstinence in Medieval Wedlock* (Princeton: Princeton University Press, 1993)

R. Endres, 'Heinrichs *hôchvart*', *Euphorion* 61 (1967), 267–94

Hans Martin von Erffa, *Ikonologie der Genesis* (Stuttgart: Deutscher Kunstverlag, 1989–95)

G. R. Evans, *Alan of Lille: the Frontiers of Theology in the Later Twelfth Century* (Cambridge: Cambridge University Press, 1983)

G. R. Evans, *The Language and Logic of the Bible: the Earlier Middle Ages* (Cambridge: Cambridge University Press, 1984)

J. M. Evans, *'Paradise Lost' and the Genesis Tradition* (Oxford: Clarendon, 1968)

Inga-Stina Ewbank, 'The House of David in Renaissance Drama', *Renaissance Drama* 8 (1965), 3–40

Ronald Finch, 'Guilt and Innocence in Hartmann's *Der arme Heinrich*', *Neuphilologische Mitteilungen* 73 (1972), 642–52

Stanley Eugene Fish, ' "Not so much a Teaching as an Intangling": Milton's Method in *Paradise Lost*', in *Milton*, ed. Alan Rudrum (London: Aurora, 1970), pp. 104–35

Rodney Fisher, 'Hartmann's *Gregorius* and the Paradox of Sin', *Seminar* 17 (1981), 1–16

M. Flunk, 'Das Protevangelium (Gen. 3. 15) und seine Beziehung zum Dogma der unbefleckten Empfängnis Marias', *Zeitschrift für katholische Theologie* 28 (1904), 642–63

Leonard Forster, 'From the *Schwabenspiegel* to Pfefferkorn: a Study in *Makulatur*', in *Medieval German Studies Presented to Frederick Norman* (London: Institute of Germanic Studies, 1965), pp. 282–95

David C. Fowler, *The Bible in Early English Literature* (London: Sheldon, 1977)

Wallace Fowlie, *Love in Literature* (Bloomington: Indiana University Press, 1965)

Peter France, ed., *New Oxford Companion to Literature in French* (Oxford: Clarendon, 1995)

Grace Frank, *The Medieval French Drama* (Oxford: Clarendon, 1954)

Christopher Frayling, *Strange Landscape* (Harmondsworth: Penguin, 1995)

W. H. C. Frend, *Saints and Sinners in the Early Church* (London: Darton, Longman and Todd, 1985)

Northrop Frye, *The Great Code: the Bible and Literature* (London: RKP, 1982)

C. Fudge, 'Aspects of Form in the Cornish Ordinalia', *Old Cornwall* 8 (1973–9), 457–64 and 491–8

H. Fuhrmann, 'Konstantinische Schenkung und Silvesterlegende in neuer Sicht', *Deutsches Archiv für Erforschung des Mittelalters* 15 (1959), 523–40

Peter F. Ganz, 'Dienstmann und Abt. "Gregorius peccator" bei Hartmann von Aue und Arnold von Lübeck', in *Festschrift für Werner Schröder*, ed. Ernst-Joachim Schmidt (Berlin: Schmidt, 1974), pp. 250–75

Helen Gardner, *Religion and Literature* (London: Faber, 1971)

Christoph Gerhardt, 'Der Phönix auf dem dürren Baum' and 'Arznei und Symbol', in *Natura loquax: Naturkunde und allegorische Naturdeutung vom Mittelalter bis zur frühen Neuzeit*, ed. Wolfgang Harms and Heimo Reinitzer (Frankfurt/M: Lang, 1981), pp. 73–108 and 109–82

K. Dieter Goebel, *Untersuchungen zu Aufbau und Schuldproblem in Hartmanns 'Gregorius'* (Berlin: Schmidt, 1974)

Elisabeth Gössmann, 'Typus der Heilsgeschichte oder Opfer morbider Gesellschaftsordnung?' *Euphorion* 68 (1974), 42–80

Robert M. Grant, *A Short History of the Interpretation of the Bible* (London: Black, rev. edn, 1965)

H. Grauert, 'Die konstantinische Schenkung', *Historisches Jahrbuch* 3 (1882), 3–30

Robert Graves and Raphael Patai, *Hebrew Myths: the Book of Genesis* (New York: McGraw-Hill, 1966)

Douglas Gray, *Robert Henryson* (Leiden: Brill, 1979)

Reinhold Grimm, 'Die Paradiesesehe: eine erotische Utopie des Mittelalters', in *[Festschrift] für Wolfgang Mohr*, ed. F. Hundschnurcher and U. Müller (Göppingen: Kümmerle, 1972), pp. 1–25

Arthur Groos, 'Time Reference and the Liturgical Calendar in Wolfram von Eschenbach's *Parzival*', *Deutsche Vierteljahresschrift* 49 (1975), 43–65

R. D. Haage, 'Der "mystische Dreischritt" und der "Märchenschluß" im *Armen Heinrich*', *Leuvense Bijdragen* 73 (1984), 145–62

Alois M. Haas, *Parzivals* tumpheit *bei Wolfram von Eschenbach* (Berlin: Schmidt, 1964)

Mary-Bess [= M. E. B.] Halford, *Illustration and Text in Lutwin's Eva und Adam. Codex Vindob. 2980* (Göppingen: Kümmerle, 1980)

M. E. B. Halford, 'The Apocryphal *Vita Adae et Evae*: Some Comments on the Manuscript Tradition', *Neuphilologische Mitteilungen* 82 (1981), 412–27; 83 (1982), 222

Oliver Hallich, *Poetologisches, Theologisches: Studien zum Gregorius Hartmanns von Aue* (Frankfurt/M: Lang, 1995)

H. W. Hanson, *Apes and Ape Lore in the Middle Ages and the Renaissance* (London: Warburg Institute, 1952)

Peter Happé, *John Bale* (New York: Twayne, 1997)

Peter Happé, 'John Bale, 1495–1563', *Jesus College, Cambridge Report* 93 (1997), 18–22

O. B. Hardison, *Christian Rite and Christian Drama in the Middle Ages* (Baltimore and London: Johns Hopkins Press, 1965)

Wolfgang Harms, *Homo viator in bivio* (Munich: Fink, 1970)

Nigel Harris, 'The Presentation of Clerical Characters in Hartmann's *Gregorius* and in the *Vie du pape saint Grégoire*', *Medium Aevum* 64 (1995), 189–204

Stephen G. Harroff, *Wolfram and his Audience* (Göppingen: Kümmerle, 1974)

D. E. Hart-Davies, *The Genesis of Genesis* (London: Clarke [1932])

Gerhard Hasel, *Old Testament Theology: Basic Issues in the Current Debate* (Grand Rapids, Michigan: Eerdmans, 4th edn, 1991)

Walter Haug, 'Gottfried von Strassburgs *Tristan*: Sexueller Sündenfall oder erotische Utopie?' in *Kontroversen, alte und neue: Akten des VII Internationalen Germanisten-Kongresses (Göttingen 1985)* (Tübingen: Niemeyer, 1986), I, 41–52

Betty Hill, 'The Fifteenth-Century Prose Legend of the Cross before Christ', *Medium Aevum* 34 (1965), 203–22

F. E. Hutchinson, *Milton and the English Mind* (London: English Universities Press, 1949)

Zbigniew Izydorczyk, ed., *The Medieval Gospel of Nicodemus: Texts, Intertexts and Contexts in Western Europe* (Tempe, Arizona: Medieval and Renaissance Texts and Studies, 1997)

G[ ] J[ ], *The Poetical Register* (London, 1723: repr. Farnborough: Gregg, 1969)

Timothy R. Jackson, *The Legends of Konrad von Würzburg* (Erlangen: Palm und Enke, 1983)

Timothy R. Jackson, 'Abraham and Engelhard: Immoral Means and Moral Ends', in

Connections: Essays in Honour of Eda Sagarra, ed. Peter Skrine et al. (Stuttgart: Heinz, 1993), pp. 117–26

Adolf Jacoby, *Ein bisher ungeachteter apokrypher Bericht über die Taufe Jesu* (Strassburg: Trübner, 1902)

Danielle Jacquart and Claude Thomasset, *Sexuality and Medicine in the Middle Ages* (Princeton: Princeton University Press, 1988)

Martin Jones, 'Changing Perspectives on the Maiden in *Der arme Heinrich*', in *Hartmann von Aue: Changing Perspectives*, ed. T. McFarland and Silvia Ranawake (Göppingen: Kümmerle, 1988), pp. 211–31

Marinus de Jonge and Johannes Tromp, *The Life of Adam and Eve and Related Literature* (Sheffield: Academic Press, 1997)

Peter Jentzmik, *Zu Möglichkeit und Grenzen typologischer Exegese in mittelalterlicher Predigt und Dichtung* (Göppingen: Kümmerle, 1973)

Stanley J. Kahrl, *Traditions of Medieval English Drama* (London: Hutchinson, 1974)

Stanley J. Kahrl, 'Secular Life and Popular Piety in English Medieval Drama', in *The Popular Literature of Medieval England*, ed. Thomas J. Heffernan (Knoxville: University of Tennessee Press, 1985), pp. 85–107

Marianne E. Kalinke, 'Hartmann's *Gregorius*: a Lesson in the Inscrutability of God's Will', *Journal of English and Germanic Philology* 74 (1975), 486–501

N. R. Ker, *Medieval Libraries of Great Britain* (London: Royal Historical Society, 2nd edn, 1964)

Peter Kesting, '*Diu rehte warheit*: zu Konrads von Würzburg *Engelhard*', *Zeitschrift für deutsches Altertum* 99 (1970), 246–59

K. C. King, 'The Mother's Guilt in Hartmann's *Gregorius*', in *Medieval German Studies Presented to F. Norman* (London: IGS, 1965), pp. 84–93

Pamela M. King, 'The Morality', in *The Cambridge Companion to Medieval English Theatre*, ed. Richard Beadle (Cambridge: Cambridge University Press, 1994), pp. 240–64

W. Kirkconnell, *The Celestial Cycle* (Toronto: UTP, 1952, repr. New York: Gordian, 1967)

Dorothea Klein, *Bildung und Belehrung* (Stuttgart: Heinz, 1988)

Carl Klimke, *Das volkstümliche Paradiesspiel* (Breslau: Marus, 1902; repr. Hildesheim: Olms, 1977)

David Knowles, *The Evolution of Medieval Thought* (London: Longmans, 1962)

Barbara Könneker, *Die deutsche Literatur der Reformationszeit* (Munich: Winkler, 1975)

A. K. Krappe, 'The Legend of Amicus and Amelius', *Modern Language Review* 18 (1923), 152–61

Pierre Labriolle, *History and Literature of Christianity from Tertullian to Boethius*, trans. Herbert Wilson (London: Kegan, Paul, Trench, 1924)

Peter Lamarque, 'Fiction and Reality', in *Philosophy and Fiction: Essays in Literary Aesthetics*, ed. Peter Lamarque (Aberdeen: Aberdeen University Press, 1983), pp. 52–72

Sanford V. Larkey, 'Leprosy in Medieval Romance', *Bulletin of the History of Medicine* 35 (1961), 77–80

A. van der Lee, 'De mirabili divina dispensatione et ortu beati Gregorii pape', *Neophilologus* 53 (1969), 30–47, 120–37 and 251–6

John Leonard, *Naming in Paradise: Milton and the Language of Adam and Eve* (Oxford: Clarendon, 1990)

Israel Lévi, 'Éléments Chrétiens dans le *Pirke Rabbi Eliezer*', *Revue des études Juives* 18 (1889), 83–9

C. S. Lewis, *Arthurian Torso* (Oxford: Clarendon, 1948)

C. S. Lewis, *English Literature in the Sixteenth Century* (Oxford: Clarendon, 1954)

C. S. Lewis, *They Asked for a Paper* (London: Bles, 1962)

C. S. Lewis, *Studies in Medieval and Renaissance Literature*, ed. W. Hooper (Cambridge: Cambridge University Press, 1966)

R. W. B. Lewis, *The American Adam: Innocence, Tragedy and Tradition in the Nineteenth Century* (Chicago and London: University of Chicago Press, 1955)

Carl Lofmark, 'The Advisor's Guilt in Courtly Literature', *German Life and Letters* 24 (1970/1), 3–13

Roger Sherman Loomis, ed., *Arthurian Literature in the Middle Ages* (Oxford: Clarendon, 1959)

Roger Sherman Loomis, *The Development of Arthurian Romance* (London: Hutchinson, 1963)

Henri de Lubac, *Exégèse médiévale: les quatre sens de l'Écriture* (Paris: Aubier, 1959–64)

Victor Luzarche, 'Le drame et la légende d'Adam au moyen-âge', *Revue contemporaine* 20 (1855), 5–38

Diane Kelsey McColley, *A Gust for Paradise: Milton's Eden and the Visual Arts* (Urbana and Chicago: University of Illinois Press, 1993)

Winder McConnell, '*Sacrificium* in Hartmann von Aue's *Der arme Heinrich*', *Neuphilologische Mitteilungen* 84 (1983), 21–8

J. B. McLean, 'Hartmann von Aue's Religious Attitude and Didacticism in his *Gregorius*', *Rice Institute Pamphlets* 39 (1952), 1–17

Robert E. McNally, *The Bible in the Early Middle Ages* (Westminster, Maryland: Newman, 1959)

Martin McNamara, *The Apocrypha in the Irish Church* (Dublin: IAS, 1975)

J. M. R. Margeson, *The Origins of English Tragedy* (Oxford: Clarendon, 1967)

John Margetts, 'Observations on the Representation of Female Attractiveness in the Works of Hartmann von Aue', in *Hartmann von Aue: Changing Perspectives*, ed. Timothy McFarland and Silvia Ranawake (Göppingen: Kümmerle, 1988), pp. 199–210

Andrew Martin, 'The Genesis of Ignorance: Nescience and Omniscience in the Garden of Eden', *Philosophy and Literature* 5 (1981), 3–20

C. W. Marx, 'The Problems of the Doctrine of the Redemption in the ME Mystery Plays and the Cornish *Ordinalia*', *Medium Aevum* 54 (1985), 20–32

C. W. Marx, *The Devil's Rights and the Redemption in the Literature of Medieval England* (Cambridge: D. S. Brewer, 1995)

Achim Masser, *Bibel, Apokryphen und Legenden: Geburt und Kindheit Jesu in der religiösen Epik des deutschen Mittelalters* (Berlin: Schmidt, 1969)

Edward Scott Matthews, 'Rational Inquiry and Communities of Interest: Anselm's Argument and the Friars' (Ph.D. Diss., Lancaster, 1996)

Georg Megas, 'Das Χειρωγραφον Adams', *Zeitschrift für die neutestamentliche Wissenschaft* 27 (1928), 305–20

Peter Meister, *The Healing Female in the German Courtly Romance* (Göppingen: Kümmerle, 1990)

Peter Meredith, 'The Direct and Indirect Use of the Bible in Medieval English drama', *Bulletin of the John Rylands Library* 77 (1995), 61–77

Volker Mertens, *Gregorius Eremita* (Munich: Artemis, 1978)

Volker Mertens, 'Gregorius', in *Die deutsche Literatur des Mittelalters: Verfasserlexikon* (Berlin: de Gruyter, 1978–), III, 244–8

Volker Mertens, 'Verslegende und Prosalegendar: Zur Prosafassung von Legendenromanen in "Der Heiligen Leben" ', in *Poesie und Gebrauchsliteratur in deutschen Mittelalter*, ed. Volker Honemann (Tübingen: Niemeyer, 1979), pp. 265–89

Almut Agnes Meyer, *Heilsgewißheit und Endzeiterwartung im deutschen Drama des 16. Jahrhunderts* (Heidelberg: Winter, 1976)

Heinz Meyer, *Die Zahlenallegorese im Mittelalter: Methode und Gebrauch* (Munich: Fink, 1975)

Gretchen Mieszkowski, 'The Reputation of Criseyde', *Transactions of the Connecticut Academy of Arts and Sciences* 43 (1971), 71–153

Andrew Robert Miller, 'German and Dutch Legends of the Wood of the Cross before Christ' (D.Phil. Diss., Oxford, 1992)

J. Hillis Miller, 'Literature and Religion', in *Relations of Literary Study*, ed. James Thorpe (New York: MLA, 1967), pp. 111–26

Mary V. Mills, *The Pilgrimage Motif in the Works of the Medieval German Author Hartmann von Aue* (Lewiston and Lampeter: Mellen, 1996)

Werner Monselewski, *Der barmherzige Samaritaner: eine Auslegungsgeschichtliche Untersuchung zu Lukas 10, 25–37* (Tübingen: Mohr, 1967)

R. S. Moxon, *The Doctrine of Sin* (London: Allen and Unwin, 1922)

Lynnette R. Muir, *Liturgy and Drama in the Anglo-Norman Adam* (Oxford: Blackwell, 1973)

Maria S. Müller, *Der Poet der Moralität: Untersuchungen zu Hans Sachs* (Berne, Frankfurt/M, New York: Peter Lang, 1985)

Brian Murdoch, 'The Garments of Paradise: a Note on the *Wiener Genesis* and the *Anegenge*', *Euphorion* 61 (1967), 375–82

Brian Murdoch, *The Fall of Man in the Early Middle High German Biblical Epic* (Göppingen: Kümmerle, 1972)

Brian Murdoch, 'The River that Stopped Flowing: Folklore and Biblical Typology in the Apocryphal Lives of Adam and Eve', *Southern Folklore Quarterly* 37 (1973), 37–51

Brian Murdoch, 'An Early Irish Adam and Eve', *Medieval Studies* 35 (1973), 146–77

Brian Murdoch, *The Recapitulated Fall: a Comparative Study in Medieval Literature* (Amsterdam: Rodopi, 1974)

Brian Murdoch, 'Genesis and Pseudo-Genesis in Late Medieval German Poetry', *Medium Aevum* 45 (1975), 70–8

Brian Murdoch, 'Das deutsche Adambuch und die Adamlegenden des Mittelalters', in *Deutsche Literatur des späten Mittelalters*, ed. W. Harms and L. P. Johnson (Berlin: Schmidt, 1975), pp. 209–24

Brian Murdoch, 'Die sogenannte *Wârheit*', in *Akten des V. internationalen Germanistenkongresses* (Berne and Frankfurt/M: Lang, 1976), II, 404–13

Brian Murdoch, 'Adam', 'Adambuch', 'Adams Klage', 'Adam-Predigtparodie',

'Immessen', in *Die deutsche Literatur des Mittelalters, Verfasserlexikon*, 2nd edn by Kurt Ruh (Berlin: de Gruyter, 1977–), I, 44–7, 61–2; IV, 366–8

Brian Murdoch, 'The Breton *Creation Ar Bet* and the Medieval Drama of Adam', *Zeitschrift für celtische Philologie* 36 (1977), 157–79

Brian Murdoch, 'Devils, Vices and the Fall: Dramatic Patterns from the Medieval Mystery to Bidermann's *Cenodoxus*', *Maske und Kothurn* 23 (1977), 15–30

Brian Murdoch, 'Hartmann's *Gregorius* and the Quest of Life', *New German Studies* 6 (1978), 79–100

Brian Murdoch, 'Eve's Anger: Literary Secularisation in Lutwin's *Adam und Eva*', *Archiv* 215 (1978), 256–71

Brian Murdoch, 'Naming the Beasts: Tom Scott and the Poet's Paradise', *Chapman* 26 (= 6/ii, Spring, 1980), 37–45

Brian Murdoch, '*Pascon agan Arluth*: the Literary Position of the Cornish Poem of the Passion', *Studi Medievali* 22 (1981), 822–36

Brian Murdoch, *Old High German Literature* (Boston: Twayne, 1983)

Brian Murdoch, 'Eden to Sauchiehall Street: Variations on a Myth in Modern Poetry', *Lines Review* 86 (September, 1983), 12–23

Brian Murdoch, 'Creation, Fall and After in the Cornish Mystery Play *Gwreans an bys*', *Studi Medievali* 29 (1988), 685–705

Brian Murdoch, '*Peri hieres nousou*: Approaches to the Old High German Medical Charms', in *Mit regulu bithuungan*, ed. J. Flood (Göppingen: Kümmerle, 1988), pp. 142–60

Brian Murdoch, 'Adam *sub gratia*: zur Bußszene in Hartmanns *Gregorius*', *Archiv* 227 (1990), 122–6

Brian Murdoch, 'The Origins of Penance: Reflections of Adamic Apocrypha and of the *Vita Adae* in Western Europe', *Annals of the Archive of Ferran Valls I Taberner's Library* 9/10 (1991), 205–28

Brian Murdoch, '*Drohtin, uuerthe so*! Zur Funktionsweise der althochdeutschen Zaubersprüche', *Jahrbuch der Görres-Gesellschaft* NS 32 (1991), 11–37

Brian Murdoch, 'Jacob Ruf's *Adam und Heva* and the Protestant Paradise-Play', *Modern Language Review* 86 (1991), 109–25

Brian Murdoch, *Cornish Literature* (Cambridge: D. S. Brewer, 1993)

Brian Murdoch, 'Sethites and Cainites: Narrative Problems in the Early Middle High German Genesis Poems', in *Festschrift for R. A. Wisbey*, ed. A. Stevens et al. (Berlin: Schmidt, 1994), pp. 83–97

Brian Murdoch, '*Trost in Verzweiflung*: an Analysis of an Early Middle High German Fragment', *Neuphilologische Mitteilungen* 96 (1995), 187–201

Brian Murdoch, 'Dos piezas dramáticas en verso del Génesis, una germana y una celta, de finales de la Edad Media', *Acta Poetica* 16 (1995), 349–68

Brian Murdoch, 'Schöpfung, fal und erlösung: Hans Sachs and Genesis 1–3', in *Hans Sachs and Folk Theatre in the Late Middle Ages* ed. R. Aylett and P. Skrine (Lewiston: Mellen, 1995), pp. 63–80

Brian Murdoch, 'Various Gospels', *Studi Medievali* 3/36 (1995), 776–96

Brian Murdoch, 'Legends of the Holy Rood in Cornish Drama', *Studia Celtica Japonica* 9 (1997), 19–34

Brian Murdoch, '*Parzival* and the Theology of Fallen Man', in *A Companion to*

Wolfram's Parzival, ed. Will Hasty (Columbia, SC: Camden House, 1999), pp. 143–58

Brian Murdoch, 'The *Mors Pilati* in the Cornish *Resurrexio Domini*', *Celtica* 23 (1999), 211–26

Adolfo Mussafia, 'Sulla leggenda del legno della croce', *Sitzungsberichte der kaiserl. Wiener Akademie der Wissenschaften*, phil.-hist. Cl. 63 (1869), 165–216

Dieter von der Nahmer, *Die lateinische Heiligenvita* (Darmstadt: WBG, 1994)

R. Morton Nance, 'The Plen an Gwary or Cornish Playing Place', *Journal of the Royal Institution of Cornwall* 24 (1935), 190–217

Allardyce Nicoll, *British Drama: an Historical Survey* (London: Harrap, 4th edn, 1947)

Kenneth J. Northcott, 'Paradisaical Love in Early Middle High German Literature', in *Taylor Starck Festschrift*, ed. Werner Betz (The Hague: Mouton, 1964), pp. 164–75

(Ernst) Friedrich Ohly, *Sage und Legende in der Kaiserchronik* (Münster, 1940, repr. Darmstadt: WBG, 1968)

Friedrich Ohly, 'Die Suche in Dichtungen des Mittelalters', *Zeitschrift für deutsches Altertum* 94 (1965), 171–84

Friedrich Ohly, *Schriften zur mittelalterlichen Bedeutungsforschung* (Darmstadt: WBG, 1977)

Friedrich Ohly, *Süsse Nägel der Passion* (Baden-Baden: Loerner, 1989)

Friedrich Ohly, *Der Verfluchte und der Erwählte: vom Leben mit der Schuld* (Opladen: Westdeutscher Verlag, 1976), trans. Linda Archibald, *The Damned and the Elect* (Cambridge: Cambridge University Press, 1992)

Friedrich Ohly, *Ausgewählte und neue Schriften zur Literaturgeschichte und zur Bedeutungsforschung*, ed. Uwe Ruberg and Dietmar Peil (Stuttgart and Leipzig: Hirzel, 1995), reviewed by D. H. Green, *Modern Language Review* 92 (1997), 783–5

F. Ohrt, *Die ältesten Segen über Christi Taufe und Christi Tod in religionsgeschichtlichem Lichte* (Copenhagen: Levin and Munksgaard, 1938)

R. L. Ottley, *Studies in the Confessions of St Augustine* (London: Robert Scott, 1919)

Elaine Pagels, *Adam, Eve and the Serpent* (Harmondsworth: Penguin, 1988)

Albert Pauphilet, 'La vie terrestre d'Adam et Ève', *Revue de Paris* 5 (1912), 213–24

J. A. Phillips, *Eve: the History of an Idea* (San Francisco: Harper and Row, 1984)

F. P. Pickering, *Essays on Medieval German Literature and Iconography* (Cambridge: Cambridge University Press, 1980)

Rosemary Picozzi, 'Allegory and Symbol in Hartmann's *Gregorius*', in *Essays . . . in Honor of Joyce Hallamore*, ed. M. Batts and M. Stankiewicz (Toronto: University of Toronto Press, 1968), pp. 19–33

Stuart Piggott, *Ancient Britons and the Antiquarian Imagination* (London: Thames and Hudson, 1989)

William H. Poteat, 'Birth, Suicide and the Doctrine of Creation', in *New Essays on Religious Language*, ed. Dallas M. High (New York: Oxford University Press, 1969), pp. 162–77

Angelique M. L. Pragsma-Hajenius, *La légende du bois de la croix dans la littérature française médiévale* (Paris: Van Gorcum, 1995)

G. Prochnow, 'Mittelhochdeutsche Silvesterlegenden und ihre Quellen', *Zeitschrift für deutsche Philologie* 33 (1901), 145–212

Eleanor Prosser, *Drama and Religion in the English Mystery Plays* (Stanford, CA: Stanford University Press, 1961)

Esther C. Quinn, *The Quest of Seth for the Oil of Life* (Chicago: University Press, 1962)

Jos. M. von Radowitz, *The Saints in Art*, trans. Christopher Benson (Rome: Victoria, 1898)

Barbara C. Raw, *Anglo-Saxon Crucifixion Iconography* (Cambridge: Cambridge University Press, 1990)

Margaret J. C. Reid, *The Arthurian Legend* (Edinburgh: Oliver and Boyd, 1938)

Paul Remy, 'La lèpre: thème littéraire au moyen âge', *Le Moyen Age* 52 (1946), 195–242

Peter Richards, *The Medieval Leper and his Northern Heirs* (Cambridge: D. S. Brewer, 1977)

Paul Riessler, *Altjüdisches Schrifttum außerhalb der Bibel* (Heidelberg: Winter, 1928)

A. G. Rigg, '*De motu et poena peccati*: a Latin Poem on the Causes and Effects of Sin', in *Literature and Religion in the Later Middle Ages (Philological Studies in Honor of Siegfried Wenzel)*, ed. Richard G. Newhauser and John A. Alford (Binghampton, NY: Medieval and Renaissance Texts and Studies, 1985), pp. 161–77

D. W. Robertson and Bernard F. Huppé, *Piers Plowman and Scriptural Tradition* (Princeton: University Press, 1951)

Anke Roeder, *Die Gebärde im Drama des Mittelalters* (Munich: Beck, 1974)

Ernst Rose, 'Problems of Medieval Psychology as Presented in the 'klein gemahel' of Heinrich the Unfortunate', *Germanic Review* 22 (1947), 182–7

Steven Rose, Introduction in *Genesis: Authorised King James Version* (Edinburgh: Canongate, 1998), pp. vii–xiv

Hellmut Rosenfeld, *Der mittelalterliche Todestanz* (Cologne and Graz: Böhlau, 3rd edn, 1974)

Kurt Ruh, 'Hartmanns Armer Heinrich: Erzählmodell und theologische Implikation', in *Medievalia Litteraria: Festschrift für Helmut de Boor zum 80. Geburtstag*, ed. Ursula Hennig and Herbert Kolb (Munich: Beck, 1971), pp. 315–29

D. S. Russell, *The Old Testament Pseudepigrapha* (London: SCM, 1987)

Hugh Sacker, *An Introduction to Wolfram's Parzival* (Cambridge, Cambridge University Press, 1963)

Gerhard Schmidt, *Die Armenbibeln des XIV Jahrhunderts* (Graz: Böhlau, 2nd edn, 1969)

Klaus M. Schmidt, 'Frauenritter oder Artusritter? Über Struktur und Gehalt von Ulrichs von Zatzikhoven *Lanzelet*', *Zeitschrift für deutsche Philologie* 98 (1979), 1–18

Hans Schottmann, 'Gregorius und Grégoire', *Zeitschrift für deutsches Altertum* 94 (1965), 81–108

Jens-Peter Schröder, *Arnold von Lübecks Gesta Gregorii Peccatoris* (Frankfurt/M: Lang, 1997)

Walter Johannes Schröder, *Der Ritter zwischen Welt und Gott* (Weimar: Böhlau, 1952)

Walter Johannes Schröder, *Die Soltane-Erzählung in Wolframs 'Parzival'* (Heidelberg: Winter, 1963)

Meinolf Schumacher, *Sündenschmutz und Herzensreinheit: Studien zur Metaphorik der Sünde in lateinischer und deutscher Literatur des Mittelalters* (Munich: Fink, 1996)

Ute Schwab, *Lex et Gratia: der literarische Exkurs Gottfrieds von Strassburg und Hartmanns Gregorius* (Messina: Università, 1967)

Paul Schwarz, *Die neue Eva: der Sündenfall in Volksglaube und Volkserzählung* (Göppingen: Kümmerle, 1973)

Werner Schwarz, 'Free Will in Hartmann's *Gregorius*', *Beiträge*, Tübingen 89 (1967), 128–50

R. W. Scribner, *The German Reformation* (London: Macmillan, 1986)

Leslie Seiffert, 'The Maiden's Heart', *Deutsche Vierteljahresschrift* 37 (1963), 384–405

J. L. Sharpe, 'The Second Adam in the *Apocalypse of Moses*', *Catholic Biblical Quarterly* 35 (1973), 35–46

Kerry Shea, 'The H(i)men Under the Kn(eye)fe: Erotic Violence in Hartmann's *Der arme Heinrich*', *Exemplaria* 6 (1994), 385–403

Samuel Singer, 'Zu Wolframs *Parzival*', in *Abhandlungen zur germanischen Philologie: Festgabe für Richard Heinzel* (Halle/S: Niemeyer, 1898), pp. 353–436

Beryl Smalley, *The Study of the Bible in the Middle Ages* (Oxford: Blackwell, 3rd edn, 1983)

Erich Smith, *Some Versions of the Fall: the Myth of the Fall of Man in English Literature* (London: Croom Helm, 1973)

George D. Smith, *The Teaching of the Catholic Church* (London: Burns Oates and Washbourne, 1948)

Ann Snow, 'Heinrich and Mark, Two Medieval Voyeurs', *Euphorion* 66 (1972), 113–27

Karl Stackmann, '*Der Erwählte*: Thomas Manns Mittelalterparodie', *Euphorion* 53 (1959), 61–74

Walter Stein, 'Christianity and the Common Pursuit', *Northern Miscellany* 1 (1953), 47–64

Sandro Sticca, *The Planctus Mariae in the Dramatic Tradition of the Middle Ages*, trans. Joseph R. Berrigan (Athens, GA, and London: University of Georgia Press, 1988)

Lorraine Kochanske Stock, 'The Reenacted Fall in Chaucer's *Shipman's Tale*', *Studies in Iconography* 7/8 (1981–2), 135–45

Michael Stone, *A History of the Literature of Adam and Eve* (Atlanta: Scholars Press, 1992)

Michael Stone, 'The Fall of Satan and Adam's Penance', *Journal of Theological Studies* 44 (1993), 143–56

Michael Stone, 'Jewish Tradition, the Pseudepigrapha and the Christian West', in *The Aramaic Bible: Targums in their Historical Context*, ed. D. R. G. Beattie and M. J. McNamara (Sheffield, 1993 = *Journal for the Study of the Old Testament*, Supplementary Series 166), pp. 431–49

Hilda Swinburne, 'The Miracle in *Der arme Heinrich*', *German Life and Letters* NS 22 (1969), 205–9

Petrus W. Tax, '*Felix culpa* und *lapsit exillis*: Wolframs *Parzival* und die Liturgie', *MLN* 80 (1965), 454–69

Petrus W. Tax, 'Wolfram von Eschenbach's *Parzival* in the Light of Biblical Typology', *Seminar* 9 (1973), 1–14

197

Winfried Theiß, *Exemplarische Allegorik: Untersuchungen zu einem literarhistorischen Phänomen bei Hans Sachs* (Munich: Fink, 1968)

Neil Thomas, 'The Ecumenical Ideal in Wolfram von Eschenbach Revisited', *Amsterdamer Beiträge zur älteren Germanistik* 50 (1998), 111–29

John J. Thompson, *The Cursor Mundi: Poem, Texts and Contexts* (Oxford: Blackwell, 1998)

Barbara Thoran, *Studien zu den österlichen Spielen des deutschen Mittelalters* (Göppingen: Kümmerle, 2nd edn, 1976)

E. M. W. Tillyard, *The Elizabethan World Picture* ([1943] Harmondsworth: Penguin, 1963)

Frank J. Tobin, *'Gregorius' and 'Der arme Heinrich'* (Berne and Frankfurt/M: Lang, 1973)

Frank J. Tobin, 'Fallen Man and Hartmann's *Gregorius*', *Germanic Review* 50 (1975), 85–98

Hope Traver, *The Four Daughters of God* (Bryn Mawr, Penn.: Bryn Mawr College Monographs, 1907)

Fritz Tschirch, 'Schlüsselzahlen', in *Festgabe für Leopold Magon* (Berlin: Deutsche Akademie der Wissenschaften, 1958), pp. 30–53

Fritz Tschirch, 'Gregorius der *heilaere*' (1964) in his *Spiegelungen* (Berlin: Schmidt, 1966), pp. 245–77

Rosemond Tuve, *A Reading of George Herbert* (London: Faber, 1952)

D. J. Unger, *The First-Gospel* (St Bonaventure, NY: Franciscan Institute, 1954)

Annette Volfing, *Heinrich von Mügeln, Der meide kranz: a Commentary* (Tübingen: Niemeyer, 1997)

Fred Wagner, 'Heinrich und die Folgen', in *German Narrative Literature of the Twelfth and Thirteenth Centuries: Studies Presented to Roy Wisbey*, ed. Volker Honemann and others (Tübingen: Niemeyer, 1994), pp. 261–74

Christine Wand, *Wolfram von Eschenbach und Hartmann von Aue* (Herne: Verlag für Wissenschaft und Kunst, 1989)

Peter Wapnewski, *Wolframs Parzival: Studien zur Religiosität und Form* (Heidelberg: Winter, 1955)

Peter Wapnewski, *Hartmann von Aue* (Stuttgart: Metzler, 5th edn, 1972)

Marina Warner, *Alone of All Her Sex* (London: Weidenfeld and Nicolson, 1976)

Rainer Warning, *Funktion und Struktur* (Munich: Fink, 1974)

Hermann J. Weigand, 'Die epischen Zeitverhältnisse in den Graldichtungen Crestiens und Wolframs', *PMLA* 53 (1938), 917–50

H. J. Weigand, 'Thomas Mann's Gregorius', *Germanic Review* 27 (1952), 10–30 and 81–95

David A. Wells, 'Fatherly Advice: the Precepts of "Gregorius", Marke and Gurnemanz and the School Tradition of the "Disticha Catonis" ', *Frühmittelalterliche Studien* 28 (1994), 296–332

Horst Wenzel, 'Der "Gregorius" Hartmanns von Aue: Überlegungen zur zeitgenössischen Rezeption des Werkes', *Euphorion* 66 (1972), 323–54

P. B. Wessels, 'Wolfram zwischen Dogma und Legende' (1955), in *Wolfram von Eschenbach*, ed. Heinz Rupp (Darmstadt: WBG, 1966), pp. 232–60

Claus Westermann, *Genesis 1–11* (Darmstadt: WBG, 1972)

Jessie L. Weston, *From Ritual to Romance* (Cambridge: Cambridge University Press, 1920)

Hugh White, *Nature and Salvation in Piers Plowman* (Cambridge: D. S. Brewer, 1988)

Robert Wildhaber, *Jakob Ruf: ein Zürcher Dramatiker des 16. Jahrhunderts* (St Gallen: Wildhaber, 1929)

Maurice Wiles, *The Christian Fathers* (London: SCM Press, 2nd edn, 1977)

Basil Willey, *The Seventeenth-Century Background* ([1934] Harmondsworth: Penguin, 1962)

Charles Williams, 'The Way of Exchange' [1941], reprinted in *Selected Writings*, ed. Ann Ridler (London: Oxford University Press, 1961), pp. 122–31

H. B. Willson, 'Symbol and Reality in *Der arme Heinrich*', *Modern Language Review* 53 (1958), 526–36

H. B. Willson, 'Hartmann's *Gregorius* and the Parable of the Good Samaritan', *Modern Language Review* 54 (1959), 194–203

H. B. Willson, '*Amor inordinata* in Hartmann's *Gregorius*', *Speculum* 41 (1966), 86–104

H. B. Willson, ' "Marriageable" in *Der arme Heinrich*', *Modern Philology* 64 (1966), 95–102

H. B. Willson, '*Ordo* and the Portrayal of the Maid in *Der arme Heinrich*', *Germanic Review* 44 (1969), 83–94

Ludwig Wolff, *Arnold Immessen* (Einbeck: Geschichtsverein, 1964)

Rosemary Woolf, *The English Religious Lyric in the Middle Ages* (Oxford: Clarendon, 1968)

Rosemary Woolf, *The English Mystery Plays* (Berkeley and Los Angeles: University of California Press, 1980)

Rosemary Woolf, *Art and Doctrine: Essays on Medieval Literature*, ed. Heather O'Donoghue (London: Hambledon Press, 1986)

Reinhard Wunderlich and Bernd Feininger, eds, *Zugänge zu Martin Luther (Festschrift für Dietrich von Heymann)* (Frankfurt/M: Lang, 1997)

Marianne Wynn, 'Heroine without a Name: the Unnamed Girl in Hartmann's Story', in *German Narrative Literature of the Twelfth and Thirteenth Centuries: Studies Presented to Roy Wisbey*, ed. Volker Honemann et al. (Tübingen: Niemeyer, 1994), pp. 245–59

David N. Yeandle, '*Schame* in the Works of Hartmann von Aue', in *German Narrative Literature of the Twelfth and Thirteenth Centuries: Studies Presented to Roy Wisbey*, ed. Volker Honemann et al. (Tübingen: Niemeyer, 1994), pp. 193–228

Rainer Zäck, *Der guote sundaere und der peccator precipuus* (Göppingen: Kümmerle, 1989)

BIBLICAL INDEX

GENERAL INDEX

Names such as Adam and Eve, and themes which run through the entire work, such as 'penance,' 'baptism' or 'original sin,' are not listed here.